# THE BUTTERFLIES OF BRITAIN AND EUROPE

*Text by*

**Lionel G. Higgins**

*Illustrated by*

**Brian Hargreaves**

Collins, London

William Collins Sons & Co Ltd
London · Glasgow · Sydney · Auckland
Toronto · Johannesburg

First published 1983


Paperback edition ISBN 0 00 219702 2
Hardback edition ISBN 0 00 219708 1

Filmset by Jolly & Barber Ltd, Rugby
Made and printed in Great Britain
by William Collins Sons & Co Ltd, Glasgow

# Contents

# About this book

**The Range.** In this book are illustrated all the butterflies known to occur in western Europe, numbering about 393 different species, and a large number of subspecies and local forms. Our area is bounded in the north and west by the oceans, in the south by the Sahara Desert, and in the east by the Bosphorus, Dardanelles and USSR. It includes the Baltic countries, Poland, Czechoslovakia, East Germany, Romania, Bulgaria and the Atlantic and Mediterranean islands, in all of which the butterflies are closely related to those of Britain and central Europe.

**The illustrations.** All species and major subspecies of butterflies are illustrated. They have been painted in natural sizes from actual specimens, the undersides shown on the right. In many European butterflies males and females differ, and both sexes are shown in almost all such species. Individual and local variation in wing-markings is very common, and the specimens have been chosen to show average patterns.

**The Text.** It is assumed that most specimens can be identified by comparison with the coloured illustrations, making long, verbal descriptions unnecessary. In the brief textual accounts of each species and subspecies, emphasis is given to distinctive specific characters, to comparison with related species and to the names of larval food-plants. The text does not include records of occasional vagrant individuals from other countries, which cannot be regarded as forming part of our natural fauna. 'E.' at the end of a description indicates that that species is found only in Europe. Maps mentioned in bold type refer to the British distribution maps on pages 237–243.

**The Maps.** The maps show the geographical ranges within the region of all resident butterflies. In all cases the breeding range of each species or of the nominate subspecies and of additional subspecies is marked in a solid colour. In the case of the few known migrant species the resident areas are marked in a solid colour and the areas of migrant dispersal in lines of the same colour. It is not to be supposed that any butterfly will occur everywhere within the marked areas. Almost all butterflies live in colonies which may be sparsely scattered, but more commonly in certain areas which will

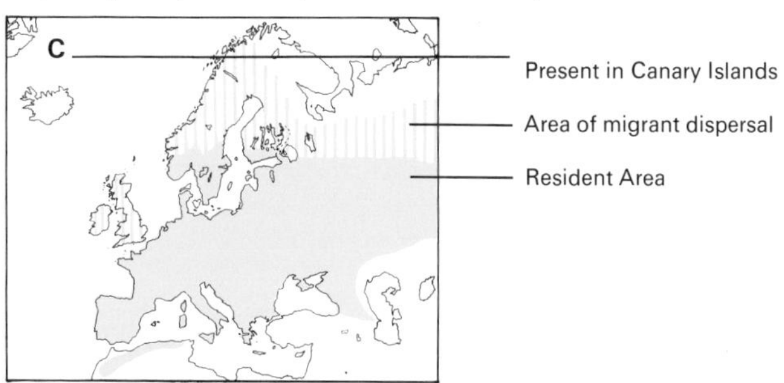

be mentioned in the text, where more detailed information, often with the actual localities where local species have been found, is given. The Atlantic islands, which form part of our region, are indicated on the map by the letters C=Canary Islands, M=Madeira, Az=Azores.

In many cases butterflies are known to occur far beyond the eastern frontiers of our region. It follows that distribution maps drawn only for western Europe are often misleading. In this book their scope is extended to cover European Russia to the Urals, Asia Minor, the Caucasus and Northern Iran.

The maps show the main features of the eastern ranges of our western butterflies, although lacking the precision which is possible today for western Europe: information about European Russia is hard to find. They do not show forms known only outside Europe – except in a few instances of adjacent subspecies.

**Systematic Arrangement and Nomenclature.** The species are listed in the order generally accepted in modern literature as most suitable. The Skippers (Hesperiidae) are placed at the end of the series, which begins with the Swallowtails. The nine principal sytematic groups, known as Families, are named, short accounts of their distinctive characters are given and natural groups are indicated in the text as an aid to identification. The nomenclature employed is most simple. Each species is described under its English name followed immediately by the appropriate Latin name. English names are not available for many subspecies mentioned in the text.

**Names, Species and Subspecies.** The accepted scientific term for a 'kind' of anything is a 'species'. The word is used freely in this book in which most of the butterflies have two names, one in English (vernacular) and one in Latin (scientific). Why is this necessary? The English names are meaningful to many British readers, perhaps more easily remembered, but they do not have international status. The use of Latin names, introduced by the great Swedish naturalist Linnaeus and employed since 1758 in the vast entomological literature, supplies names that are truly international and much better devised for expressing the natural relationships of different species of butterflies.

The Latin specific name is always double (binominal). The first word is a group name, the generic name, e.g. *Papilio*, used for a whole group or *genus* of similar kinds of butterflies, all of which have certain characters in common. The second name, the specific name, e.g. *machaon*, is adjectival and identifies the *species*, it indicates a particular sort of *Papilio*, with special characters among all those others which qualify to belong to the group (*genus*). It is found that butterflies vary, for example, *Papilio machaon* flying in the Himalayas is not quite the same as the European kind, although both are so much alike that they must be closely related. Those from the Himalayas form a geographical race, known as a *subspecies*, indicated by a third name following the specific name, for example, *Papilio machaon sikkimensis* (a trinomen). In practice it is usual to make contractions by writing only the initial letters of the first two words, in contexts where this would not lead to confusion, so that *Papilio machaon sikkimensis* would become *P.m.sikkimensis*.

## The Life History of a Butterfly

The life of every butterfly is divided into four phases. It begins as an egg, usually very small, the egg-shell often beautifully sculptured, making an elaborate pattern peculiar to the group or species in question. There are characteristic features in the eggs of each of the principal butterfly families recognised in modern classification.

**The Egg.** This is usually laid upon a leaf of the correct larval food plant. Most butterflies are extremely fussy, since the larva will eat only its proper food, often a single kind of plant, sometimes indeed, an uncommon species. In some way the female is able to identify the correct leaf in a bank of mixed vegetation, so that when the egg hatches the caterpillar does not need to go far in search of food. How this is possible is rather a mystery. Probably the female butterflies are able to smell or taste the plant with the sense organs (pulvilli) on their feet.

**The Larva (Caterpillar).** Within the tiny egg the insect develops into a larva, a grub-like creature with many legs. Within two or three weeks the egg may hatch, the larva escaping by eating a hole in the egg-shell, and beginning a phase of active life, of which the primary objective is growth. Larval skins do not grow or stretch as the little larva gets bigger, so it will be obliged to change its skin three or four times before growth is complete. Sometimes the egg will not hatch at once, but will remain dormant for several months, perhaps through the winter, to hatch in the spring. Larvae are helpless, soft and unable to move fast to get away from their many enemies, so most of them learn to hide. Their skins are coloured with subtle patterns making them hard to see as they feed, and often they feed only at night. In some cases, instead of hiding away, the larva makes itself unattractive by growing hair or spines. The caterpillars of our common Peacock and Small Tortoiseshell butterflies do just this, their black spiny larvae may swarm over a patch of nettles, but the birds do not seem to be interested.

Peacock caterpillars seem to be unattractive to birds

**The Pupa (Chrysalis).** When fully grown the larval butterfly casts aside its larval skin to become a chrysalis (pupa), in some ways an inactive phase, but demanding great metabolic activity within. The digestive apparatus of the larva has to be altered to the simple sucking organs of the butterfly; wings have to be developed; the elaborate reproductive organs must be fashioned, all of which must demand a great deal of energy. The complete change-over can be completed in a miraculously short time, perhaps in two or three weeks.

Most butterfly pupae are fixed by caudal (cremastral) hooks to something firm, the stem of a plant or tree, but others may be pendulous, hanging by the cremaster, or supported, often in a vertical position, by a silken girdle (Papilionidae, Pieridae, Lycaenidae). The chrysalis is enclosed within a sheath of firm chitin, the insect's substitute for bone. The essential changes from larval anatomy are largely completed during the last stages of larval life, and the eyes, antennae, legs, proboscis and wings can all be seen through the chitin as soon as the pupa is formed. Many species pass the winter as a pupa, a convenient method of hibernation.

**The Imago (Butterfly).** At the appointed time the chitinous pupal case splits and the butterfly emerges with its adult organs and legs fully formed, but with its wings folded and imperfectly developed. They are fully expanded in half an hour or less by the efforts of the insect. The butterfly crawls to a position with its wings hanging down, and then it expands them by pumping its body fluid along its wing-veins, at this stage soft and flexible, but soon to become rigid, to hold the wing perfectly flat.

Usually the birth cycle is completed in three to twelve months. Extreme

The Queen of Spain Fritillary, *Issoria lathonia*, is a species easily recognised by its underwing pattern. The position, with the wings not quite fully closed, shown left, is typical for a resting butterfly

The Small Tortoiseshell, *Aglais urticae*, may be seen flying early in the year for it hibernates as an imago.

limits probably are between twenty-one days and two years. The final phase of life now begins, the objective is to mate and lay eggs, the commencement of the new generation. Its biological objective completed, the individual dies.

This is the life story of every butterfly, but the duration varies in different species. In a majority the cycle takes a whole year, and the final butterfly phase, the *imago* (plural *imagines*), appears only once during twelve months, in a single annual generation (single-brooded). In other cases, such as the Small Whites, species which first emerge early in the year, the eggs from the first brood soon hatch and, with abundant food material, the larvae grow rapidly and, when fully developed, imagines produce a second generation (brood) later in the same year (double-brooded). Sometimes a third annual brood may appear in early autumn when conditions are favourable. In such cases the wing-markings of the first and later broods will probably differ, sometimes considerably (seasonal polymorphism).

How long does the species live as an imago? Usually for quite a short time, perhaps for two or three weeks, and in order to see such species active as butterflies, the colony must be visited at the appropriate time of the year. In a few species – the Brimstones among them – the diapause is passed as imagines, and such butterflies live for several months in this state, but again the biologically active stage in spring lasts for a few weeks only.

**Hibernation (Diapause).** Like most other insects, all butterflies enjoy the warmth and sunshine of summer, but they have to arrange some method of living through the cold winter when there is little or no food. Many have solved this problem by hibernating: they become dormant, without any sign of life, and the normal physiological functions are greatly altered. In this state insects are able to live for months without food or drink and to survive freezing temperatures. Some species hibernate as eggs (ova), fully exposed upon a branch of the food plant; others as larvae, usually very small in first or second instars, usually somewhat sheltered in a tussock of grass; others again as pupae, exposed upon the dried stem of a bush; a very few hibernate as imagines, among them the Peacock, Small Tortoiseshell and the Brimstone, which pass the winter months hidden in a hollow tree or a thick bush.

Such butterflies go into hibernation in the autumn soon after emerging from the pupa and without showing any sign of sexual activity. At the end of the winter they wake up and immediately mate, fertilised eggs are laid, and soon afterwards the old butterflies die leaving the eggs to hatch and the next generation to develop during the summer. As a rule closely related butterflies all adopt the same hibernation policy, as shown below for the Europeans in the following list.

Hibernation

| | |
|---|---|
| as ova | **Lycaenidae** (Blues): Hairstreaks, Silver-studded Blue, Idas Blue |
| | **Papilionidae**: Apollo Butterfly (*Parnassius apollo*) |
| as larvae | **Lycaenidae**: all Coppers, species of the genera *Polyommatus, Agrodiaetus, Lysandra, Aricia* |
| | **Nymphalidae**: most species excepting the genera *Nymphalis, Vanessa* and close relatives |
| | **Satyridae** (Browns): most species |
| | **Pieridae** (Whites): Black-veined White, Clouded Yellows (*Colias*) all species |
| | **Hesperiidae** (Skippers): probably most species, but information is often indefinite |
| as pupae | **Papilionidae** (Swallowtails): all species except the Apollo |
| | **Pieridae** (Whites): all genera except *Aporia* and *Colias* |
| as imagines | **Nymphalidae**: the genera *Nymphalis, Vanessa* and allies excepting *Cynthia* |
| | **Pieridae** (Whites): Brimstone (*Gonepteryx rhamni*) in Europe |

In the case of the Red Admiral, it has been suggested that hibernation may be as a pupa or as an imago. This aspect of butterfly life has not attracted much attention. It is hard to explain why one or other of these different methods of hibernation should appeal so strongly to different butterfly families or generic groups. In some cases – Brimstones – it is thought that the sexes mate in the autumn, but only the fertilised females hibernate. It seems that there are different mechanisms for determining times of onset and of termination of the diapause, and in butterflies the length of daylight is an important factor. Under artificial conditions the onset can be delayed by maintaining adequate light. By so doing a Large White (*Pieris brassicae*) has been bred continuously for ten years.

## The Anatomy of a Butterfly

In all insects the body is divided into three parts – the head, the chest (thorax), which carries the legs and wings, and the abdomen, which carries the digestive and generative organs.

**The head** includes two large, compound eyes which take up a lot of room. Each eye has many hundreds of small lenses, a fixed focus, and its surface is sufficiently curved to give a wide field of vision. Its practical efficiency is excellent. Below the eyes is the *proboscis*, a minute pipe through which the insect can suck up water and liquid food. A butterfly does not have any jaws. On each side of the proboscis are the *palpi*, small, paired triple-jointed organs of variable size. On the top of the head between the eyes are two *antennae*, in butterflies more or less expanded at their apices into bulbous *clubs*. Each antenna is an important sensory organ, the shaft provided with short hairs, important receptors in the insect's sensory system, which warn of aerial vibrations indicating nearby noise and movement. The antennae also help to maintain balance during flight.

A narrow neck connects the head with **the chest** (*thorax*) stoutly constructed with rigid plates of hardened chitin. It forms a firm base for three pairs of legs, two pairs of wings and their muscles. Each functional leg has a thigh (*femur*), a shin (*tibia*) and a five-jointed foot (*tarsus*) ending in a pair of claws, but this structure varies in different species. In particular the front leg is always vestigial in the Fritillaries, Satyrids and their relatives.

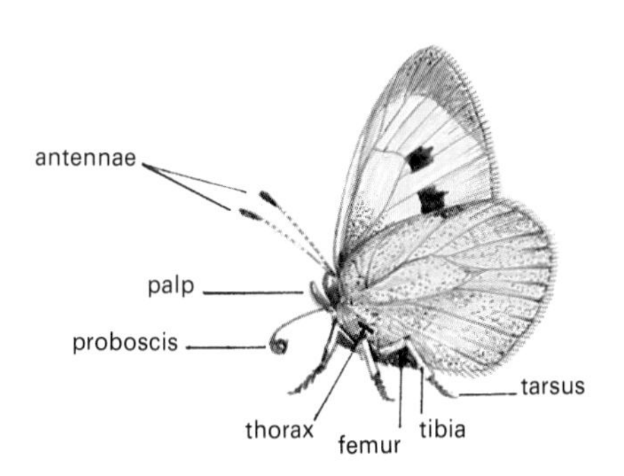


The anatomy of a Large White, *Pieris brassicae*.

**The wings** are composed of a thin chitinous membrane supported by minute tubes known as veins. In almost all butterflies the wings are covered by scales, thousands of tiny, flat platelets, often beautifully grooved, lying in rows across the wing to which they are fixed by peg-and-socket attachments. The scales are of two types. First are the cloaking scales which provide the wing-markings, usually by actual pigments, although the gleaming green and blue tones which are so striking (as for instance in the Common Blue) are produced by diffraction of light (interference colours). Secondly, in many but not in all species, there are specialised 'scent scales' (*androconia*), present only in males, which are of many shapes but always quite unlike the cloaking scales. They are concerned with sexual attraction, probably through the secretion and dispersal of aphrodisiac or identifying scents (*pheromones*) to which the female will react.

The vivid blue of the Adonis Blue, *Lysandra bellargus*, is a 'rainbow' colour, produced by light diffraction from the grooved wing scales.

**Variation: Polymorphism.** Excluding variation of subspecific (geographical) importance, local variation in wing markings and size may be quite marked in some, but not in all butterflies. If samples of a sensitive species, such as the Small Copper, taken in different localities or at different times of the year, are compared, differences will be seen. As a rule the most obvious variation will be in the dark upperside markings, emphasised in some, reduced in others, especially well illustrated in many Whites and Small Fritillaries, for example the Spotted Fritillary (*Melitaea didyma*). Similar but more pronounced changes occur in the late broods of bigenerate species (see page 9). Since the same effects appear in many different butterflies, it is assumed that they are produced, at least partly, in response to local conditions of humidity, temperature, altitude, and other features of the differing biotopes, as the basic characters of the wing patterns are usually unaltered in variation of this type. Not all the variation seen in different generations can be explained so simply. In the Map Butterfly (*Araschnia levana*), the orange-buff, black-spotted first brood is followed in late summer by a second brood with very different dark wing markings (page 108), a most uncommon situation.

Recurrent abnormal markings may appear in species with relatively constant wing patterns. The upperside colour of the Small Copper (*Lycaena phlaeas*) is normally orange-red, and the usual seasonal changes are well developed in specimens taken in warm or cold climates. Occasional rare specimens occur in which the upperside ground colour is white or pale yellow. Other striking examples of recurrent variation among the Lycaenids appear in the blue female forms of the Chalkhill Blue (f. *syngrapha*). It is known that in both these examples the abnormality is due to a genetic factor (a recessive gene, sex-linked in *Lysandra coridon*). Blue female forms of other related Blues may be explained, no doubt, in the same way.

Another type of variation is seen in some dimorphic species, species which commonly appear in two distinct forms. The white and yellow female forms of some Clouded Yellows (*Colias* spp.) are examples, in a situation which has been examined by several entomologists. It is now known that in *Colias* the colour forms are controlled by genes present in both parents, but the 'gene for white' is unable to show itself in the male, it is 'sex controlled'. The dimorphic females (f. *valesina*) of our common Silver-Washed Fritillary (*Argynnis paphia*) are controlled by a similar mechanism.

Probably the greatest extent of variation (polymorphism) within our region is to be found in the Ringlets (the genus *Erebia*). There can be no doubt that this is a very special case involving both sexes. In all species the wing markings are similar, consisting of fulvous spots or bands, which may be prominent or, in other races of the same species, reduced, even to the point of obliteration. The various different forms (phenotypes) are certainly racial, that is, each is confined to certain mountain groups, but the extreme forms are usually connected by populations with intermediate characters. Many of these phenotypes appear to be true subspecies, genetically controlled no doubt, but at present the extreme variation is not understood as it appears in such species as the Woodland Ringlet (*Erebia euryale*); Silky Ringlet (*E. gorge*); the Sooty Ringlet (*E. pluto*) and many others.

Males of *Colias* butterflies, such as this Berger's Clouded Yellow, *Colias australis*, never show the dimorphic white form which is usual in females.

## The Distribution of Butterflies

All butterflies are highly specialized insects, each species adapted to live in a certain type of habitat (biotope). A few species adapted to live in the rather variable conditions present today in lowland Europe are widely distributed in what may be regarded as a diffuse colony, extending for hundreds or thousands of miles, but this is unusual. Most butterflies live in restricted (localised) colonies, each separated from one another perhaps by many miles. The suitability of the habitat will depend upon the presence of the required food-plant and such features as altitude, temperature, sunshine or shade and other characters difficult to analyse. If a butterfly occurs at all, it is usually correct to assume that a colony is established somewhere near; truly vagrant specimens of local species are rarely seen.

In all parts of the world and in all habitats, butterflies occur where the native plants grow best. They are rarely attracted by the foreign trees and shrubs so often planted for display in public gardens. In lowland areas the roadside hedges and grass verges may be productive. These are natural nature reserves, but only too often in agricultural districts they will be lifeless, the normal relationship between plants and living creatures destroyed by insecticides and weed-killing sprays. Elsewhere, light woodland broken by clearings, with indigenous plants growing naturally, will usually support many species. Similar conditions are often present on the middle altitude slopes of mountains, when these are at once too rocky and too steep for practical cultivation. Moorlands are habitats for several local species including small Fritillaries, Blues and Satyrs. Many different biotopes are found among mountains, where conditions vary so greatly between the sheltered valley levels and the high alpine areas above the tree-line. For this reason the greatest variety of species is found in mountainous regions such as the Alps, Pyrenees and Balkan countries. Northern and southern mountain slopes often differ in vegetation so both need inspection. Species absent at low altitudes may appear at the 1500–1800m levels, a little below the tree-line. Beyond this, at 2000m or over in central Europe, the exciting alpine fauna will be at its best from late June to early August, with small Fritillaries, Blues and Skippers flying over the Rhododendron and Vaccinium slopes and various Ringlets round the rocks and moraines. The same or similar butterflies are to be found in the arctic and sub-arctic regions of Scandinavia, where alpine conditions occur at low altitudes, in some places down to sea level.

**Migration and Vagrancy.** True migration such as is known to occur in eels, turtles, birds and fish rarely if ever happens among European butterflies, but the Monarch Butterfly in North America does behave in this way. The species spends the winter hibernating in the warm Gulf States, then in spring it flies some 1,500 miles to breed in the northern States. To pass the next winter the new generation returns to the same roosting trees used by its parents. In Europe migration or dispersal within the region does occur in many species. The stimulus that prompts migrant activity is not understood.

We may suppose that discovery of additional food supplies and extra living space are obvious objectives, and biologically frequent dispersal is necessary to ensure constant 'gene-flow' to maintain the genetic constitution of the individual species. In all cases enough individuals remain behind to maintain a colony at its proper strength. In Europe there does appear to exist a decided drift northwards that is difficult to explain. There is not the same urge to fly to the south. The Pale Clouded Yellows and the Small Tortoiseshell do not occur in North Africa, where the Red Admiral is quite rare (occasional).

Over 20 species of European Butterflies are recognized as 'wanderers', i.e. they display migratory movements, and of these the most interesting are those which frequently or regularly emigrate beyond their usual distribution frontiers. Great Britain is especially well placed to illustrate these movements, since unusual species can arrive there only after crossing the sea, and are recognised immediately. I have selected six European species which deserve special attention.

RED ADMIRAL *Vanessa atalanta.* This species is resident in Europe where it hibernates as an imago during the winter months. Females emerge from hibernation in March or April to lay eggs which will produce one or two generations of butterflies through summer and into autumn, the latter always much the most abundant. It is well known that the species makes migratory movements in various directions. These include annual emigrations in summer north of latitude 48°N or thereabouts, which appears to be the northern limit of the usual hibernation area. The migrations are extensive, reaching the Baltic countries, Scandinavia and Britain, where the butterflies appear every year in late May or June, usually in rather small numbers. They are able to breed freely, and it is not until the second generation appears in August/September that the species becomes a common garden insect, widely distributed in the country. In Britain the numbers vary greatly, with occasional seasons of great abundance when it reaches every part of England, Ireland and Scotland. Today many authors doubt whether hibernation in these islands is ever successful, and it was thought that the entire second generation must die at the end of each year. No doubt many do die, but it seems probable that many others escape from Britain and other northern areas in a southerly migration which is now accepted by many authors as an annual incident of importance. The situation of the principal European base of the Red Admiral is uncertain. The species is rather uncommon in many parts of central and southern Europe, including the Balkan countries and Spain. With an unstable immigrant population it is not possible to map precisely the probable distribution for any single year in Britain.

CLOUDED YELLOW *Colias crocea.* This butterfly, common in southern Europe, is seen most years as a rare immigrant, usually only occasional specimens flying over lucerne fields near the south coasts of England and Ireland. Occasionally there are large immigrations when, by late summer, the species becomes widely distributed almost everywhere in Great Britain, but it is erratic, sometimes quite absent for several successive years. It sometimes breeds in the lucerne, and during mild winters breeding colonies may be established and maintained for a year or two.

PALE CLOUDED YELLOWS *Colias hyale* and *Colias australis.* These are much less common immigrants and quite erratic, but most years reported once or twice from the coastal counties of southern England. The Pale Clouded Yellow (*Colias hyale*) is said to be more common than Berger's Yellow (*C. australis*).

CAMBERWELL BEAUTY *Nymphalis antiopa.* This species is of special interest as it appears to approach Britain from the east. Usually it is a rare immigrant, but occasionally it appears in large numbers, amounting to an 'invasion' in 1976.

LARGE WHITE *Pieris brassicae.* It is not always recognised that this is one of Britain's most common immigrants. Usually the foreign individuals can be recognised by distinctive seasonal changes in wing markings which differ from those of native specimens flying in Britain at the same date. A notable immigration of this species occurred in 1979.

The following rare European immigrants have been recorded from time to time from the coastal districts of southern England: Queen of Spain Fritillary (*Issoria lathonia*), Bath White (*Pontia daplidice*), Bloxworth Blue (*Everes argiades*), Lang's Short-tailed Blue (*Syntarucus pirithous*), Long-tailed Blue (*Lampides boeticus*).

PAINTED LADY *Cynthia cardui.* Of the non-European immigrants to Britain, this is the most important. The life history differs from that of the Red Admiral in one important matter. The species breeds continuously; that is to say the generations follow one another without a diapause and pupal stages are rather short. This arrangement is not uncommon among exotic species which live in climates which are never very cold and a pause for hibernation is not necessary. We are reminded that, with a vast distribution in tropical and sub-tropical countries, the Painted Lady is truly a tropical butterfly, which only briefly ventures north from Africa into the temperate climate as an immigrant but is unable to survive the European winter. The story goes as follows. At the African base, perhaps Algeria, imagines emerge in March or April and disperse quickly across the Mediterranean Sea into Europe. There the immigrants breed to produce one, or often two, native European generations through summer and autumn. The first immigrants rarely arrive in Britain before late May or June. These are most constant along the southern coasts of England and Ireland, where the immigration can be fairly termed annual, but further north and inland records in May are more erratic. Soon after arrival the immigrants begin to breed and native British individuals, as with the Red Admiral, appear in late July and early August, soon becoming common and often widely distributed in Scotland and sometimes reaching even to the Hebrides and Orkney Islands. Everywhere within the British Isles the species shows a marked preference for coastal areas, but of course many do travel inland. During autumn the number of individuals in Britain declines. No doubt many die, but it seems probable that many others join in a southerly migration as in the case of the Red Admiral. There are many records of butterflies, including Painted Ladies, moving south in autumn over some of the high passes across the Pyrenees. Sudden mass migrations, possibly at night, may be the explanation of the sudden disappearance of abundant local populations, which have been reported more than once in the literature. In the Painted Lady it is noteworthy that the hind-wing underside does not show the dark, cryptic markings present in related hibernating species such as the Small Tortoiseshell and Peacock.

AMERICAN PAINTED LADY *Cynthia virginiensis.* Resident in the Canary Islands (Tenerife etc) in recent years has been recorded many times from the coastal areas of south-western Europe. By some authors it is now accepted as resident in southern Portugal (Serra da Monchique etc).

MONARCH BUTTERFLY *Danaus plexippus.* This American species is a well-known wanderer, occasionally recorded from coastal areas of Portugal, western Spain and other improbable localities in western Europe. The species is resident in the Canary Islands, but whether our occasional immigrants come from there or from North America is uncertain.

**Distribution.** Many readers, examining the distribution maps in this book, might conclude that butterflies behave in the most irrational manner, often present locally in curious places and unexpectedly absent elsewhere for no apparent reason. There must be reasons for these patterns of distribution, and often they can be explained by known geological facts. By estimating the ages of rare fossil butterflies, it is known that many kinds have been present in the world for millions of years, through almost infinite ages. During this period the shapes of our continents have altered, islands have been isolated, mountains have been pushed up and all sorts of things have happened to disturb the distribution of living creatures. Butterflies, like all insects, do move about, extending their distributions when, for some reason, a new area becomes more acceptable and withdrawing in the presence of adverse conditions.

During the last two million years or so, as everyone must know, there have been 'Ice Ages' in northern Europe, when great areas of land became frozen. These events were immensely important for all creatures living at that time, including butterflies, which had to migrate to seek shelter in warmer places, known as refuge areas (Refugia). Important refugia were established in northern China and eastern Siberia ('Angaraland'), in eastern Turkey and Armenia (Pontic refuge), and in Spain and North Africa. In these places creatures could maintain themselves ready to repopulate the frozen areas when conditions improved, and from them are derived many of the butterflies that are found in Europe today.

The broad lowlands north of the Alps were inhospitable moorlands during the ice ages, but whenever the climate improved these lands were colonised by butterflies from the east, the so-called Euro-Siberian fauna, established today from France and England across southern Scandinavia and Germany to Mongolia, Siberia and sometimes even to Japan and North America. These butterflies form an important group in our fauna, including, for example: the Heath Fritillary (*Mellicta athalia*); the Large Heath (*Coenonympha tullia*); the Dryad (*Minois dryas*) and many other species distributed now from the coast of the Atlantic to the Pacific Ocean.

Very different species occur at high altitudes in the Alps and on other mountains, flying at levels where trees and herbaceous plants are replaced by short grass and low scrub (*Vaccinium* etc). The same, or closely related species, fly also at lower levels elsewhere when similar conditions exist, especially on the moorlands and barren tundra of arctic Scandinavia and northern Russia. The relationship is so close that alpine and arctic creatures are accepted by zoologists as forming a specialised Boreoalpine (Oreo-tundral) fauna. The distribution of these butterflies is remarkably extensive, such characteristic species as the Ringlets (*Erebia*) occur north of the tropics, throughout the northern hemisphere, in arctic and sub-arctic areas and on high mountains in Europe, Asia and in North America, with marked concentration in the European Alps. Because of their exceptionally wide distribution, it is thought that these represent an ancient, pre-glacial fauna, dating from a time when the geography of the world was very different.

In southern Europe and North Africa many kinds of butterflies are to be found which never occur north of the Alps. Most of these 'Ponto-Mediterraneans' are derived from the Pontic refuge area of western Asia, members of the great Mediterranean sub-region, which includes all countries bordering the Mediterranean Sea, extending eastwards across Turkey and western Asia to Iran in the east, and to the Canary Islands and Madeira in the west. The fauna is especially rich in 'Blues' (Lycaenidae) and 'Browns' (Satyridae). Evidence of antiquity is provided by the presence of localised species and discontinuous ranges (Nevada Grayling, page 152, for example), which can be explained by the known geographical changes associated with the development of the Mediterranean Sea. The consequent withdrawals and isolation of various species provided the best possible conditions for the development of distinct subspecies, which have made this area of special interest to all entomologists, providing many fascinating problems of distribution.

**Geography.** As zoogeographical regions, the names of the old countries, such as Dalmatia, Bosnia etc. are more meaningful than the modern Yugoslavia, which includes representatives of several different faunas. Especially important is the term Macedonia, including part of Bosnia and of north-western Greece, an area which seems to have exceptional zoogeographical significance.

# The Identification of Butterflies

Many butterflies can be recognised easily by comparison with the illustrations, but others are difficult to identify even for experienced collectors. For beginners attention to the following points will be useful.

Wing markings are often variable in extent but not in position. In cold, humid conditions black markings may be unusually extensive ('heavy') the actual striae wide, especially in Nymphalid butterflies, Fritillaries etc. In warm, dry areas black markings are often reduced, vestigial or absent, as in late-brood specimens from southern Europe, but in such specimens the arrangement of important features is not changed. In particular, eyespots (ocelli) often vary greatly in size. In the variable and puzzling group of Ringlets (*Erebia*) and in other satyrid species, the upperside presence of fulvous areas and eyespots are exceptionally inconstant. Always examine both surfaces. In many butterflies important markings are present on the undersides of the hind-wings. This is especially true of the Blues (Lycaenidae) in which the exact arrangement of spots etc. may show specific characters.

Size is usually of little importance in identification, as it is so variable in many species. In difficult conditions, for instance in southern Europe, when food plants are scarce during dry weather at the end of summer, late brood specimens will be small.

In writing and interpreting descriptions of butterflies, because it is necessary to define exact areas on the wings, the wing's topography and nomenclature must be understood by the reader.

As shown in the diagrams overleaf, the principal areas of the wing are known as the costa (front edge), inner margin (back edge), the outer margin, and the subdivision of its surface, i.e. the basal, discal, postdiscal, submarginal, marginal, subapical, and apical areas.

The diagrams also show the principal wing veins: costal vein, radial (subcostal) vein, and median (cubital) vein, which together divide into the distal veins. The veins are numbered 1–12 on the forewing, and from 1–8 on the hindwing. Areas between these veins are termed spaces, which take the number of the vein immediately below. In most species, half-way across the wings, the radial and median veins are joined together by the discoidal veins to form an important enclosed space, the discoidal cell ('cell'), said to be 'closed' when the cross-veins are well developed and 'open' when they are not present (as in the hindwing only of Purple Emperors and Marsh Fritillary etc.).

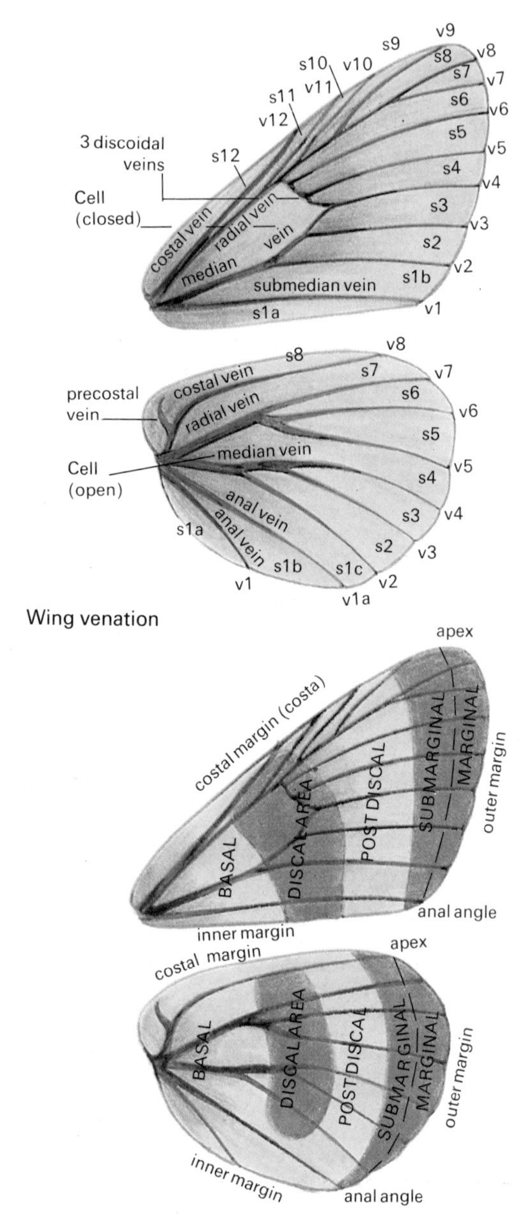


Wing venation

Principal areas of the wing

# Glossary

**Bigenerate** Having two annual generations ('broods').

**Biotope** Conditions of life in a given area, including all factors such as altitude, vegetation, temperature etc.

**Caudal** Relating to, or in the position of, the tail.

**Cline** A character gradient; a gradual change through a series of populations of any character such as size, colour, etc.

**Cremaster** The structure at the anal extremity of the pupa including hooks by which the pupa is suspended. Adj. cremastral.

**Diapause** At any time of the year, a period of suspended animation during which the creature does not feed and appears to sleep.

**Dimorphism** Occurrence of two distinct forms within the same species, e.g. in Clouded Yellows, females often yellow or white.

**Double-brooded** See Bigenerate.

**Endemic** In relation to butterflies, confined in distribution to a certain area or country.

**Eurasia** The continents of Europe and (Palaearctic) Asia taken together.

**Fauna** Collective name for all living creatures within a specified area, especially of a named group, e.g. European fauna, Butterfly fauna etc.

**Fennoscandia** Name for Scandinavia and Finland taken together.

**Form** =f. Of butterflies, a distinct variant, constant or inconstant, not classed as species or subspecies, e.g. female form (♀f), seasonal form, local form (or morph).

**Girdle** Of butterflies, the silken thread which supports the pupa in the Swallowtails and Whites.

**Holarctic Region** Europe, Asia and America north of the tropics.

**Homonym** A name already given to another species within the same genus.

**Imago (pl. imagines)** The fourth (breeding) phase in the life of every butterfly.

**Invalid name** A scientific name which fails to conform with the Rules of the International Code for Nomenclature.

**Irrorated** Minutely speckled or dotted with coloured scales.

**Larva** Immature free-living form that develops into the adult, breeding, form by metamorphosis. In butterflies the caterpillar.

| | |
|---|---|
| **Mimicry** | Of butterflies, close resemblance of shape or markings to different and frequently unrelated species for protection; e.g. A fly mimics a wasp. |
| **Nominate subspecies** | The subspecies first described and therefore giving its name to the whole species. |
| **N Africa** | That part of North Africa within the region covered: Morocco, Algeria and Tunisia. |
| **Ocellus** | A spot like an eye with a central pupil. |
| **Osmaterium** | A red, filamentous organ behind the head of Papilionid larvae, erected when the creature is excited. |
| **Palaearctic Region** | The zoological region that includes Europe and Asia north of the Himalayas and Africa north of the Sahara, i.e. the Old World north of the tropics. |
| **Phenotype** | The characters of external shape and markings. |
| **Pilose** | Set with fine, short bristles like the pile of a carpet. |
| **Pupa** | The immobile, non-feeding stage between larva and imago when metamorphosis takes place; the chrysalis. |
| **Region** | The region dealt with in this book, including western Europe and north-western Africa, as defined in the Preface. |
| **Stria** | A short, finely drawn streak or line. |
| **Subspecies** | A geographical race of a recognised species, with recognisable characters and distinct distribution. |
| **Synonym** | A later name for a species already described and named. |
| **Taxon (pl. taxa)** | Of insects, a recognisable group, often unnamed although suitable for a valid name, as subspecies, species or any higher category. |
| **Taxonomy** | The theory and practice of classifying organisms. |
| **Type specimen** | The actual specimen described by the author of the description when naming a species or subspecies. |

## Abbreviations used in the Text

| | |
|---|---|
| ♂ | male |
| ♀ | female |
| f | form |
| fw | forewing |
| hw | hindwing |
| upf | upperside forewing |
| uph | upperside hindwing |
| unf | underside forewing |
| unh | underside hindwing |
| ups | upperside |
| uns | underside |
| pd | postdiscal |
| gc | ground-colour |
| gen. | generation (i.e. brood, gen.1 = first brood) |
| v | vein |
| s | space |
| dc | discal or discoidal (wing area) |
| esp. | especially |
| spp. | species (plural) |
| ssp. | subspecies |
| N | North |
| S | South |
| E | East |
| W | West |
| NW | Northwest |
| SW | Southwest |
| NE | Northeast |
| SE | Southeast |
| E. | Endemic, of a butterfly, occurring only in a specified region or country. |

# PAPILIONIDAE
## The Swallowtails, Apollos and their allies

In this very large family all species have six functional legs, with simple double claws, the hind-wings with a single anal vein, and other anatomical peculiarities. All larvae have an osmaterium behind the head, a red filamentous organ which is exposed and erected when the creature is excited.

The butterflies fall into three distinct groups. The Swallowtails, a very large group with about 500 mostly tropical species; the Apollos with about 40 species, only present in the north temperate (Holarctic) region, many of them found only at high alpine levels on the great mountains of C Asia and Siberia; and a small number of rather curious butterflies, only three or four in our region, with unusual characters, not closely related to any large group, regarded as relict forms (i.e. representing geologically ancient types almost extinct today).

**The Swallowtails** Usually large butterflies, among them some of the largest in the world, almost all with 'tails' on the hind-wing. They are beautifully marked; males and females often differ, the females especially are often modified to mimic inedible species belonging to entirely different families. The larval food plants include a great variety of herbs and the leaves of deciduous trees. A large tropical group lives upon species of *Aristolochia*. In all European species the sexes are similar, ♀ often slightly larger.

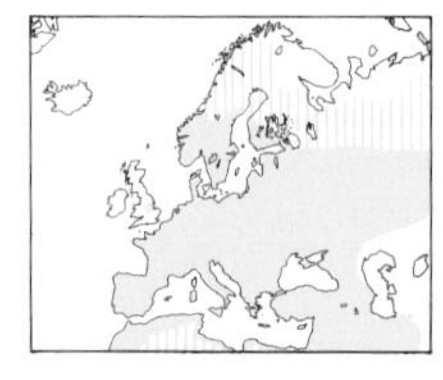

**SWALLOWTAIL** *Papilio machaon*. ♂ upf wing-bases broadly dark; unf submarginal band straight-edged. ♀ larger, otherwise similar. Common and widely distributed throughout C and S Europe but in NW Africa more local. Flies in open country and flowery meadows from sea level to 1800m, April–May and June–July. Larval food plants Umbelliferae including *Selinum* (Milk Parsley), *Foeniculus* (Fennel), *Angelica* etc. *Dictamnus* and Rutaceae. There are two annual broods, gen.1, ups yellow, markings very dark; gen.2 in July–August, ups paler yellow, dark markings more or less powdered with pale scales. In N Europe, including England, often a single brood in May–June. The species is a vagrant, continental specimens of gen.2 occasionally reach England. Range extends across temperate Asia to Japan and N America. Larva p. 226 **Map 1**

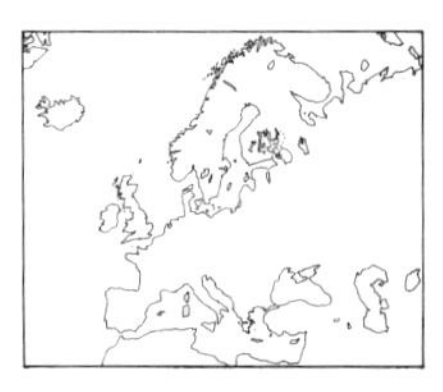

**CORSICAN SWALLOWTAIL** *Papilio hospiton*. Like the Swallowtail but unf dark submarginal band is wavy; tail of hw short. Flies on Corsica and Sardinia in a single prolonged brood, May–July, often in mountains, over heather and low scrub at 700–1500m. Fennel is said to be the only larval food plant. The species is now local and uncommon. E.

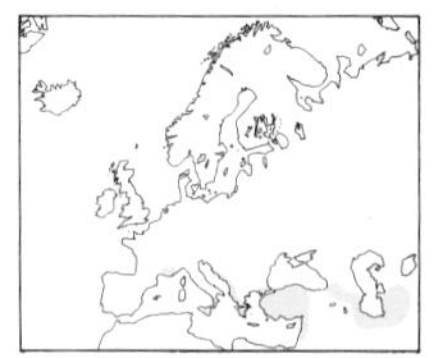

**SOUTHERN SWALLOWTAIL** *Papilio alexanor*, upf bright yellow with 4 black bars. ♀ larger, otherwise similar. Very local in scattered colonies, often near the northern Mediterranean coasts; France, in Provence, Var, Basses Alpes (Valley of the Tinée), Ardèche, Drôme, Isère; Italy, on the eastern slopes of the Maritime Alps, the Aspromonte, but usually rare; Sicily, Yugoslavia in Dalmatia, Istria; Greece, local but sometimes common on Corfu, Peloponnesos, etc. Flies in open country from lowlands to 1500m, attracted by thistles, in a single prolonged brood, May–July. Larval food plants Umbelliferae, including *Trinia*, *Seseli*, *Ptychotis*. Range extends to Lebanon, Iran and C Asia.

Swallowtail

Corsican Swallowtail

Southern Swallowtail

**SCARCE SWALLOWTAIL** *Iphiclides podalirius*. Upf with 6 black bars, tail long. Flies in open country from lowlands to 1600m, usually near food plants *Prunus spinosa*, more rarely *Crataegus*, *Sorbus* or cultivated fruit trees, April–June, July–September. Two annual broods; gen.1 ups markings black, abdomen and hw body-groove black; gen.2 ups markings usually grey, body groove not black. The degree of seasonal change depends partly upon habitat and locality. Larva p. 230.

*I. p. podalirius*, throughout Europe from Pyrenees northwards; ups palest yellow or 'off-white' in gen.2. Range extends across Europe and Asia to China.

*I. p. feisthamelii*, in parts of S France, Spain, Portugal and N Africa; larger, ♀ in gen.1 yellow, black markings emphasized; in gen.2 often still larger, and hw more elongate. E.

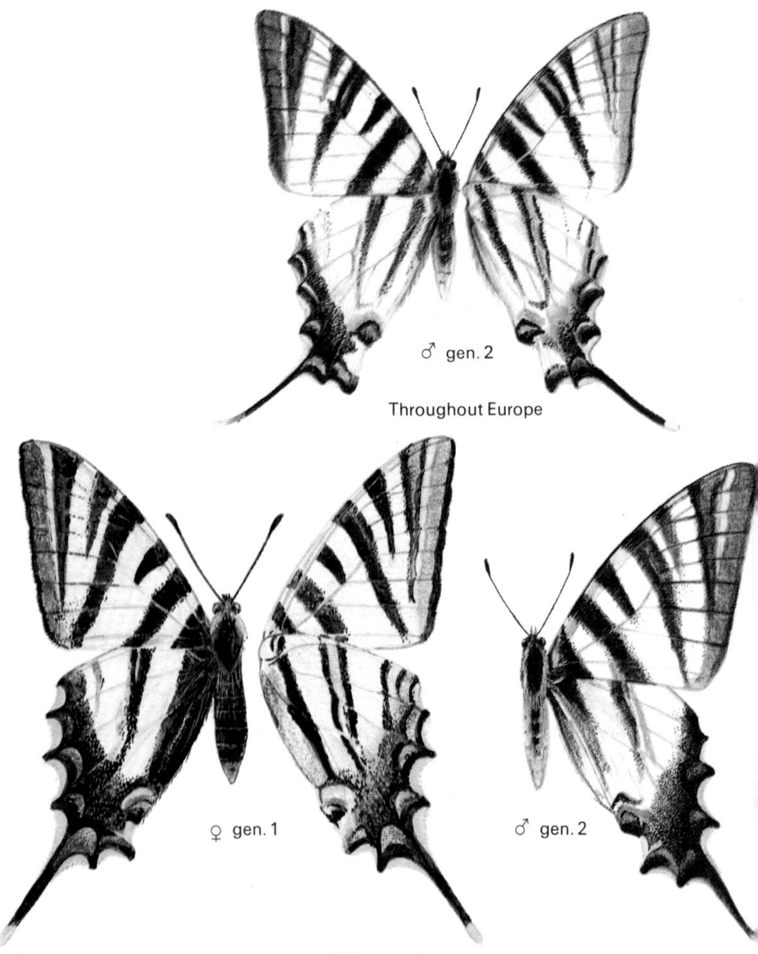




**Scarce Swallowtail**

♂ f. *medesicaste*

♀ f. *honoratii*
SE France, etc

♀ f. *canteneri*
Morocco

**Spanish Festoon**

**The Festoons.** Interesting butterflies with unusual markings, not closely related to the Swallowtails, but to other primitive species which survive today in western, central and eastern Asia. The larvae are rather plump with short, fleshy papillae on the back and sides. The slender pupa lies upon the ground to which it is fixed by silken threads attached to the top of its head. In all species larval food plants are *Aristolochia*.

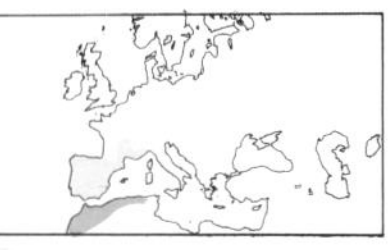
*Z.r. rumina*
*Z.r. africana*

**SPANISH FESTOON** *Zerynthia rumina*. Upf red spots in cell and at cell-end; vitreous window present near apex. Flies in SW Europe, February–May, in a single brood over open heathland etc. lowlands to 1500m. E.

*Z. r. rumina*, in SE France, Spain, Portugal, of medium size; red basal spot present uph (f. *medesicaste*), perhaps racial in France; ups may be deep yellow, ♀-f. *canteneri*, not rare in France; a ♀-f. *honoratii* occurs occasionally.

*Z. r. africana* occurs in Morocco, very large, markings brilliant, best developed at low levels near the coast, f. *canteneri* common. Inland, at altitudes of 1500m specimens are smaller.

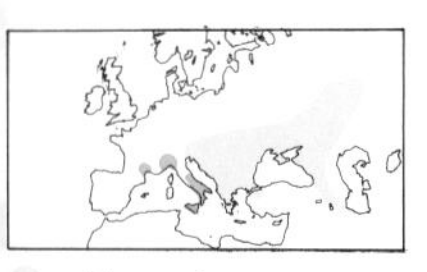
*Z.p. polyxena*
*Z.p. cassandra*

**SOUTHERN FESTOON** *Zerynthia polyxena*. Upf lacks red spots in cell and vitreous window near apex. Local from S France and eastwards; Austria, Yugoslavia and Greece. Flies April–June in rough, stony places from lowlands to 1000m. Larva p. 228.

*Z. p. polyxena* in C and E Europe, ups not heavily marked, upf a single red costal spot present in s9; ups gc sometimes deep yellow f. *ochracea*.

*Z. p. cassandra*, only in SE France, ups heavily marked, upf lacks red costal spot; unh reddish markings prominent; colonies very local.

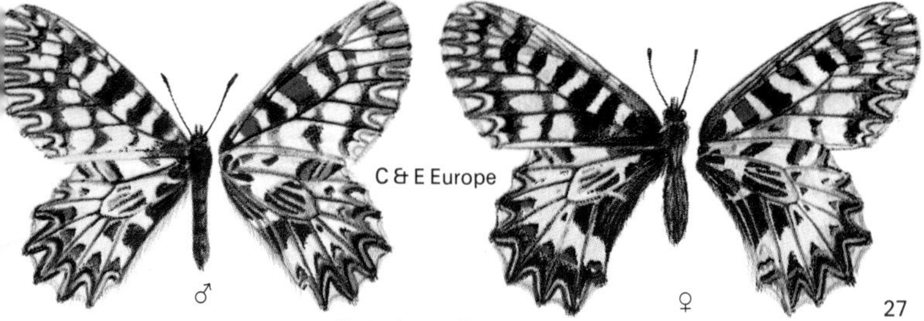
C & E Europe
♂ ♀

**Southern Festoon**

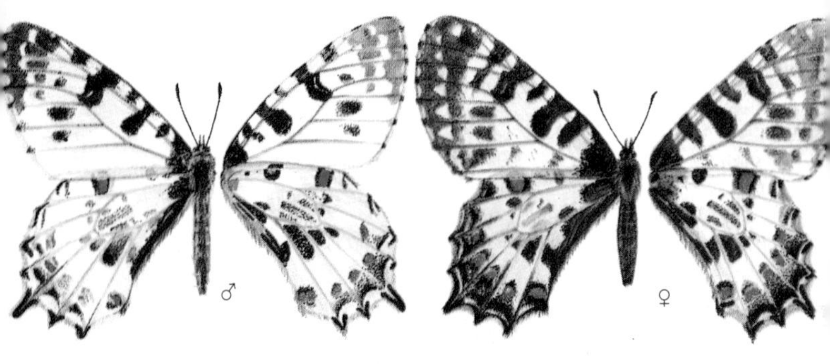

SE Romania to N Greece

♂ Crete

**Eastern Festoon**

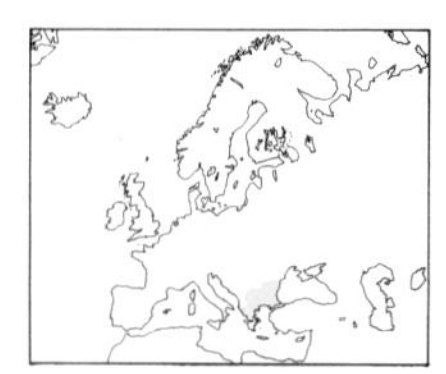

Z.c. ferdinandi
Z.c. cretica

**EASTERN FESTOON** *Zerynthia cerisyi*. Hw outer margin deeply scalloped, often with short tail on v4. Flies in S Balkans and eastwards to Iran, on open rocky ground from lowlands to 1500m, in a single brood in April–June.

*Z. c. ferdinandi*, the large European race, local in SE Romania, Dobrogea, Bulgaria and N Greece. Flies April–June, often in hot valleys at low altitudes. ♀ ups dark markings extended. Larval food plants *Aristolochia* species.

*Z. c. cretica*. smaller, outer margin of hw evenly rounded. Only on western Crete, flying in March/April, from lowlands to 1000m (Omalos).

**FALSE APOLLO** *Archon apollinus*. Uph has 6 large red and blue submarginal spots. Has been recorded from SE Europe, but such reports have never been confirmed. Flies over rough, stony ground in February and later, from lowlands to 1500m, often in mountainous country. Larval food plant *Aristolochia hastata*. Range confined to Asia Minor, Syria, Lebanon and Israel.

♂

**False Apollo**

**The Apollos.** These butterflies form a most distinct group, almost all with white thinly scaled wings. In many species the markings are similar, the hind-wings with characteristic round, red spots, absent on the Clouded Apollos. They fly at various altitudes up to 4000m. All species are single-brooded, occurring principally in the mountains of Europe, Asia and N America, and three species are found in our region. After mating females have a horny structure (sphragis) underneath the end of the abdomen. These lovely creatures are among the most characteristic butterflies to be seen in the Pyrenees and Alps, but unhappily they have disappeared from many places where they were common formerly. In many countries today there are large areas where they are protected, and interference of any kind is forbidden.

**APOLLO** *Parnassius apollo*. Antennae yellow-grey, *inconspicuously ringed darker grey*; ♂ uph grey marginal markings *usually present*. Occurs June–August in Fennoscandia at low levels, but at 1000–1800m or more on the mountains of C and S Europe, flying over flowery slopes. Range extends across Russia and W Asia to the Urals and Caucasus Mts and eastwards to W Siberia. Larval food plants *Sedum*, esp. *S. album*. Within the European distribution area there are many named local subspecies. Larva p. 230.

*P. a. apollo* in S Scandinavia, large, wings densely scaled, snow white.

*P. a. hispanicus* in C Spain, ups grey markings reduced, red spots small, in rare specimens spots may be yellow.

*P. a. nevadensis* in S Spain on Sierra Nevada, hw spots orange-yellow.

*P. a. rhodopensis* on Balkan Mts, large, uph red spots large.

*P. a. geminus* Switzerland (Valais), ♂ gc faintly yellowish, hw red spots small.

*P. a. pumilus* S Italy (Aspromonte) small, ♂fw 28–29mm, hw red spots very small.

*P. a. siciliae* in N Sicily, ups grey markings reduced, red spots small.

**Apollo**

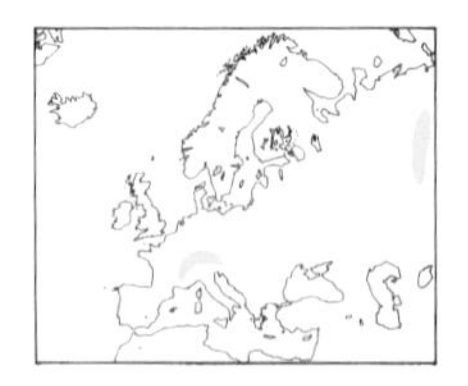

**SMALL APOLLO** *Parnassius phoebus*. Antennal shaft clearly *ringed black and white*; in fw a small red spot in s10 near costa; ♂ uph grey submarginal and *marginal markings lacking*. Range extends across Russia and Siberia to Kamschatka and N America. Flies July–August. Larval food plant *Saxafraga*.

*P. p. sacerdos* the European race, not rare in July–August in the Alps, flying at 2000m and over. In f. *cardinalis* (figured) the red hw spots are united by a black band.

*P. p. styriacus* with heavier black ups markings, occurs in the E Alps.

*P. p. gazeli* upf red costal spot absent, grey marginal borders present. Very local in the Maritime Alps.

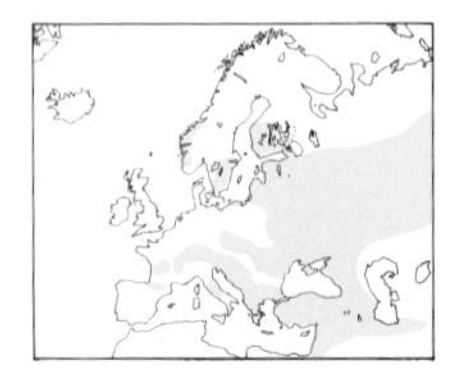

**CLOUDED APOLLO** *Parnassius mnemosyne*. Small, ups without red markings. Black markings scanty, extended in ♀ and in ♀–f. *melaina* ups widely suffused with grey and markings indistinct. Larval food plant *Corydalis*. Widely distributed in N and C Europe from valley levels to 1800m, often in hilly districts; in S Europe including Sicily, only in mountains. Absent from C and S Spain. Flies May–June. Range extends to the Caucasus and C Asia. Larva p. 224.

*P. m. mnemosyne*, upf grey apical area lacks white spots, the common form in N and C Europe, ♀–f. *melaina* common.

*P. m. athene*, in Greece and other countries of N Mediterranean, upf grey apical area encloses five or six white spots, Peloponessos only ♀–f. *melaina* rare.

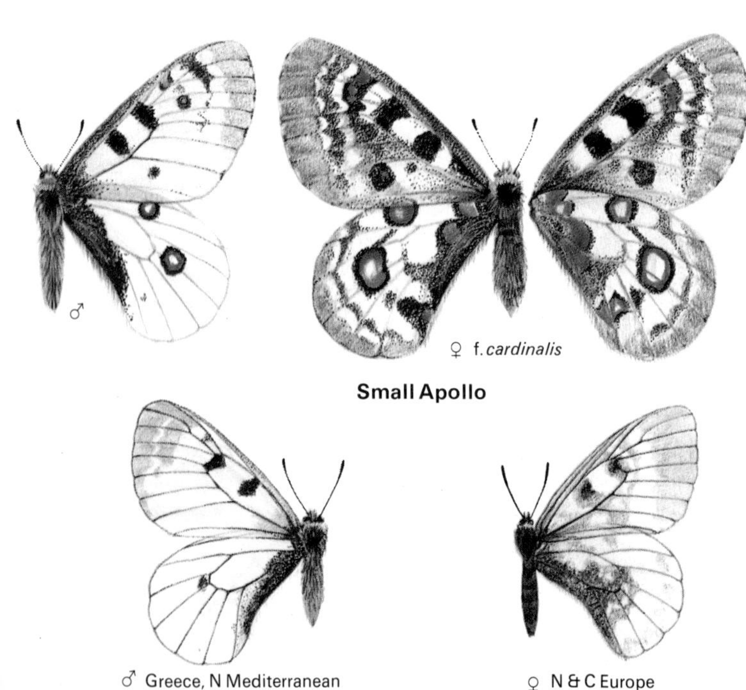


**Small Apollo**



**Clouded Apollo**

# PIERIDAE
## The Whites, Clouded Yellows and their allies

This large Family is well represented in every country, with about 40 species in our region. These butterflies are distantly related to the Swallowtails, with three pairs of functional legs, but their claws are divided to make two pairs on each foot. The ova are characteristic, about 2½ times as tall as they are wide. Not all the species are white, many are yellow and some with red markings. Some are great travellers, seen occasionally in large numbers, flying over the sea many miles from land. In England, any Clouded Yellows seen are immigrants from S Europe. Another well-known migrant is the Large White.

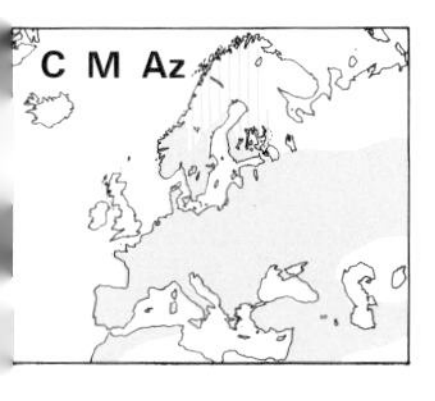


**LARGE WHITE** *Pieris brassicae*. ♂ upf milk-white, black apical border extends along outer margin to v3; uph black costal mark on costa at v7; unf with black pd spots in s1 and s3. ♀ upf more heavily marked with black pd spots in s1 and s3. Usually flies from April through summer to September in two or more broods, from sea level to 1800m. Range extends widely from N Africa and W Europe across temperate Asia to Siberia; occurs also in the Himalaya Mts. Two subspecies in our region. Larva p. 228. **Map 2**

*P. b. brassicae* in Europe and N Africa. First brood unh yellowish, suffused with dark scales; late broods unh white, suffusion minimal or absent. Larval food plants various Cruciferae, *Tropaeolum* etc. Flies April–June and July–September.

**Large White**

*P. b. cheiranthi* on Canary Islands, Tenerife, La Palma, Gomera. Both sexes larger, black markings extended, unf black pd spots joined together. ♀ ups hw yellow, upf pd spots greatly enlarged and fused. Food plant esp. *Tropaeolum*. On Madeira, f. *wollastoni*, characters are intermediate, black markings usually extended, ♂ fw black marginal border extends to v2; ♀ upf black pd spots frequently fused. Flies over the *maquis*, usually at 1000m or more. Said to fly throughout the year.

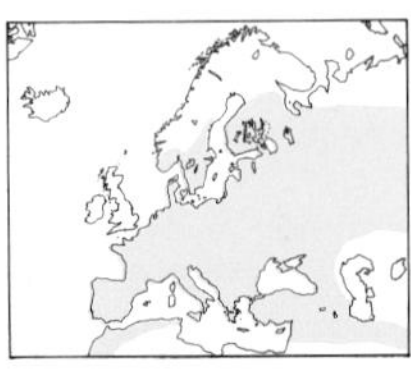

**Black-veined White**

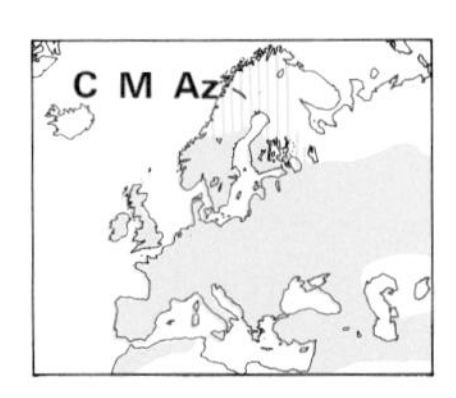

**BLACK-VEINED WHITE** *Aporia crataegi*. ♂ white, veins lined black. ♀ similar but upf discal area broadly un-scaled, membrane exposed for a variable extent, membrane sometimes faintly brown. Flies May–June in a single brood in open country from sea level to 1800m. Often common in N Africa and Europe to S Fennoscandia but extinct in Britain. Range extends across temperate Asia to Siberia and Japan. Larva p. 224.

**The Small Whites.** The five following species form a difficult group. All have two or three annual broods showing well-marked seasonal variation.

**SMALL WHITE** *Artogeia rapae*. Upf apical mark extends further along costa than down outer margin, postdiscal *spot round*, not connected with outer margin. Very common and widespread in open country in N Africa and Europe to 70°N. Flies throughout the summer, from sea level to 1800m. First brood ups markings grey, late broods often larger, markings black; in hot localities (e.g. Crete) upf apical mark may be enlarged, triangular. Larval food plants Cruciferae. Range extends across Europe and Asia to Siberia and N America (introduced). Larva p. 228. **Map 3**

**SOUTHERN SMALL WHITE** *Artogeia mannii*. Like the Small White. Upf apical black mark extending down outer margin to vein 4 or vein 3, post-discal spot *not round*, externally flat or concave. Common locally in S Europe from NE Spain to S Romania and Greece including Sicily. It is very local and rare in Middle Atlas, Morocco. Absent from Corsica, Sardinia, and other Mediterranean Islands. Flies at low levels throughout summer, but rising to 1500m in N Africa. First brood ups markings black, small, unh powdered with dark scales; late broods ups more heavily marked, esp.♀ with postdiscal spot upf clearly joined to outer margin along veins 3, 4; unh yellow. Larval food plant *Iberis sempervirens*. Range extends to Asia Minor, Caucasus and C Asia.

**MOUNTAIN SMALL WHITE** *Artogeia ergane*. ♂ unf without black markings, but dark discal spot may show through from ups. ♀ usually yellowish, upf grey apex and discal markings larger. Flies in April and later throughout the summer, in rocky places from low levels to 1500m. Very local in E Spain, and SE France, more common eastwards across Italy to Balkans, S Romania and Greece. Larval food plant *Aethionema*. European specimens are often small. Range extends across W Asia to N Iran.

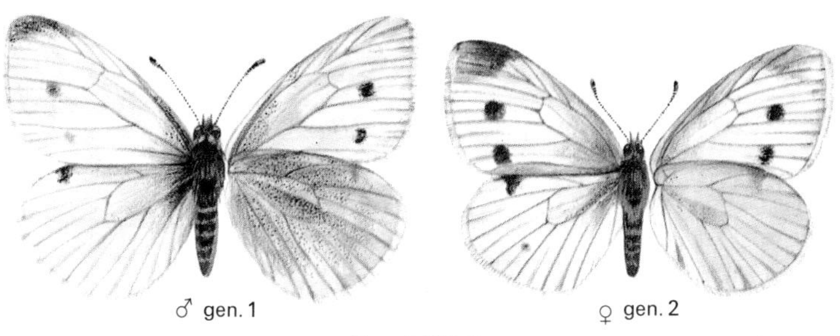


**Small White**

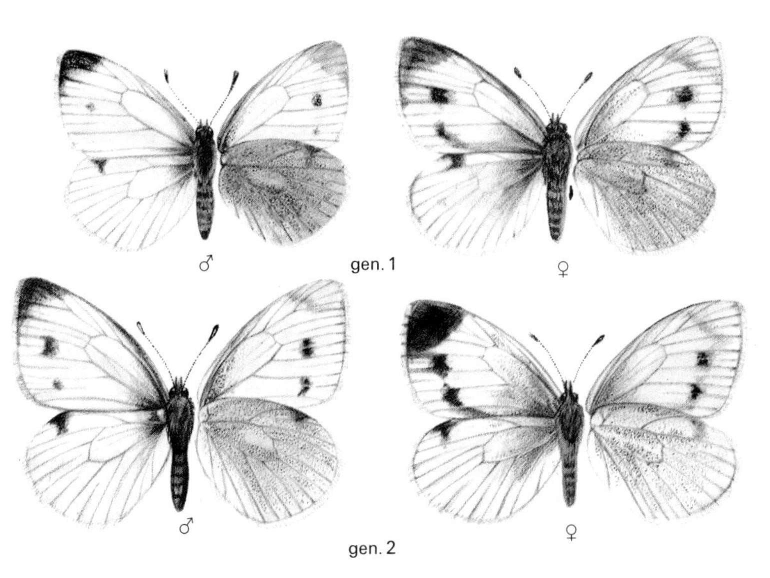


**Southern Small White**

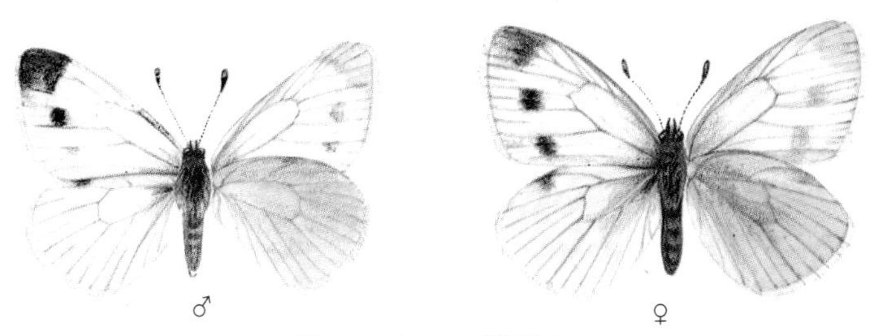


**Mountain Small White**

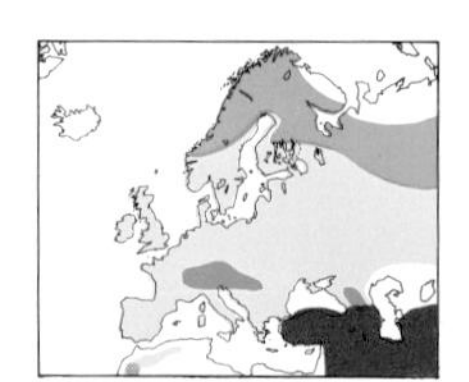

A.n. napi
A.n. adalwinda
A.n. bryoniae
A.n. segonazaci
A.n. pseudorapae

**GREEN-VEINED WHITE** *Artogeia napi*. Like the Small White, ♂ upf with or without black pd spot in s3; unh all veins more or less lined dark. ♀ upf with additional black pd spot in s1. Flies in April and later in two broods with marked seasonal dimorphism. In early brood ups black markings well developed; in late broods, f. *napaeae*, black markings reduced, unh dark lining of veins greatly reduced or vestigial, and easily confused with the Small White. Widely distributed in W Europe, very local and scarce in N Africa, with several local races. Larval food plant *Biscutella*. Range extends across W Asia to the S Urals, Caucasus, and N Iran. Larva p. 226. **Map 4**

*A. n. adalwinda*, ♂ like *A. napi* of first brood, ♀ ups widely suffused grey-brown. Racial in Fennoscandia in a single brood in arctic regions.

*A. n. bryoniae*, ♂ ups black veins prominent; ♀ ups heavily marked and suffused grey-brown. Flies at 1500m and upwards, in a single brood in the Alps, Tatra and Carpathians, but in N Balkans *A. n. flavescens*, darkly suffused specimens fly with others normally marked from 200m upwards. Also occurring in SE Europe, f. *subtalba*, unh the yellow shade absent.

*A. n. maura*, in Algeria, common locally around water springs at 1000m, flies in May and later. Probably represents *A. n. napi* in N Africa.

*A. n. segonzaci*, large, all dark markings emphasized, occurs in the High Atlas, Morocco, flying in June at 2800m in a single brood?

*A. n. atlantis*, flies in Morocco in the Middle Atlas, in May at 1400m, like *A. n. napi* the pd black spot in s3 prominent, rare and local.

*A.n. pseudorapae*, markings on unh vestigial or absent, flies in late broods in Turkey and in other hot countries.

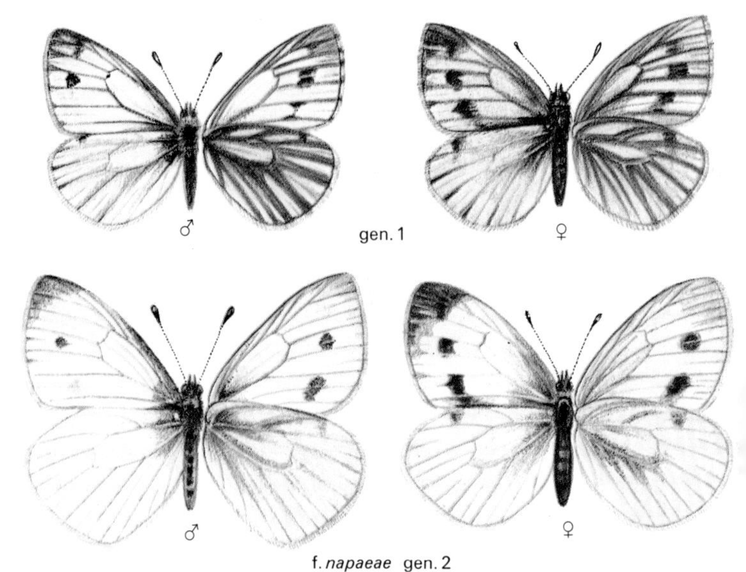


f. *napaeae* gen. 2

**Green-veined White**

**Green-veined White**

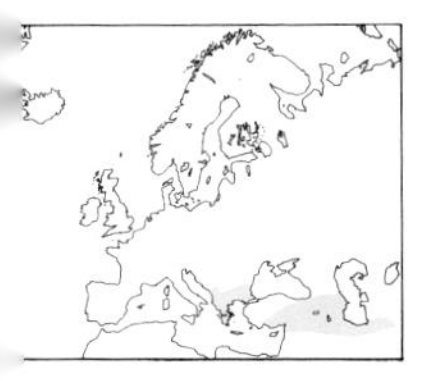

**KRUEPER'S SMALL WHITE** *Artogeia krueperi*. ♂ like *Artogeia napi*, upf a short triangular costal mark present before wing apex. Flies in April and later, in rocky places, from lowlands to 2000m, seasonal variation marked. In first brood unh broadly suffused dark green-grey, in later broods suffusion reduced and finally vestigial and yellowish. Occurs in Europe only in S Balkans and Greece. Larval food plant *Alyssum saxatile*. Range extends across W Asia to N Iran and C Asia, southwards to Oman.

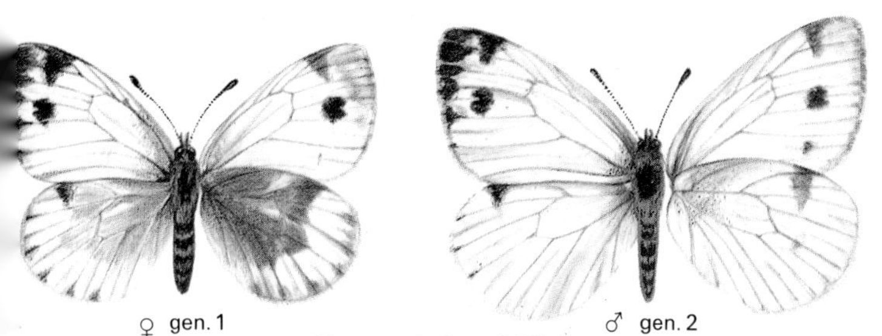


**Krueper's Small White**

**Bath and Peak Whites** The three species following are remarkable for their extensive geographical distributions.

**BATH WHITE** *Pontia daplidice*. Unf with black pd spot in s1b; unh has an isolated white spot in cell. Widespread and common throughout N Africa and S and C Europe. Flies from March all summer in open country at all altitudes to 2000m. Unh in first brood markings dark green, becoming yellow-green in late summer. Larval food plants *Arabis*, *Reseda*, *Sinapis* etc. The species is a notable migrant, seen occasionally in England. Range extends across all temperate Asia including the Himalayas. Larva p. 228.

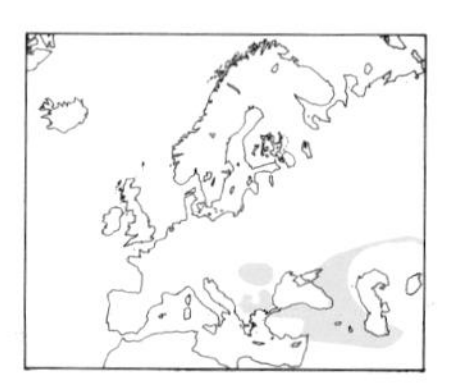

**SMALL BATH WHITE** *Pontia chloridice*. Like the Bath White, often smaller, unh *white marginal marks between veins elongate* and very regular. In Europe occurs only in Bulgaria, S Yugoslavia (Macedonia), N Greece and European Turkey. Flies at low altitudes in 2 annual broods, April–May and in June. Prefers rocky slopes with rough vegetation, a very local species. Larval food plants not known. Range extends eastwards to the Caucasus, N Iran, and S Siberia. In N America represented by the subspecies *beckeri*.

**PEAK WHITE** *Pontia callidice*. Unh with an elongate white mark in cell and *large submarginal chevrons*; veins broadly lined green in a lattice pattern. Occurs locally on the highest mountains, Pyrenees and Alps. Flies in a single brood May–June over grassy slopes at 2000m and over. Larval food plants *Erysimum pumilum* and *Reseda glauca*. Range extends to the Caucasus, Iran and Himalayas and across Siberia, also in Lebanon (Cedar Mt). In N America represented by the subspecies *occidentalis*.

**Dappled Whites and Orange-tips.** These form another Holarctic group with distinct anatomical characters, not closely related to the Small Whites. It is well represented in Western N America, especially in California.

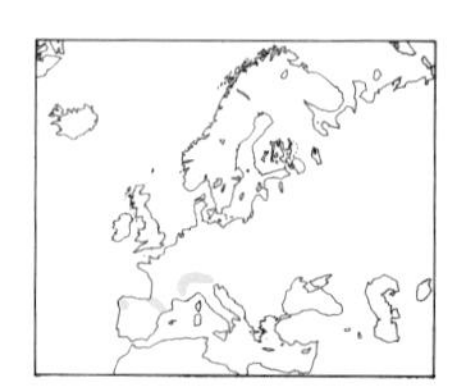

**DAPPLED WHITE** *Euchloe ausonia*. Upf discoidal mark narrow, angled, reaching costa; hw costal margin slightly angled at vein 8. ♀ ups black markings enlarged, hw yellowish. A mountain species, flying in a single brood in June–early July, over alpine pastures at 1500–2000m or more. Occurs in the Cantabrian Mts (Picos de Europa), Pyrenees and W Alps. Larval food plants *Iberis*, *Sisymbrium* and *Barbarea*. Eastern range uncertain, represented in N America by the form *ausonides*, flying in the western mountains at altitudes of 1000–2500m.

♂ gen. 2 ♀ gen. 1

**Bath White**

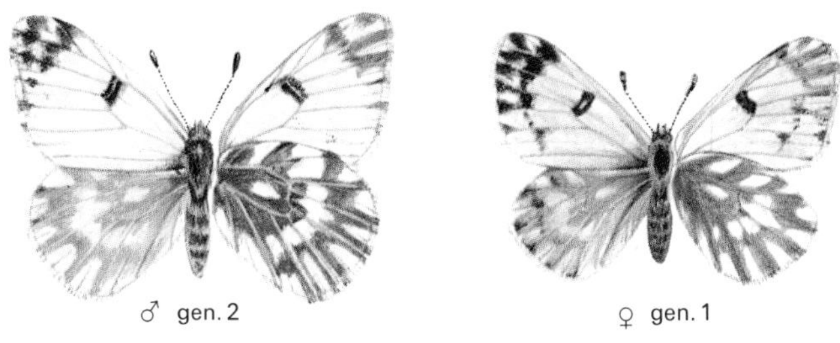

♂ gen. 2 ♀ gen. 1

**Small Bath White**

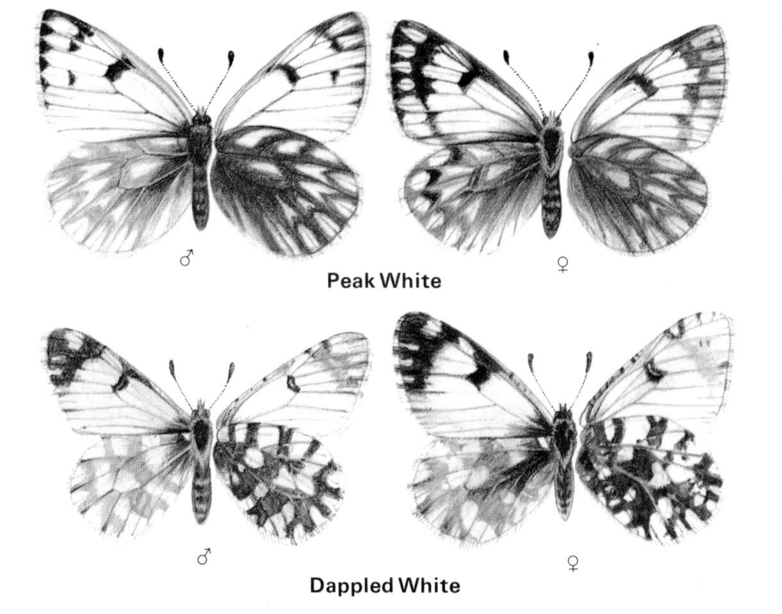

♂ ♀

**Peak White**

♂ ♀

**Dappled White**

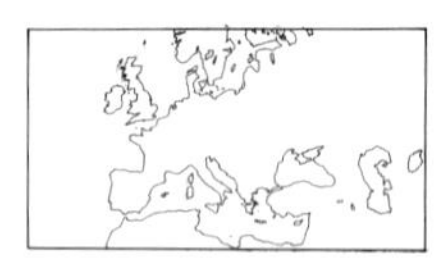

**CORSICAN DAPPLED WHITE** *Euchloe insularis.* Small; upf grey discoidal spot narrow, extending along costa; unf discoidal spot very small; unh white spots small, numerous. Flies May–June on Corsica and Sardinia from sea-level to 1200m, but rare at high altitudes. Generally very local and uncommon in open country. Larval food plant *Hirschfeldia incana*. E.

**FREYER'S DAPPLED WHITE** *Euchloe simplonia (crameri).* Like the Dappled White but upf the black discoidal (costal) mark larger, rarely joins the *costal border*; unh the white spaces sometimes nacreous. Widely distributed in Morocco and S Europe, extending north to S Switzerland (Rhône Valley), N Italy, Balkans and Greece. Flies at low altitudes in April–May or later, and in most localities a second brood, often slightly larger, appears after a short interval. Larval food plant *Iberis* etc. Range extends to Asia Minor, Lebanon, Caucasus, W Himalayas and NW America (*E. s. hyantis*).

The taxon *E. simplonia*, probably includes several distinct biological species, not yet recognized and defined.

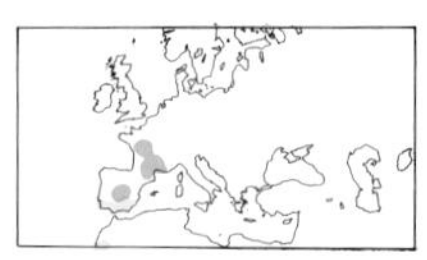

E.t. tagis
E.t. bellezina

**PORTUGUESE DAPPLED WHITE** *Euchloe tagis.* Like the Dappled White but smaller; hw evenly rounded, no angle at vein 8. Flies in a single brood at 1000m in Europe, but up to 1500m in Morocco. Locally variable with two subspecies.

*E. t. tagis*, in Portugal, Morocco and S Spain, unh greenish with a few small white spots. Very local but in colonies may be abundant. Flies in April or later. Larval food plant *Iberis pinnata*. E.

*E. t. bellezina*, in C Spain (Aranjuez) and France in Ain and Provence. Usually slightly larger, unh the white markings more regular and better defined. Flies in March–May, usually at moderate altitudes in open, hilly country. E.

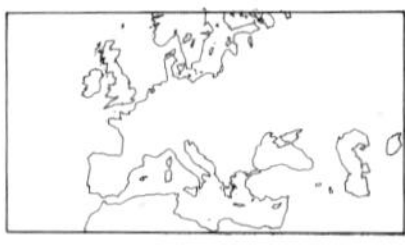

**PECH'S WHITE** *Euchloe pechi.* Small, ♂ upf lacking white spots in the apical grey mark; unh green with a single, small, white discal mark. Known only from the Djebel Aures in Algeria, flying at 1500m in April. Larval food plant not known. E.

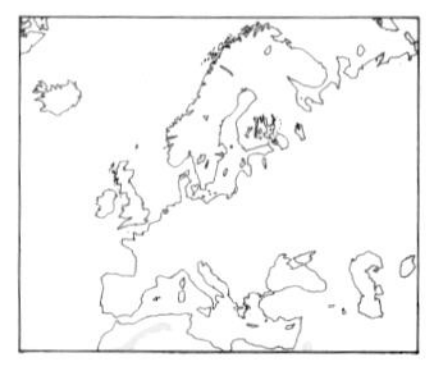

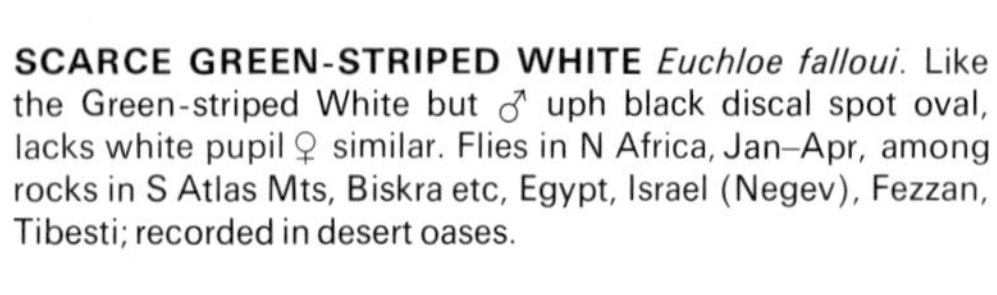

**SCARCE GREEN-STRIPED WHITE** *Euchloe falloui.* Like the Green-striped White but ♂ uph black discal spot oval, lacks white pupil ♀ similar. Flies in N Africa, Jan–Apr, among rocks in S Atlas Mts, Biskra etc, Egypt, Israel (Negev), Fezzan, Tibesti; recorded in desert oases.

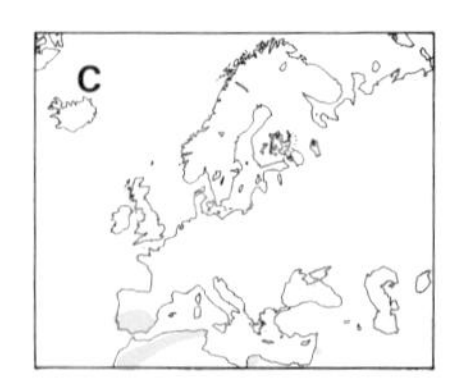


**GREEN-STRIPED WHITE** *Euchloe belemia.* ♂ ups like the Scarce Green-striped white but upf black discal spot large, enclosing a white stria. Flies in two annual broods, March–May and May–June, usually at low altitudes, over flowery slopes. Larval food plant *Iberis*, *Sisymbrium* etc.

*E. b. belemia*, in Spain, Portugal and N Africa. First brood January–March, unh green, white stripes regular and well defined. Late brood similar but unh yellow-green, white stripes irregular, not well defined. Range extends to Sinai, Lebanon etc with long disjunctions.

*E. b. hesperidum*, in Canary Islands on Gran Canaria, Tenerife, Fuerteventura, small, flies in two broods at 1500m and upwards.

**Green-striped White**

Larval food plants *Cheiranthus*, *Sisymbrium bourgaeanum*. Different colonies vary slightly in size of individuals.

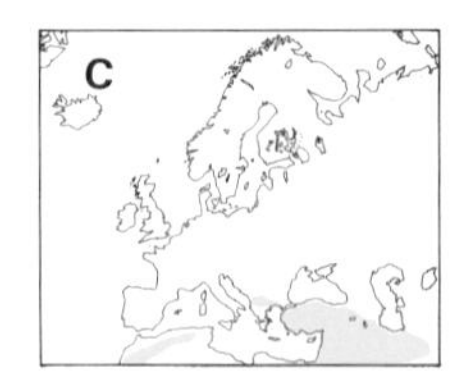


**GREENISH BLACK-TIP** *Elphinstonia charlonia*. Ups yellow, fw apex dark brown. Said to fly in two annual broods, at various dates from January to October, usually recorded in March–June, at various altitudes from valley levels to 1600m, often in rocky places. Larval food plant *Mathiola tessala*.

*E. c. charlonia*, widely distributed in N Africa, on the southern slopes of the Atlas Mts and in semi-desert country in Algeria, Tripolitania etc. Also on the Atlantic Islands of Lanzarote and Fuerteventura.

*E. c. penia*, in rare, widely separated colonies in S Yugoslavia, N Greece etc. Individuals slightly larger, ups deeper tone of yellow. Flies in June. The range extends widely across W Asia and Arabia with considerable local variation.

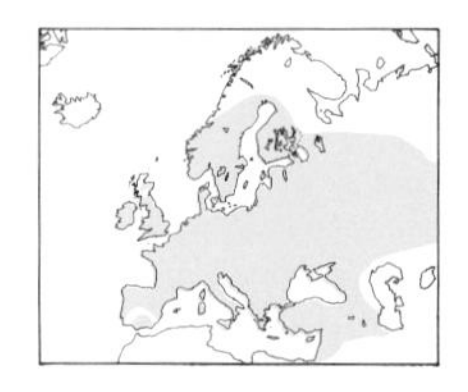

**ORANGE-TIP** *Anthocharis cardamines*. ♂ ups white; upf apex broadly red; unh markings mottled green. ♀ similar, upf lacking red apical mark. Usually common throughout W Europe to 66°N, absent from Balearic Islands, Malta, Elba. Flies from sea level to 1500m, in April–May often common in light woodland, roadsides etc. Larval food plant *Sisymbrium*, *Cardamine*. Range extends across temperate Asia to E Siberia and Japan. Larva p. 226. **Map 5**

*A.b.belia*
*A.b.euphenoides*

**MOROCCAN ORANGE-TIP** *Anthocharis belia*. ♂ ups yellow; upf apex broadly red; unh markings dark stripes in a lattice pattern. ♀ ups white upf dark discal spot prominent, apex yellowish bordered grey; unh yellow. Flies from valley levels to 1500m or more. Locally variable.

*A. b. belia* in Morocco, Algeria, Tunisia, unh markings reddish, in S Morocco often vestigial. Flies March–May. Larval food plant *Biscutella lyrata*.

*A. b. euphenoides* in Spain, Portugal and SE France, Italy in Cottian Alps north of Turin and C Abruzzi. Unh markings well defined, grey-green. Flies March–June. Larval food plant *Biscutella laevigata*.

♂ N Africa

♀ Yugoslavia & Greece

**Greenish Black-tip**

♂

♀

**Orange Tip**

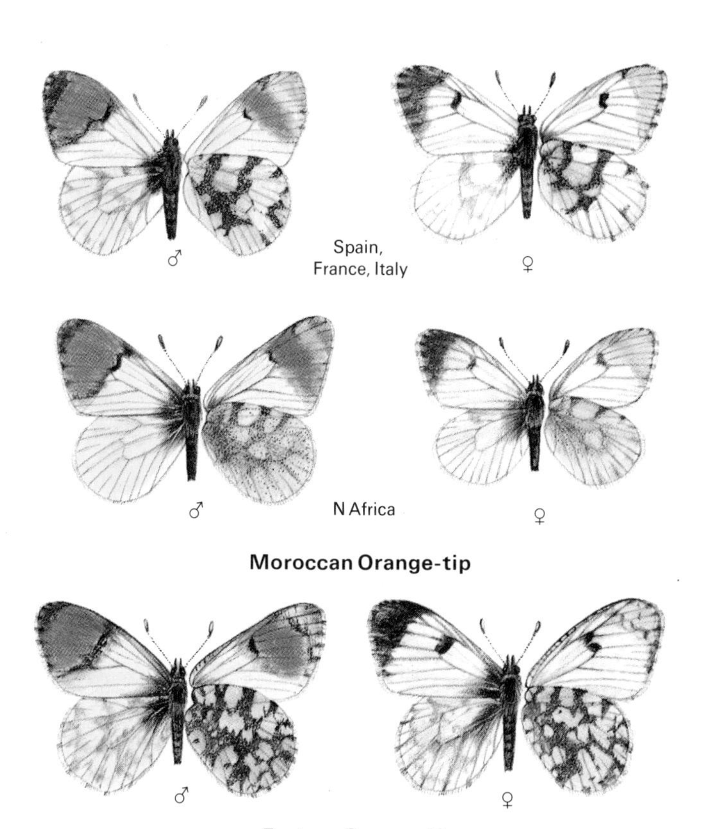


**Moroccan Orange-tip**

♂

♀

**Eastern Orange-tip**

**EASTERN ORANGE-TIP** *Anthocharis damone*. ♂ like the Orange-tip but ups yellow; unh yellow with mottled green markings. ♀ ups white; unh yellow, markings as in ♂. Flies April–May at 1000m or more in a single brood, local in Sicily (Mt Etna) and in S Italy (Calabria), S Yugoslavia, Greece (Mt Parnassus). Larval food plant *Isatis tinctoria*. Range extends to Syria, Lebanon, Trans-Caucasus and Iraq, always very local.

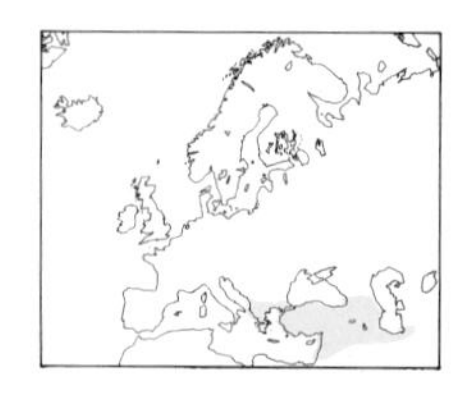

**GRUNER'S ORANGE-TIP** *Anthocharis gruneri*. ♂ ups like the Orange-tip but small, pale yellow; unh green with irregular white spots. ♀ white, grey *discal spot large*, joining costa. In Europe only in Greece, mainland and Peloponnessus, Macedonia, Albania and Turkey. Flies April–May, on open, stony ground in a single brood, from low levels to 1000m. Larval food plant *Aethionema saxatile*. Range includes Asia Minor, Syria, Kurdistan and N Iran.

**SOOTY ORANGE-TIP** *Zegris eupheme meridionalis*. ♂ white, upf apex broadly dark enclosing a red mark, which is small in ♀. Occurs in Spain and Portugal, April–June in open grassy meadows at valley levels to 1000m, but at 1500m in the Middle Atlas, and at 2500m in the High Atlas. Larval food plant *Hirschfeldia incana*. Colonies often widely separated, a local species. Range extends widely across S Russia, Asia Minor, the Caucasus, Iran and Kazahkstan.

**DESERT ORANGE-TIP** *Colotis evagore nouna*. ♂ upf apical vermilion patch triangular; unh pale yellowish to sandy-red, darkest in early broods. ♀ fw apex rounded, upf often with dark stripe below v1, variable vermilion patch small, narrow, black-bordered. Occurs in N Africa in rocky desert areas with *Capparis*, larval food plant. Occasional in S Spain (Murcia) not permanently resident. Flies from February through summer until October, from lowlands to 1800m. Range extends widely across tropical Africa to Arabia. The butterfly is our single representative of a large tropical group, not closely related to the European Orange-tips.

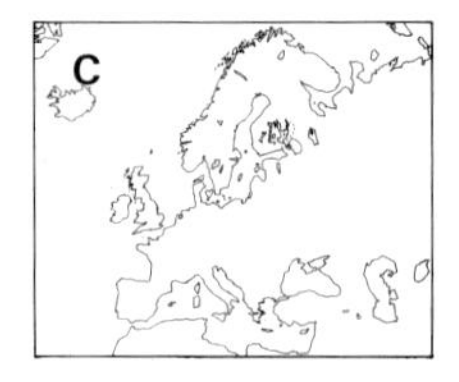


**AFRICAN MIGRANT** *Catopsilia florella*. ♂ ups greenish-white, discal spot very small, unf a hair-tuft from inner margin. ♀ similar but lacks hair-tuft, upf costa narrowly dark. Occurs in the Canary Islands on Tenerife, Gran Canaria and Gomera, flying at low levels, often in public gardens, in May and later. Larval food plant *Cassia*, grown in the islands as an ornamental plant. Range is most extensive across tropical Africa and Asia. First identified on the Canary Islands in 1964 on Tenerife, on Gomera since 1974. A dimorphic yellow-brown ♀-form occurs in Africa, not yet reported from the Canary Islands.

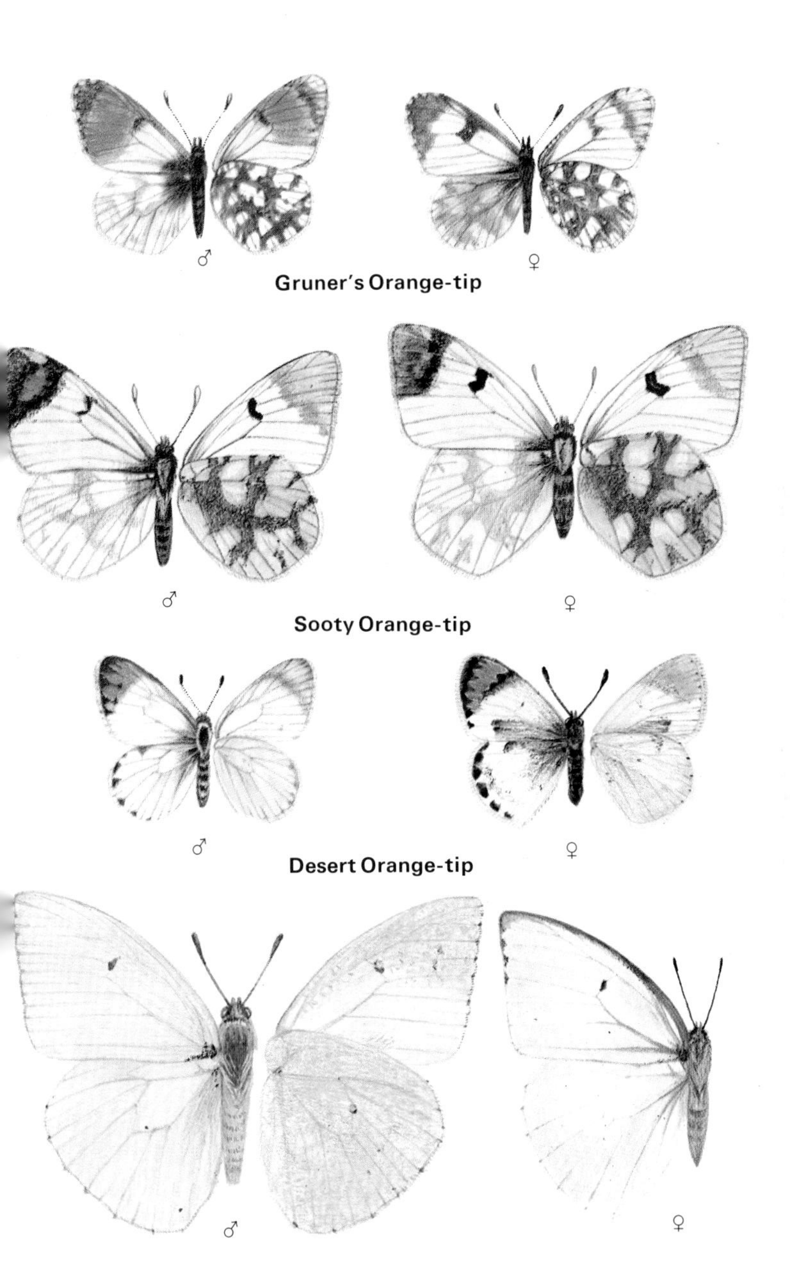
♂
♀
Gruner's Orange-tip
♂
♀
Sooty Orange-tip
♂
♀
Desert Orange-tip
♂
♀
African Migrant

**The Clouded Yellows.** This is an important group. Twelve species occur in our region, and many others are present in the great mountains of C Asia and N America, several also in S America on the Andes, and two in tropical Africa. It is noteworthy that so many species occur only in the Arctic, or on mountains at very high altitudes. Structurally they differ in several ways from other butterflies. In all but three of the European species a sex-brand is present on the hind-wing upperside.

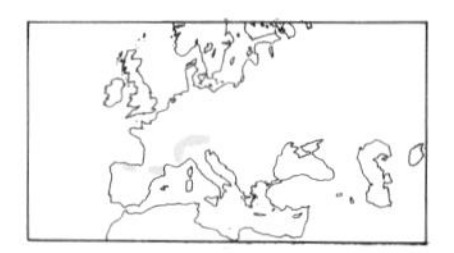

**MOUNTAIN CLOUDED YELLOW** *Colias phicomone*. Ups. ♂ greenish-yellow, hw yellow discal spot usually prominent on both surfaces. ♀ pale greenish-white. In both sexes ups more or less suffused with dark grey. Flies at 1800m or more, June–August. Larval food-plants *Hippocrepis comosa* and other vetches (*Vicia*). Not rare in the Pyrenees, Asturias and in the main chain of the Alps. Distinguish by locality from the Pale Arctic Clouded Yellow. Larva p. 224.

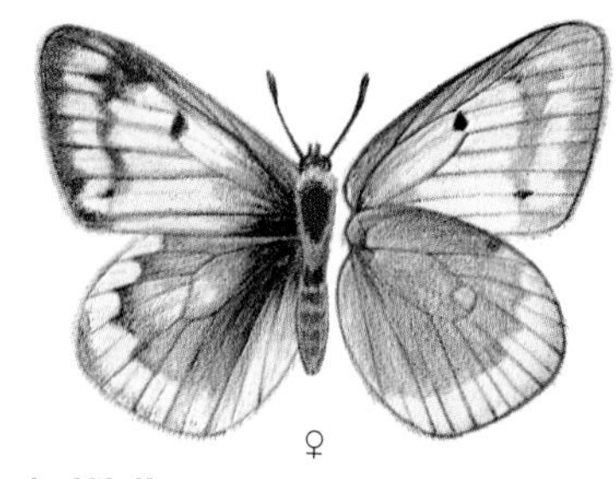


Mountain Clouded Yellow

**PALE ARCTIC CLOUDED YELLOW** *Colias nastes werdandi*. Like the Mountain Clouded Yellow but ups without dark suffusion; hw yellow discal spot very small or absent. ♀ greenish-white, ups veins lined dark, black markings extended. Flies in Fennoscandia, not south of 66°N, often in hill country, May–June. Larval food plant *Astragalus alpinus*. Range extends to arctic Siberia, Greenland and Labrador.

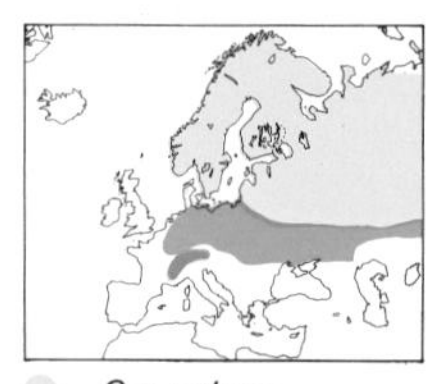

*C.p.palaeno*
*C.p.europome*
*C.p.europomene*

**MOORLAND CLOUDED YELLOW** *Colias palaeno*. Ups black marginal borders solid; unh submarginal markings absent. Flies over bogs and heaths with *Vaccinium* brushwood, at various altitudes. Larval food plant *Vaccinium uliginosum*. Range extends across Europe and Russia to N America. Larva p. 226.

*C. p. palaeno*, flies June in Fennoscandia to 70°N, ♂ ups very pale yellow, fringes red, upf a small, dark discal spot is usually present. ♀ ups white, dark marginal borders less well defined along inner margins.

*C. p. europome*, flies June–July on Moorlands in the Vosges, Jura, Bavaria and elsewhere in Germany, Czechoslovakia etc. ♂ like *C. p. palaeno* but bright butter yellow, upf a small, black discal spot is present, dark marginal borders wide; ♀ generally 'off-white,' occasional specimens yellow, uncommon – f. *illgneri*.

*C. p. europomene*, in the Alps of Switzerland etc, flying July at 600m or more, like *C. p. europome*, often slightly smaller, ♂ upf black discal spot absent; unh lightly suffused grey. ♀ usually white but yellow specimens f. *illgneri* not uncommon.

**EASTERN PALE CLOUDED YELLOW** *Colias erate.* ♂ ups bright butter yellow, upf black marginal borders sometimes crossed by a few vestigial yellow veins. ♀ yellow, upf black marginal borders enclosing yellow spots. Occasional in N Greece, S Yugoslavia, Bulgaria and Turkey, constant only in Romania. Flies in two broods, May and August–September, in open country at valley levels. Larval food plant not recorded. Range extends across the steppe country of Russia and C Asia to Kashmir.

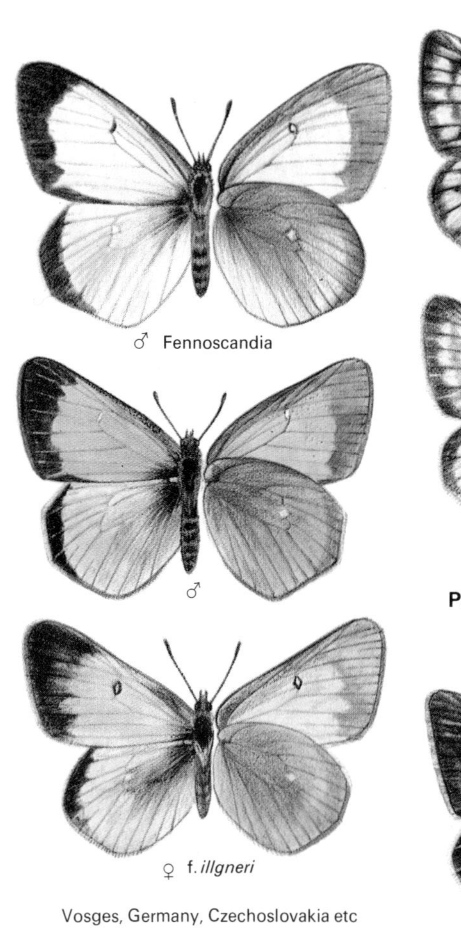

♂ Fennoscandia

♂

♀ f. *illgneri*

Vosges, Germany, Czechoslovakia etc

**Moorland Clouded Yellow**

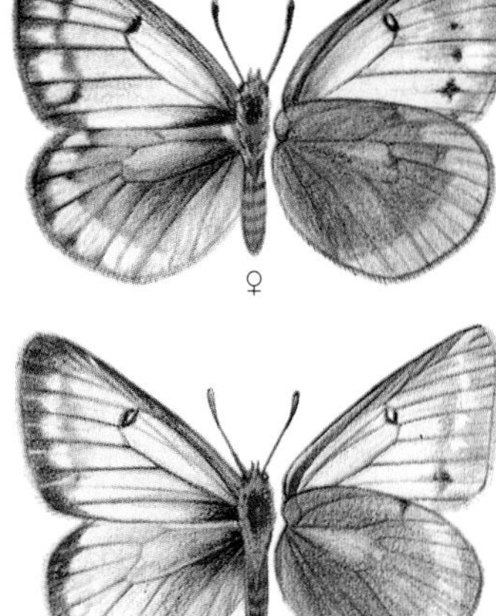

♀

♂

**Pale Arctic Clouded Yellow**

♂

**Eastern Pale Clouded Yellow**

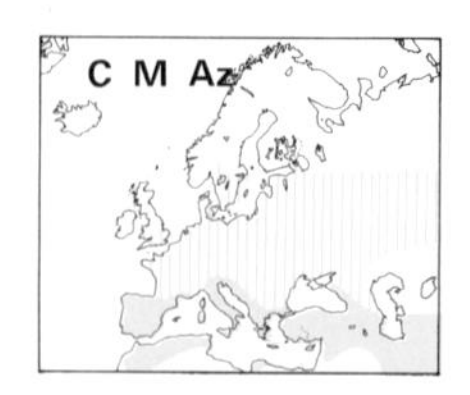


**CLOUDED YELLOW** *Colias crocea*. ♂ ups deep yellow, dark marginal borders crossed by yellow veins; unf well-defined submarginal black spots in spaces 1b,2,3. ♀ ups yellow; black marginal borders of both wings include pale yellow spots; ♀-f. *helice*, ups 'off-white,' uncommon with occasional intermediates. Widely distributed and resident in N Africa and S Europe and as a migrant north of the Alps to 66°N. Flies in April–May and later in open country from lowlands to 2000m. Larval food plants various Leguminosae, esp. Vetches. Range includes Fezzan, Cyrenaica, and across W Asia to Iran.
*Note*. The species is a vigorous migrant. It hibernates successfully in S Europe and other warm countries, flying northwards in spring to reach north-central Europe, including England, by June, where a late brood is established to fly in August. Such specimens probably perish. It is unlikely that the species is truly resident anywhere north of the Alps. Larva p. 224.

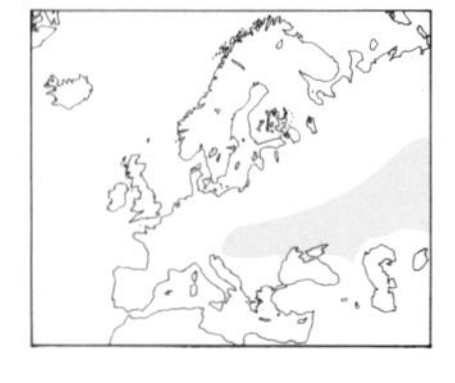

**LESSER CLOUDED YELLOW** *Colias chrysotheme*. Small, fw pointed; ♂ ups orange-yellow, upf costa faintly greenish, black marginal border crossed by yellow veins well defined. ♀ upf costa broadly greenish, in other respects like the Clouded Yellow. Occurs in E Austria (Burgenland), Moravia, Hungary, Slovakia and Romania. Flies in two broods, May and late July–August, at low levels over the grass slopes on the steppe country. White and pale yellow ♀-forms are rare. Larval food plant *Vicia hirsuta*. Range extends to the Caucasus and S Siberia.

♂

♀

**Lesser Clouded Yellow**

**GREEK CLOUDED YELLOW** *Colias libanotica heldreichii*. ♂ large, ups *dusky orange*, dark marginal borders crossed by yellow veins; unh yellow-green. ♀ unh *smooth blue-green*, discal spot white, *small*. Confined to the high mountains of Greece, Mt Parnassus, Mt Chelmos etc. Flies in June–July at 1800m or more. A white ♀-form is not uncommon. Larval food plant *Astragalus cyleneus*. Range extends to Asia Minor, Lebanon, Iran.

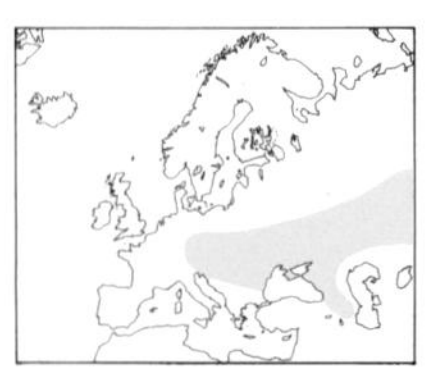

**DANUBE CLOUDED YELLOW** *Colias myrmidone*. ♂ ups bright orange-yellow, marginal borders *solid black*. ♀ ups like the Clouded Yellow, uph has pale submarginal spots, pale or white forms not rare; unf black *submarginal spots near anal angle not prominent*. Flies in May and again in July–August. Local in E Europe, Hungary, Romania, Austria to Munich, over heaths and open places. Larval food plant *Cytisus capitatus*. Range extends across Russia to the Ural Mts.

**Clouded Yellow**

**Greek Clouded Yellow**

**Danube Clouded Yellow**

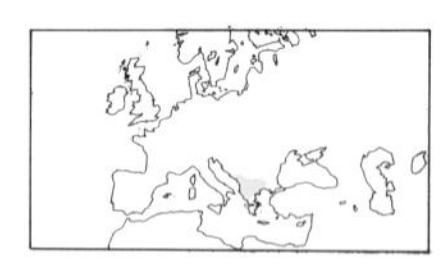

**BALKAN CLOUDED YELLOW** *Colias balcanica.* Larger than the Danube Clouded Yellow, ♂ *ups reddish-orange*, wing-borders *solid black*. ♀ upf *base dusky*, uph *base suffused grey*; a white ♀–form *rebeli* is rare. Occurs in Yugoslavia, from Mt Trebević to Macedonia on Mt Perister, flying in July in light woodland at 1500m or more. Larval food plant not known. E.

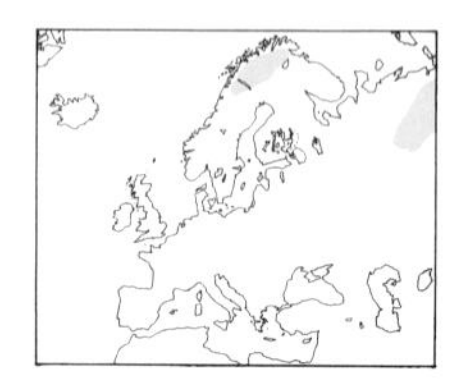

**NORTHERN CLOUDED YELLOW** *Colias hecla sulitelma.* ♂ small, ups orange-yellow, upf discal spot small; unh base green. ♀ ups yellow submarginal spots usually prominent; unh green. Within the region, only in Fennoscandia not south of 68°N. Flies in late June–July, at sea level rising to 1000m (Mt Nuolja). Larval food plant *Astragalus alpinus*. Range extends across arctic Europe and Asia, Greenland and N America (circumpolar).

**PALE CLOUDED YELLOW** *Colias hyale.* ♂ pale yellow, fw *pointed*, apex *broadly black* or dark grey; uph discal spot *pale*. ♀ ups dark markings as in ♂. Resident in E Europe, Austria, Romania, Balkans, often seen in C Europe, probably absent from Spain. Flies in S Europe in May–June and August–September, often at low levels over clover fields but rising to 1800m, the late brood often common. Larval food plants *Vicia, Coronilla, Medicago* (Lucerne). Range extends across Russia to the Urals, Caucasus, Altai Mts and C Asia. Larva p. 224.

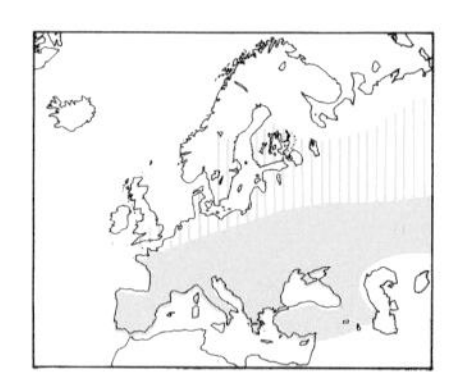

**BERGER'S CLOUDED YELLOW** *Colias australis.* ♂ like the Pale Clouded Yellow, upf *brighter yellow*, dark apical markings *less extensive*, basal shade restricted to space 1a, not invading cell; uph discal spot *bright orange*, prominent. ♀ like the Pale Clouded Yellow, black markings may be less extensive. A yellow ♀–f. *inversa* not uncommon. Resident chiefly in SW Europe, France, Spain, Italy, Mediterranean islands and Greece. Flies May–June and August–September. May fly with the Pale Clouded Yellow, distinction often most difficult. Larval food plants *Hippocrepis comosa* (Horse-shoe Vetch), *Coronilla*. The species is strongly migratory, occasionally reaches England. Range extends to Asia Minor.

♂

♀

**Berger's Clouded Yellow**

**Balkan Clouded Yellow**

**Northern Clouded Yellow**

**Pale Clouded Yellow**

**The Brimstones.** The Brimstone Butterflies are unusual in their strongly falcate forewings with rather anomalous venation, as in the Clouded Yellows. The basal segments of the palpi are exceptionally long, and the feet are without pulvilli. A striking feature is present in their curious life history. In W Europe the single annual brood emerges in late summer, and very soon the butterflies hide away for winter hibernation without mating. They come out again in March or April, mate at once and eggs are laid which produce the new brood in late summer. It seems possible that this behaviour pattern is adjusted for W Europe only. In N Africa fresh specimens of the Brimstone and the Cleopatra are flying already in June. In the Canary Islands, the local *cleobule* is said to fly throughout the year, except perhaps during October and November.

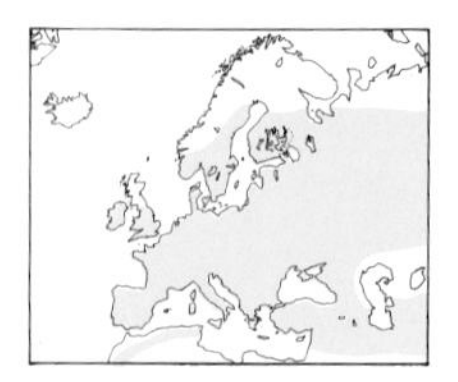

**BRIMSTONE** *Gonepteryx rhamni.* ♂ ups both wings lemon-yellow; hw outer margin angled at vein 3. ♀ ups greenish-white. Widespread and usually common in N Africa and Europe to 65°N, absent from Crete and the Atlantic islands. Flies in June–July and later, and hibernated specimens appear in March–April in N Europe, from sea level to 1600m, a single brood in Europe, perhaps two broods in N Africa. Large specimens, f. *meridionalis* occur locally in S Europe and N Africa. Larval food plant *Rhamnus*. Range extends across Russia and W Asia to Siberia and Japan. **Map 6**

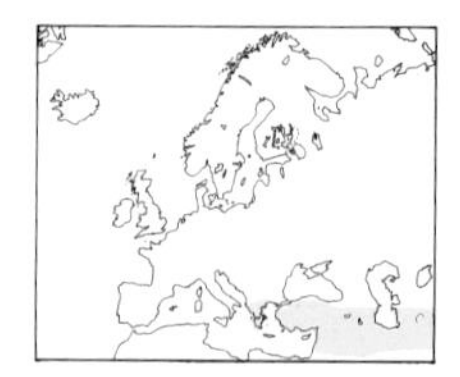

**POWDERED BRIMSTONE** *Gonepteryx farinosa.* Like *G. rhamni* in size and markings; ♂ ups the tone of lemon-yellow is paler, *the hw obviously paler than the fore-wing.* In fresh males upf appears slightly roughened on close examination, due to the upturned apices of the scales, which do not lie flat as in *G. rhamni.* ♀ similar to *G. rhamni.* Flies in May–June in a single brood, usually at low or moderate altitudes in hilly country. In Europe occurs only in Greece, Albania and Turkey, perhaps also in Yugoslav Macedonia. Range extends across W Asia to N Iran. Larval food plant *Rhamnus.*

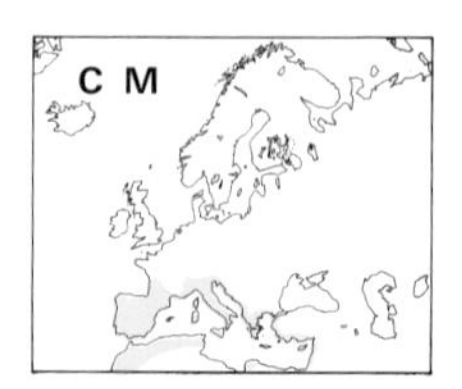


**CLEOPATRA** *Gonepteryx cleopatra.* ♂ like the Brimstone, but upf with a deep orange flush. ♀ greenish-white, uph often slightly flushed yellow. It occurs widely distributed in S Europe from sea level to 1000m or more, and to 1700m in N Africa. Hibernated individuals appear in early spring, the first brood in June–July, perhaps a partial second brood in late summer in some localities. Range extends to Asia Minor, Cyprus and Lebanon. Larva p. 224.

*G. c. cleopatra* in N Africa, upf yellow marginal border 5–6mm wide. In W Europe f. *europaea*, upf yellow marginal border usually narrower. In Greece the females often have a marked yellow flush uph, which may be widely suffused upf in some specimens.

*G. c. maderensis*, on Madeira, ♂ upf intense orange, yellow marginal border 2–3mm, thorax and dorsum of abdomen dark grey, prominent. Flies from April through summer, often among mountains up to 1000m.

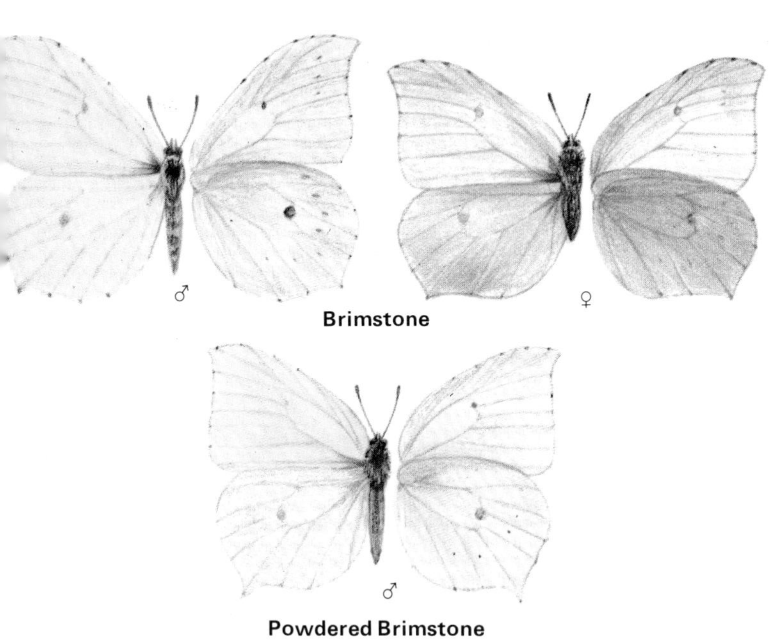

♂ ♀

**Brimstone**

♂

**Powdered Brimstone**

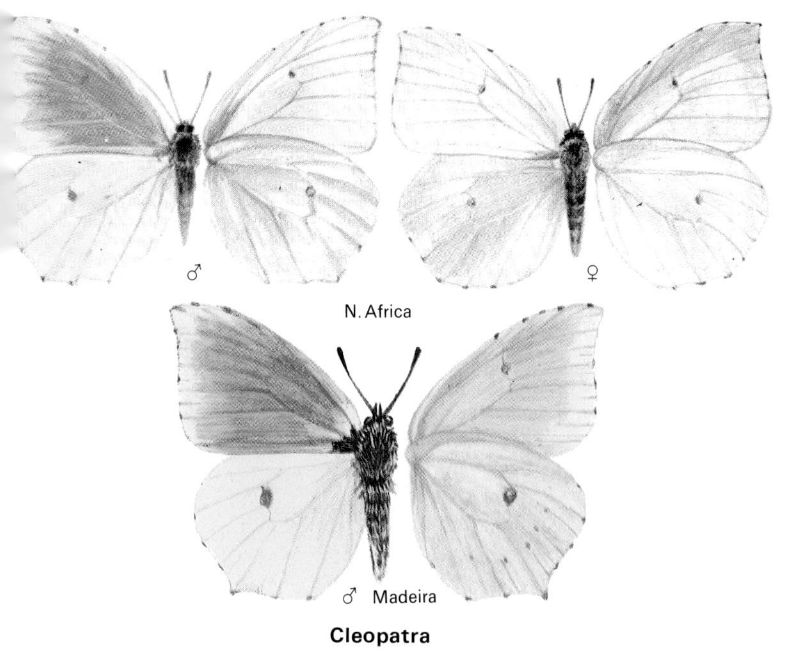

♂ ♀

N. Africa

♂ Madeira

**Cleopatra**

♂ Tenerife & Gomera

♂ La Palma ♀

**Cleopatra**

*G. c. cleobule*, on Canary Islands, Tenerife and Gomera, usually large, upf suffused orange-yellow to outer margin; ♀ ups suffused yellow or faintly orange upf; hw marginal angle at v3 reduced. Said to fly every month except November.

*G. c. palmae*, on La Palma, like *G. c. cleobule* but upf paler, yellowish; ♀ uph yellow but upf almost white, lightly flushed yellow along costa to apex. The species is not recorded from the eastern group of islands. In all areas ♂♂ are dimorphic, unf costa and all hw pale green or – f. *italica* – yellow, the latter rare in France, Spain and N Italy. The f. *italica* is common (50%?) in Morocco, C and S Italy, Sicily and Greece, probably preponderates in the Canary Islands and is constant in the Balearics, Corsica, Sardinia, Crete, Elba and in all Asiatic specimens examined.

**The Wood Whites.** The Wood Whites are small, fragile insects, which occupy a special position among the Whites, with several unusual features. In the fore-wing all veins (12) are present, but the cell is extremely short, less than a quarter of the full length of the wing. All our species are very widely distributed in Eurasia, where they are the only representatives of a large South American group with over 70 species, none of them white, but with curious and often mimetic wing-markings.

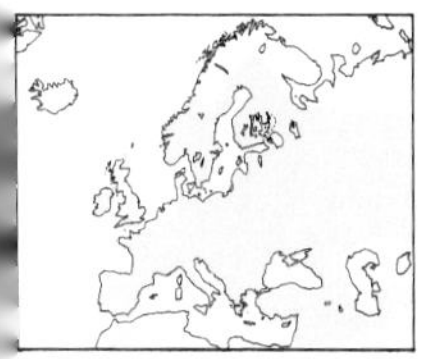

**WOOD WHITE** *Leptidea sinapis.* Antennal club black, extreme apex chestnut brown with white patch beneath. Occurs in Morocco Er Rif and Middle Atlas and is widely distributed in Europe to 66°N. Flies in two or more broods, May–June and July–August, from valley levels to 1500m, always in light woodland. Seasonal variation is marked: first brood, upf apical mark grey; unh mottled yellow and grey; ♀ upf apical mark vestigial. Second brood, ♂ upf apical mark smaller, dense black; unh markings vestigial or absent. ♀ apical mark usually absent. Larval food plants various Papilionaceae, esp. *Lotus*. Range extends across Russia and temperate Asia to E Siberia. Larva p. 224. **Map 7**

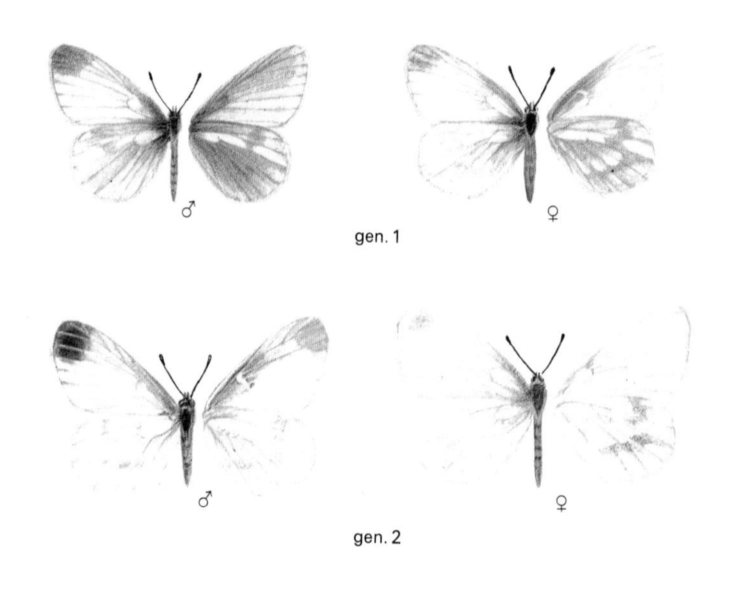


**Wood White**

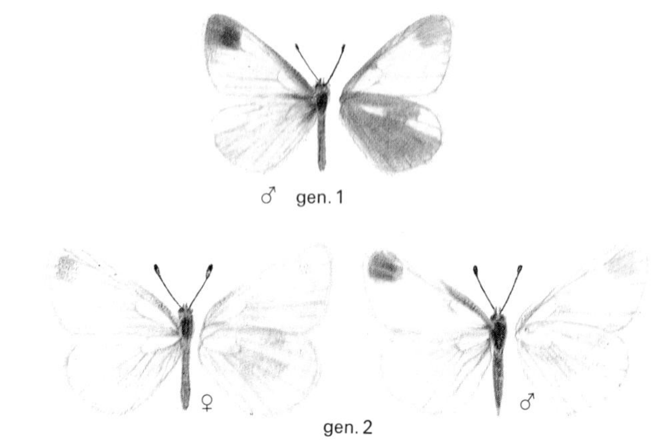
♂ gen. 1

♀ ♂
gen. 2

**Eastern Wood White**

**EASTERN WOOD WHITE** *Leptidea duponcheli.* Like the Wood White; fw apex pointed; antennal club without white mark beneath. Local in SE France, northwards to Briancon; S Yugoslavia (Skopje); Greece, Bulgaria, Albania and Turkey, Flies in two broods, April–June and July–September, at low levels in mountainous districts. First brood ♂ unh grey with small white areas at base and apex; ♀ upf grey apical mark often divided by veins. Second brood ♂ upf apical mark black, small; unh flushed yellow, otherwise usually unmarked; ♀ upf apical mark grey, greatly reduced, often absent. Larval food plants various Papilionaceae. Range extends widely across W. Asia to Iran.

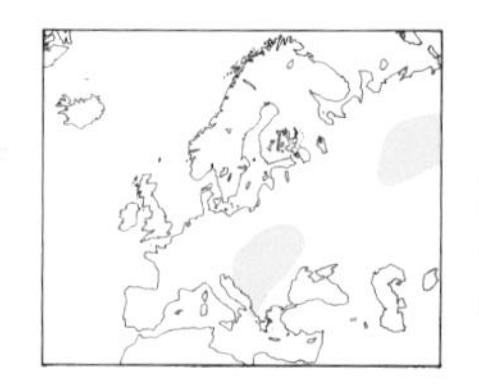

**FENTON'S WOOD WHITE** *Leptidea morsei.* In the European race, first brood: f. *croatica*, small, fw with definite apical peak at vein 6; upf veins 3, 4, 5, darkened to form a streaky, apical mark; unh yellowish marbled grey, but cell area remains white; ♀ falcate apical peak better developed. Second brood: f. *major* larger, ♂ paper-white, upf apical *peak not constant*, apical black mark dense; unh markings pale grey; antennal tip brown, white beneath. Occurs very locally in Czechoslovakia, Austria, Romania, Yugoslavia in Croatia and W to Fiume (furthest W). Flies April–May and June–July in mountainous country, at valley levels in light woodland. Females rarely leave the woods. Larval food plant *Lathyrus verna* and *L. niger*. Commonly associated with the Common Glider (p. 102) with the same food plants. Range extends across Siberia to Japan.

**Fenton's Wood White**

♂ gen. 2

# LYCAENIDAE
## Blues, Hairstreaks and their allies

This is one of the largest families, including over a quarter of all the butterflies in the region. Male fore-leg well formed, with a single long tarsal segment, ending in a single claw; the precostal vein of the hind-wing is absent. The larvae are short, flat like a woodlouse, with a lateral ridge, differing greatly from the larvae of all other butterflies. Many have a 'honey gland' on their backs which secretes a clear liquid, of which ants are very fond. Some of them actually live for part of their lives in the ant's nests. The pupae are usually attached to the food-plant by the cremastral hooks and a girdle, head upwards like a Pierid. Almost all the butterflies are small, difficult to identify, as the characters often are similar through quite large specific groups.

**The Silverlines.** These small butterflies are our only representatives of a specialized group widely spread across the dry, semi-desert regions of Africa and Asia. On the uppersides they are golden yellow, looking very like the Coppers, although there is no evidence of close relationship. The hw undersides are marked rather strangely with rows of ocelli or spots, often with gleaming metallic silvery scales, and the hind-wings have delicate, short tails near the anal angles. The sexes are similar.

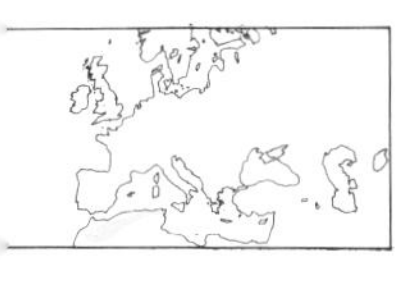

**DONZEL'S SILVER LINE** *Cigaritis zohra*. Upf submarginal spots well developed, uph basal row of black spots short, postdiscal row irregular; unh with rows of small, silver spots broadly ringed yellowish and bordered black. Flies on dry hillsides at 1000m or more with a single brood in April–May. Local in Morocco, Algeria and Tunisia. Larval food plant not known E.

**ALLARD'S SILVER LINE** *Cigaritis allardi*. Like *C. zohra*. Both sexes upf submarginal spots well developed; uph basal row of spots extends to space 1c, postdiscal row short; unh ground-colour white, prominent, markings as in *C. zohra*. A single brood flies in April–May, on dry hillsides, very local at 1000m or more in Morocco, Algeria and Tunisia. Larval food-plant not known. E.

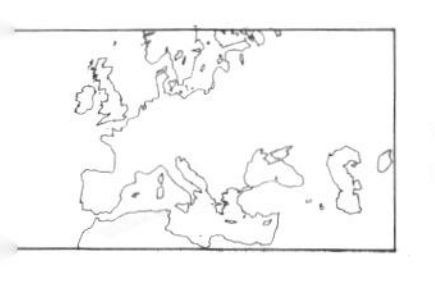

**COMMON SILVER LINE** *Cigaritis siphax*. Like *C. zohra* but upf submarginal black spots not well developed, small; uph costal border broadly dusky, black discal spot exposed, pd row of spots acutely angled; unh variable, markings almost obscured by some shade of brown. Flies in a single brood in March or later, often at lower altitudes. Very local in Algeria and Tunisia, not recorded from Morocco. E.

♀

**Donzel's Silver Line**

♂

**Allard's Silver Line**

♀

**Common Silver Line**

**The Large Hairstreaks.** These butterflies are the western representatives of a large group which is widespread in SE Asia. They occur especially in China, Formosa and Assam, there forming an important tribe. All their larvae feed upon forest trees.

*Q.q. quercus*
*Q.q. iberica*

**PURPLE HAIRSTREAK** *Quercusia quercus.* ♂ ups gleaming purple-blue but somewhat variable. ♀ upf has a smaller area of royal blue at wing base and along the inner margin. Range extends widely across Europe and W Asia. Two subspecies within the region. Larva p. 228. **Map 8**

*Q. q. quercus.* Uns grey, pale pd stripe firmly marked across both wings. Flies in July–August, usually at valley levels, in S and C Europe to 62°N, but replaced in most of Spain and in N Africa by the following subspecies.

*Q. q. iberica.* Uns pale yellow-grey, pd stripe not firmly marked, often vestigial. Occurs June–July in mountains in C and S Spain, and in N Africa up to 2000m. Colonies with intermediate characters occur in N Spain. In all cases the larval food plants are species of oak or ash. E.

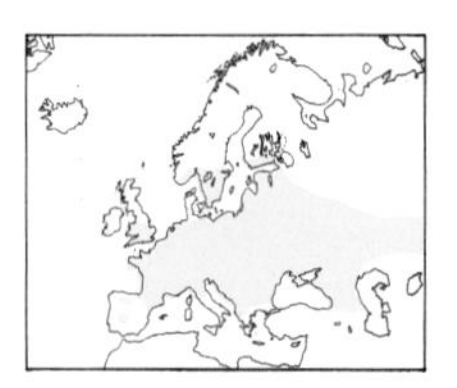

**BROWN HAIRSTREAK** *Thecla betulae.* ♂ ups dark brown, on fw often with a vestigial yellow pd mark; ♀ upf with broad orange pd band. Flies July–August at low or moderate levels in light woodland in C Europe to 62°N, and recorded from Cantabrian Mts and from N Greece, but rare in the south. Larval food plants Plum, Sloe and more rarely Birch and Beech. Range extends across temperate Asia to Amurland and Korea. **Map 9**

**SPANISH PURPLE HAIRSTREAK** *Laeosopis roboris.* ♂ ups purple-blue with black marginal borders; unh pale grey, submarginal spots yellow. ♀ similar, upf blue area reduced. Flies in June–July, from valley levels to 1500m, almost always around Ash (*Fraxinus*). Only in SW Europe. E.

**The Small Hairstreaks.** In this group external characters are well defined, with little indication of close relationship to the Large Hairstreaks. All species fly in a single brood in late June–July.

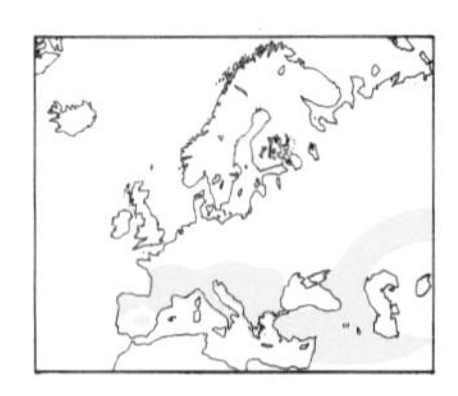

**SLOE HAIRSTREAK** *Nordmannia acaciae.* Often small, ups brown, upf lacking a fulvous pd patch; unh with three or more yellow submarginal lunules, the lunule in s2 largest, with a black marginal spot prominent, ♀ ups sometimes has vestiges of paler markings; a black anal hairtuft present. Local but widely distributed in S Europe to 47°N, reaching S Germany and Czechoslovakia in the east, absent from Mediterranean Islands. Flies June–July from sea level to 1400m, often around bushes of Sloe (*Prunus spinosa*), larval food plant. Eastern range uncertain.

**ILEX HAIRSTREAK** *Nordmannia ilicis.* ♂ ups dark brown, upf with or without a fulvous pd patch; unh usual markings of white striae *well developed*, 3–6 red submarginal spots internally and externally bordered black, *white marginal line usually well defined*. ♀ often larger, upf fulvous pd patch (f. *cerri*) common, esp in Spain etc, black anal hair tuft absent. Occurs June–July on rough ground among dwarf oaks, from sea level to 1500m, generally common in S Europe but more local and rare northwards to 58°N. Absent from Britain, Corsica, Sardininia, Crete, S Spain, Portugal. Range extends to Asia Minor and Lebanon. Larval food plant oak, esp. dwarf species.

♂ S & C Europe

♀ Spain & N Africa

**Purple Hairstreak**

♂

♀

**Brown Hairstreak**

♂

♀

**Spanish Purple Hairstreak**

♂

♀

**Sloe Hairstreak**

♂

♀ f. *cerri*

**Ilex Hairstreak**

N.e. esculi
N.e. mauretanica

**FALSE ILEX HAIRSTREAK** *Nordmannia esculi.* Like *N. ilicis*, uns white pd striae not well developed, often vestigial or absent; unh red submarginal spots usually small, but well formed and clearly separated, narrowly bordered black, *white marginal line vestigial.* Hw tail often appears prominent. ♀ often larger, upf sometimes with ill-defined fulvous pd mark. Flies June–July from valley levels to about 1200m. Larval food plants dwarf oaks. Two subspecies. E.

*N. e. esculi.* Uns markings well developed. Occurs June–July in SE France, E Pyrenees, Portugal and Spain, except Galicia and northern coastal districts, also in Balearic Islands. Similar species. Ilex hairstreak, which also occurs in SE France and in N Spain (Asturias Mts, Bronchales distr.).

*N. e. mauretanica.* Uns paler grey-brown, markings usually vestigial. Occurs in Morocco, Algeria and Tunisia, in the Middle Atlas, flying at 1500m or more.

In the three species following, males have a small, oval sex-brand upf above the cell.

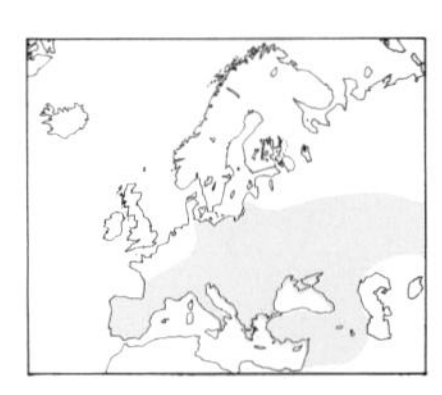

**BLUE-SPOT HAIRSTREAK** *Strymonidia spini.* Easily distinguished *unh by the blue mark at the anal angle.* In C and S Spain; ♀-f. *vandalusica*, upf with fulvous pd patch. Flies June–July over rough ground with brushwood, from valley levels to 1600m, widely distributed in S and C Europe to 58°N, but absent from Mediterranean islands. Larval food plants *Prunus, Rhamnus* etc. Range extends across Asia to the Amur. Larva p. 230.

**WHITE LETTER HAIRSTREAK** *Strymonidia w-album.* ♂ unf white pd stripe *firmly marked near costa but incomplete*; unh at anal angle shows *white 'W'-mark*, red submarginal lunules fused to form a tapering band. Sexes similar. Flies July at low or moderate levels near trees of Elm, Wych Elm etc. larval food plants, often seen at bramble flowers. Local but widely distributed in S and C Europe to 60°N, including England and S Scandinavia, Balkans and Greece. Absent from E Pyrenees, Portugal and Mediterranean Islands except Sicily; very local in N Spain. Range extends across temperate Asia to the Pacific. Larva p. 226. **Map 10**

**BLACK HAIRSTREAK** *Strymonidia pruni.* ♂ ups medium brown, *uph orange submarginal lunules present* in spaces 1b, 2, 3, often prominent; unh orange submarginal lunules *in complete series*, often present also unf, edged internally with black spots. Flies June–July at low altitudes, often near Blackthorn (Prunus), larval food plant. Local in C Europe from N Spain to 56°N, and eastwards to the Baltic countries, Balkans and N Greece. Absent from Portugal, peninsular Italy and Mediterranean islands, Ireland, local in C England. Range extends across Russia and Siberia to Japan. Larva p. 228. **Map 11**

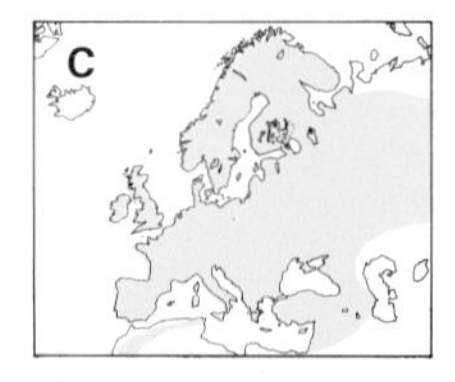


**GREEN HAIRSTREAK** *Callophrys rubi.* ♂ upf has a small, oval sex-brand above cell. Ups grey-brown, uns green, white pd striae often vestigial or absent, *eyes bordered white.* Common throughout Europe and in N Africa, from Morocco to the North Cape. The single brood flies in April or later, often at valley levels rising to 2000m or more in mountains in open country with low scrub. In Morocco and S Spain upperside often paler, red-brown, f. *fervida.* Larval food plants Heather, Gorse, Vaccinium etc. Range extends across Russia and Siberia to Sakhalin. **Map 12**

♂ Spain & Portugal

♀ N Africa

**False Ilex Hairstreak**

♂

♀ f. *vandalusica*

**Blue Spot Hairstreak**

♂

**White Letter Hairstreak**

♀

**Black Hairstreak**

♂

**Green Hairstreak**

♂

**Chapman's Green Hairstreak**

**CHAPMAN'S GREEN HAIRSTREAK** *Callophrys avis.* Both sexes ups red-brown, upf a small sex-brand above cell; uns green, unf a short white pd stripe, unh a white stripe runs to space 1b; *eyes not bordered white.* Occurs in SE France flying April–May at low altitudes. In Tunisia and E Algeria *C. a. barreguei*, slightly smaller, ups darker brown. Larval food plant *Arbutus unedo.* E.

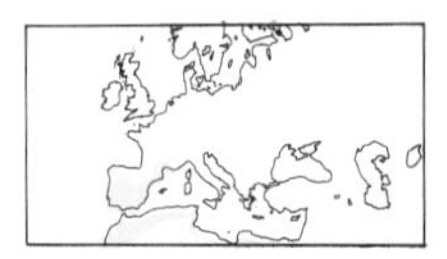

**PROVENCE HAIRSTREAK** *Tomares ballus.* ♂ ups brown, radial and cubital veins lined by androconial scales; unh blue-green with a few white spots. ♀ ups fulvous orange, unh as in ♂. The single brood flies in January or later, on rough ground, usually at low altitudes, but rising in N Africa to 1600m. Very local in SE France, more common in the Atlas Mts in Morocco, Algeria and Tunisia. Range extends to Egypt. Larval food plants uncertain, perhaps *Lotus*. Larva p. 230.

Provence Hairstreak

Nogel's Hairstreak

♂ f. *undulatus*

Moroccan Hairstreak

**MOROCCAN HAIRSTREAK** *Tomares mauretanicus.* ♂ ups like the Provence Hairstreak, but uph often with a small, red anal mark; unh brown with indistinct, dark markings. Unf very variable, individually and locally; ♂–f. *undulatus*, uph red anal mark enlarged; ♂–f. *sabulosus*, upf with orange discal patch; ♀ ups orange-fulvous, uph extent of orange variable, sometimes greatly reduced (see figure). In both sexes unf black spots often irregular, fused together or series incomplete. A single brood flies in January–April on rough, stony slopes, at low altitudes near the coast but at 1500m or more in the Atlas Mts. Occurs in Morocco, Algeria (and Tunisia?). Larval food plants *Hedysarum pallidum* and *Hippocrepis multisiliquosus*. E.

**NOGEL'S HAIRSTREAK** *Tomares nogellii dobrogensis.* ♂ fw 11–12mm, ups grey-brown, unmarked; unh grey, orange-red submarginal, pd and sub-basal transverse bands defined by small, black spots. ♀ upf discal area orange-red, otherwise similar. Only in Romanian Dobrogea, flying at valley levels in June. Distribution little understood. Larval food plant not known.

**The Coppers.** This is a large tribe including about 50 species, distributed almost equally in Eurasia and in N America. Excepting the Sooty Copper, on ups males of the European species are gleaming, golden-red, with or without markings of black spots in a conventional pattern, usually present in females. The tribal characters are well marked; the egg is deeply pitted in a distinctive pattern; the larva is almost cylindrical, the lateral ridge, usually present in Lycaenid larvae, is greatly reduced; the dorsal gland is absent. There are additional anatomical peculiarities, and the species are easily recognized by the possession of two black spots in the cell in the fore-wing underside.

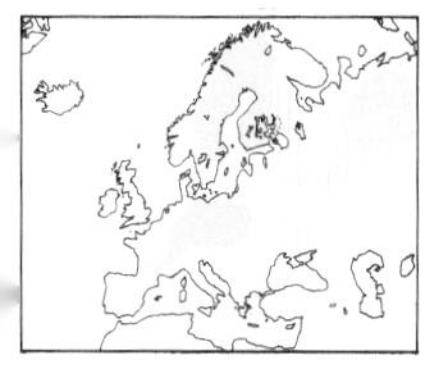

**VIOLET COPPER** *Lycaena helle.* Small, ♂ ups a violet suffusion masks the wing-markings; unh has a narrow white band before the submarginal spots. ♀ ups red-gold, lacking violet suffusion. Occurs on damp moorland and bogs in Fennoscandia, France, Jura, N Switzerland, Germany etc. A very local species, flying May–July at low levels, rarely rising to 1500m. Larval food plant *Polygonum* (Knotgrass). Range extends across N Russia to the Caucasus and C Asia. This attractive little butterfly has suffered severely from drainage of wet land, and it has become scarce almost everywhere. Larva p. 226.

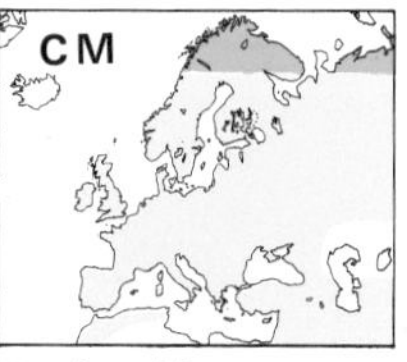


*L.p.phlaeas*
*L.p.polaris*

**SMALL COPPER** *Lycaena phlaeas.* ♂ upf red-gold with black markings; *uph black with red submarginal band.* ♀ similar. Flies in April and later, up to October, in two or more broods, from sea level to 2000m or more, widely distributed in NW Africa, Europe and Asia to Japan, also in the Himalaya Mts, N America, and C Africa, on the high mountains of Uganda. Larva p. 226.

**Map 13**

*L. p. phlaeas.* In Morocco, Algeria and Tunisia, Europe and temperate Asia excluding the boreal areas. Both sexes unh grey-brown or reddish; in warm localities and late broods ups more or less suffused fuscous – f. *elea*; uph with small, blue postdiscal spots – f. *caeruleopunctata*, common in temperate regions.

*L. p. polaris.* In Fennoscandia north of 62°N, unh pale grey, common locally to 70°N, usually flying at low altitudes.

*L. p. phlaeoides.* On Madeira, unh grey-brown, a narrow pale grey band is present after the obscure discal spots; on ups late brood specimens usually very dark.

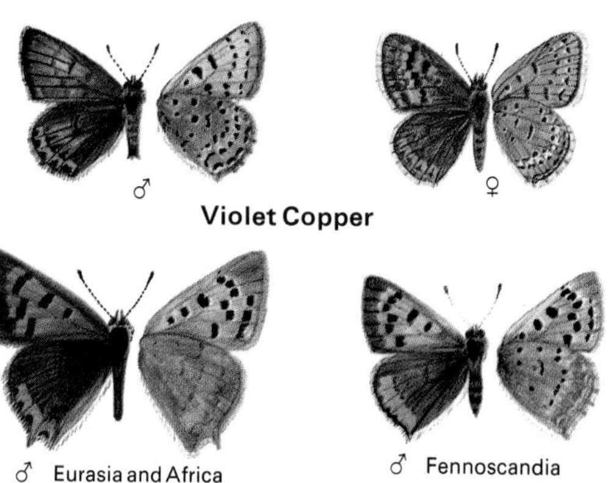


**Violet Copper**

**Small Copper**

**LARGE COPPER** *Lycaena dispar.* ♂ upf red-gold, a *black discal spot* is present; unh pale blue-grey with usual markings. ♀ upf with black pd spots but *submarginal series not developed*; uph black, submarginal band golden. Widely distributed in N and C Europe, local variation not marked except in size.

*L. d. dispar.* Large, ♂ fw 18–20mm, occurs in scattered colonies in fenland districts of N Holland (Friesland). Flies in June in a single brood. Formerly occurred in fenland districts of England (Cambridgeshire etc.) but extinct there since 1850. Larval food plants *Rumex hydrolapatha, R. aquaticus.*

*L. d. rutila.* Usually slightly smaller, unh grey ground colour often less brilliant, sometimes slightly shaded yellowish. Flies, May–June and August–September, *usually in two broods*; the second brood often small ♂ fw 16mm. Widely distributed in rough country with wet ditches and damp meadows, from France, especially in NE, Germany and northwards to the Baltic countries (Estonia), N Italy, Czechoslovakia and E Europe including Greece, S Russia and east to Crimea, Caucasus and C Asia. Flies from valley levels to 800m, often in hilly country. Larval food plants Docks, *Polygonum*, rarely *Iris pseudoacorus.*

*Note.* A colony of the Dutch form has been maintained since 1908 at Woodwalton Fen in Huntingdonshire, England.

*H.v. virgaureae*
*H.v. miegii*

**SCARCE COPPER** *Heodes virgaureae.* ♂ ups gleaming red-gold; *unh yellow-grey* with *small, white postdiscal markings.* ♀ ups paler yellow-gold with the usual black markings. Widely distributed in Europe to 66°N, absent from England, Mediterranean Islands and N Africa. Occurs July–August on flowery slopes in open country at all altitudes to 2000m. Larval food plants *Rumex* species. The range extends across Russia to the Caucasus and Siberia.

*H. v. virgaureae.* Generally distributed in C Europe, more local in S Italy, Balkans and Mainland Greece. ♂ ups unmarked. ♀ ups markings well defined. At high altitudes often small.

*H. v. montanus.* Small, ups black wing-borders wide, sometimes with a small, black discal spot; ♀ ups pale yellow-grey, markings and ground-colour more or less obscured by grey suffusion. In the far north, in Fennoscandia, *H. v. oranulus*, similar, very small, ♂ ups dark wing borders wide.

*H. v. miegii.* In Spain large, ♂ upf with black discal spot and *smaller postdiscal spots near wing-apex* in spaces 2–6. ♀ large, brightly marked.

**GRECIAN COPPER** *Heodes ottomanus.* Like *H. virgaureae miegii* but smaller. ♂ unh yellow-grey, *marginal band* red. ♀ similar, ups black markings prominent. Occurs in SE Europe, in Dalmatia, Montenegro and Greece, often in coastal areas. Flies in flowery meadows, road margins etc. at low altitudes up to 1000m, in two broods, May–June and August–September but these dates are variable according to altitude etc. Larval food plants not known. Range extends to Asia Minor.

♀ N Holland

♂ France to C Asia

**Large Copper**

♂

♀

C Europe, Italy, Balkans

♂ Spain

♂ Fennoscandia etc

**Scarce Copper**

♂

♀

**Grecian Copper**

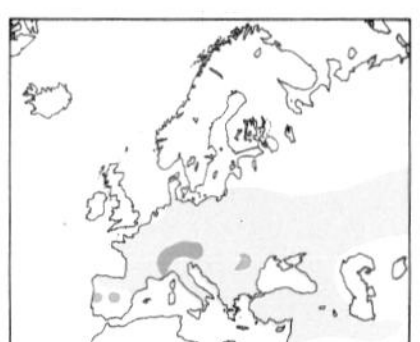

H.t. tityrus
H.t.t. f. bleusei
H.t. subalpinus

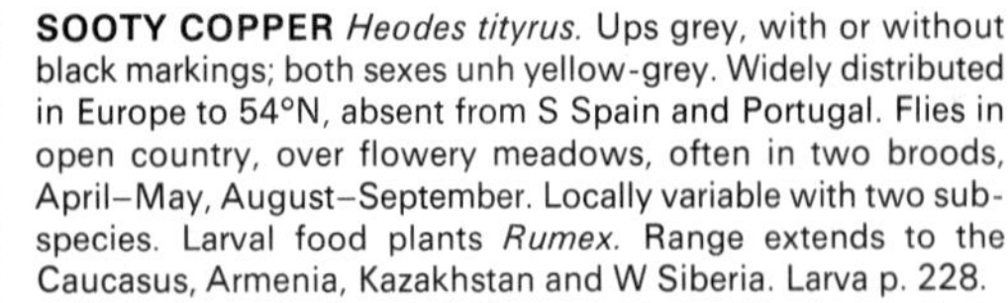

**SOOTY COPPER** *Heodes tityrus.* Ups grey, with or without black markings; both sexes unh yellow-grey. Widely distributed in Europe to 54°N, absent from S Spain and Portugal. Flies in open country, over flowery meadows, often in two broods, April–May, August–September. Locally variable with two subspecies. Larval food plants *Rumex.* Range extends to the Caucasus, Armenia, Kazakhstan and W Siberia. Larva p. 228.

*H. t. tityrus,* in S and C Europe at low altitudes, rarely to 1000m. ♂ ups grey, black markings fully developed. ♀ upf orange-yellow, uph marginal lunules orange. In C Spain (Guadarrama) f. *bleusei*: ♂ upf discal area orange, black markings complete, in late brood hw often tailed at vein 2.

*H. t. subalpinus,* at high altitudes, from Basses Alpes to the Hohe Tauern. Both sexes ups dark grey, markings often absent; in ♀ ups traces of orange markings often present. Flies in July in a single brood. Colonies with intermediate characters are not uncommon at intermediate levels.

H.a. alciphron
H.a. gordius
H.a. heracleanus

**PURPLE-SHOT COPPER** *Heodes alciphron.* Widely distributed in Europe to the Baltic coast, very local in Morocco. Locally variable with three subspecies. Flies June–July. Larval food plants *Rumex.* Range extends across Russia to the Caucasus, N Iran and W Siberia. Larva p. 228.

*H. a. alciphron,* in the Jura; Germany, Slovakia etc. ♂ ups suffused violet-grey; ♀ variable; ups heavily suffused dark brown. Flies at low altitudes, rarely to 1000m. Absent from England and NW Europe. In SE Europe and Greece f. *melibaeus*: ♂ ups yellowish, violet suffusion reduced; ♀ usually dark with some orange markings; flies at high levels.

*H. a. gordius,* in Spain, Pyrenees, Alps etc. A mountain form, flies at 1500m and above, both sexes ups gleaming fulvous red, black markings well developed; ♀ uph often black.

*H. a. heracleanus,* only in the High Atlas, Morocco. Large, ups yellow. Flies at 2700m.

**LESSER FIERY COPPER** *Thersamonia thersamon.* ♂ uph slightly dusky, orange submarginal band usually prominent. ♀ upf markings complete, uph black, orange marginal band prominent. Occurs in Italy and E Europe including the Balkans and Greece. Flies in local colonies, in two broods, April–May and July–August, on flowery slopes, at low levels to 1000m or a little more. In the second brood, f. *omphale,* hw often has a short tail at vein 2. Larva p. 230.

**MOROCCAN COPPER** *Thersamonia phoebus.* Small, ♂ ups pale golden; ♀ similar, uph suffused grey. Occurs in W Morocco, near Marrakesh. Flies May–July at lowland levels rising to 1500m. Larval food plant *Rumex* species. E.

**FIERY COPPER** *Thersamonia thetis.* ♂ ups red-gold, upf black marginal border expanded near apex, unh very pale yellow-grey. ♀ ups with usual black markings, unh as in male. In Europe only present in Greece, perhaps also in S Yugoslavia. Flies July–August at 1800m and over, at alpine levels on high mountains. A filamentous tail sometimes present on hw at vein 2. A second brood in late summer has been described. Larval food plant not known. Range extends to Lebanon, Iraq and Iran.

S & C Europe

♀ High altitudes

**Sooty Copper**

Jura, Germany, Slovakia

Spain, Pyrenees, Alps

High Atlas

**Purple Shot Copper**

**Lesser Fiery Copper**

**Fiery Copper**

**Moroccan Copper**

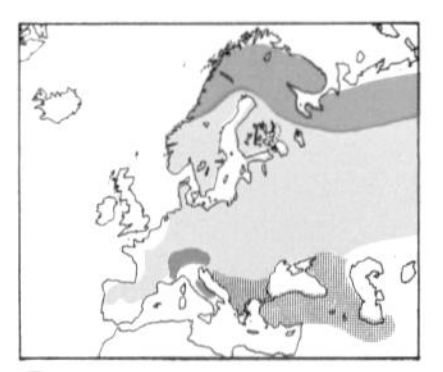

P.h. hippothoe
P.h. stiberi
P.h. eurydame
P.h. leonhardi
P.h. candens (non-European, not described)

**PURPLE-EDGED COPPER** *Palaeochrysophanus hippothoe.* ♂ ups *red-gold, often with violet reflections.* ♀ ups with usual black markings frequently masked by fuscous suffusion. Local but widely distributed in Europe from N Spain to 70°N, flying in a single brood at sea level in N Norway to 2000m in the Alps, usually in damp meadows. Range extends across Russia to the Caucasus and Siberia. Larva p. 228.

*P. h. hippothoe*, in C Europe including N Spain, and S Fennoscandia. ♂ upf with small black discal spot, otherwise unmarked; uph anal area and inner margin broadly black. ♀ ups markings often obscure. Flies June–July from valley levels to 1800m.

*P. h. stiberi*, in boreal areas of Scandinavia. ♂ like *P. h. hippothoe*; ♀ upf *bright yellow-gold, markings small but complete*; uph black, yellow submarginal band prominent.

*P. h. eurydame*, in Maritime Alps, C Alps and Abruzzi, flying at altitudes of 2000m or over. ♂ ups bright red-gold, upf *lacking discal black spot and violet flush.* ♀ ups usually heavily suffused fuscous, least dark in the Abruzzi. E.

*P. h. leonhardi*, in Balkans and Greece. Often large, markings like *P. h. hippothoe* but *distinctive characters present in ♂ genitalia.* Graded with specific rank by many authors. Range extends with related subspecies to Turkey and N Iran.

**Purple-edged Copper**

**Tiger Blues and allied species.** The six species following all look out of place in our region, unlike our familiar 'Blues'. They belong to a large group of similar butterflies widely distributed in tropical Africa and Asia. Many feed upon thorny desert bushes such as Mimosa, *Paliurus* and *Zizyphus.*

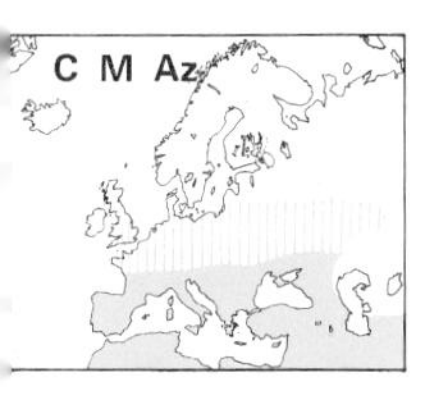


**LONG-TAILED BLUE** *Lampides boeticus.* ♂ hw tailed; uph with prominent black anal spot, unh with white submarginal band. ♀ ups wings with wide fuscous borders. Resident and widely distributed in N Africa and S Europe, occasional in C Europe. Flies throughout the summer, May–October, in open country at all altitudes. It is strongly migratory and appears each year in N Europe; occasionally seen in S England. Range practically world-wide, except in arctic regions. Larval food plants in Europe, *Colutea,* living inside the seed-pods. Larva p. 230.

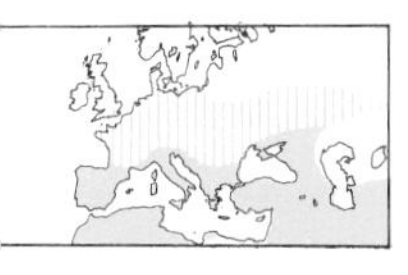

**LANG'S SHORT-TAILED BLUE** *Syntarucus pirithous* (syn. *S. telicanus*). ♂ hw tailed; upf wings blue without dark markings, unh white markings confused. ♀ upf suffused brown, dark and pale markings present. Flies March–October. Resident and common in N Africa and S Europe, rare and occasional north of the Alps, strongly migratory; has been seen in S England. Larval food plants Leguminosae, brooms etc. Range extends to Crimea, Caucasus, Himalayas. Larva p. 230.

**CANARY BLUE** *Cyclyrius webbianus.* ♂ ups deep purple-blue; unh postdiscal band white. ♀ ups golden brown; unh as male. Occurs on Tenerife and on other Canary Islands of the western group. Flies May and later, from 600m on La Palma to 3400m on the volcano at Tenerife, especially abundant among the pine trees. Larval food plants include *Cytisus, Spartocytisus, Adenocarpus* and *Lotus.*

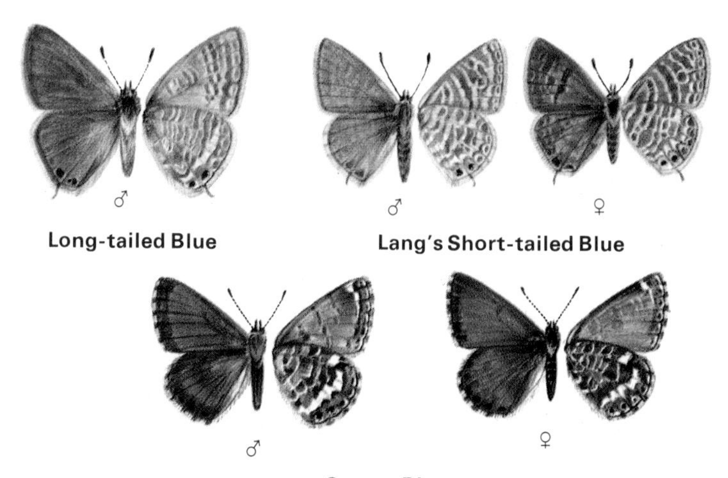


**Long-tailed Blue**

**Lang's Short-tailed Blue**

**Canary Blue**

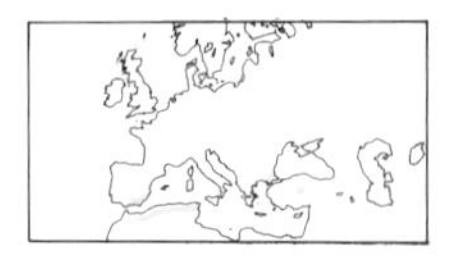

**COMMON TIGER BLUE** *Tarucus theophrastus.* ♂ upf discal spot dark. ♀ ups brown with white markings. Occurs at low levels in N Africa, and in the coastal areas of SE Spain. Flies May–June and July–August, always around bushes of *Zizyphus vulgaris*, the larval food plant. Range extends widely across most of Africa, Arabia and W Asia eastwards to India.

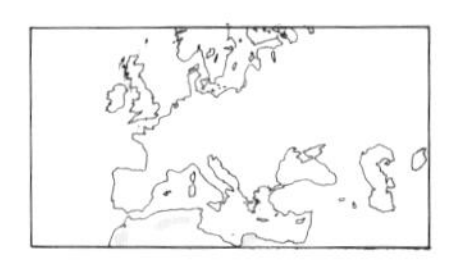

**MEDITERRANEAN TIGER BLUE** *Tarucus rosaceus.* ♂ upf grey discal spot narrow; unf black postdiscal markings form almost continuous lines. ♀ uph white markings clearly defined. Occurs April and later in Morocco (Agadir) and Algeria, beyond Blida, flying over low desert scrub. Reported from Tunisia. Range extends to Arabia, Iraq and Iran.

**LITTLE TIGER BLUE** *Tarucus balkanicus.* ♂ upf with discal and postdiscal dark markings. ♀ ups dark, wing bases flushed blue; uph lack postdiscal white spots. Occurs in hot coastal districts in Dalmatia, Montenegro, Albania, Greece, and in Algeria and Tunisia, flying April and later at low levels around bushes of *Paliurus*, larval food plant. Identification of the Tiger Blues is especially difficult in specimens from the S Mediterranean coasts and should be checked by anatomical examination.

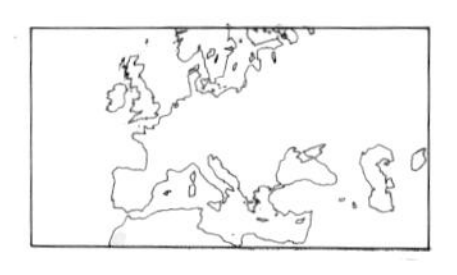

**AFRICAN BABUL BLUE** *Azanus jesous.* ♂ ups blue; unh with *several basal and marginal round, black spots.* ♀ similar, ups dusky brown, upf discal spot conspicuous. Occurs especially in coastal areas of W Morocco. Flies April–September, around *Acacia* bushes (Mimosa), larval food plant. Continental range very extensive in Africa, Syria etc.

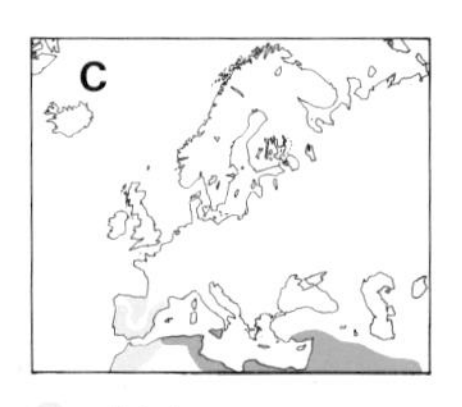


*Z.k.knysna*
*Z.k.karsandra*

**AFRICAN GRASS BLUE** *Zizeeria knysna.* ♂ *ups violet blue, brown wing-margins wide*; *uns pale brown*, markings small. ♀ ups brown, wing-bases often suffused blue, uns as in ♂. Flies April–August or later, at low or moderate altitudes, often in wet places and over short grass. Occurs on the Canary Islands, in NW Africa, S Spain and S Portugal. Larval food plants *Medicago, Oxalis* etc.

*Z. k. karsandra*, not distinguishable by markings, but male genitalia with a small distinctive character. Widely distributed in E Algeria, Tunisia and eastwards across Asia to Australia. Considered specifically distinct by some authors.

♂ ♀

**Common Tiger Blue**

♂ ♀

**Mediterranean Tiger Blue**

♂ ♀

**African Babul Blue**

**Little Tiger Blue**

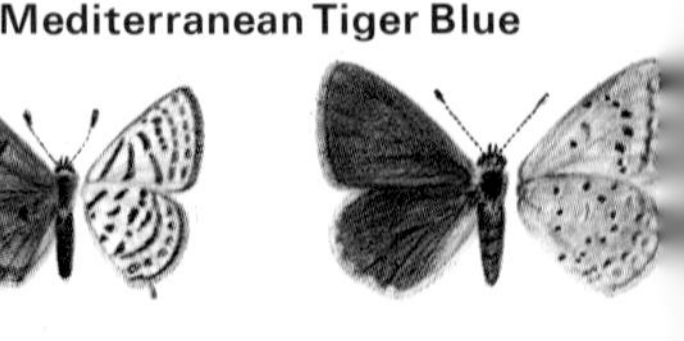

**African Grass Blue**

## The Short-tailed Blues. Three species.

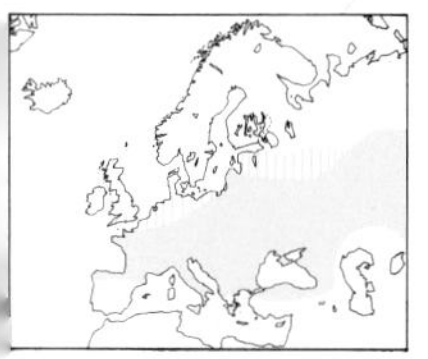

**SHORT-TAILED BLUE** *Everes argiades.* A short 'tail' present on hw at v2. ♂ unf *pd spots in a straight row*; unh *orange marginal lunules* present in s2 and s3. ♀ ups brown, sometimes flushed blue at base of fw; uns as in ♂. Flies April and later, usually in two broods, at valley levels rising to 1000m. Larval food plants Trefoil and other small Leguminosae. Widely distributed from N Spain to the Baltic countries (Estland) but always local and absent from wide areas, extends SE to N Yugoslavia, records from Greece not confirmed. Range extends across Russia to E Siberia and Japan.

♂

**Short-tailed Blue**

♂

♂

**Eastern Short-tailed Blue**

**Provençal Short-tailed Blue**

**EASTERN SHORT-TAILED BLUE** *Everes decoloratus.* ♂ hw tail short; upf *black discal spot not prominent*, marginal *dark border 1–2mm wide*; unf postdiscal spots in spaces 1b,2,3, *not in straight line*; unh black marginal spot in s2 minute. ♀ ups brown (black when fresh). Widely distributed in SE Europe, Austria, Hungary, Slovakia, Balkans and N Greece. A lowland butterfly, prefers sheltered, flowery places, roadside hedges etc. Distinguish from Provençal Short-tailed Blue, ♂ upf dark discal spot absent, marginal black borders linear. Larval food plant not recorded. Flies April–September. Range uncertain.

**PROVENÇAL SHORT-TAILED BLUE** *Everes alcetas.* ♂ ups medium blue, black marginal border linear, upf *discal dark spot absent*; unf postdiscal spots in spaces 1b,2,3, *not in straight line*; unh marginal black spot in s2 very small, may be capped with *small orange mark.* ♀ ups dark brown (black); uns as in male. Occurs in S Europe in scattered colonies from Spain and S France to Greece and the Balkans, southern slopes of the Alps and on Corsica. Flies April–September, in two broods, in open flowery places at low altitudes rising to 1000m. Larval food plants small Leguminosae, esp. *Coronilla varia.* Probably ranges to Ural Mts but information poor.

**The Little Blues.** In the following three closely related species the hind-wings are without tails.

C.m.minimus
C.m.trinacriae

**LITTLE BLUE** *Cupido minimus.* ♂ ups brown, wing-bases dusted powder-blue; uns pale grey, markings small. ♀ ups brown; uns as in ♂. Widely distributed in Europe, principally on calcareous soils, from S Spain to 68°N, including Ireland and eastwards to the Balkans and Greece. Absent from the Mediterranean islands except Sicily. Flies April–July in a single brood from valley levels to 2000m; at high altitudes and in the far north, emerging in June. In the S Alps, f. *alsoides*, very large specimens in some colonies. Range extends to the Caucasus, C Asia and Siberia. Larva p. 230. **Map 14**

*C. m. trinacriae*, flies in Sicily, very small and ups dark, only an occasional blue scale, occurs in late April–May, from sea level to 1000m.

*C. m. carswelli*, local in S Spain (Murcia); ups brown, without blue scales. Larval food plants flowers of small Leguminosae.

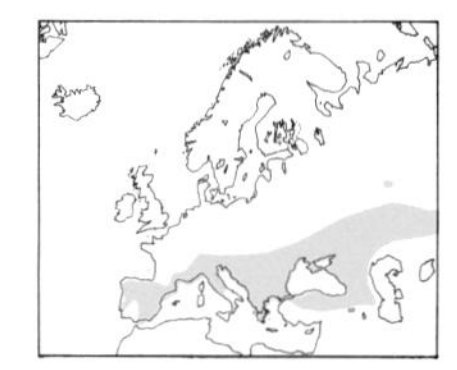

**OSIRIS BLUE** *Cupido osiris.* ♂ ups violet blue, black marginal borders linear; uns white, unh lacks a black marginal spot in s2. ♀ ups black, uns as in ♂. Occurs in C and N Spain, S France and east across S Europe including S Switzerland to the Balkans and Greece, often uncommon, always local. Absent from Mediterranean islands except Corsica. Flies May–July over sheltered, flowery banks usually in hilly country. From 500–1500m altitudes, perhaps with two annual broods. Larval food plants flowers of small Leguminosae, esp. Onobrychis. Range extends to Asia Minor and C Asia.

♂

**Lorquin's Blue**

♂

**Little Blue**

♂

**Osiris Blue**

**LORQUIN'S BLUE** *Cupido lorquinii.* ♂ ups *dark blue*, with a small discal spot, black *marginal borders wide*; uns pale grey; unf lacks a cell-spot, markings as in the Little Blue. ♀ ups dark grey (black), often with some blue scales at wing-bases. Occurs in N Africa, and very local in S Spain (Malaga, Granada). Flies late April–May, usually in mountains, at 200m or more in Spain, rising to 1500m in Morocco. Larval food plants not recorded. E.

The following four isolated species are not related to any large group.

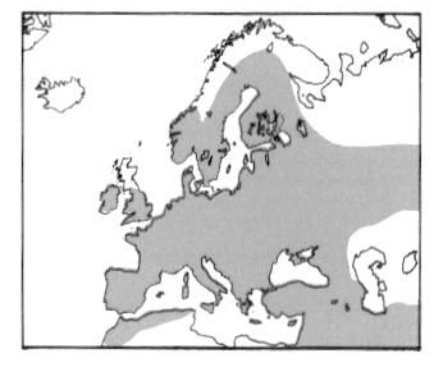

**HOLLY BLUE** *Celastrina argiolus.* ♂ ups sky-blue with black wing-margins; uns paper white with small black markings. ♀ ups paler blue, upf (first brood) wing margin wide; or (late brood) enlarged, upf discal area alone remaining blue. Occurs throughout the region, often common, flying April–May and August at all altitudes from sea level to 2000m, often in light woodland. Larval food plants Ivy, Holly, Buckthorn etc. Range extends across temperate Asia to Japan and from coast to coast in N America. Larva p. 230. **Map 15**

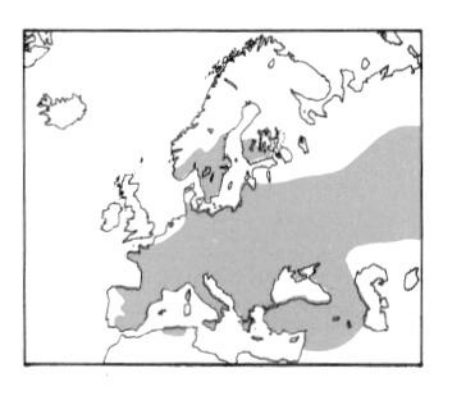

**THE GREEN-UNDERSIDE BLUE** *Glaucopsyche alexis.* ♂ uns grey; unf variable, postdiscal spots usually large, displaced towards margin; unh base usually broadly green. ♀ ups dark brown, uns as in ♂. Widely distributed in Europe from Spain to S Scandinavia and eastwards. Absent from England, Balearic Islands, Crete and Sardinia. Flies April–June from valley levels to 1200m on flowery slopes. In Algeria and Tunisia. *G. a. melanoposmater*: unf postdiscal spots reduced or absent; unh green basal shade absent. Larval food plants *Astragalus, Cytisus.* Range extends across Russia and C Asia to the Amur.

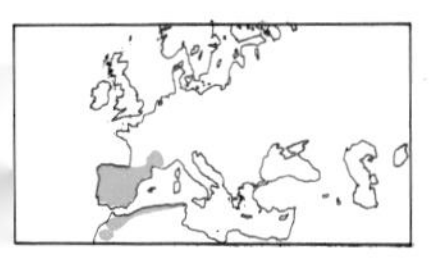

**BLACK-EYED BLUE** *Glaucopsyche melanops.* ♂ ups like the Green-underside Blue; uns brown; unh submarginal and other markings inconspicuous. ♀ ups dark brown (black), blue basal suffusion variable. Occurs in SE France, E Pyrenees and in N Italy (Liguria). In Spain and N Africa, *G. m. algirica*, larger, markings not distinctive. Local but not rare, flying April–May among tall heather at various altitudes to 2000m or more. Larval food plants *Dorycnium, Genista* and flowers of *Lotus.* E. Larva p. 224.

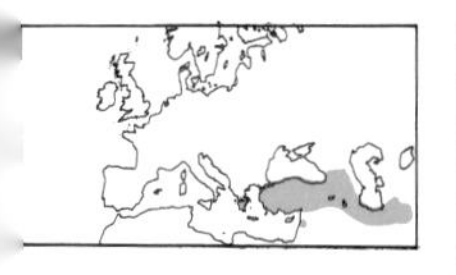

**ODD-SPOT BLUE** *Turanana panagaea taygetica.* ♂ ups blue, dark marginal borders wide; unf large black pd spot in s3 displaced outwards. ♀ ups brown, uns markings as in ♂. Within the region, occurs only in Greece at altitudes of 2000m or more, in the Peloponnesos (Taygetus Mts). Flies July–August in a single brood. Range extends to Asia Minor, Lebanon, Iran and C Asia.

♂

♀ gen. 1

♀ gen. 2

**Holly Blue**

♂

**Green-underside Blue**

♂

**Black-eyed Blue**

♂

**Odd-spot Blue**

**The Large Blues.** The extraordinary life histories of these butterflies remained a mystery until 1915. In that year the late Bagwell Purefoy and F. W. Frohawk were trying to breed the Large Blue in Devonshire; but their efforts were unsuccessful. The little caterpillars, feeding upon the flowers of Thyme, would grow in captivity until they changed their skins for the third time (third instar), when they always ceased to feed and soon died, while in the field no more larvae could be found. One day in September, Captain Purefoy noticed a small, red ant carrying a little larva in its mouth. He followed the ant until it disappeared into its nest, still carrying the larva. This observation allowed Captain Purefoy to understand what happened to the larvae at this time, and the astonishing story was fully established during the next two years.

In the early autumn the young larva, in its third instar, ceases to feed upon Thyme. It wanders about until it meets a red ant, which will pick it up and carry it to the ants' nest. Here it is carefully looked after by the ants who 'milk' it for the secretion from the dorsal gland. The larva now becomes a cannibal, eating the young ant-larvae until it is ready to change into a pupa, and in this stage it hibernates through the winter in the warm ants' nest. In May or June the butterfly hatches out, crawls out of the nest, dries its wings and flies away. It was soon discovered that all the *Maculinea* butterflies have developed the same original method for safe and comfortable hibernation.

**Alcon Blue**

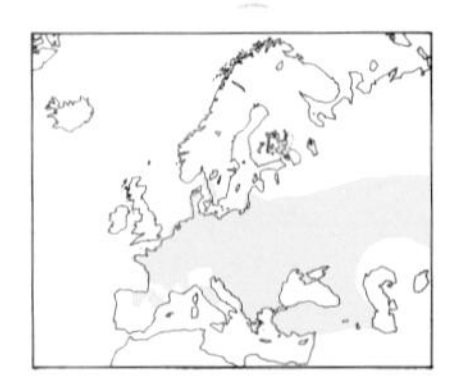

**ALCON BLUE** *Maculinea alcon.* Like the Large Blue. ♂ ups postdiscal spots absent; uns pale brown; unh blue basal suffusion absent or vestigial, no basal spot in space 1c. ♀ upf postdiscal spots small. Occurs in two forms, connected by intermediates.

*M. a. alcon*, ♂ ups dull pale blue, black marginal borders ill-defined. ♀ ups brown, upf basal blue suffusion small if present. Local in N Europe including S Sweden, NE France, Germany etc. Flies July, in a single brood at low altitudes over damp fields, moorlands and around the shores of the Bavarian lakes. Larval food plant *Gentiana pneumonanthe.*

*M. a. rebeli*, ♂ ups rather bright blue, black marginal wing borders well defined. Chiefly in mountains, in France and eastwards, local in the Alps, Apennines and Balkans to N Greece. Flies July rarely at low levels, chiefly over subalpine slopes at 1200–1800m. Also in N Spain (Santander and Teruel), E Pyrenees (Aulus), often in dry localities e.g. Dolomites. Larval food plants *Gentiana cruciata, G. germanica.* Ranges across Europe to C Asia and W Siberia.

♂

♂ f. *obscura*

**Large Blue**

*M.a. arion*
*M.a. ligurica*

**LARGE BLUE** *Maculinea arion.* ♂ ups blue, black postdiscal spots more or less developed; unh grey, basal green suffusion prominent, black spot present at base of space 1c. ♀ upf postdiscal black markings enlarged. From C and N Spain widely distributed in Europe to 62°N, including the Balkans and Greece (Pindos Mts). Extinct in England, absent from S Spain, Portugal and Mediterranean islands except Corsica. At high levels in the Alps, f. *obscura*, ups widely suffused dark grey. In the E Maritime Alps, *M. a. ligurica*, ups brilliant blue in both sexes. Flies at all levels to 1800m, in a single brood June–July, flying over slopes with Thyme, larval food plant, and ant larvae later. Ranges across Russia, Siberia and China to Japan.

**SCARCE LARGE BLUE** *Maculinea teleius.* Like the Large Blue. ♂ ups pale blue, postdiscal spots present but small; unh brown, no blue-green basal shade. ♀ ups wide marginal borders and wing-veins fuscous. Very local in C Europe to 53°N, NE France, Switzerland, not south of Rhône Valley, Bavaria, C Germany, Austria etc. Italy in a few southern alpine valleys, Carniola. Absent from Balkans. Flies in July on wet moorlands and meadows from lowlands to 1800m. Larval food plant *Sanguisorba.* Continental range extends to the Caucasus, Siberia and Japan.

♂ ♀

**Scarce Large Blue**

**DUSKY LARGE BLUE** *Maculinea nausithous.* ♂ ups like the Scarce Large Blue, ups marginal borders very wide; uns coffee brown, unh without marginal markings. ♀ ups brown, blue area usually quite obsolete. Occurs in N Spain (Soria), SE France (Ain, Isère, Savoie), N Switzerland, Germany and eastwards to Austria. Flies June, a single brood over marshy lowlands, borders of lakes etc.; a very local and often rare species. Larval food plant *Sanguisorba officinalis.* Range extends across Russia to the Caucasus, C Asia and W Siberia.

**Dusky Large Blue**
♂

**IOLAS BLUE** *Iolana iolas.* Large, ♂ ups lustrous blue, unmarked. ♀ ups wing margins broadly suffused fuscous, but variable. Local in S and C Spain, SE France, S Switzerland (Rhône valley) etc., Apennines and Balkans to Greece (Peloponnesos), also in Algeria. Flies May–June in a single brood from lowlands to 1800m, often among mountains, around bushes of *Colutea* (Senna). Larval food plant *Colutea*, larvae living within the pods. Ranges across Asia Minor, Iraq and Iran to C Asia. Larva p. 230.

♂ ♀
**Iolas Blue**

**The Baton Blues.** The five (or six) species following are unusual in their long wing fringes, strongly chequered black and white. Several butterflies closely related to this group occur in western N America.

*P.b. baton*
*P.b. schiffermuelleri*

**BATON BLUE** *Pseudophilotes baton.* ♂ ups pale powder blue; uns grey, markings black spots; unh submarginal lunules red, prominent. ♀ ups dark brown (black), upf small basal blue suffusions common; uns as in ♂. Occurs widely from the Pyrenees across Europe to 48°N. Flies April–May and August–September in two broods at low levels, a single brood at high levels, rising to 1800m, on flowery banks with *Thymus serpillus* (Thyme), larval food plant. Two subspecies occur in Europe. Distinguished by genitalia structure.

*P. b. baton*, in W Europe, N Portugal, N Spain (Cantabrian Mts), Pyrenees, France, Switzerland, Italy to Venezia Giulia, Sicily, Corsica and Sardinia. E.

**Baton Blue**

**Panoptes Blue**

**Bavius Blue**

**False Baton Blue**

*P. b. schiffermuelleri*, in E Europe, Austria, Hungary, Yugoslavia including Slovenia, Romania, Bulgaria and Greece. Range extends to the Caucasus, Himalayas, C Asia and Siberia, including additional subspecies. These two subspecies, are graded species by many authors.

**PANOPTES BLUE** *Pseudophilotes panoptes.* Like the Baton Blue. ♂ ups darker blue; uns pale brown, markings brown spots; unh red submarginal lunules absent or vestigial. ♀ ups dark brown. Replaces the Baton Blue in C and S Spain. Flies in two broods, April–May and July, on rough ground with Thyme, at altitudes of 800–2000m. E.

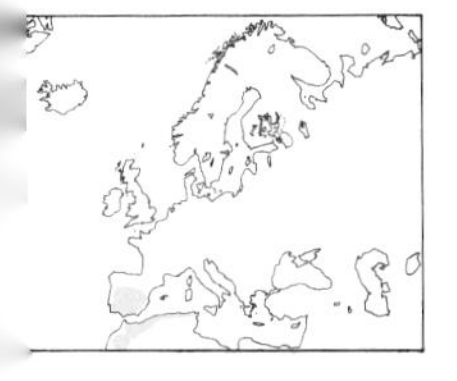

**FALSE BATON BLUE** *Pseudophilotes abencerragus.* Like the Baton Blue. ♂ ups dark, steel-blue, black wing-margins broad; unh red submarginal lunules vestigial if present. ♀ ups dark grey-brown, blue dusting at wing bases minimal. Occurs in Morocco, Algeria, Tunisia, also in S and C Spain and Portugal, north to Madrid and Cuenca. Flies April and later in a single brood, from lowlands to 800m, very local in colonies. Larval food plants *Thymus vulgaris*, perhaps also *Erica arborea* and *E. scoparia*, feeding on the flowers. E.

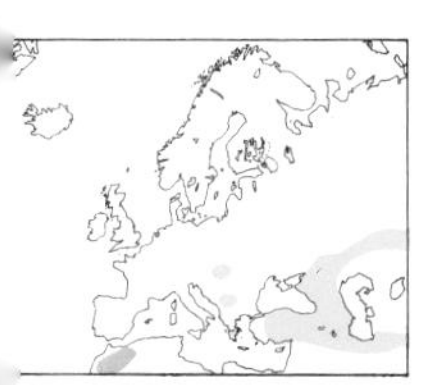

*P.b. bavius*
*P.b. fatma*

**BAVIUS BLUE** *Pseudophilotes bavius.* ♂ ups rather dark blue, black marginal borders wide; uph submarginal lunules orange-red; unh series of orange-red submarginal lunules conspicuous, complete. ♀ ups black with blue basal flush on both wings. Flies May. Two subspecies occur in Europe, distinguished principally by anatomical characters.

*P. b. bavius*, in Romania (Cluj etc.), Macedonia and Greece (Peloponnesos). ♂ ups red submarginal lunules present in spaces 1c,2,3; unh seven lunules in complete series. ♀ ups black, uph and unh, seven red submarginal lunules present on both surfaces. Larval food plant *Salvia*? Range extends across Asia Minor to Caucasus and Kazakhstan.

*P. b. fatma*, in Morocco and Algeria. ♂ ups brighter tone of blue, uph and unh seven red submarginal lunules on both surfaces. ♀ ups blue suffusions extensive. Larval food plant *Salvia*? Graded with specific rank by some authors. The two subspecies are distinguished by male genitalia.

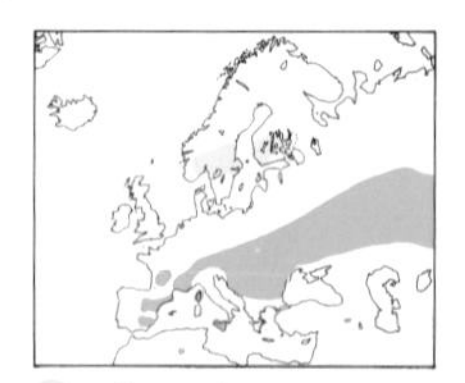

S.o. orion
S.o. lariana

**CHEQUERED BLUE** *Scolitantides orion.* Uns both sexes white, boldly marked with jet-black spots and unh red submarginal lunules. Flies May–July. Two subspecies with widely different distributions.

*S. o. orion*, in S Sweden and S Finland. ♂ ups blue, pale blue marginal lunules well defined within the fuscous marginal borders, upf black discal spot prominent. ♀ ups somewhat suffused dark, otherwise as in ♂. Very local at low altitudes. Larval food plants *Sedum.* Range extends to N Russia.

*S. o. lariana*, in S Europe, from E Spain to Greece, including Sicily and Corsica. ♂ ups black, upf blue basal suffusion obscure, variable. ♀ black, blue basal flush vestigial if present. Local at low altitudes on rough ground, rare above 1000m. Larval food plants *Sedum telephium* and *S. album.* Range extends to the Caucasus, C Asia, Siberia and Japan.

**Chequered Blue**

**Polyommatine Blues.** In many respects all the following butterflies resemble one another closely, in their anatomy and on the undersides in their wing-markings, with rows of small, black spots arranged in a similar standard pattern. All 45 species are closely related, and with an even larger number of similar species that fly in Asia, form an important tribe (Polyommatini). They are characteristic of the Palaearctic Region, especially of the Mediterranean Subregion, and are not found in such numbers and such variety anywhere else in the world.

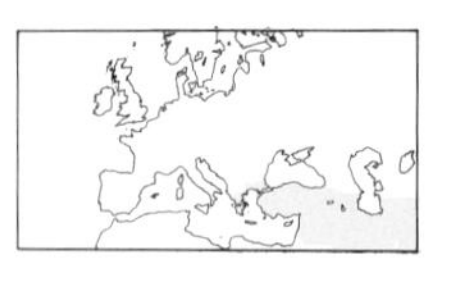

**GRASS JEWEL** *Freyeria trochylus.* Very small, ♂ ups brown; uph two to four orange submarginal lunules near anal angle. Sexes similar. In Europe occurs only in Greece, Turkey and Crete, flying close to the ground at low altitudes throughout the summer, over dry stony slopes. Range most extensive, across tropical and sub-tropical Africa and Asia. Larval food plant Heliotrope. One of the world's smallest butterflies.

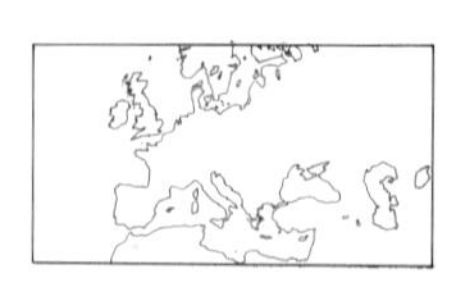

**VOGEL'S BLUE** *Plebejus vogelii.* ♂ ups pale brown with orange submarginal bands, fringes chequered black and white. ♀ similar or with small white ups marks internal to marginal borders. Only known from Morocco, Middle Atlas (Taghzeft Pass); flies August in a single brood, at 2000m. Larval food plant *Erodium cheiranthifolium.* E.

**Vogel's Blue**

**Grass Jewel**

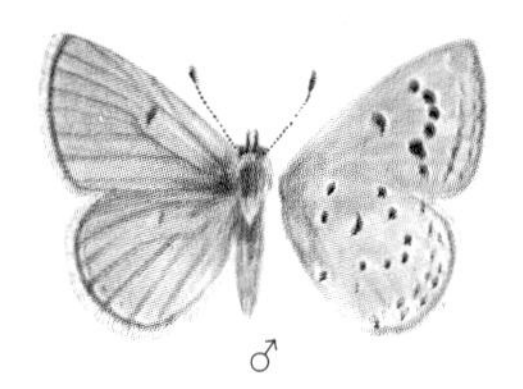

♂

♀

♀ W Algeria & Morocco

**Martin's Blue**

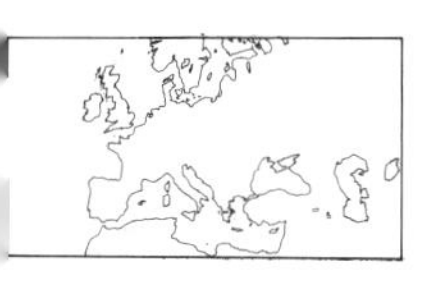

**MARTIN'S BLUE** *Plebejus martini*. ♂ ups pale lavender blue upf small discal spot present; unf black postdiscal spots prominent; unh yellow submarginal lunules small. ♀ ups dark brown with blue basal flush; uph has four or five submarginal orange lunules. Occurs especially in E Algeria. In W Algeria and Morocco *P. m. allardi*: unf postdiscal black spots not prominent. Flies May on open heath-like slopes at moderate to high altitudes. Larval food plant not known. E.

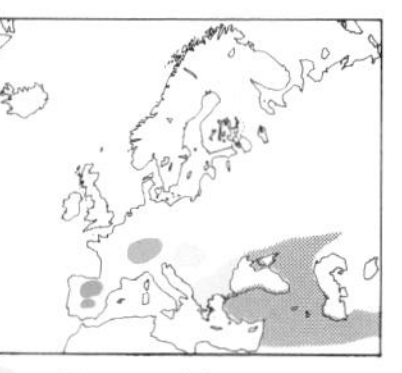

*P.p. sephirus*
*P.p. trappi*
*P.p. hespericus*
*P. p. ssp.* (not European, not described)

**ZEPHYR BLUE** *Plebejus pylaon*. A complex species with several colour forms. ♂ ups shining blue, upf lacks black discal spot. ♀ ups brown, without blue basal flush; uph orange submarginal lunules present at least in spaces 1c,2,3; unh marginal spots do not have iridescent green pupils, ♂ tibia spined. Flies May–June over flowery slopes at various altitudes, often in mountains, rising to 1800m, colonies always extremely localized. Larval food plant *Astragalus*. In Europe the species occurs in three areas; 1. SE Europe at valley levels; Greece as a mountain butterfly. 2. SW Switzerland and S Tirol. 3. Spain. In each area characters are distinct. Range extends across S Russia to the Urals.

*P. p. sephirus*, in Greece, Bulgaria, S Romania. ♂ ups bright blue; ♀ uph orange submarginal lunules well developed. Both sexes of medium size.

*P. p. trappi*, in SW Switzerland and Tirol, usually larger, ♂ ups darker blue; uph black marginal spots often present with dark marginal border wider. ♀ uph orange marginal lunules vestigial if present.

*P. p. hespericus*, in Spain. ♂ ups variable, f. *hespericus* large, ups pale gleaming blue, Sierra de Alfarcar, Sierra Navada; near Alberracin smaller; in f. *galani* near Aranjuez, Toledo etc. ups slightly darker blue. Other minor colour forms have been named.

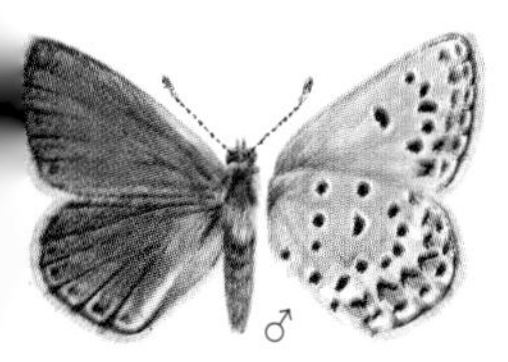

♂

SW Switzerland, Tyrol

♀

Greece, Bulgaria, S Romania

♂ Spain

**Zephyr Blue**

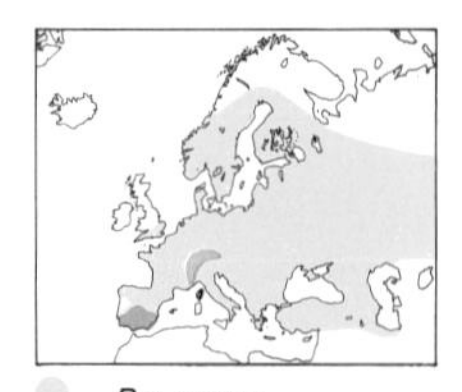

P.a. argus
P.a. aegidion
P.a. hypochionus
P.a. corsicus

**SILVER-STUDDED BLUE** *Plebejus argus.* ♂ ups blue, black marginal borders variable. ♀ ups brown, often with blue basal suffusion. In both sexes fore-tibia with prominent terminal spine. In both sexes unh black marginal spots have iridescent green pupils. Widely distributed but local throughout Europe to 68°N. Absent from Scotland, Ireland, Sicily, Sardinia, Crete, small Mediterranean islands and N Africa. Flies May–August at low levels rising to 1800m, with two or perhaps three broods in south. Very variable with several named subspecies. Larval food plants *Lotus, Medicago* etc. Range extends to the Caucasus, Siberia and Japan. Larva p. 230. **Map 16**

*P. a. argus*, in C Europe at low levels. Small, ♂ upf black marginal border 1mm; uns pale grey, dark markings small. ♀ ups brown.

*P. a. aegidion*, in the Alps, flying in July at high altitudes in a single brood. Small, ♂ upf black marginal border 2–3mm.

*P. a. hypochionus*, in C and S Spain. Larger, ♂ ups marginal border 1–2mm, uns pale grey-white, in Pyrenees similar.

*P. a. corsicus*, in Corsica. Like *P. a. argus*, but un markings rather pale grey-brown, spots not conspicuous. ♀ ups blue suffusions extensive.

♂ C Europe

♀ Corsica

♂ Spain

## Silver-studded Blue

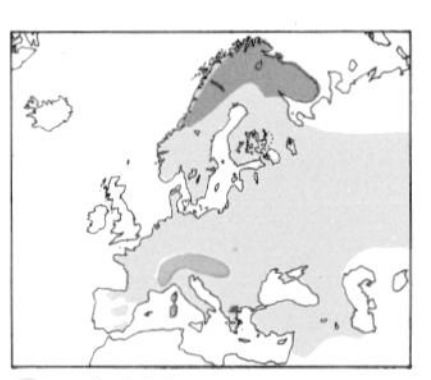

L.i. idas
L.i. haefelfingeri
L.i. lapponicus
L.i. bellieri
L.i. magnagraeca

**IDAS BLUE** *Lycaeides idas.* A variable, complex species. ♂ like the Silver-studded Blue, but fore-tibia lacks a spine; ups marginal borders black, variable, often linear; unh marginal spots black with shining, green pupils. ♀ ups brown, with or without blue suffusions. Widespread throughout Europe to 70°N. Absent from Britain, Sicily, Crete and small Mediterranean islands. Larval food plants small Leguminosae. Range extends to the Altai Mts, perhaps further east. Flies June–July.

*L. i. idas*, in S Fennoscandia, N and C Europe. Small, ♂ ups black marginal borders narrow; uns markings small. ♀ ups brown. Flies in a single brood from lowlands to 1000m or more. In S Alps, *L. i. alpinus*, often larger, ♂ uns pale grey.

*L. i. haefelfingeri*, at high altitudes in Switzerland, Albula Pass etc., small, ♂ ups black margins linear, uns medium brown. ♀ ups brown.

*L. i. calliopis*, Basses Alpes, Hautes Alpes. Rather small, ♂ uns pale grey. ♀ ups blue suffusion often marked, uns brown. Local, usually in mountains from valley levels to 1500m or more, always near *Hippophae rhamnoides*, larval food plant; attended by ants.

*L. i. lapponicus*, boreal regions of Fennoscandia. Small, ♂ uns grey. ♀ ups often with blue suffusions.

*L. i. bellieri*, Corsica and Sardinia. ♂ small, ups black marginal borders 1–2mm or more; uns spots large, prominent. ♀ ups blue basal suffusion common.

*L. i. magnagraeca*, N Greece and S Yugoslavia. Large, ♂ ups black wing-margins 2mm, veins lined black. ♀ ups brown, orange marginal lunules prominent, in complete series.

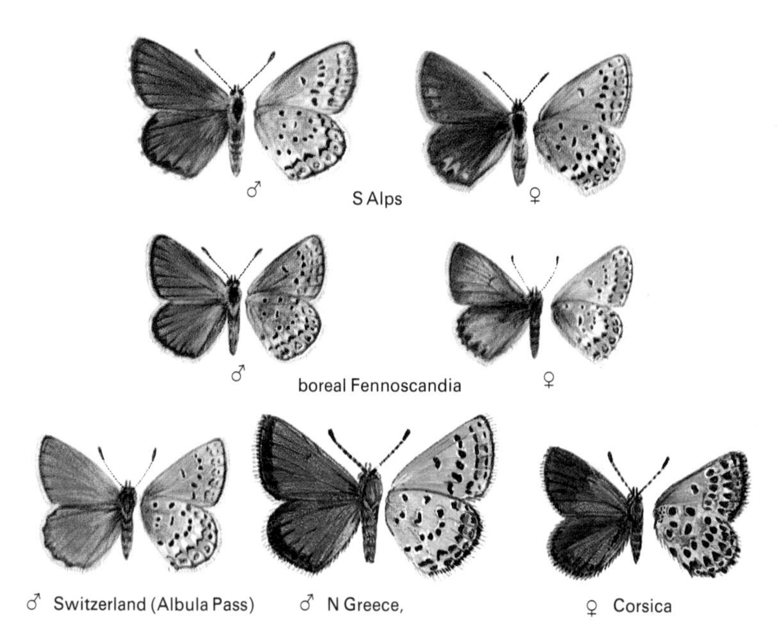

♂ S Alps ♀

♂ boreal Fennoscandia ♀

♂ Switzerland (Albula Pass) ♂ N Greece, ♀ Corsica

**Idas Blue**

**REVERDIN'S BLUE** *Lycaeides argyrognomon.* Like *L. i. alpinus*, often rather large. ♂ ups clear bright blue, some veins lined black, marginal black borders 1–2mm; uns grey-white; unh marginal spots pupilled shining green, the black chevrons, internal to the orange submarginal band, replaced by almost flat, black lunules. ♀ ups brown, uns pale grey. Widespread but local in Europe except boreal regions and Spain. Known to occur from France and S Scandinavia eastwards to Austria, Romania and Greece. Specific identification by external markings is uncertain, and anatomical examination is necessary. The exact distribution of the species is uncertain at present. Flies June–July.

**CRANBERRY BLUE** *Vacciniina optilete.* ♂ ups dark, purple-blue; unh a yellow submarginal lunule prominent in space 2. ♀ ups brown; uns as in ♂. Occurs widespread in Fennoscandia, on moorlands and bogs of NE France, Germany, Czechoslovakia etc., and at high altitudes in the Alps and in Macedonia on the Schar Planina. Flies July at various altitudes, always associated with *Vaccinium uliginosum*, larval food plant. Extends across Asia to the Kurile islands and Japan; widespread in subarctic and boreal N America. Larva p. 230.

♂

**Reverdin's Blue**

♂

**Cranberry Blue**

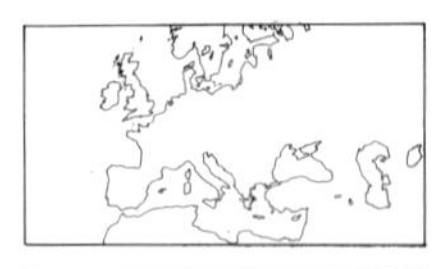

**CRETAN ARGUS** *Kretania psylorita.* Small, ♂ ups grey-brown, uph with small lunules pale yellow. ♀ similar, ups yellow submarginal lunules well developed. Occurs late May–June, on Crete, flying on Mt Ida at 1600m and over, and restricted to this mountain. Associated with a spiny *Astragalus.* E.

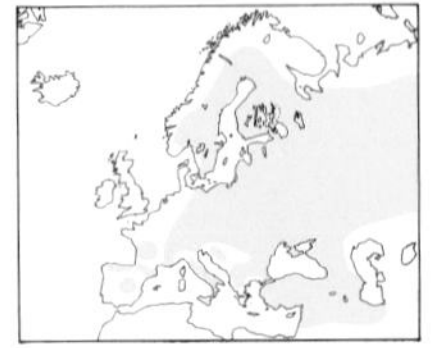

**GERANIUM ARGUS** *Eumedonia eumedon.* Ups brown, unmarked; uns pale brown, marking spots black, white-ringed; unh a short white stripe from the discal spot along vein 4 is distinctive when present. Sexes similar. Widespread in Fennoscandia to 70°N, and in mountainous districts of C and S Europe, from Spain (Cantabrian Mts), Pyrenees, C France and the Alps, to Carpathians, Apennines and Balkans, Greece and Sicily. Absent from NW Europe and from the Mediterranean islands except Sicily. Flies July in a single brood, at low levels in Fennoscandia, in C Europe more often among mountains, at altitudes of 1000m, rising to 2400m. In Fennoscandia and E Europe, f. *fylgia*; the white stripe unh is absent: in the high North, f. *borealis,* often small, uns pale grey-brown, markings less distinct. Larval food plant *Geranium pratense.* Range extends across Asia Minor to the Caucasus, S Urals, Lebanon, Iran, Altai Mts and Siberia.

♂

**Cretan Argus**

♂

♂ f. *borealis*

**Geranium Argus**

**The Brown Arguses.** These four small, brown butterflies have an enormous distribution across Europe and Asia to Siberia and the Himalayas. Local variation in wing-markings and in anatomy is very slight. The sexes are similar, but the ♀ often slightly larger, ups markings better developed. In order to define species within this complex, breeding experiments have been undertaken between forms of the Brown Argus and of the Mountain Argus, to find out if they are genetically compatible. It has been found that these two species do not hybridize successfully, and on these grounds they are considered specifically distinct. Other forms from N Africa, Spain, and Balkans have not been analysed in this way, and in the arrangement given here no attempt has been made to refer to all the many forms and subspecies that have been described and named.

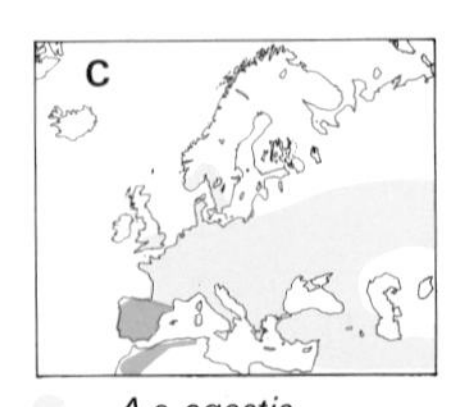

*A.a. agestis*
*A.a. cramera*

**BROWN ARGUS** *Aricia agestis.* Small, ups orange-red submarginal lunules well developed, upf sometimes incomplete near wing apex; unh postdiscal black spot in space 6 clearly out of line with the other spots in the row. ♀ ups red submarginal lunules often enlarged. Occurs in N Africa, S and C Europe to about 55°N, including S England. Flies in two or more broods, April–May and July–August, at low altitudes, not over 1200m. Larval food plants *Helianthemum, Erodium* and other Geraniaciae, also *Centaurea* species. Locally variable with two major subspecies in Europe. Larva p. 228. **Map 17**

*A. a. agestis,* from the Pyrenees to S England and Denmark, eastwards to Romania, Greece, and the larger Mediterranean islands except the Balearics. ♂ uns usually pale grey-brown. Range extends across Russia to Asia Minor, Iran, C Asia and the Himalayas.

*A. a. cramera*, in Morocco, Algeria, Tunisia, Portugal and Spain, north to the foothills of the Pyrenees, Balearic islands and Canaries. ♂ uns darker grey-brown (first brood) or brown (late broods). Further distinguished by a small character in the male genitalia. E.

*A.a. artaxerxes*
*A.a. allous*
*A.a. montensis*

**MOUNTAIN ARGUS** *Aricia artaxerxes.* Small, ♂ ups submarginal lunules orange-yellow, usually vestigial, often absent; uns markings as for the Brown Argus. ♀ ups submarginal lunules usually vestigial, but often better developed. Flies June–July in N Europe, Alps, Carpathians etc. in a single brood, with four subspecies distinguished by wing-markings. Larval food plant *Helianthemum*. Range extends across N Russia to the Urals, Caucasus and Altai Mts. **Map 18**

*A. a. artaxerxes*. Flies in Scotland and N England. ♂ upf discal spot white; uns discal and pd spots white with minute black pupils. ♀ similar. In N England occasional specimens occur f. *salmacis*, with white markings incomplete, transitional to *A. a. allous*.

*A. a. allous.* Usually slightly larger, ups discal spot not white, red submarginal lunules variable, on upf partly developed or vestigial but at high altitudes f. *inhonora*, often absent; uph lunules more often partly developed. Absent from S England, Massif Central of France and Apennines.

*A. a. montensis* (Large Argus). ♂ ups submarginal orange lunules incomplete, rarely vestigial or absent; uns pale yellow-grey, unh pd spot in space 8 only slightly out-of-line. ♀ similar but ups submarginal lunules yellow and series complete on both wings. Occurs in a single brood flying in July among mountains from 1200m upwards. In N Africa, Spain and S France, also in Hungary, Tatra and Romanian Carpathians (Bucegi, Retezat Mts).

*A. a. macedonica* (Balkan Argus). ♂ fw 13.5–14mm, ♀ slightly larger. A large form, ups both sexes very dark, fw usually unmarked, hw orange lunules reduced, inconspicuous. Widespread as a mountain butterfly in Hungary (Bükk Mts), Romania (Damogled), Yugoslavia, N Greece, Bulgaria.

♂ England to C Asia

♀ Canary Is.

**Brown Argus**

♂ Scotland & N England

♂ Continental Europe

♂ N Africa & Spain etc

**Mountain Argus**

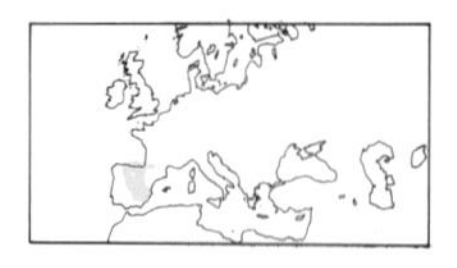

**SPANISH ARGUS** *Aricia morronensis*, like *A. a. allous*. ♂ ups submarginal lunules reduced to small, yellow marks upf in spaces 2,3; unh submarginal lunules yellow, present in space 1b to space 7, a white stripe along vein 4 prominent. Sexes similar. Distributed in Spain and N Portugal in widely scattered colonies. Very local, flying July–August in a single brood, on rough, stony slopes at 1000–2000m or more. Larval food plant *Erodium*. E.

**BLUE ARGUS** *Aricia anteros*. ♂ ups pale, gleaming blue; upf small discal spot present, dark marginal border 1mm; unh postdiscal spot in space 6 slightly out of line. ♀ ups brown; uns as in ♂. Occurs in Yugoslavia, Dobrugea, Albania, Bulgaria and Greece. Occasional and rare in its northern range. A mountain butterfly, usually seen at 1000–1700m, flies June–July in a single brood. Larval food plant not recorded. Range extends across Asia Minor to Transcaucasus.

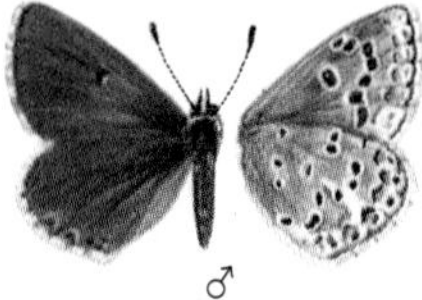

♂

**Spanish Argus**

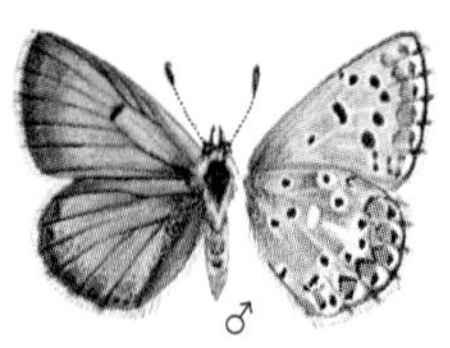

♂

**Blue Argus**

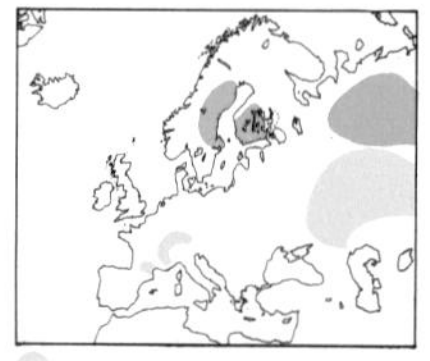

P.n.nicias
P.n.scandica

**SILVERY ARGUS** *Pseudaricia nicias*. ♂ ups pale blue, fuscous marginal borders very wide; unh white stripe along vein 4 prominent, postdiscal row of spots not irregular. ♀ ups brown. Flies July in a single brood, local and usually uncommon. Larval food plants *Geranium pratense* and *G. silvaticum*.

*P. n. nicias*, E Pyrenees (Val d'Aran) and main chain of the Alps from France to the Stilfserjoch, ♂ ups blue areas restricted by fuscous marginal borders 3–4mm wide. Occurs in mountains at 1000–2000m. Local but not rare. E.

*P. n. scandica*. in S Sweden and S Finland. ♂ ups brightly marked, marginal borders 2mm. Flies in light woodland at low levels. Range extends to N Russia (Komi).

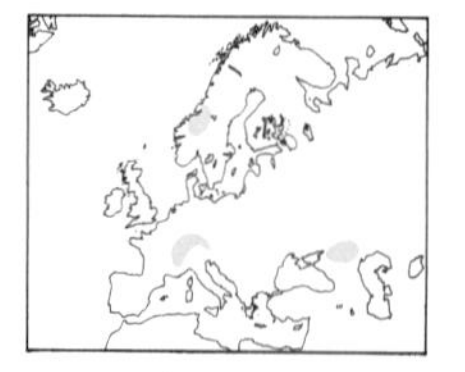

**ALPINE ARGUS** *Albulina orbitulus*. . ♂ ups bright, shining blue, unmarked; unh basal and pd spots white. ♀ ups brown; unh markings as in ♂. Occurs on the Alps, from Basses A to the Grosser Glockner and the Triglav (Julian Alps), local in S Norway. In the Alps flies at high altitudes, 1800m or more, over open alpine slopes of grass and flowers, flies July in a single brood. In Scandinavia occurs on the Dovrefjeld, Jotunfjeld and in Jämtländ at lower altitudes to 1000m. Absent from the Pyrenees, Carpathians and Balkans. Larval food plants *Astragalus* species. Continental range extends to Altai Mts, C Asia and Siberia.

♂

**Silvery Argus**

♂

**Alpine Argus**

*A.g.glandon*
*A.g.zullichi*
*A.g.aquilo*

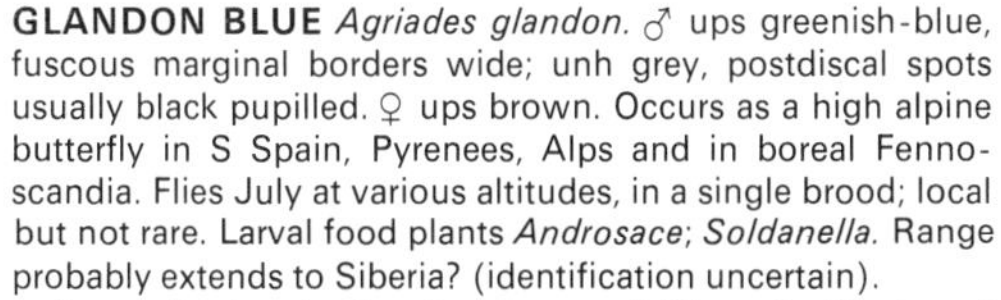

**GLANDON BLUE** *Agriades glandon.* ♂ ups greenish-blue, fuscous marginal borders wide; unh grey, postdiscal spots usually black pupilled. ♀ ups brown. Occurs as a high alpine butterfly in S Spain, Pyrenees, Alps and in boreal Fennoscandia. Flies July at various altitudes, in a single brood; local but not rare. Larval food plants *Androsace*; *Soldanella.* Range probably extends to Siberia? (identification uncertain).

*A. g. glandon*, in the Pyrenees and Alps, at altitudes of 1800m and over. Locally common. In f. *alboocellatus*, unh postdiscal spots lack black pupils, a constant race in Bavarian Alps (Nebelhorn etc.).

*A. g. zullichi*, very local in S Spain, Sierra Nevada. Small, unh rather pale, markings well developed.

*A. g. aquilo*, only in boreal Fennoscandia. ♂ ups pale; uns dark submarginal lunules prominent on both wings.

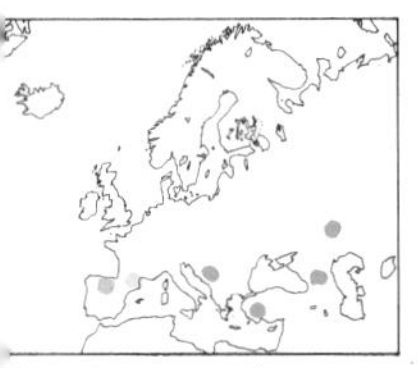

*A.p.pyrenaicus*
*A.p.asturiensis*
*A.p.dardanus*

**GAVARNIE BLUE** *Agriades pyrenaicus.* ♂ ups pale grey, black marginal borders linear, unh discal and pd spots white. ♀ ups brown. Very local in Europe as a mountain butterfly, flying at high altitudes. Larval food plants *Gregoria*; *Androsace*; *Soldanella*. Flies July. Range extends to Asia Minor and Caucasus, further Asiatic distribution uncertain.

*A. p. pyrenaicus*, in the C Pyrenees: Cauterets, Gavarnie etc; Absent from E Pyrenees and Andorra. ♂ ups an even tone of lustrous, pale grey. Flies over grassy alpine slopes at 1800m and over, locally common.

*A. p. asturiensis*, flies in the Cantabrian Mts on Picos de Europa, at 2000m and over, in local abundant colonies. Like *A. p. pyrenaicus* but ♂ ups has white pd marks between veins.

*A. p. dardanus* (='*glandon dardanus*') in Balkans, only known from Ćvrstniča and Vran Planina in Herzegovina, flying at high altitudes. Very small, ups grey-blue, marginal borders narrow; unh postdiscal spots in spaces 4,5 vestigial or absent. Occurs on Turkish Mt Olympus, Caucasus and reported from S Russia (Voronesh) and C Asia.

♂ ♀ Pyrenees & Alps ♂ f. *alboocellatus*

♂ Spain ♂ Fennoscandia

**Glandon Blue**

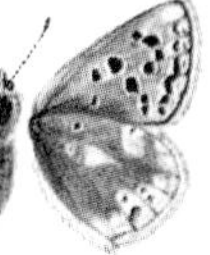

♂ C Pyrenees ♂ Cantabrian Mts ♀ ♂ Balkans

**Gavarnie Blue**

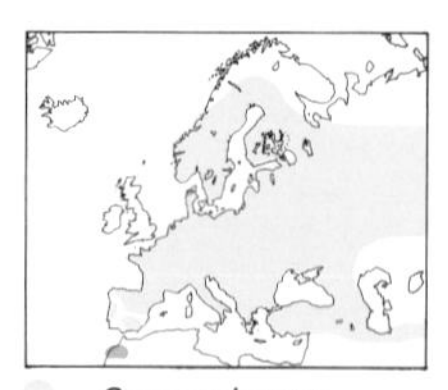

C.s. semiargus
C.s. maroccanus

**MAZARINE BLUE** *Cyaniris semiargus.* ♂ ups violet-blue; uns without marginal markings. ♀ ups brown. Widely distributed and often common in C Europe to 68°N, more local in Spain and Portugal, very local in Morocco. Flies June–August in a single brood, in open country, hayfields etc, from sea level to 1800m or more. Larval food plants *Trifolium, Anthyllis, Melilotus* etc. Range extends throughout temperate Europe and Asia to Mongolia.

*C. s. semiargus*, from Spain (Sierra Navada) northwards to Scandinavia and eastwards to Hungary and Greece, extinct in England, absent from the Mediterranean islands of Sardinia and Crete and from the Balearics. At high altitudes in Bulgaria and Greece, f. *parnassia*, unh with small, grey marginal spots at anal angle, sometimes with an orange lunule in s2, said to be sufficiently common to be considered racial in some localities (Mt Parnassos; Mt Timphristos).

*C. s. maroccana*, only in the High Atlas. ♂ normal; ♀ ups blue basal suffusions well marked. Flies at 2600m in open places with flowers.

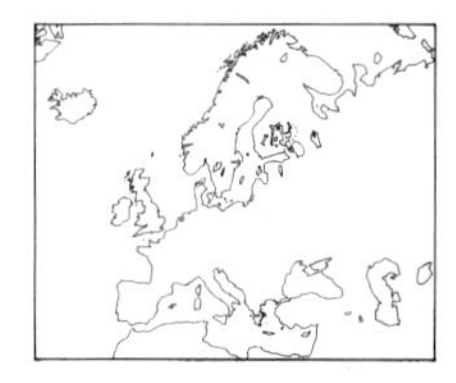

**GREEK MAZARINE BLUE** *Cyaniris helena.* ♂ ups like the Mazarine Blue but much smaller; unh with large submarginal lunules pale orange in spaces 1c,2,3. ♀ ups black, orange lunules present on both surfaces of hw. Only known in Greece (Peloponnesos), on Taygetus Mts and Mt Chelmos. Flies June–July at 1500m on the mountains. Larval food plant *Anthyllis vulneraria.* Perhaps specifically distinct but closely related to *Cyaniris antiochena* (Lebanon) and to *C. mesopotamica* (Iraq).

♂
**Mazarine Blue**

♂
**Greek Mazarine Blue**

## Anomalous Blues.

Twenty species following all lack a cell-spot unf and all have similar genitalia characters, implying a close relationship, although colour and wing patterns are variable. The distribution areas are almost confined to the Mediterranean region, extending eastwards to the Caucasus and Iran. Because specific features are so badly expressed in the wing patterns and male genitalia, identification often depends upon chromosome examination, a difficult and laborious process applicable only to fresh material prepared in the field.

### Uppersides brown in both sexes: Anomalous Blues

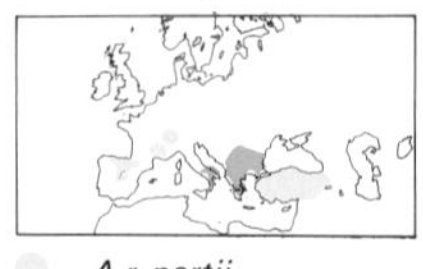

A.r. partii
A. pelopi

**RIPART'S ANOMALOUS BLUE** *Agrodiaetus ripartii.* ♂ fw 16–17mm, ups dark brown, upf androconial patch in pd area, fringes dark; unh pale brown, a white stripe present from wing base along v4 strongly marked. ♀ ups slightly darker, fringes paler; unh white stripe usually emphasized. Local in NE and C Spain, SE France (Nice, etc), S Italy (Lucania). In Macedonia, Bulgaria and Greece, *Agrodiaetus pelopi*, very similar, is locally

♂
Anomalous Blue

♂
Ripart's Anomalous Blue

♂
Oberthur's Anomalous Blue

common. Flies July–August at low or moderate altitudes in hot, rocky places. Larval food plant *Onobrychis*. Range extends widely across Asia Minor.

**ANDALUSIAN ANOMALOUS BLUE** *Agrodiaetus violetae*. Like *Agrodiaetus ripartii*, ups 'chestnut brown,' androconial patch extensive; uns pale cream colour, marginal markings not well defined, unh a pale stripe usually present, sometimes reduced or absent. ♀ slightly smaller, uns a darker tone of yellow-brown unh pale stripe less prominent. Described from the Sierra de Almijara, S Spain, flying at 1150m in early August, not illustrated.

**HIGGINS'S ANOMALOUS BLUE** *Agrodiaetus nephohiptamenos*. ♂ fw 15–17mm, ups medium brown, veins darkened, fringes noticeably pale; unh a white stripe well developed. ♀ uns slightly darker tone of brown, vestigial marginal brown markings often present. Described from N Greece, flying at 1600m or more late July. Appears to be very local and uncommon. *Agrodiaetus galloi*, recently described, resembles *A. nephohiptamenos* closely, probably the same species. The pale fringes uph are equally noticeable. Described from S Italy in Reggio Calabria. Not uncommon on Monte Pollino flying on grass slopes at 1500m, not illustrated.

**White stripe unh vestigial or absent**

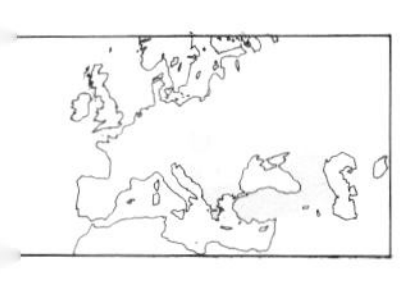

**ANOMALOUS BLUE** *Agrodiaetus admetus*. Like Ripart's Blue, but unh the white basal stripe is absent, rarely vestigial or represented by a triangular pd mark, submarginal and marginal markings are present on both wings ups. ♀ similar, often smaller. Occurs in widely scattered colonies in the Romanian Dobrugea, Bulgaria, Macedonia and Greece, flying at low altitudes to 1000m. Larval food plant *Onobrychis*. Range extends to Asia Minor.

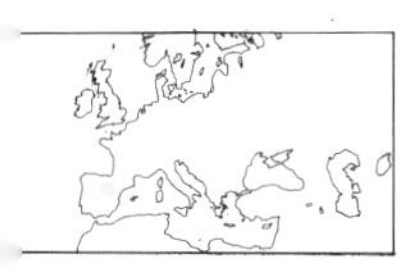

**OBERTHUR'S ANOMALOUS BLUE** *Agrodiaetus fabressei*. ♂ like the Anomalous Blue, uns the usual pd markings well developed, but unh the pale stripe is absent, with vestigial marginal markings. ♀ similar, usually smaller. Flies July–August in widely scattered colonies from low altitudes to 1500m in NE Spain, Teruel; Albarracin; Burgos etc.

Grecian Anomalous Blue  Agenjo's Anomalous Blue

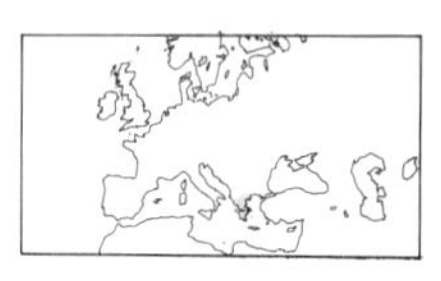

**GRECIAN ANOMALOUS BLUE** *Agrodiaetus aroaniensis* resembles *A. fabressei* closely. Unh the white stripe is absent, or rarely vestigial, and faintly marked marginal spots are often present unh. Reported from Macedonia (Skopje) and Greece, mainland and Peloponnesos (Mt Chelmos). Larval food plant not known. Flies July. The relationship of this butterfly to the Spanish *A. fabressei* is unclear at present.

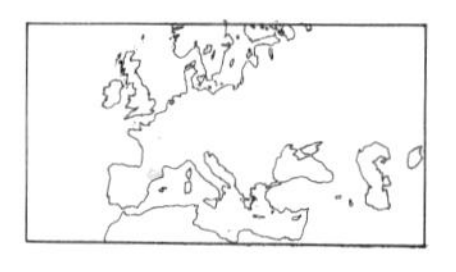

**AGENJO'S ANOMALOUS BLUE** *Agrodiaetus agenjoi.* ♂ usually large; ups dark brown, veins darkened; uns usual markings well defined, unh lacking a pale stripe, vestigial marginal spots present in each space. ♀ smaller, ups darker veins more obvious. Flies July–August in NE Spain (Catalonia) at low altitudes in very localized colonies. The larger size and general appearance of *A. agenjoi* does not suggest a close relationship with *A. fabressei.*

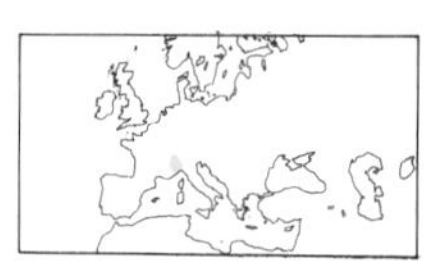

**PIEDMONT ANOMALOUS BLUE** *Agrodiaetus humedasae,* recently described, is similar. This is a relatively large species, ups dark brown, unh lacking a pale stripe and with darker marginal spots faintly visible in each space. It flies August in the Cogne valley, W Switzerland, at low altitudes.

*Note.* Specific identification of the nine species recorded above is unsatisfactory and the relationships of the taxa to one another are unclear. Additional species or subspecies may be described in the future, and the arrangement given above, including little more than published names and localities, is to be considered provisional.

**Male uppersides blue, grey or milk-white**

**CHELMOS BLUE** *Agrodiaetus iphigenia nonacriensis.* ♂ ups bright, shining blue, *black marginal borders linear;* uns pale yellow grey, unh a pale stripe from wing-base to s3 firmly marked. ♀ ups brown. In Europe known only from Mt Chelmos in S Greece, flying July at 1300–1800m. Larval food plant not known. Provisionally associated with the Asiatic *Agrodiaetus iphigenia.*

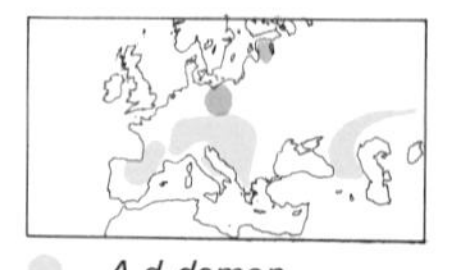

*A.d. damon*
*A.d. ultramarinus*

**DAMON BLUE** *Agrodiaetus damon.* ♂ ups shining sky-blue, marginal borders *fuscous, 3–4mm wide;* unh pale yellow-brown, a white stripe firmly marked. ♀ ups brown, fringes brown; unh darker yellow-brown. Occurs in scattered colonies in C and N Spain, across S and C Europe to Estonia, Yugoslavia

and Greece. Most often seen July–August among mountains with calcareous rocks, often common from valley levels to 2000m. Larval food plant *Onobrychis*. Range extends to Caucasus, Altai Mts and W Siberia. Larva p. 228.
*A. d. ultramarinus* ♂ ups dark blue in Estonia, Poland etc. Spanish specimens, f. *noguerae*, are usually small (variable).

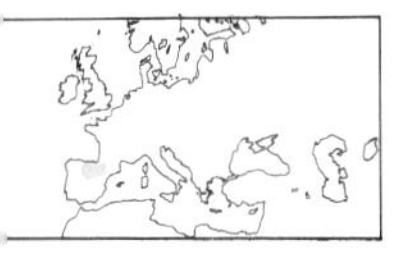

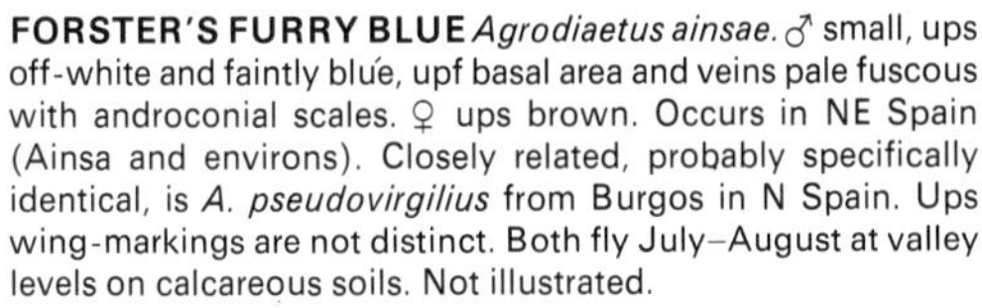

**FORSTER'S FURRY BLUE** *Agrodiaetus ainsae*. ♂ small, ups off-white and faintly blue, upf basal area and veins pale fuscous with androconial scales. ♀ ups brown. Occurs in NE Spain (Ainsa and environs). Closely related, probably specifically identical, is *A. pseudovirgilius* from Burgos in N Spain. Ups wing-markings are not distinct. Both fly July–August at valley levels on calcareous soils. Not illustrated.

*A.d. dolus*
*A.d. vigilius*
*A.d. vittatus*

**FURRY BLUE** *Agrodiaetus dolus*. ♂ ups pale blue to off-white; upf with brown basal suffusion of androconia; uns pale grey or faintly brownish; unh with or without pale stripe from base to space 3. ♀ ups brown, fringes white. Occurs July–August in N Spain, SE France and peninsular Italy. Larval food plants *Onobrychis*, *Medicago sativa*. E.

*A. d. dolus*, in SE France, Var, Bouches du Rhône, Alpes Maritimes. ♂ ups pale blue; unh pale stripe not well defined. In NE Spain (Barcelona), *A. d. fulgens*, similar, but unh basal stripe even less well defined, more often absent.

*A. d. virgilius*, in peninsular Italy (Abruzzi) to S Italy (Pietrapertosa), in widely scattered colonies. ♂ ups white or faintly blue, upf basal area, veins etc. all fuscous; unh pale yellow-grey, pale stripe absent. Colour tones vary slightly in different colonies.

*A. d. vittatus*, in S France, Massif Central, Lozère, Aveyron. Small, ♂ upf white, wing-base faintly blue, fuscous suffusion very extensive, including uph; unh pale brown, pale stripe well developed.

♂

**Chelmos Blue**

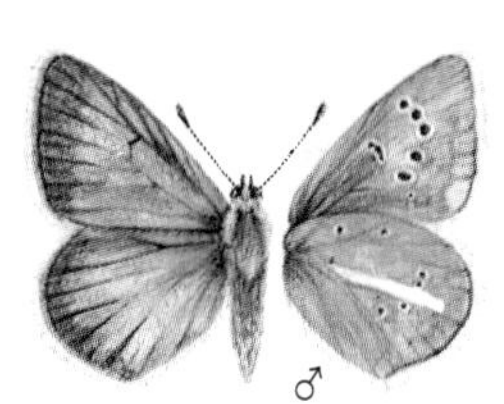

♂

**Damon Blue**

♂ Italy

♂ SE France to Alpes Maritime

**Furry Blue**

**CHAPMAN'S BLUE** *Agrodiaetus thersites.* ♂ ups like the Common Blue (p. 000). ♀ ups brown, with or without orange submarginal lunules. Widespread in Morocco and Europe to 50°N, flying in two or more broods, May–July, in open places and fields with *Onobrychis* (Sanfoin), larval food plant, lowlands to 1600m or more. Range extends to Lebanon, Iran and C Asia.

*A.e. escheri*
*A.e. dalmaticus*
*A.e. ahmar*

**ESCHER'S BLUE** *Agrodiaetus escheri.* ♂ ups bright blue, black marginal lines narrow, fringes white, partially chequered black on hw. ♀ ups brown, blue basal suffusion rare, yellow submarginal lunules often prominent, rarely absent. Widely distributed to 47°N in Europe, rare and very local in Morocco. Flies June–July. Larval food plant *Onobrychis.*

*A. e. escheri*, in SW Europe from Spain to S France, Switzerland in Rhône Valley and Alps of N Italy. ♂ ups bright blue. Flies at altitudes of 800–1800m, most commonly among mountains. Local but not rare.

*A. e. dalmaticus*, in S Yugoslavia (Herzegovina, Dalmatia, Macedonia) and Greece (Peloponnesos and mainland). Large, ♂ ups pale blue, gleaming. ♀ ups yellow marginal lunules not well developed. Widely distributed, esp. in western coastal areas, on Mt Chelmos; Mt Parnassos, Mt Olympos and north to Macedonia.

*A. e. ahmar*, in Middle Atlas, Morocco, small, rather pale blue, an undistinguished form flying at 1800m, very local and rare.

*A. e. splendens*, in C Italy, Florence and C Apennines, l'Aquila etc. ♂ like *E. e. dalmaticus* but often small, fw 14mm, ups pale shining blue. ♀ ups orange submarginal lunules well developed. Flies at 1000m or over.

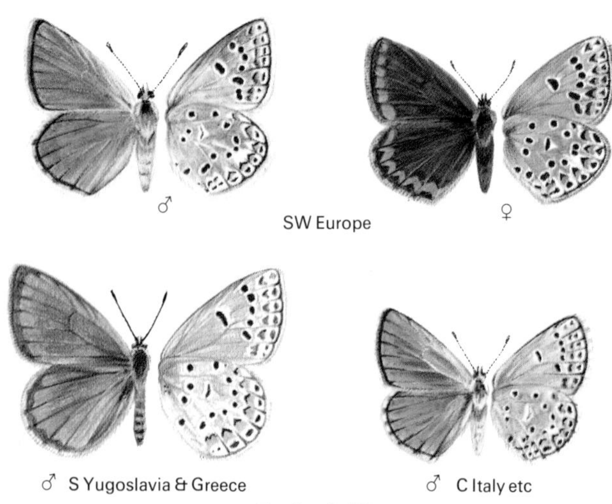


**Escher's Blue**

**Chapman's Blue**

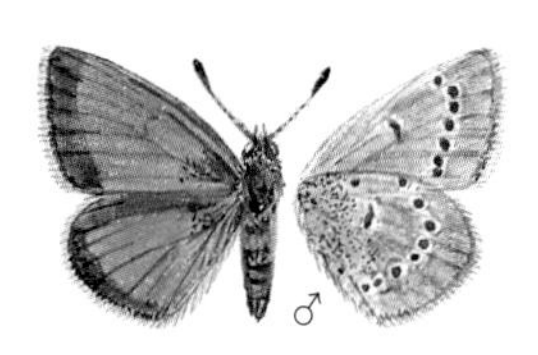

**Pontic Blue**

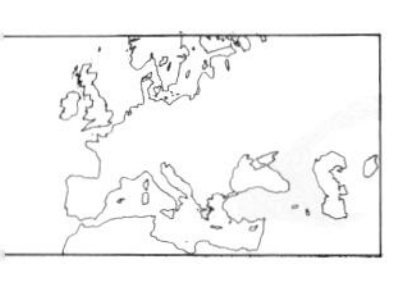

**PONTIC BLUE** *Agrodiaetus coelestinus.* Like the Mazarine Blue, ♂ ups dark blue, marginal borders 2–3mm wide, black; unh grey with small markings, green basal suffusions wide. ♀ ups brown. In Europe occurs on Mt Chelmos (Greece, Peloponnesos), flying June–July at 1200–1500m or more. Larval food plant *Anthyllis vulneraria.* Range extends to the Urals, Caucasus and Kazakstan.

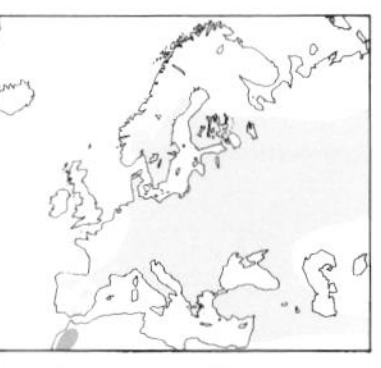

*A.a. amanda*
*A.a. abdelaziz*

**AMANDA'S BLUE** *Agrodiaetus amanda.* Large; ♂ ups gleaming sky-blue, marginal borders fuscous, 2–4mm wide; uns pale grey, black spots in usual pattern clearly white-ringed, hw base suffused blue-green, submarginal lunules yellow. ♀ ups dark brown; uns paler brown, white-ringed black spots prominent. Widespread in Europe to 65°N. Flies June–July from lowlands to 1500m in a single brood, usually seen near *Vicia cracca* (Tufted Vetch) larval food plant. Range extends across W Asia to Iran, Turkestan and W Siberia.

*A. a. amanda*, in all Europe, ♂ ups blue shade slightly variable. ♀ ups yellow submarginal lunules absent or (rarely) vestigial. Absent from Britain.

*A. a. abdelaziz*, in Morocco, ♂ ups slightly paler blue. ♀ ups yellow submarginal lunules large, well developed on both wings.

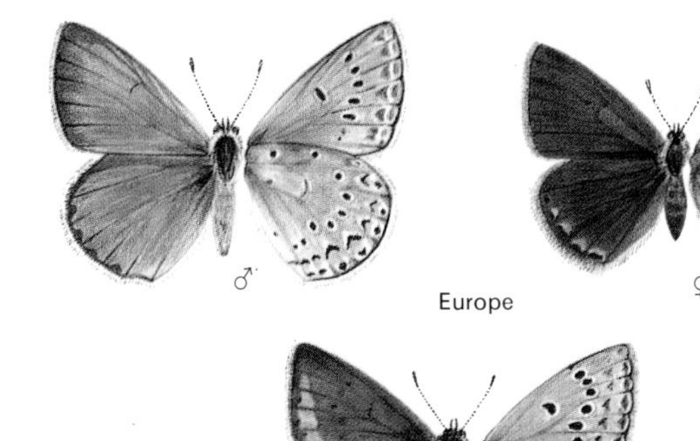

♂ Europe ♀

♀ Morocco

**Amanda's Blue**

**TURQUOISE BLUE** *Plebicula dorylas*. ♂ ups sky-blue, black marginal borders linear; uns margins white. ♀ ups brown, with or without basal blue suffusions. Widely distributed in S and C Europe to 60°N, including S Sweden, Latvia, Carpathians, Balkans and Greece; very local in N Spain. Absent from NW Europe and Mediterranean islands except Sicily (?). Flies May–July in two broods. Common on flowery slopes from 1000–1800m. Larval food plants *Melilotus, Trifolium, Thymus* etc. Range extends to Asia Minor.

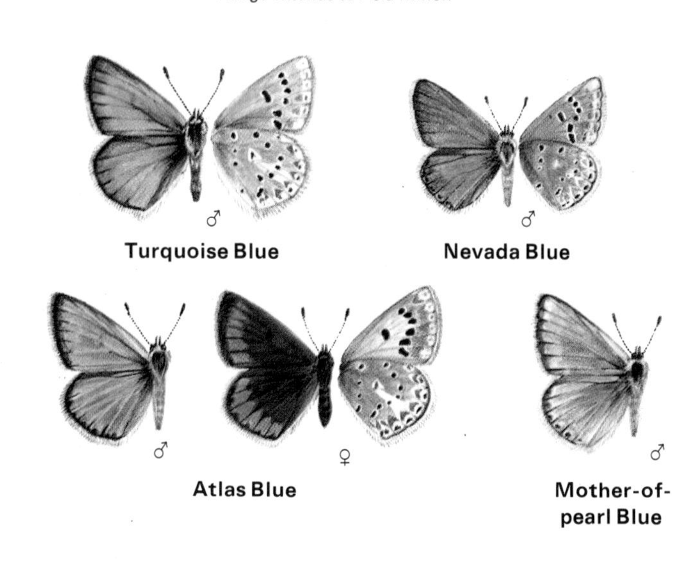


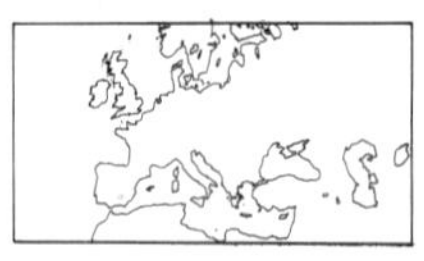

**NEVADA BLUE** *Plebicula golgus*. Like the Turquoise Blue but smaller. ♂ ups fw pointed, deeper tone of blue; uns pale grey-brown. ♀ ups brown. Known only from S Spain, Sierra Nevada, flying July at 2500m over stony slopes. Flies in a single brood. E.

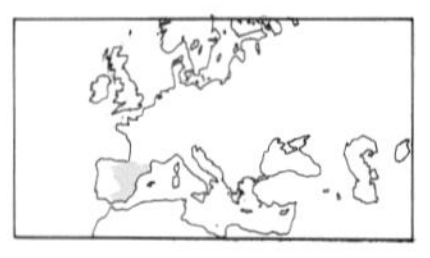

**MOTHER-OF-PEARL BLUE** *Plebicula nivescens*. ♂ ups pale, shining silver-grey; uns like the Turquoise Blue. ♀ ups brown. Local, but widely distributed in E. Spain, from Granada to Catalonia and Burgos, absent from W Spain, furthest north at Aulus. Flies June–July in a single brood at altitudes of 1000–2000m. Larval food plants *Trifolium, Melilotus*. E.

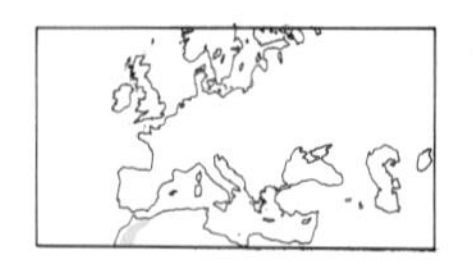

**ATLAS BLUE** *Plebicula atlantica*. ♂ ups very pale sky-blue; uns like the Turquoise Blue. ♀ ups the orange submarginal lunules very large; unf black discal and postdiscal spots prominent. Only in Morocco, local but widespread in colonies at 2000–2300m, Middle Atlas, Taghzeft Pass; High Atlas, Toubkal Massif. Flies May–June on stony slopes in two broods. Larval food plant not known. E.

**The Chalk-hill Blues.** These butterflies resemble those of the preceding section in their anatomy, but they have a standard pattern of wing-markings which is entirely different. They are especially associated with limestone mountains. The wing-markings are so similar in all species that the specific identity of several forms is still a subject for argument, while local and specific variation in the ups ground-colour is most confusing, especially in Spain. The fringes of both wings are chequered black and white. Larval food plants include *Coronilla, Astragalus, Hippocrepis* etc. The larvae are attended by small red ants, which are said to carry the larvae, found at a distance from the ant's nest, to a convenient place easily available for 'milking'.

The arrangement adopted below follows closely the proposals of the late H. de Lesse, who made a special study of these butterflies, basing his suggestions on the chromosome numbers, which differ between species and in different areas, but which are normally constant in a given colony.

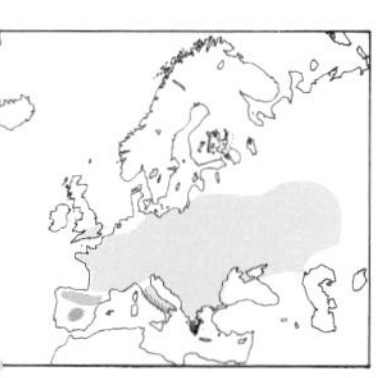

*L.c. coridon*
*L.c.c.* f. *asturiensis*
*L.c.c.* f. *caelestissima*
*L.c.c.* f. *apennina*
*L.c. graeca*

**CHALK-HILL BLUE** *Lysandra coridon.* Ups fringes white chequered black. ♂ ups pale, silvery blue, marginal borders fuscous, 2–3mm wide. ♀ ups brown, or f. *syngrapha* more or less suffused with blue. Widespread in Europe from Spain to S England and eastwards to Austria, the Balkans, Greece and to the Ukraine. Striking blue colour forms occur in Spain, including in Cantabrian Mts, Burgos etc f. *asturiensis*, ♂ ups pale blue; in Teruel, at Albarracin etc f. *caelestissima*, ♂ gleaming ups sky-blue, both graded distinct species by some authors. f. *caerulescens*, ♂ like f. *caelestissima*, ups slightly darker grey-blue, the gleaming reflection almost completely absent, in contrast with the brighter f. *caelestissima* in which it is most prominent. Flies in late July–August among the colonies of f. *caelestissima* in the provinces of Teruel and Cuenca (Montes Universales etc), usually less common than the bright blue form. In C Italy there is f. *apennina*, ♂ ups pale blue, fuscous marginal borders narrow. The species is absent from Sicily and other Mediterranean islands and from S Spain and Portugal. A small race, *L. c. graeca*, ♂ ups pale yellowish-grey, occurs locally on mountains of mainland Greece. In all areas the species flies June–August in a single brood on calcareous soil, at all altitudes from lowlands to 2000m, in open country. Larval food plant *Hippocrepis, Astragalus coronilla*. E. Larva p. 228.
**Map 19**

♂

♂ f. *asturiensis*

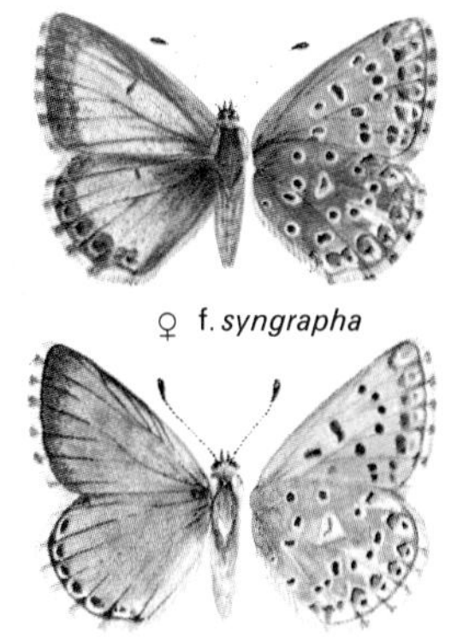

♀ f. *syngrapha*

♂ f. *caelestissima*

**Chalk-hill Blue**

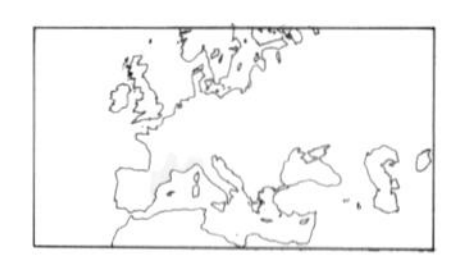

**PROVENCE CHALK-HILL BLUE** *Lysandra hispana*. Like the Chalk-hill Blue. ♂ ups pale, silvery blue; ♀ brown. Local in S France, in Provence, E Pyrenees, Basses Alpes etc; also in NE Spain, in Catalonia and southwards to Valencia; and in N Italy, in Liguria and Emilia. Flies in two broods April–June and August–September, on open flowery banks, not above 1000m altitude. Larval food plants *Coronilla*, *Astragalus* etc. The blue ♀–f. *syngrapha* does not occur in this species.

**MACEDONIAN CHALK-HILL BLUE** *Lysandra phillipi*. ♂ ups pale, gleaming blue, markings on both surfaces like *L. coridon*. By external characters it is probably indistinguishable from *L. c. asturiensis* (Asturias Mts), and clearly distinct from the widely distributed *L. c. graeca*. A claim to specific rank is supported by chromosome study. The species was discovered recently on a mountain in NE Greece, flying at 700–1900m in late July. Not illustrated.

**SPANISH CHALK-HILL BLUE** *Lysandra albicans*. Like the Chalk-Hill Blue; ♂ ups pale grey to off-white (variable), faintly blue in some colonies. ♀ ups brown. Widespread in Spain, from Granada to the foothills of the Pyrenees and Cantabrian Mts. Very pale in hot localities in the south, but in Teruel, *L. a. arragonensis*, darker, ups flushed grey-blue. Also known from the Middle Atlas, Morocco, *L. a. berber*, ♂ ups very pale, local and rare. Flies July–August. Larval food plants Pea, *Hippocrepis*, *Astragalus* etc. Symbiotic with ants. E.

**ADONIS BLUE** *Lysandra bellargus*. ♂ ups vivid sky-blue, black marginal borders linear; ♀ ups brown, often with blue ups suffusion. Widespread in Europe from Portugal and Spain to S England and the Baltic, eastwards to the Balkans and Greece. Flies in two annual broods, May–June and July–August, at all altitudes from sea level to 1800m. Often on calcareous soil but local in many districts. Larval food plant *Hippocrepis comosa* and other small Leguminosae. Range extends across Asia to Iraq, the Caucasus and N Iran (?). Larva p. 224 **Map 20**

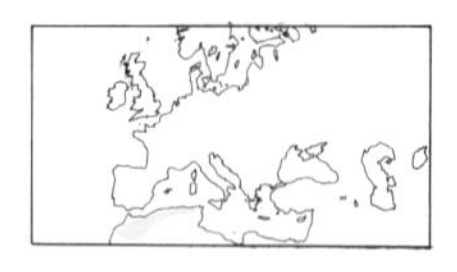

**SPOTTED ADONIS BLUE** *Lysandra punctifera*. Like the Adonis blue, ups white fringes strongly chequered; uph black submarginal spots constant. ♀ ups brown, blue suffusion frequent. Widespread in Morocco and Algeria in the Middle Atlas Mts at 1500m and over. Not recorded from Tunisia. Flies in two broods, May–June and September, second brood small. Larval food plant not known. E.

**MELEAGER'S BLUE** *Meleageria daphnis*. Usually large; hw outer margin slightly scalloped near anal angle; ♂ ups pale, shining blue, black marginal borders narrow; unf cell-spot not always present; uns pale grey with small markings. ♀ hw more deeply scalloped near anal angle; ups bright blue with fuscous costal and marginal borders, or ♀–f. *steeveni* ups heavily suffused dark grey. Widespread in S and C Europe, from NE Spain across S and C France, S Switzerland and Italy to Austria, the Balkans and Greece. Absent from Mediterranean islands except Sicily. Flies June–July in a single brood from valley levels to 1400m or more. Larval food plants include *Astragalus* and Thyme. Range extends to Asia Minor, Lebanon, Caucasus and N Iran.

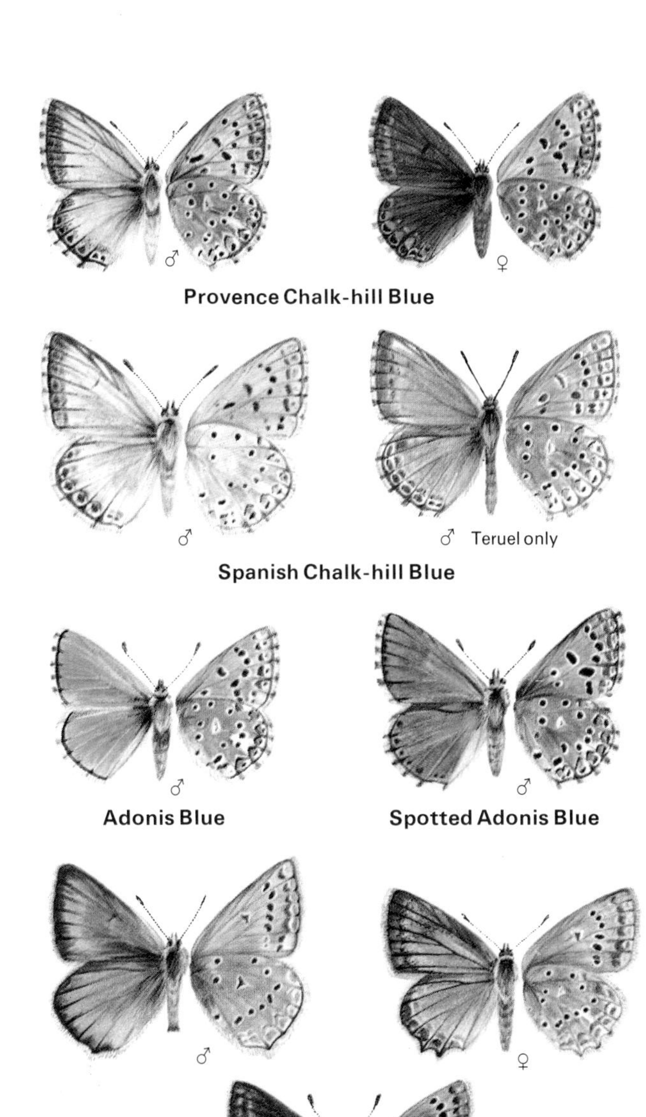


**Provence Chalk-hill Blue**

♂ ♂ Teruel only

**Spanish Chalk-hill Blue**

♂ ♂

**Adonis Blue** **Spotted Adonis Blue**

♂ ♀

♀ f. *steeveni*

**Meleager's Blue**

**The Common Blues.** The three species following, which include the Common Blue, do not look in any way unusual, but their anatomical characters are quite distinct. On the fore-wing underside in each species, there is a small cell-spot, which allows easy recognition, e.g. from Chapman's Blue, and from others with similar markings.

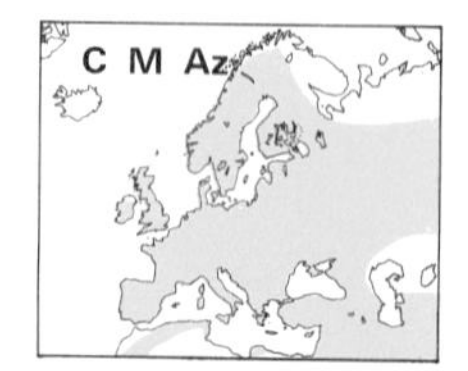


**COMMON BLUE** *Polyommatus icarus*. ♂ ups blue with narrow black marginal lines; unf a black spot present in the cell. ♀ ups brown, with or without blue suffusion; unf as in ♂. In N Africa and Europe, common and very widely distributed to 70°N, including the Atlantic and Mediterranean islands. In hot countries and late brood specimens, ♂ often small; f. *celinus*, ups pale blue. Flies through the summer April–October in a succession of broods, in open country, meadows etc., from sea level to 2000m or over. Larval food plant small Leguminosae, clovers, trefoil etc. Range extends to W Asia, the Caucasus and eastwards across Siberia to Sakhalin. **Map 21**

*Note*. This common butterfly can be confused with other species unless the cell-spot unf is noticed. In rare cases f. *icarinus*, this spot is vestigial or absent.

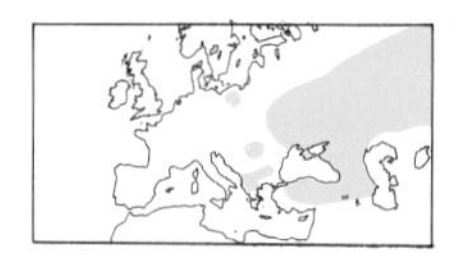

**FALSE EROS BLUE** *Polyommatus eroides*. Like the Common Blue. Ups gleaming sky blue, the black *marginal lines 1–2mm wide*. ♀ ups brown. An eastern species, occurs in E Prussia, Czechoslovakia, Bulgaria, Macedonia and N Greece. Flies in a single brood June–July in mountainous country at 1200–1800m altitude, in colonies. Larval food plant not known. Range extends to the Caucasus and C Asia.

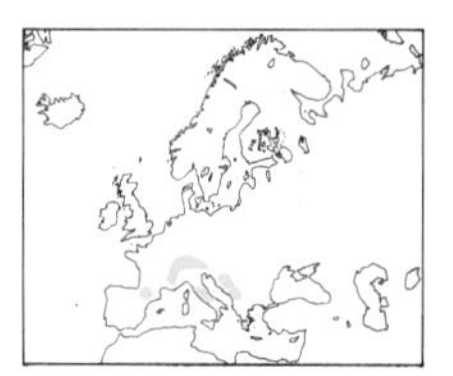

**EROS BLUE** *Polyommatus eros*. Like the False Eros but smaller. ♂ fw 13–14mm ups paler, shining blue, black marginal borders 1–1.5mm; uns grey-brown, markings like the Common Blue. ♀ ups grey-brown, blue basal suffusions common. In Europe widespread at high altitudes in the Mts of Cantal, Pyrenees, Alps and Apennines, flying June–August over grassy slopes. Larval food plants small Leguminosae including *Onobrychis*, *Astragalus* etc. Range extends to the Altai Mts and W Siberia. In S Greece, *P. eros menelaos*; slightly larger, ♂ fw 14–17mm, ups markings as in *eros eros*; unh submarginal orange lunules rarely prominent. ♀ ups grey-brown; uns markings well defined. Flies on the Langhada Pass, Taygetos Mts, in June–early July.

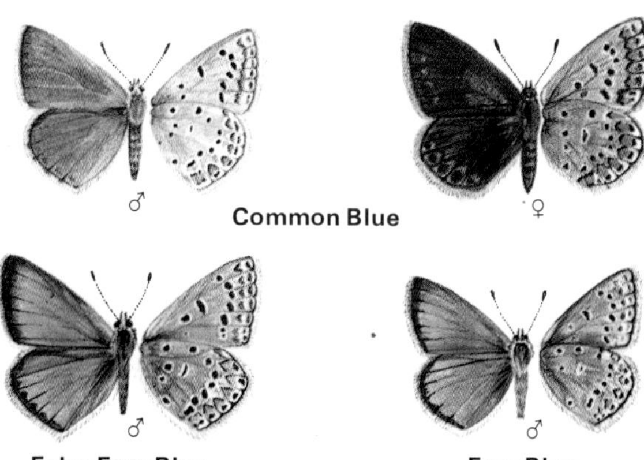


Common Blue

False Eros Blue

Eros Blue

# RIODINIDAE

This family is of special interest as its members all have certain anatomical characters showing relationship to the Blues (Lycaenidae). In ♂♂ the front legs are small and useless for walking, the tarsus without claws, reduced to a single segment. ♀♀ have six fully developed legs with normal claws. The larva is flat, like the larva of a Lycaenid, woodlouse-shaped, with short, pale hair, but it lacks a 'honey gland.' This is an important group in S America with many curious forms, often mimetic of inedible species, but in Europe there is only a single species, the Duke of Burgundy Fritillary, looking so much like a small Fritillary, although it differs in so many ways. With the exception of a few little known species living in the mountains of SW China, this is the only representative of the Family that occurs in the vast Palaearctic Region.

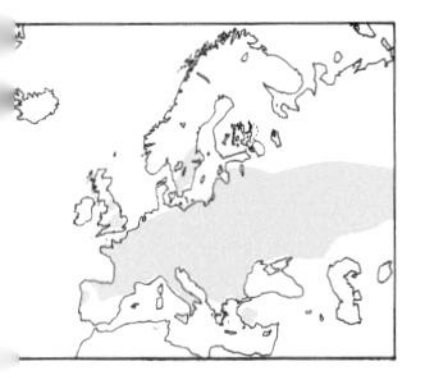

**DUKE OF BURGUNDY FRITILLARY** *Hamearis lucina*. ♂ fore-wing apex pointed; unh cinnamon-brown with white basal and discal bands. ♀ forewing apex rounded, markings similar. Widely distributed but local in C Europe to 60°N, including England. Absent from S Spain, NW Germany, Holland, Ireland and Mediterranean islands except Sicily; in Denmark only on Zeeland. Usually a lowland species, flying in fields and open woodland, rarely rising to 1200m or more. In S Europe, f. *praestans*, often large, flying in two broods, May–August; in gen.2, f. *schwingenschussi*, with extended dark ups markings, the hind-wing almost black. Larval food plants *Primula* species, esp. *P. veris* (Cowslip). Range extends across temperate Europe to the Ural Mts. Larva p. 226. **Map 22**

**Duke of Burgundy Fritillary**

# LIBYTHEIDAE

Butterflies of middle size or less, related to the Nymphalidae. The forewing apex elongate, wings usually dark brown with white or yellow markings. Antenna thickened gradually to a blunt apex, club not well defined. ♂ fore-leg small, with single tarsal segment, without claws, useless for walking; ♀ fore-leg with five tarsal segments and claws, fully functional. The most striking character is the great length of the palpi, almost as long as the head and thorax together. The distribution is remarkable. The butterflies are migrants. Although only 10–12 species are known, these are distributed on every continent, and usually only a single species will be present over a vast area.

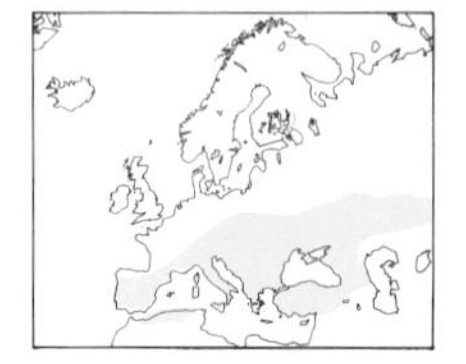

**NETTLE-TREE BUTTERFLY** *Libythea celtis*. Upf fulvous markings extensive. Sexes similar. Occurs especially in Mediterranean countries from N Africa to the southern slopes of the Alps and from Portugal and Spain to Greece. Flies June–August at all altitudes to 1500m or more. Larval food plant *Celtis australis* (Nettle Tree). Hibernates as a butterfly in early autumn; eggs are laid in the spring to produce the single annual brood. Occurs on all the larger Mediterranean islands, and vagrant specimens may appear almost anywhere. Range extends across S Europe and temperate Asia to Japan. Larva p. 228.

**Nettle-tree Butterfly**

## NYMPHALIDAE

Ova barrel-shaped or conical, ribbed and reticulate. Larvae usually with spines or hairy warts, arranged in longitudinal rows. Pupa suspended by the tail (cremaster), without a girdle. In the butterfly, in both sexes, the front legs are small, without claws and useless for walking. Many species are large; the uppersides brightly coloured with red, yellow etc.; the undersides often dull with confused, cryptic patterns. They are not poisonous, and many are eaten by birds and lizards. This is a most extensive family with hundreds of different species, including some of the smallest and many of the largest and most handsome species known. About 18% of our resident butterflies belong here, including many common species such as the Peacock, the Tortoiseshells and the Red Admiral.

**Emperors and allied species.** In appearance and in anatomical characters the following species differ greatly from those already described. They are related to large groups with many species that live principally in the warm or tropical forest regions of Ethiopian Africa and eastern Asia. The larvae are variable, but never have regular longitudinal rows of spines or bristles. The larval food plants are forest trees.

**TWO-TAILED PASHA** *Charaxes jasius*. ♂ ups dark brown with wide fulvous borders; hw with two short tails. ♀ similar, larger. Locally common, flying in two broods, May–June and August–September, in coastal areas of Portugal, S and E Spain, extending inland widely across Sevilla, Cordoba and Badajoz, and Balearic Islands; also near coasts in S France, Corsica, Sardinia, Elba and W Italy; less common in Yugoslavia and Greece, including Corfu; rare in N Africa. Always associated with *Arbutus unedo* (Strawberry Tree), larval food plant. Range extends to coastal areas of Turkey and Cyprus, and in well-marked subspecies to Abyssinia and C Africa.

**Two-tailed Pasha**

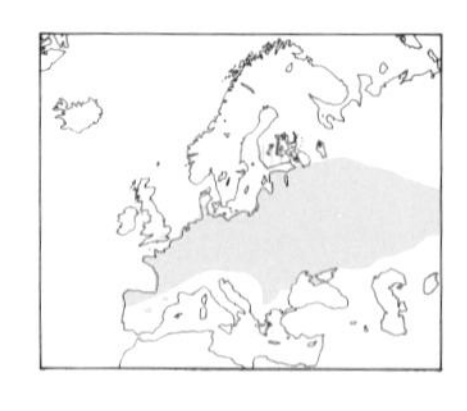

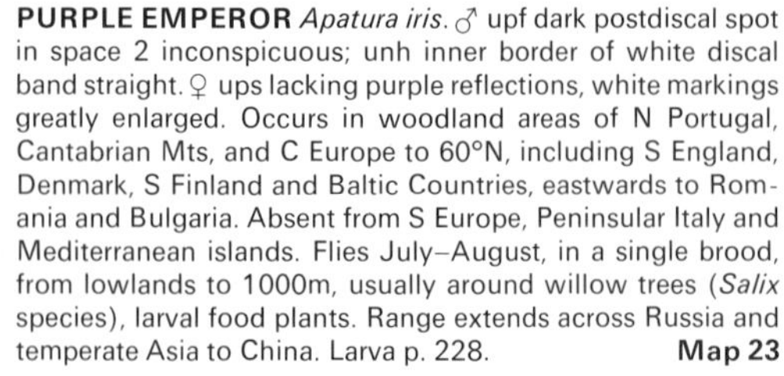

**PURPLE EMPEROR** *Apatura iris*. ♂ upf dark postdiscal spot in space 2 inconspicuous; unh inner border of white discal band straight. ♀ ups lacking purple reflections, white markings greatly enlarged. Occurs in woodland areas of N Portugal, Cantabrian Mts, and C Europe to 60°N, including S England, Denmark, S Finland and Baltic Countries, eastwards to Romania and Bulgaria. Absent from S Europe, Peninsular Italy and Mediterranean islands. Flies July–August, in a single brood, from lowlands to 1000m, usually around willow trees (*Salix* species), larval food plants. Range extends across Russia and temperate Asia to China. Larva p. 228. **Map 23**

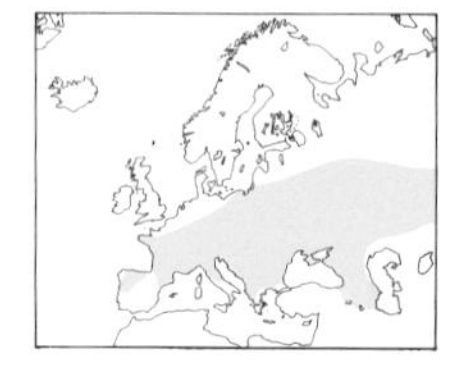

**LESSER PURPLE EMPEROR** *Apatura ilia*. ♂ like the Purple Emperor but smaller; upf dark spot in space 2 conspicuous, ringed orange; unh white discal band not well defined, inner border not straight. ♀ ups grey-brown, lacking purple reflections, white markings enlarged. Occurs in N Portugal, N Spain, especially Catalonia, Pyrenees and across C France to Jura, Vosges and eastwards to Austria, Romania and Balkans including NW Greece. Absent from England, Mediterranean islands and Italy south of Rome. In all localities dimorphic, with f. *clytie*, pale areas yellow instead of white, dark areas paler brown, exposing uph six round, postdiscal spots. Flies usually at low levels, in valley bottoms, in two broods May–June and August–September in southern localities, sometimes a single brood in its northern range. Larval food plants Willows and Poplars, esp. *P. tremula* and *P. nigra*. Range extends from Europe to the Ural Mts and again in E Asia. Larva p. 226.

*A. i. barcina*, in Andorra and Catalonia, uph white discal band wider, more regular; f. *clytie* uncommon in this area.

**Purple Emperor**

Andorra & Catalonia

N Portugal to NW Greece

**Lesser Purple Emperor**

Freyer's Purple Emperor

Poplar Admiral

**FREYER'S PURPLE EMPEROR** *Apatura metis*. Like the Lesser Purple Emperor but upf the pd spot in s2 very small; uph the pd dark spots are replaced by a brown band. ♀ similar, pale markings slightly enlarged. All specimens seen have been clytoid forms, with all pale markings yellow. Occurs in E Europe, in Austria, Hungary, Romania and Bulgaria. Flies May/June–August, at low altitudes around willow trees, in two broods. The butterfly occurs again in China, E Siberia, Korea and Japan.

**POPLAR ADMIRAL** *Limenitis populi*. ♂ large, ups dark grey with white and orange-yellow markings. ♀ similar, ups white markings enlarged. Widely distributed but local in C Europe to 66°N, commonest north of the Alps. Absent from the Pyrenees and S and W France, Spain, Portugal, Britain, Peninsular Italy and Greece. In ♂ ups white markings sometimes vestigial, f. *tremulae*. Flies June–July in a single brood, often at valley levels rising to 1200m or more. Larval food plants Poplar species, esp. *P. tremulae*. Range extends across Russia and Siberia to Japan. Larva p. 234.

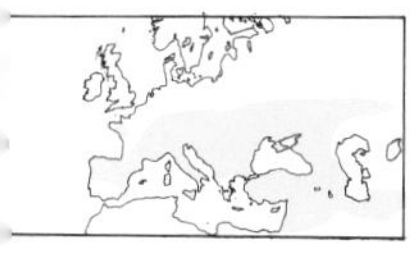

**SOUTHERN WHITE ADMIRAL** *Limenitis reducta*. Unh a single row of dark, postdiscal spots. Sexes similar. Widespread and often common in S Europe to 50°N, absent from Balearic Islands and Crete. Flies May–July, in one or more broods through summer, often in light woodland. Larval food plant *Lonicera* (Honeysuckle). Range extends across W Asia to the Caucasus, Lebanon, Iraq and Iran. Larva p. 234.

**WHITE ADMIRAL** *Limenitis camilla*. Unh two rows of dark postdiscal spots beyond the white discal band. Sexes similar. Widespread in C Europe to 56°N, including S England; very local and generally rare in N Portugal and N Spain, and east to Romania and N Balkans. Absent from SE France, Htes and Basses Pyrénées, from Italy south of Rome, S Balkans, Greece and Mediterranean islands. Flies June–July, usually a single brood, at valley levels to 1000m or little more, always in woodland. Larval food plant *Lonicera* (Honeysuckle). Continental range extends to C Asia, the Amur, Ussuri and Japan. Larva p. 234 **Map 24**

**Southern White Admiral**

**White Admiral**

**COMMON GLIDER** *Neptis sappho.* Uph with white discal band and postdiscal white spots. Sexes similar. Only in E Europe, in Hungary, Czechoslovakia, Romania and N Yugoslavia (Croatia), extending to Salzburg and Gradisca and recently taken in N Greece. Flies in two broods, May–June and July–September at low altitudes in woodlands, a very local species. Larval food plant *Lathyrus verna* (Vetchling). Range extends across Russia and Siberia to Japan.

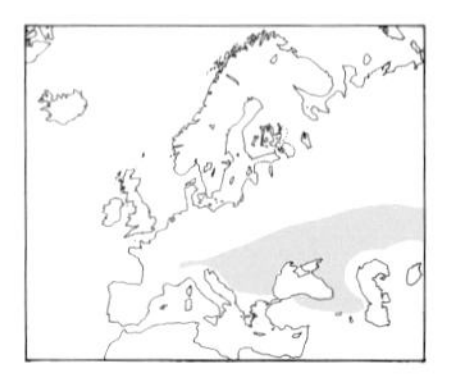

**HUNGARIAN GLIDER** *Neptis rivularis.* Uph with white discal band but lacking white postdiscal spots. Sexes similar. Rather widely distributed from Salzburg eastwards through the Danube countries to Romania and Bulgaria; with occasional colonies in warm alpine valleys in S Switzerland (Bignasco, Lugano, Monte Bré etc.) and N Italy (Susa, Turin, Merano, Bolzano, Venezia Giulia etc.). Flies usually in two broods May–June and July–September in mountainous country from valley levels to 1500m or more. Larval food plants *Spiraea* species. Continental range extends across Russia and Siberia to the Amur and Japan. Larva p. 234.

## The Vanessids.

This large group is remarkable for its extensive distribution on all Continents, and for the vast intercontinental ranges of some of the species. The striking individual wing markings of the Red Admiral, the Painted Lady, the Camberwell Beauty and others, are remarkably constant, so that geographical (subspecific) variation is rare, in spite of the extensive distributions. The explanation could be the migratory instinct which appears in many of these butterflies, maintaining gene-flow throughout enormous areas. The Painted Lady is exceptional in this respect, as one of the world's most successful migrant butterflies. All European species, except the Painted Lady, hibernate as butterflies (imagines), emerging in spring to mate and lay their eggs. The sexes are similar. All species appear to have a strong urge to migrate and/or disperse, and it is difficult to know in what regions they are truly resident throughout the year.

*N.p.polychloros*
*N.p.erythromelas*

**LARGE TORTOISESHELL** *Nymphalis polychloros.* Upf dark wing borders sharply defined; fore-legs *hair black.* Sexes similar. Flies June–July in a single brood and again in spring after hibernation, at low altitudes, rising in mountains to 1800m. Larval food plants willow, elm and other trees, larvae living in nests and companies. Range extends to S Russia, W Asia, the Caucasus, C Asia and W Siberia. **Map 25**

*N. p. polychloros*, in Europe, widely distributed to 60°N, S Fennoscandia and the Mediterranean islands. Ups yellow-brown. Locally not uncommon but becoming rare or absent in some localities.

*N. p. erythromelas*, in N Africa, in the Middle Atlas Mts, Ups bright red-brown (most striking in fresh specimens). Locally common.

**YELLOW-LEGGED TORTOISESHELL** *Nymphalis xanthomelas.* Ups like the large Tortoiseshell, but uph dark wing-borders internally not sharply defined; fore-legs hair dull buff (not black). Rare in E Europe, esp. Romania, Poland, E Germany, and occasional migrant specimens further west to Czechoslovakia, S Sweden, Denmark etc. Flies July–September near woodland, usually at low levels. Larval food plant willow trees, larvae living in companies. Range extends to C Asia, China and Japan.

♂

Common Glider

♂

Hungarian Glider

♂

Large Tortoiseshell

♂

Yellow-legged Tortoiseshell

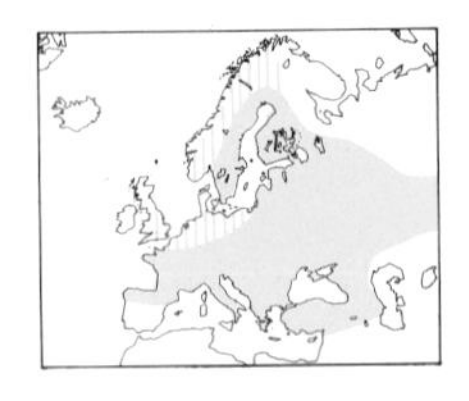

**CAMBERWELL BEAUTY** *Nymphalis antiopa.* Ups purple-blue with cream-coloured marginal borders. Widely distributed in Europe to 70°N, not uncommon in the south, but absent in S Spain and Mediterranean islands; a rare immigrant in Britain. Flies June–August or later and again in spring after hibernation, from sea level to 1800m, in open country or light woodland. Larval food plants Willows, Birch etc. Range extends across temperate Asia and N America in Canada and USA.

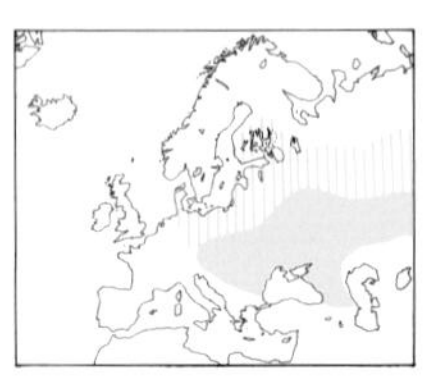

**FALSE COMMA** *Nymphalis vau-album.* Like the Large Tortoiseshell, upf with white costal mark near apex; uph a similar white costal mark. Sexes similar. Rare and local in E Europe, most frequent in Romania, in the Retezat Mts. Flies July after hibernation, usually in woodland areas in sheltered, open places, at low altitudes. Larval food plants Willow, Poplar, Beech and other forest trees. Range extends across Europe and temperate Asia to Siberia, Sakhalin, China, Japan and widely spread in N America, entirely without obvious local variation. Larva p. 234.

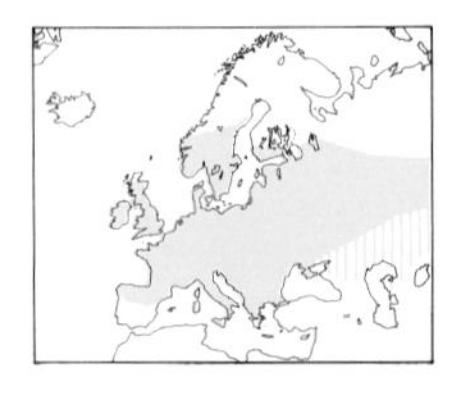

**PEACOCK** *Inachis io.* Ups a large 'peacock' eye on each wing. Widespread and common in W Europe to 60°N, including all the larger Mediterranean islands. Absent from Crete and N Africa. Flies in a single brood on flowery banks at all altitudes, in July and later, and in spring after hibernation. Larval food plants *Urtica* (Nettles) and rarely other low plants. Range extends across temperate Asia to Japan, without obvious local variation. Larva p. 232.

**Map 26**

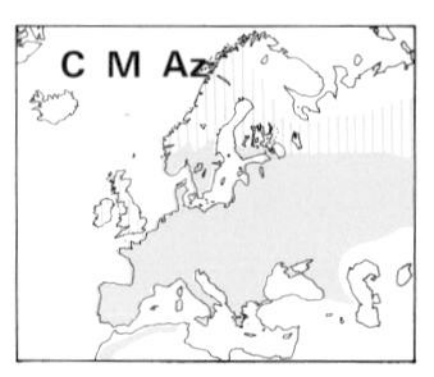


**RED ADMIRAL** *Vanessa atalanta.* Upf the red transverse band is intact, of even width across the wing. Resident and widely distributed throughout Europe northwards to about 48°N, but further north and in NW Europe including Britain, only as an immigrant during summer; rare or occasional in N Africa. Hibernates as an imago in winter. Flies in summer and early autumn in a single brood derived from hibernated individuals or immigrants. At the end of summer no doubt many of the northern immigrants will die, but it is thought that many others will fly south to districts where successful hibernation is possible. Larval food plants *Urtica* (Nettles). Resident range includes the Canary Islands, Madeira, the Azores, and across temperate Europe and Asia Minor to C Asia and Siberia, also in N America, Guatemala and ?New Zealand. Larva p. 232.

**Map 27**

**Red Admiral**

♂

Camberwell Beauty

♂

False Comma

♂

Peacock

**INDIAN RED ADMIRAL** *Vanessa indica calliroe (vulcania).* Upf red transverse band irregular, broken by black ground-colour. Occurs only on Madeira and the Canaries where it flies throuhgout the year on all the larger islands, except perhaps on Lanzarote; otherwise common in gardens and on flowery slopes elsewhere. Larval food plant *Urtica* (Nettles). Closely related to the oriental Indian Red Admiral (*V. indica indica*), widely distributed in the Far East, from the Himalayas to China and Japan. The species does not occur anywhere in W Asia, Europe or Africa, between Kashmir and the Canary Islands. No other butterfly is known with this remarkable distribution.

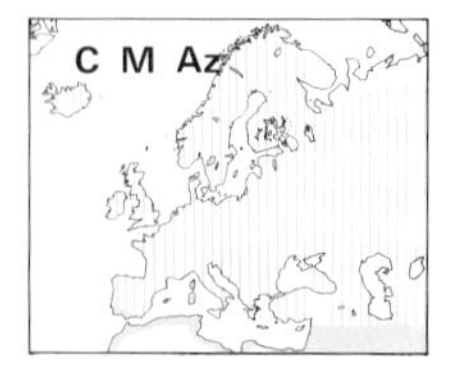


**PAINTED LADY** *Cynthia cardui.* Unh markings rather confused with five small submarginal ocelli. Common in Africa and from there an annual immigrant into Europe during March, April and later. There it breeds to produce one, or sometimes two broods during the summer and early autumn. The extent of European distribution and the rarity or otherwise of the species is most variable, depending partly upon the numbers of immigrants arriving during the spring and early summer. In favourable years the species will be widely distributed and generally common, and from time to time it may be present in great numbers with a veritable invasion even in England. Except in Malta and possibly in S Spain the species is not able to survive the European winter. With the onset of autumn no doubt many individuals die, but it is thought that many others are able to return to frost-free regions in Africa by southerly migration. Larval food plants *Carduus* (Thistles), *Urtica* (Nettles) and *Malva*. Range. Resident in the Azores, Canary Islands and Madeira, and on all continents, but absent from S. America. It is noticeable that unh the markings are not dark and cryptic as they are e.g. in the Small Tortoiseshell which hibernates through the European winter. **Map 28**

**AMERICAN PAINTED LADY** *Cynthia virginiensis.* Unh with very large submarginal ocelli in space 2 and space 5. Not common on the Canary Islands, but certainly resident on Tenerife, La Palma, Gran Canaria and La Gomera. Rare and occasional in the coastal districts of Portugal, Spain and SW France. Flies in June or later, but throughout the year in the Canary Islands. Larval food plant *Gnaphalium, Antennaria, Malva*. Range is widespread in N America, extending to Guatemala and Cuba.

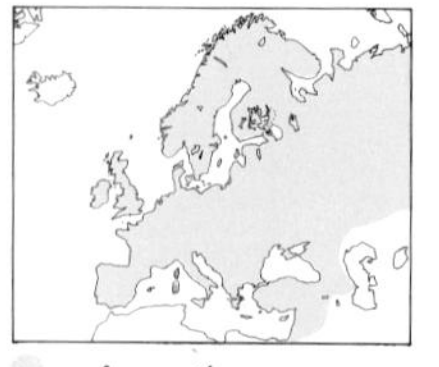

*A.u.urticae*
*A.u.ichnusa*

**SMALL TORTOISESHELL** *Aglais urticae.* Unh base black with red postdiscal band (variable). Larval food plant *Urtica* (Nettles). Range (*A. u. urticae*) extends across Russia to Siberia, the Pacific coast, Sakhalin and the Kurile Islands. Absent from N Africa. Larva p. 232. **Map 29**

*A. u. urticae*, in Europe to 70°N, including all Mediterranean islands except Corsica and Sardinia. Upf with black postdiscal spots in space 2 and space 3. Common April–August, in one or more broods, on rough ground and flowery slopes from sea level to 2000m. Migrant individuals frequent on high mountains. After hibernation appears again in March/April.

*A. u. ichnusa*, only on Corsica, Sardinia and Elba. Upf lacks black postdiscal spots in spaces 2,3; markings very bright. In Peninsular Italy and other warm localities, the postdiscal spots of *A. u. urticae* may be reduced or be vestigial, but the colour generally rather pale, without the brilliance of *ichnusa*. Flies June.

♂

Indian Red Admiral

♂

Painted Lady

♂

American Painted Lady

♂ Europe to 70°N

♂ Corsica, Sardinia, Elba

Small Tortoiseshell

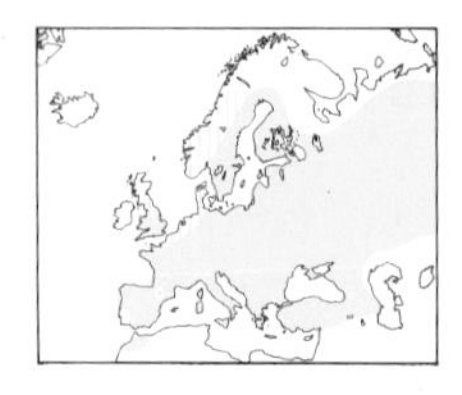

**COMMA BUTTERFLY** *Polygonia c-album*. Unh a white discal mark shaped like the letter 'C.' Generally not uncommon in Europe to 66°N, including the larger Mediterranean islands; also in Morocco, Algeria and Tunisia in the Atlas Mts. Flies in open country, light woodland etc., from sea level to 1800m, in two broods June–July and August–September, and again in spring after hibernation. Gen.1, f. *hutchinsoni*, ♂ + ♀ uns brightly marked in shades of yellow to brown. Gen.2 uns colours less brilliant, more variable; ♀ unh often dark, greenish-brown with obscure markings. The seasonal distinction not always well defined. Larval food plants Nettles, Hop, various trees etc. Range extends across temperate Asia to the Caucasus, the Amur and Sakhalin. Larva p. 232. **Map 30**

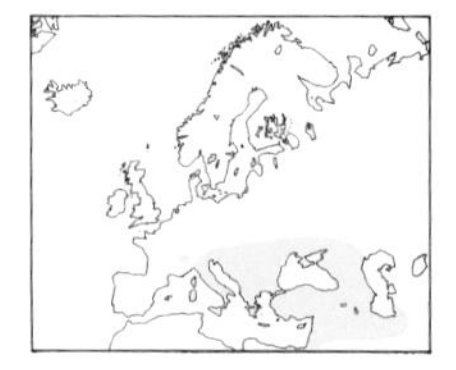

**SOUTHERN COMMA** *Polygonia egea*. Like the Comma Butterfly. Ups dark markings smaller; unh a small white discal mark line like the letter 'v' on its side. Widely distributed in SE France, Italy and SE Europe to 46°N, including the Mediterranean islands except the Balearics. Absent from Portugal, Spain and N Africa. A lowland species, often found in hot, rocky gorges or along stony paths, rare above 1000m. Flies in two broods, May–June and August–September, gen.1 in late spring, ups bright yellow-brown, uns pale; gen.2 f. *j-album*, both surfaces darker in tone; also appears for a short time in early spring after hibernation. Larval food plants Pellitory *(Parietaria)* and various trees. Range extends eastwards to C Asia and the Himalayas.

**Southern Comma**

♂ gen. 1

The following species, the Map Butterfly, is rather isolated, without any close relatives among European butterflies, but allied to the Tortoiseshells in several respects.

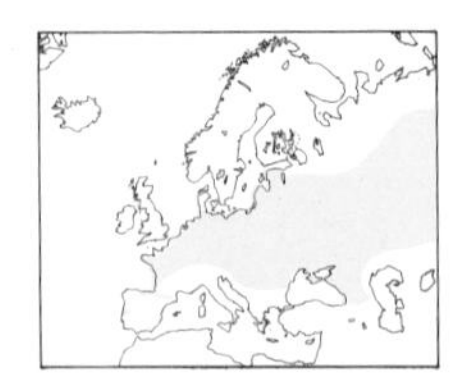

**MAP BUTTERFLY** *Araschnia levana*. Ups seasonal variation very marked; uns with pale reticulate markings. Sexes similar. Occurs commonly in C Europe, from N Spain and Pyrenees to the Baltic coast and eastwards to Romania and N Balkans. Absent from Britain, SE France and S Balkans. Flies May–June and August–September at low altitudes in light woodland, rarely over 1000m, in two broods. Gen.1 (f. *levana*), ups yellow-brown; gen.2 (f. *prorsa*) ups black with white and yellow markings. Specimens with intermediate characters not uncommon. Larval food plants *Urtica* (Nettles), the larvae living in companies. Range extends across Europe to the Caucasus, Siberia and Japan. Larva p. 232.

♂ gen. 1

♂ gen. 2 ♀

**Comma Butterfly**

♂ gen. 1

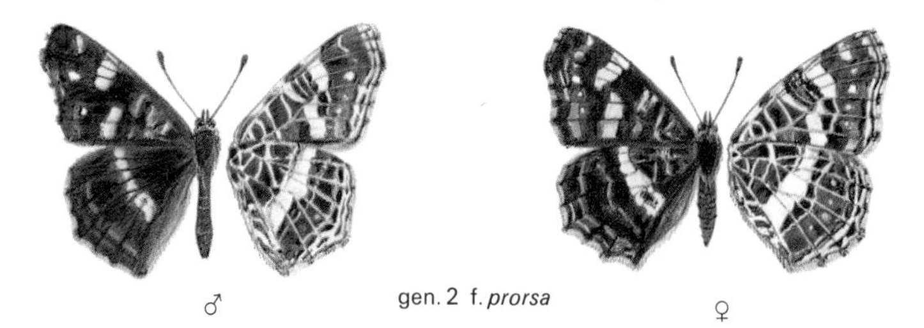

♂ gen. 2 f. *prorsa* ♀

**Map Butterfly**

**The Large Fritillaries.** On the upperside almost all Fritillaries are some shade of yellow or fulvous, marked with black spots; their larvae live upon violets. Many fly at high altitudes on mountains, or on the arctic tundra, including the Arctic Fritillary which reaches 81.42°N in Greenland, the furthest north of any butterfly. About 26 species occur within our region, with many more in Siberia and N America. This large group is particularly characteristic of the Northern Hemisphere, but a few related species fly on the high mountains in C Africa (Mt Elgon, Ruanda, Kilimanjaro) and in S America in Chile, Bolivia and Peru. This wide dispersal must mean that the origin of the group dates from an early geological period when the situations of the continents differed from that which we know today. The best specific characters appear on unh. On ups in most species the sexes are similar or nearly so, but ♂♂ usually have sex brands along the veins upf.

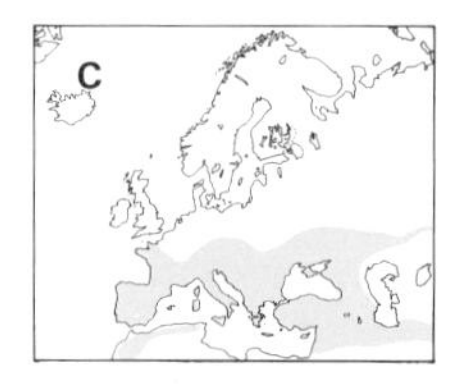


**CARDINAL** *Pandoriana pandora.* A large species. ♂ unf rosy-red. Widely distributed in S Europe, from Spain and Portugal, including the Balearics and other Mediterranean islands, to Austria, the Balkans and Greece, and north to the southern Alpine slopes; also in Morocco, Algeria and Tunisia, and in the Canary Islands on Tenerife, La Palma and La Gomera. Flies in one or two broods, from lowlands to 1700m, most common among mountains, in Europe in July, in N Africa in June and August. Larval food plants Violets. Range extends to the Caucasus, Altai Mts, C Asia and W Himalayas.

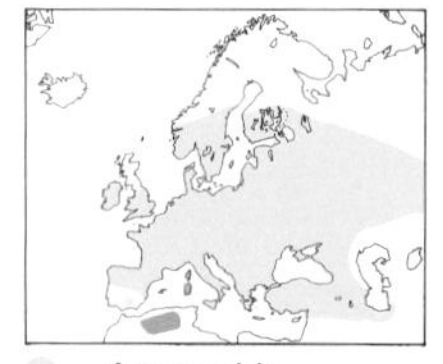

*A.p. paphia*
*A.p. immaculata*
*A.p. dives*

**SILVER-WASHED FRITILLARY** *Argynnis paphia.* ♂ ups sex-brands along veins 1–4 conspicuous; unh variable, usually green or greenish with transverse silver markings. ♀ dimorphic, ups fulvous, like ♂, or ♀–f. *valesina*, dark greenish grey, not uncommon in some localities. Widely distributed in S and C Europe to 62°N, including the larger Mediterranean islands, also in Algeria, but absent from Morocco. Occurs in light woodland, from sea level to 1800m, flying end of June. Range extends across Asia to Japan. Larva p. 234. **Map 31**

*A. p. paphia*, on the European mainland. Unh green or greenish with silver markings prominent in the ♀; ♀–f. *valesina* common locally, eg Spain. In f. *anargyria*, unh silver markings obsolete, occasional in C Italy and Spain.

*A. p. immaculata*, on Corsica, Sardinia, Elba and Giglio. Unh markings partly obsolete with generalized golden suffusion; ♀–f. *valesina* common. Specimens transitional to *immaculata* are not rare in Spain and on the mainland of Italy.

**Cardinal**

*A. p. dives*, only in Algeria (Djebel Aures, Sgag, Kabylia etc.). Unh variable, usually well marked and with golden sheen but lacking silver.

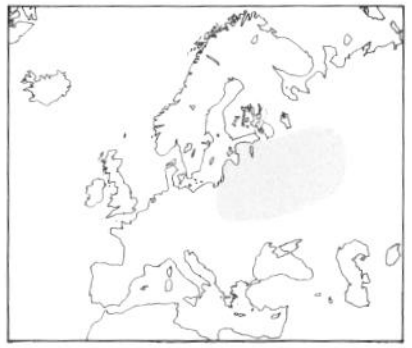

**PALLAS'S FRITILLARY** *Argyronome laodice*. ♂ upf has a small, white costal mark near apex; unh base olive yellow, distal area brown. Occurs in NE Europe, E Finland, Lithuania, E Poland, E Prussia, E Slovakia and N Romania. Flies in woodland at low altitudes, July–August. Very local and usually scarce. Larval food plant *Viola palustris*. Range extends across Russia to the Caucasus, Himalayas, Siberia and SW China.

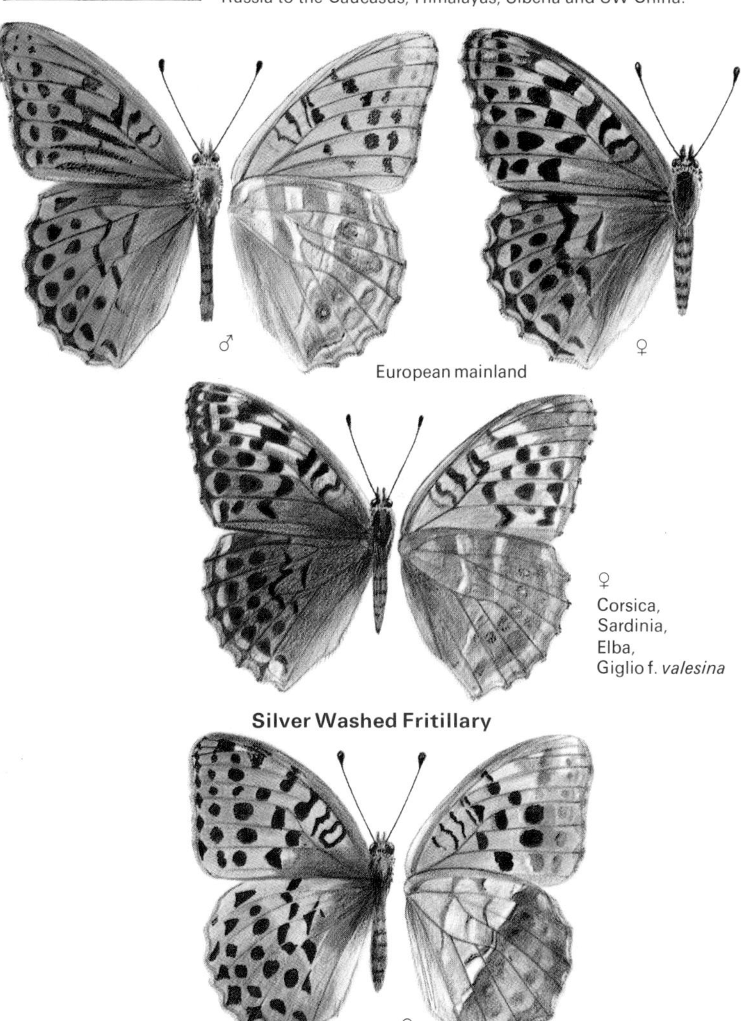


**Silver Washed Fritillary**

**Pallas's Fritillary**

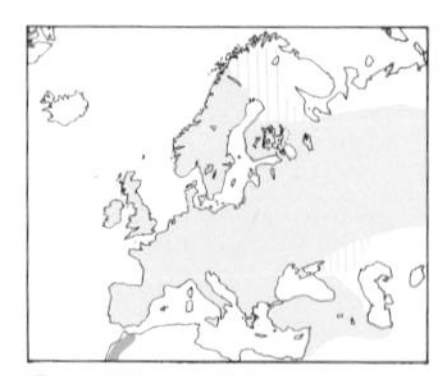

M.a. aglaja
M.a. lyauteyi

**DARK GREEN FRITILLARY** *Mesoacidalia aglaja.* ♂ unh with basal, discal and marginal silver spots, postdiscal spots absent. ♀ ups ground-colour slightly paler. Widely distributed in Europe to 70°N, also in Morocco. Absent from Mediterranean islands except Sicily. Flies July–August over flowery slopes or light woodland, from sea level to 1800m. Distribution extends across C Asia, Siberia and China to Japan. Larva p. 234.

**Map 32**

*M. a. aglaja*, on the European mainland and Sicily. ♂ ups bright fulvous; unh green marking not extensive. ♀ ups often suffused dark.

*M. a. lyauteyi*, only in Morocco. Larger, ♂ ups yellow-buff; unh green markings extensive. ♀ ups paler yellow-buff. Flies at 1500m or more, always in woodland. Absent from the High Atlas and Algeria.

F.a. adippe
F.a. chlorodippe

**HIGH BROWN FRITILLARY** *Fabriciana adippe.* Like the Dark Green Fritillary; ♂ unh with small, silver-pupilled pd spots, upf sex-brands present on veins 2+3. ♀ ups slightly paler yellow-buff. Widely distributed in Europe to 58°N. Flies June–July in a single brood, from sea level to 1600m, locally common in forest clearings, light woodland and alpine meadows. Larval food plants *Viola*. Range extensive, across Europe and temperate Asia to Siberia and Japan, including the western Himalayas, with several subspecies. Larval food plants *Viola*. Larva p. 232. **Map 33**

**Dark Green Fritillary**

*F. a. adippe*. Unh ground-colour yellow-buff. Widespread from the Pyrenees to 58°N and eastwards across Europe. Both sexes are dimorphic; f. *adippe*, unh with basal, discal and other markings bright silver; f. *cleodoxa*, unh markings outlined in brown on the buff ground-colour, lacking silver, a common form, sometimes racial e.g. Sicily, Greece etc. Both forms may fly together.

*F. a. chlorodippe*, in C and S Spain and Portugal. Unh ground-colour green; f. *cleodoxa* does not occur; upf sex-brands thin. In N Spain f. *cleodippe*, unh greenish but markings not silvered, transitional leading to *F. a. adippe*.

*Note*. In *F. adippe* the androconial scales are long, slender, but in *F. niobe* shorter and stouter.

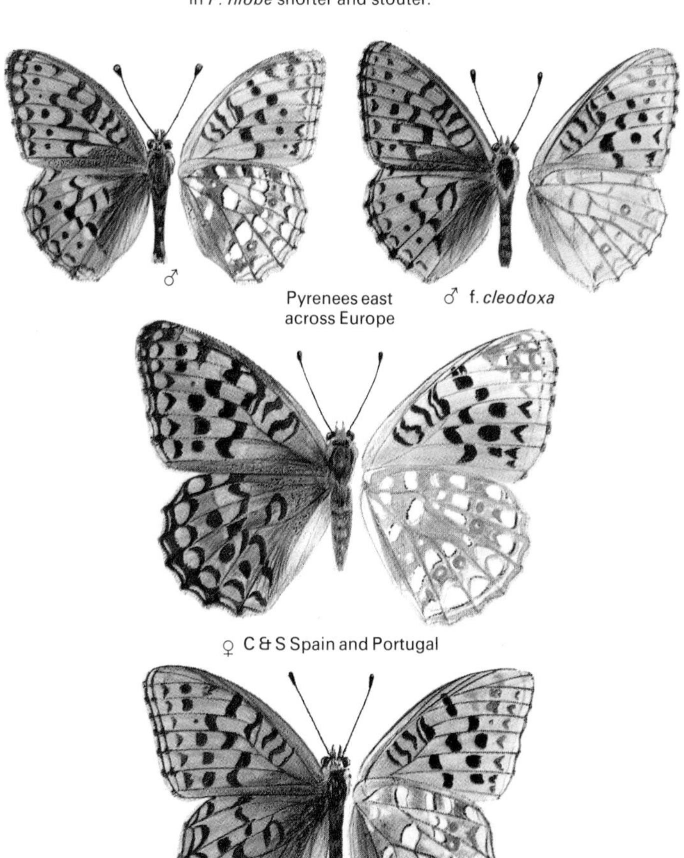

♂ Pyrenees east across Europe ♂ f. *cleodoxa*

♀ C & S Spain and Portugal

♂ N Spain f. *cleodippe*

**High Brown Fritillary**

F.n. niobe
F.n. auresiana

**NIOBE FRITILLARY** *Fabriciana niobe.* Like the High Brown Fritillary but usually smaller. ♂ upf sex-brands on veins 2,3,4, often thin, vestigial or absent; unh small postdiscal spots brown, silver-pupilled, a small yellow spot in cell, often enclosing a black pupil, placed below branching of veins 6+7, a specific character when present. ♀ ups often suffused dark. Widely distributed in Europe to 62°N; also in Morocco and Algeria. Absent from Britain and Mediterranean islands except Sicily. Flies June–July in a single brood. Larval food plants *Viola*. Range extends to the Caucasus, Iran, C Asia and W Siberia. Three subspecies. Larva p. 234.

♀

♂ f. *eris*

European mainland

♂ Morocco & Algeria

**Niobe Fritillary**

*F. n. niobe*, on Europe mainland, size variable. Unh pale buff, base sometimes faintly green. Both sexes dimorphic: f. *niobe* (type), unh basal, discal and other markings bright silver, common in C France and C Apennines, otherwise occasional; f. *eris*, unh spots not silvered, common and widely distributed. In Scandinavia (Dovrefjeld) small; f. *eris* only. Flies at all levels to 1800m, locally common in meadows and subalpine pastures. Easily confused with the High Brown Fritillary, but androconial scales are shorter and stouter.

*F. n. auresiana*, ♂ fw 29–32mm, unh green, spots all silvered but reduced in size and number, often bordered black, upf sex-brands absent. Occurs in the Middle Atlas, in Morocco and Algeria. Flying at 1500m. ♂ genitalia with small distinctive character. In the High Atlas, flying at 2600m, *F. n. astrifera*, small, ♂ fw 23–27mm.

*F. n. hassani*, large, expanse up to 57mm, ups fulvous tone intense, black markings enlarged. Occurs in Er Rif, –Targuist, Ketama, flying in late July at 1200m.

**CORSICAN FRITILLARY** *Fabriciana elisa*. ♂ like the High Brown Fritillary but smaller; ups black markings scanty: unh has many small silver spots; sexes similar. Restricted to Corsica and Sardinia, flying there June–July in the heather zone at 1000m or more. Larval food plants *Viola*.

Corsican Fritillary

Queen of Spain Fritillary

In the four species following, ♂ sex-brands are absent.

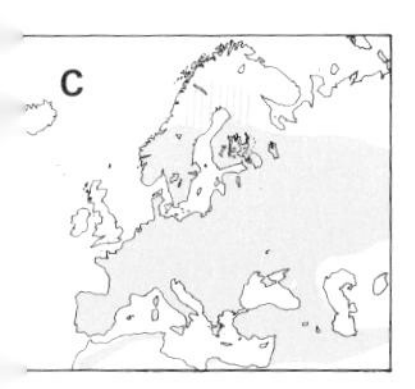


**QUEEN OF SPAIN FRITILLARY** *Issoria lathonia*. Unh with distinctive large silver spots. Widely distributed on mainland Europe to 64°N, including the larger Mediterranean islands, but occasional or absent in the NW; also throughout N Africa and in the Canary Islands on Tenerife, La Palma and Gomera. Flies April–September, in two or more broods through the summer, at all altitudes to 2000m or more, often common. The butterfly is a notable migrant, seen occasionally in England. Larval food plant *Viola*. Range extends far into the desert oases in Tripolitania etc. and eastwards to C Asia and Siberia. Larva p. 234.

**TWIN-SPOT FRITILLARY** *Brenthis hecate.* ♂ unh with two rows of black postdiscal spots. ♀ often suffused fuscous. Occurs in scattered colonies in Spain, in Soria, Teruel, Cuenca etc.; S France, very local in Var, Maritimes and Basses Alpes, Bouches du Rhône etc.; more general in E Europe, in Czechoslovakia, Hungary and Austria to N Greece; locally common in N Italy but very local in Peninsular Italy, Abruzzi, Lucania. Absent from Portugal, the Mediterranean islands and Pyrenees. Flies May–June over open ground from valley levels to 1500m or more, usually in mountainous country. Larval food plant *Dorycnium* (Leguminosae). Range extends to Iran, the Caucasus and W Siberia.

**MARBLED FRITILLARY** *Brenthis daphne.* Like the Twin-spot Fritillary. Unh a single row of dark postdiscal spots, base of space 4 usually brown. Sexes similar. Often common in S Europe, local in N and C and S Spain (Murcia) to 46°N, and eastwards to Czechoslovakia, Austria, Hungary and south to the Balkans and Greece. Absent from Portugal, and Mediterranean islands except Sicily. Flies June–July in warm valleys with *Rubus* (Bramble), rare above 1000m. Larval food plants *Rubus, Viola.* Ranges across Europe and temperate Asia to China and Japan.

**LESSER MARBLED FRITILLARY** *Brenthis ino.* Like the Marbled Fritillary but *smaller.* Ups black marginal lines continuous; unh base of space 4 yellow; ♀ ups often suffused grey. Widely distributed in C and N Europe, to 70°N. Absent from S Spain, Portugal, Britain, Mediterranean islands and Greece. Flies June–July in damp grass or marshy places from valley levels to 1500m, usually in colonies. Larval food plants *Filipendula* (Meadowsweet) and *Sanguisorba* (Great Burnet). Range extends across Europe and temperate Asia to N China and Japan.

## The Alpine Fritillaries.

Rather small butterflies, lacking sex-brands. The sexes are similar or nearly so. The anatomical characters are distinctive. One European species flies also in N America.

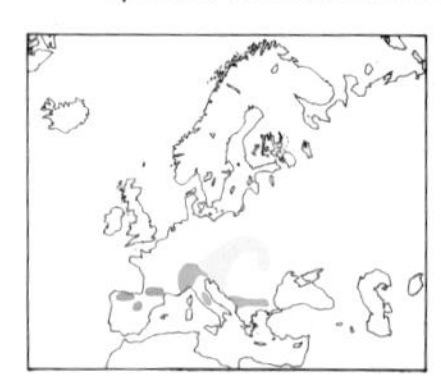

*B.p. pales*
*B.p. palustris*
*B.p. pyrenesmiscens*

**SHEPHERD'S FRITILLARY** *Boloria pales.* Hind-wing apex angled. ♂ ups black markings rather macular; uph black basal suffusion extends to reach the discoidal veins; unf *black markings scanty.* ♀ ups slightly darker. Occurs on high mountains in Alps, Tatra, Carpathians, and Apennines; very local in the Balkans. Flies July–early August at altitudes of 2000m or more, above the trees, over slopes of *Vaccinium* or grass. Larval food plant *Viola*, esp. *V. calcarata.* Range extends to the Caucasus, W Himalayas, C Asia and a series of closely related subspecies are widely distributed in Siberia. Three subspecies in Europe. Larva p. 232.

*B. p. pales*, Bavarian Alps, Austria, Tatra and Carpathians. Ups bright fulvous, discal markings macular, unh brightly variegated.

*B. p. palustris*, in W Alps, Apennines, Gran Sasso etc., Balkans on the Rila and Pirin Mts, Prenj, Durmitor. N of the Rhône valley less typical. Smaller, ups paler, yellowish, black markings thin.

*B. p. pyrenesmiscens.* Pyrenees and Cantabrian Mts. Ups paler, orange-yellow, black markings macular; uph black basal suffusion less extensive; unh paler, yellowish or greenish.

These colour phenotypes are well defined in certain areas but tend to fade into one another.

♂

♀

**Twin-spot Fritillary**

♂

♀

**Marbled Fritillary**

♂

**Lesser Marbled Fritillary**

♂

Bavarian Alps, Austria etc

♀

♂

♀

W Alps, Appenines etc

♂ Pyrenees & Cantabrian Mts

**Shepherd's Fritillary**

**MOUNTAIN FRITILLARY** *Boloria napaea.* Like the Shepherd's Fritillary, often slightly larger. ♂ ups markings linear, thin; unf *black markings very scanty*; unh colours pale, appear faded. ♀ ups often suffused dark grey with pale ground-colour. Occurs in the W Alps in France, Switzerland, Bavaria and east to the Hohe Tauern; very local in the E Pyrenees. Widely distributed in Fennoscandia, to 70°N. Flies July–August, in the Alps at 1800m, often in wet places; in Fennoscandia at low altitudes on the open moorlands, Dovrefjeld etc., but in far north usually small, f. *frigida.* Larval food plant *Polygonum* (Alpine Bistort). Range extends to the Altai Mts, Siberia; and very local in Wyoming, USA.

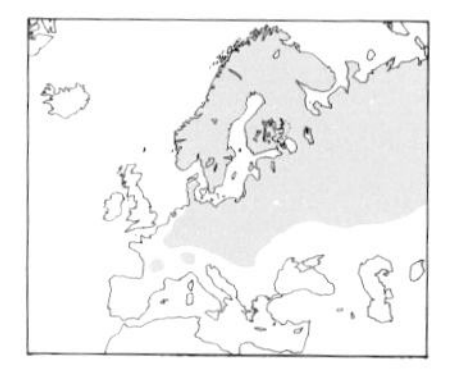

**CRANBERRY FRITILLARY** *Boloria aquilonaris.* ♂ ups rather heavily marked, discal spots prominent; unf *black markings well defined*; unh markings reddish. ♀ ups more heavily marked. Flies June–July. Widely distributed in Fennoscandia to 70°N; locally common at various altitudes on *Vaccinium* bogs in the Jura, Vosges (Ardennes), Germany, Austria, C France etc., to 1800m in Switzerland (Engadin). In some lowland colonies larger, f. *alethea*, not rare in C France. Larval food plant *Vaccinium oxycoccus.* Range extends to the Ural Mts and probably eastwards into W Siberia.

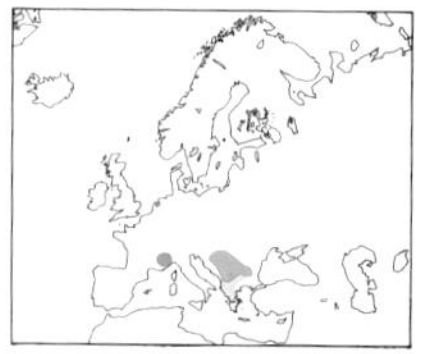

*B.g. graeca*
*B.g. balcanica*
*B.g. tendensis*

**BALKAN FRITILLARY** *Boloria graeca.* ♂ hw margin strongly angled at v8; unh six round postdiscal spots well defined. ♀ ups fulvous slightly paler; unh often mottled greenish. Occurs in mainland Greece, Veluchi Mts, etc. Macedonia (Mt Perister), very local. Flies June–July at 1800m or over. In Bulgaria and Bosnia, *B. g. balcanica*: slightly smaller and ups bright fulvous, not rare at 1600m and over in the Rilo Mts, Durmitor, Schar Planina, Prenj, Vlasulja etc. In SE France, *B. g. tendensis*: very similar, small, ♀ ups distinctly yellow; local in the Maritime Alps; also in Italian Alps, Col di Tenda; Limone Piemonte etc. In Balkans and in the Maritime Alps often accompanied by *B. pales palustris* flying at a higher altitude on the same mountain. Larval food plant not known. E.

*P.e. eunomia*
*P.e. ossianus*

**BOG FRITILLARY** *Proclossiana eunomia.* ♂ ups bright fulvous; unh with six small, white-pupilled postdiscal ocelli. ♀ ups often more or less suffused fuscous. Widespread in scattered colonies in E Pyrenees, NE France and eastwards across Germany and Czechoslovakia to Bulgaria. Flies late May–June on damp moorlands, bogs, usually at low altitudes, extremely local. In Fennoscandia *P. e. ossianus*, widespread and often common to 70°N, on wet areas, mosses and bogs: smaller, unf markings more complete, unh colour contrast often brighter; ♀ similar. Larval food plant *Polygonum, Vaccinium* etc. Range extends to the Caucasus, E Siberia, Sakhalin, Japan, and to N America in sub-artic areas and in western mountains, Colorado.

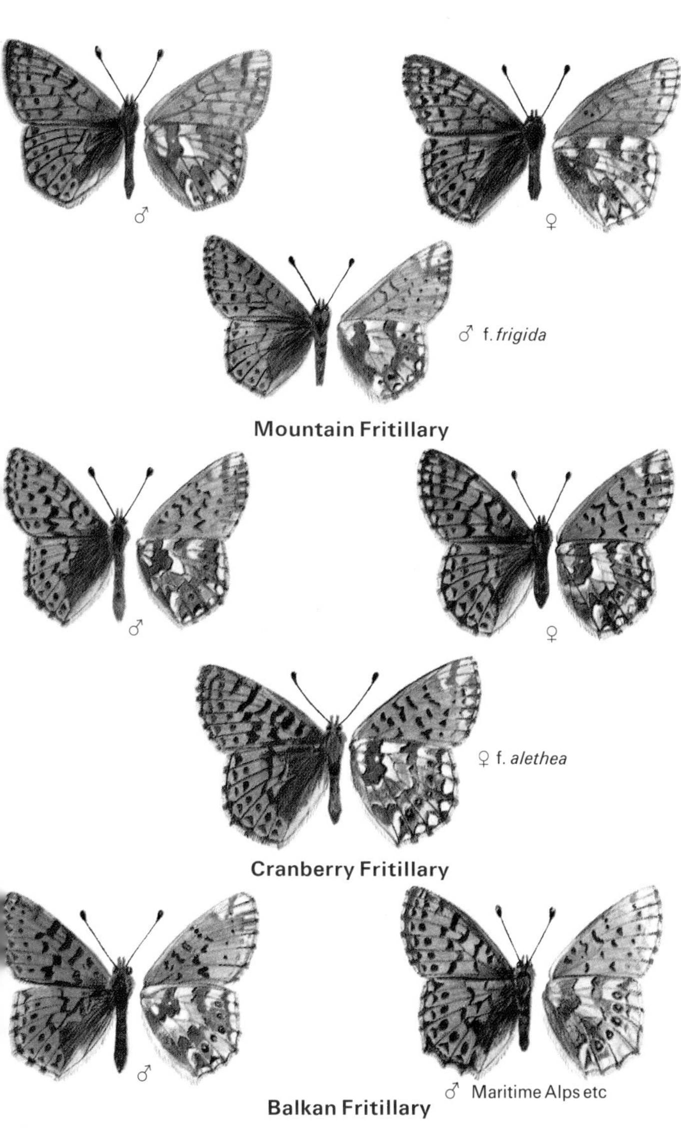

Mountain Fritillary


Cranberry Fritillary


Balkan Fritillary

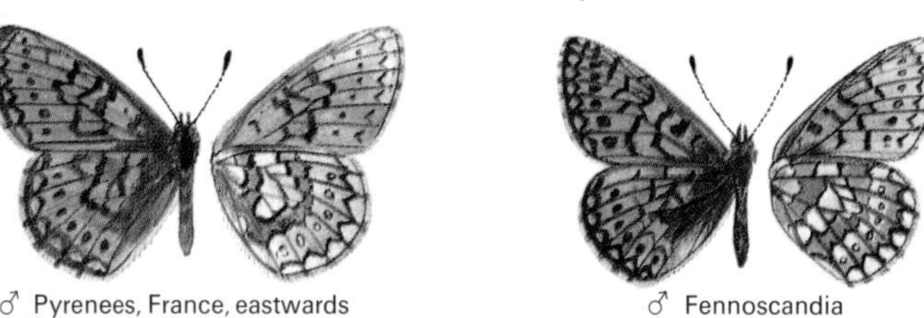

Bog Fritillary

**The Smaller Fritillaries.** An extensive Holarctic generic group, the species often restricted to high altitudes on mountains or to the Arctic regions, sometimes circum-polar. The sexes usually similar.

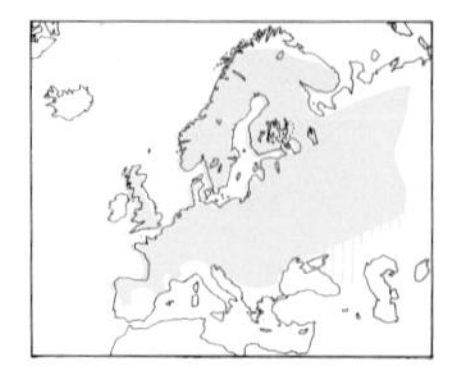

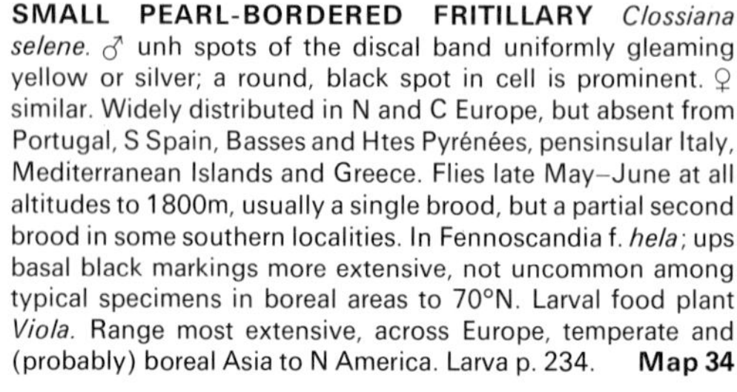

**SMALL PEARL-BORDERED FRITILLARY** *Clossiana selene.* ♂ unh spots of the discal band uniformly gleaming yellow or silver; a round, black spot in cell is prominent. ♀ similar. Widely distributed in N and C Europe, but absent from Portugal, S Spain, Basses and Htes Pyrénées, pensinsular Italy, Mediterranean Islands and Greece. Flies late May–June at all altitudes to 1800m, usually a single brood, but a partial second brood in some southern localities. In Fennoscandia f. *hela*; ups basal black markings more extensive, not uncommon among typical specimens in boreal areas to 70°N. Larval food plant *Viola.* Range most extensive, across Europe, temperate and (probably) boreal Asia to N America. Larva p. 234. **Map 34**

C.t.titania
C.t.cypris

**TITANIA'S FRITILLARY** *Clossiana titania.* ♂ unh markings rather confused, postdiscal spots connected to elongate, dark, submarginal chevrons. ♀ similar, ups often yellowish. Local but widely distributed in C Europe. Larval food plants *Viola, Polygonum.* Distribution extensive, to S Urals, Altai Mts, Siberia, and further to N America on Mt Baker, Mt Rainer and Mt Adams. Two subspecies in Europe. Larva p. 232.

*C. t. titania*. In NW Italy in the Cottian Alps (Ulzio, Crissolo); in C France, on the mountains of Isère and Auvergne (Col de Mayrand, Mt Mézenc etc.); in S Finland and Lithuania very similar (*C. t. rossica*). Ups clear orange-fulvous, black markings delicate. ♀ ups paler yellowish. Flies late June–July at 1200–1500m among scattered spruce trees or light woodland.

*C. t. cypris,* through the C and S Alps of Switzerland, Bavaria, Italy etc. to Yugoslavia (Durmitor, Trebević). ♂ ups more intense fulvous, with heavy black markings. Flies at 1500m and over, on mountain slopes, often among open spruce woodland.

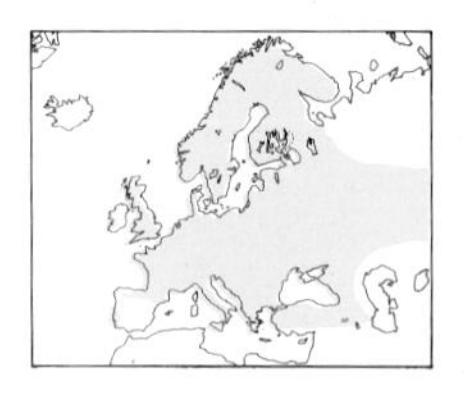

**PEARL-BORDERED FRITILLARY** *Clossiana euphrosyne.* Like the Small Pearl-bordered. ♂ unh central spot of yellow discal band bright silver, prominent. ♀ ups black markings often extended (inconstant). Very widely distributed across Europe from C Spain to 70°N and eastwards to the Carpathians, Balkans and Greece. In boreal regions, f. *fingal*: ♀ ups black markings extended, not common, among typical specimens. Flies May, June, July in light woodland and on rough mountain slopes at all altitudes to 2000m, often in a single brood, but in S Europe a partial late second brood may appear. Absent from S Spain and Mediterranean islands; very local in Ireland. Larval food plant *Viola.* Continental range extends across Europe and N Asia to the Caucasus, Siberia and Sakhalin. Larva p. 234.
**Map 35**

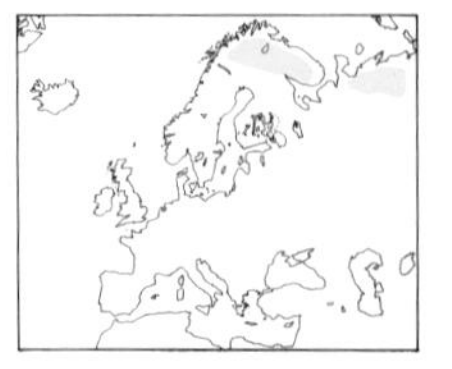

**ARCTIC FRITILLARY** *Clossiana chariclea.* Like Titania's Fritillary but smaller. ♂ unh purple-brown with striking discal band of silver spots. ♀ similar, ups often more heavily marked. A circumpolar species flying late June–July in Lapland, not south of 68°N. Often found at a low altitude 200–400m, which seems preferred to the basic level of the flat tundra. Larval food plants not recorded. Range extends to Novaya Zemlya, Greenland, Labrador, Polar Urals and NE Siberia, with little local variation.

♂

♀ f. *hela*

**Small Pearl-bordered Fritillary**

♂ NW Italy, C France etc

♂ C & S Alps etc

**Titania's Fritillary**

♂

♀ f. *fingal*

**Pearl-bordered Fritillary**

♀

**Arctic Fritillary**

**FREIJA'S FRITILLARY** *Clossiana freija.* Unh with prominent zig-zag postdiscal line in spaces 1,2,3. Sexes similar. In Baltic countries (often rare) and Fennoscandia from 60°N to North Cape. Flies May–June over moorlands and boreal tundra, usually at low levels but at 1000m or more in mountains (Dovrefjeld etc.). Larval food plants *Rubus chamaemorus* and *Vaccinium.* Range extends across N Europe and Asia to Japan; also in boreal N America and western mountains to Colorado.

Freija's Fritillary

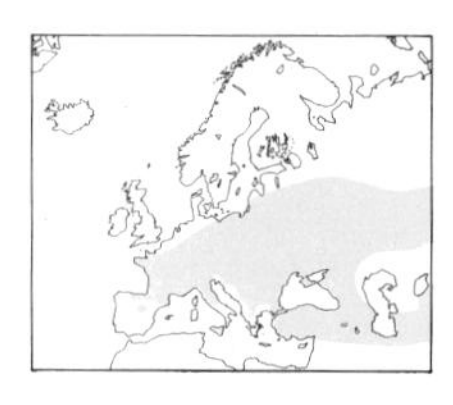

**WEAVER'S FRITILLARY** *Clossiana dia.* Small, hind-wing margin angled at vein 8; unh marbled purple-brown. Sexes similar. Widely distributed across temperate Europe from N Spain eastwards. Absent from Britain, Fennoscandia, and Mediterranean islands; in S Europe often very local or occasional. Flies May–September in light woodland in several broods throughout the summer, at low or moderate altitudes. Larval food plants *Rubus, Viola.* Range extends across S Russia and N Turkey to the Caucasus, C Asia, W Siberia and China.

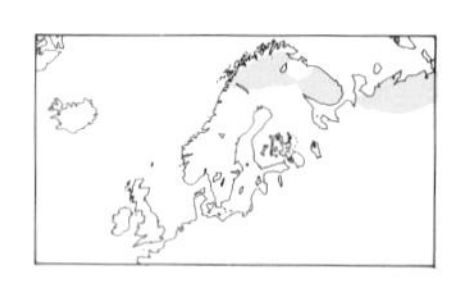

**POLAR FRITILLARY** *Clossiana polaris.* Unh with many small white markings. Sexes similar. A circumpolar species, in W Europe, only in Fennoscandia, not south of 68°N, Pallas Tunturit, Petsamo, Maalselv etc. Flies June–July, on rough slopes usually above valley levels. Larval food plant uncertain, possibly *Dryas octopetala.* Range extends across boreal Asia to N America and Greenland.

*C.t.thore*
*C.t.borealis*
*C.t.carelia*

**THOR'S FRITILLARY** *Clossiana thore.* Unh variable, marbled in shades of yellow to purple-brown, lacking white markings. Widespread but local in the Alps and in Fennoscandia. Flies June–July. Range extends across Russia and N Asia to Siberia and Japan with well-defined subspecies. Larval food plant *Viola.* Three European subspecies.

*C. t. thore*, in the Alps, esp. N Switzerland, Bavarian Alps and Dolomites. ♂ ups very dark, fulvous almost obscured by black, suffused markings. ♀ ups black suffusion slightly less extensive. Flies among spruce trees at altitudes of 1500–1700m.

*C. t. carelia*, in E Finland (Katohma jarvi etc.). ♂ ups dark suffusion less extensive; uph postdiscal area yellow but postdiscal spots and marginal border united to form a wide black band. Flies at low levels.

*C. t. borealis*, in Scandinavia, esp. mountains of Norway, from 62°N to 70°N; Saltdalen, Abisko, Inari, Altenfjord etc. ♂

ups paler, fulvous-yellow, black suffusion greatly reduced. ♀ similar. Not rare but local in the mountains at 300m or more, often in the birch zone.

**FRIGGA'S FRITILLARY** *Clossiana frigga.* Unh with conspicuous white costal and discal marks set in deep brown. Sexes similar. Widespread in Fennoscandia, not south of 60°N, most frequent in the far north; Dalecarlia, Abisko etc. Occasional in Estonia and Latvia. Prefers damp, watery bogs at low altitudes, flying June–early July, usually in colonies. Larval food plant *Rubus chamaemorus.* Range very extensive across N Asia, and boreal N America, extending south across the high western mountains to Colorado.

**DUSKY-WINGED FRITILLARY** *Clossiana improba.* Small, ♂ ups dusky, markings not well defined. ♀ ups grey suffusion less dense. In Europe only in Fennoscandia; rare and local in colonies, not south of 66°N, on hills and mountains, e.g. Altevand, near Kilpisjärvi at 400m; Abisko on Mt Nuolja at 1000m. Flies July. Larval food plant unknown. A wide circumpolar range, including Novaya Zemlya, Labrador, Alaska.

Weaver's Fritillary

Polar Fritillary

Thor's Fritillary

Frigga's Fritillary

Dusky-winged Fritillary

**The Melitaeas.** At first sight these butterflies look very much like the Smaller Fritillaries. They have a similar colour scheme, with black markings on a bright orange-fulvous ground, but there the likeness ceases. Their anatomy is most distinct, unlike any other butterflies, and they like the warm countries of S Europe instead of the colder northern moorlands and arctic tundra. The larvae have hairy warts or even spines, but these are never branched like those of the Large Fritillaries. Almost all species live on low plants such as Scabious, Gentian and Plantain. In several cases there are remarkable gaps, 'disjunctions', in the distribution patterns, with colonies separated sometimes by thousands of miles, evidence of wide dispersal in the distant past followed by widespread extinction, leaving isolated colonies which have lost all contact with other centres of distribution. Such disjunctions are not found with the Large Fritillaries. In almost all species the sexes are similar.

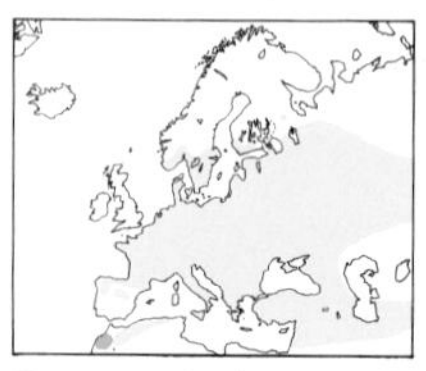

*M.c. cinxia*
*M.c. atlantis*

**GLANVILLE FRITILLARY** *Melitaea cinxia.* Uph with five round black spots in the submarginal band; unh black marginal spots small. Sexes similar, but ♀ often suffused dark. Widely distributed and locally common in N Africa, S and C Europe to 60°N, in Britain only on the Isle of Wight. Absent from Mediterranean islands except Sicily. Flies on open, flowery slopes from lowlands to 1800m or more, usually with two annual broods May–June and August–September. Larval food plants *Plantago, Centaurea* etc. Range extends across Russia and W Asia to the Caucasus, C Asia, Siberia and Sinkiang. **Map 36**

*M. c. cinxia*, throughout the Middle Atlas, Er Rif, S and C Europe. Local and seasonal variation often marked; ups black pattern often heavy and with fuscous suffusion in colder districts and at high altitudes, especially striking in females.

*M. c. atlantis*, only in the High Atlas of SW Morocco, flying in July at 2500m. Ups ground-colour pale yellow, all black markings well defined but lacking fuscous suffusion.

**FREYER'S FRITILLARY** *Melitaea arduinna.* Like the Glanville Fritillary but larger; ♂ ups fulvous, with heavy black markings; unh marginal black lunules joined to form a continuous row. The European subspecies *M. a. rhodopensis* occurs in local colonies in Macedonia, Bulgaria and NW Greece (Ioanina etc.) flying June at moderate altitudes among mountains. Larval food plant uncertain. Range extends across S Russia to Transcaucasia, Iraq and Iran.

*M.p. phoebe*
*M.p. occitanica*
*M.p. punica*

**KNAPWEED FRITILLARY** *Melitaea phoebe.* Upf orange submarginal lunule in space 3 very large; uph black spots in orange submarginal band rarely present. ♀ usually large. Widely distributed in N Africa, S and C Europe to 60°N. Absent from Britain and from Mediterranean islands except Sicily. Flies April–August in two or more broods through summer at low altitudes; a single brood in July in mountains at high levels, often common on open, flowery slopes to 1800m. Larval food plants *Plantago, Centaurea* (Knapweed). Range extends across Europe and temperate Asia to the Altai Mts, C Asia, W Siberia and N China. The species is very variable.

*M. p. phoebe*, from the Pyrenees across S and C Europe, reaching the Baltic coast, but rare and often absent in the NW. Very variable, but without clearly defined subspecies in this area. In the S Alps, f. *alternans*; florid races with ups colour contrast, bright fulvous and yellow markings; late broods in hot, dry districts often remarkably small, f. *pauper*.

*M. p. occitanica*, in Portugal and Spain. Ups alternate fulvous and yellow bands give brilliant colour-contrast, fully developed in late broods.

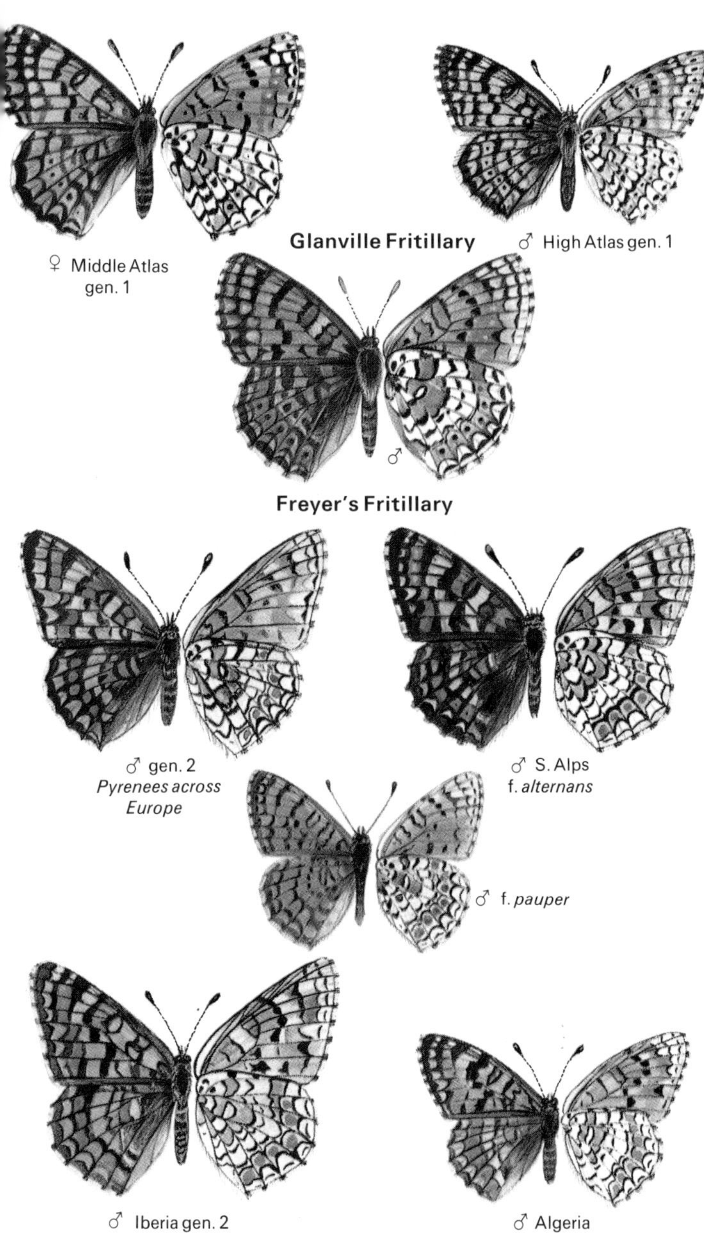


## Knapweed Fritillary

*M. p. punica*, in Algeria. Often small, ups markings very regular, lacking colour-contrast. In Morocco, f. *gaisericus* is slightly larger and markings less constant.

M.a. aetherie
M.a. algirica

**AETHERIE FRITILLARY** *Melitaea aetherie.* Like the Knapweed Fritillary. ♂ ups both wings postdiscal areas almost unmarked. ♀ ups variable. Confined to N Africa, NE Sicily and S Spain, in two poorly defined subspecies. Larval food plants *Centaurea* species. E.

*M. a. aetherie*, S Spain and S Portugal, Cadiz, Chiclana, Val da Rosal etc., in coastal areas, extremely local and uncommon. Unf black discal spots often small (inconstant). ♀ ups fuscous suffusion slight or absent. Flies late April–May over flowery slopes at low altitudes.

*M. a. algirica*, in Tunisia, Algeria and Morocco, flying at 1600m in the Middle Atlas, at 2600m in the High Atlas; also on NE Sicily, f. *perlinii*, very similar, flying near Lupo. ♀ ups heavily suffused dark grey.

**Atherie Fritillary**

M.d.f. didyma
M.d.f. meridionalis
M.d.f. occidentalis

**SPOTTED FRITILLARY** *Melitaea didyma.* ♂ ups markings often scanty, macular. ♀ ups markings more complete, often suffused dark grey, very variable. Widely distributed in N Africa, S and C Europe to 55°N. Absent from Britain and Mediterranean islands except Sicily and Elba. Flies over flowery slopes May–August, at all altitudes to 1800m, in two or more broods at low levels, a single brood at high altitudes. Larval food plants *Plantago*, *Linaria* etc. Range extends widely across temperate W and C Asia. Local and seasonal variation can be related to three principal forms, usually referred to as subspecies.

*M. didyma* f. *didyma*, in northern distribution areas. Ups black markings complete; ♀ ups dark suffusion moderate if present.

*M. didyma* f. *meridionalis*, especially in mountain races of the Pyrenees, S Alps and Balkans. ♂ ups reddish-fulvous; ♀ upf heavily suffused dark grey.

*M. didyma* f. *occidentalis*, in Portugal, Spain, N Africa, S Italy etc., especially in hot lowland areas and late broods. Ups both sexes black markings scanty, ♀ dark suffusion absent; in late summer often very small, f. *dalmatina*.

**DESERT FRITILLARY** *Melitaea deserticola*. ♂ ups like the Spotted Fritillary, black markings scanty; unh the basal orange markings broken up, each spot bordered black. Occurs in Algeria, on the southern slopes of the Atlas Mts; also recorded from Morocco. Flies probably in two broods, April–May and August. Larval food plant *Verbascum* (Mullein). Range extends to Egypt, Lebanon, Israel and Jordan.

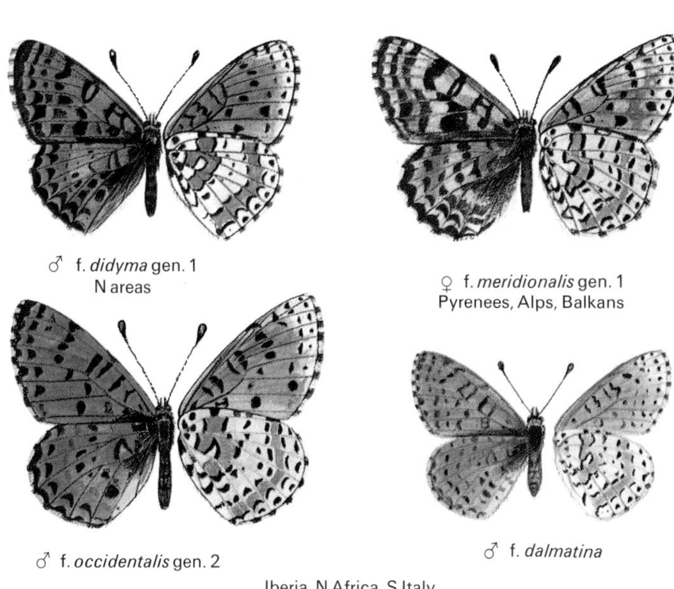

♂ f. *didyma* gen. 1
N areas

♀ f. *meridionalis* gen. 1
Pyrenees, Alps, Balkans

♂ f. *occidentalis* gen. 2

♂ f. *dalmatina*

Iberia, N Africa, S Italy

**Spotted Fritillary**

♂

**Desert Fritillary**

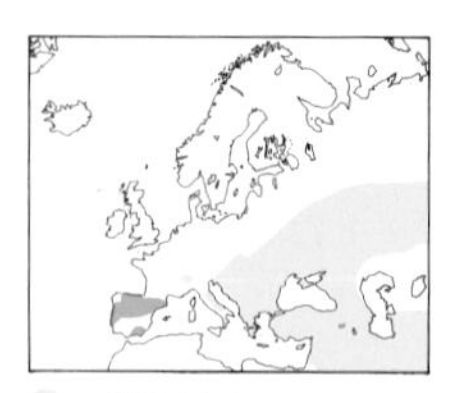

M.t.trivia
M.t.ignasiti

**LESSER SPOTTED FRITILLARY** *Melitaea trivia.* Small, like the Spotted Fritillary. Uph black postdiscal spots usually well developed; the *lower disco-cellular vein is present in the hindwing.* European distribution irregular; common in E Europe, Balkans, Romania, Austria, Czechoslovakia; very local in C Apennines, Piedmont (Susa), Lake Garda; also in N Spain and Portugal, not rare. Flies June–August, often in mountains at 500m or more. Larval food plant *Verbascum* (Mullein). Two European subspecies.

*M. t. trivia*, in SE Europe to Austria, Trieste, L. Garda and C Apennines. Ups deep orange-fulvous, black markings complete, in some favourable localities, f. *fascelis*, larger, darker (esp. Bulgaria).

*M. t. ignasiti*, widespread but local in Spain and Portugal, Sierra de Guadarrama, Catalonia, Leon, Cuenca; Serra da Estrela etc. Ups orange-yellow, submarginal lunules and other black markings often less complete and smaller. ♀ often relatively large. Genitalia structure distinctive.

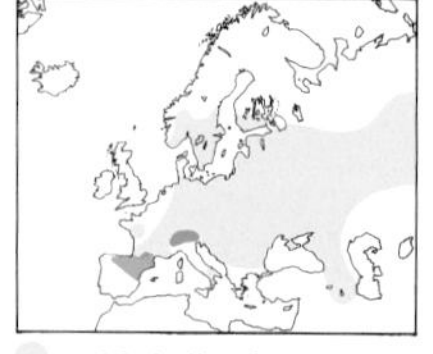

M.d.diamina
M.d.vernetensis
M.d.wheeleri

**FALSE HEATH FRITILLARY** *Melitaea diamina.* ♂ ups very dark; unh each lunule of the orange submarginal band encloses a small, round spot. ♀ ups less heavily marked, uph spots often pale, almost white. In both sexes uns marginal lines orange. Widespread across S and C Europe to 60°N; absent from Britain, Mediterranean islands and S Greece. Flies usually in a single brood June–July, but two broods in some southern localities; occurs at all levels to 1800m, in well defined colonies, often in rather damp, shady places. Larval food plants *Plantago, Veronica; Melampyrum.* Range extends across Europe and north-temperate Asia to the Altai Mts, Transbaical, Amur, China and Japan. Three European subspecies.

*M. d. diamina*, in C and E Europe, the Alps, Carpathians and Balkans. ♂ ups very dark; ♀ uph markings often pale.

*M. d. vernetensis*, in E Pyrenees, Cantabrian Mts. ♂ ups like the Heath Fritillary, well marked on orange-fulvous ground. ♀ similar, transitional forms in Hautes Pyrénées; unh markings as in *M. d. diamina.* In Catalonia (Tortosa, Planolas etc.) f. *codinai*: small, ups similar, but unh markings pale. Flies in two broods May and August.

*M. d. wheeleri*, in some warm valleys in S Alps, Reazzino, Val Cordevole, Val Degano etc. Small, ups fulvous, black markings complete and regular. Flies in two broods, May and August.

♂

♂ gen. 1 f. *fascelis*

SE Europe to Austria, Italy & Trieste

♂ Spain, E Portugal gen. 2

**Lesser Spotted Fritillary**

♂

♀

C & E Europe

♂ E Pyrenees & Cantabrian Mts

**False Heath Fritillary**

**The Heath Fritillaries.** The six species following, including the widely distributed Heath Fritillary, all have similar markings, and they are so much alike that identification, without examination of the male genitalia, can be most difficult. It is helpful to notice carefully the exact distribution areas and habitat conditions, altitudes etc. of doubtful specimens. The ranges extend to the Altai Mts and C Asia.

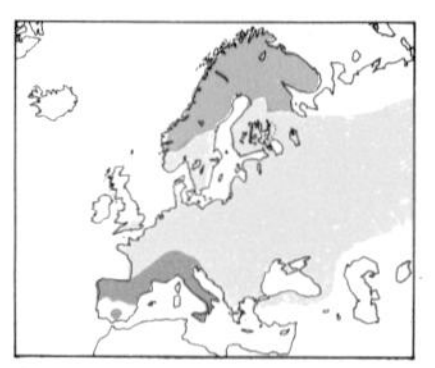

*M.a.athalia*
*M.a.norvegica*
*M.a.celadussa*

**HEATH FRITILLARY** *Mellicta athalia.* Like the False Heath Fritillary. ♂ ups fulvous with black markings in a standard pattern; unh the lunules of the submarginal band do not enclose dark spots; unf the submarginal lunules in spaces 2,3, have *prominent black internal borders.* Larval food plants *Plantago, Melampyrum.* **Map 37**

The European forms of this variable species are divided by anatomical characters into two major subspecies, not defineable by external characters, with minor local variation in size and wing-markings. A third subspecies is defined in the Arctic regions.

*M. a. athalia*, widely distributed in C and E Europe, including Britain, but excluding Italy and the south-west. Size variable, ups often heavily marked; in Balkans f. *boris*, ups black markings more regular (Bulgaria, Greece) but at high levels in the same area f. *satyra*, dark ups suffusion often very extensive. Flies usually in a single brood in July.

*M. a. norvegica*, arctic areas in Fennoscandia, extending to 70°N, very small, with neat, regular markings, genitalia structure like *M. a. athalia.* A transitional form, f. *lachares*, larger, lightly marked, occurs in S Scandinavia.

*M. a. celadussa*, occurs in S and C France, Spain, Portugal, SW Switzerland, Italy and Sicily, sometimes flies in two broods. Ups generally brightly marked, in W Spain and Portugal f. *biedermanni*, both sexes very large. In late brood specimens from warm, dry localities, often small, pale, ups black markings slender, f. *tenuicola.* In S Spain only, in the Sierra Nevada, f. *nevadensis*, ups black markings scanty, with distinctive appearance.

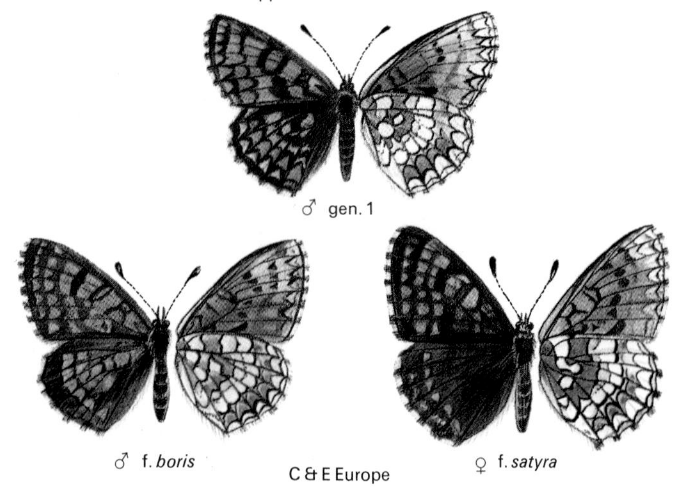

♂ gen. 1

♂ f. *boris* C & E Europe ♀ f. *satyra*

**Heath Fritillary**

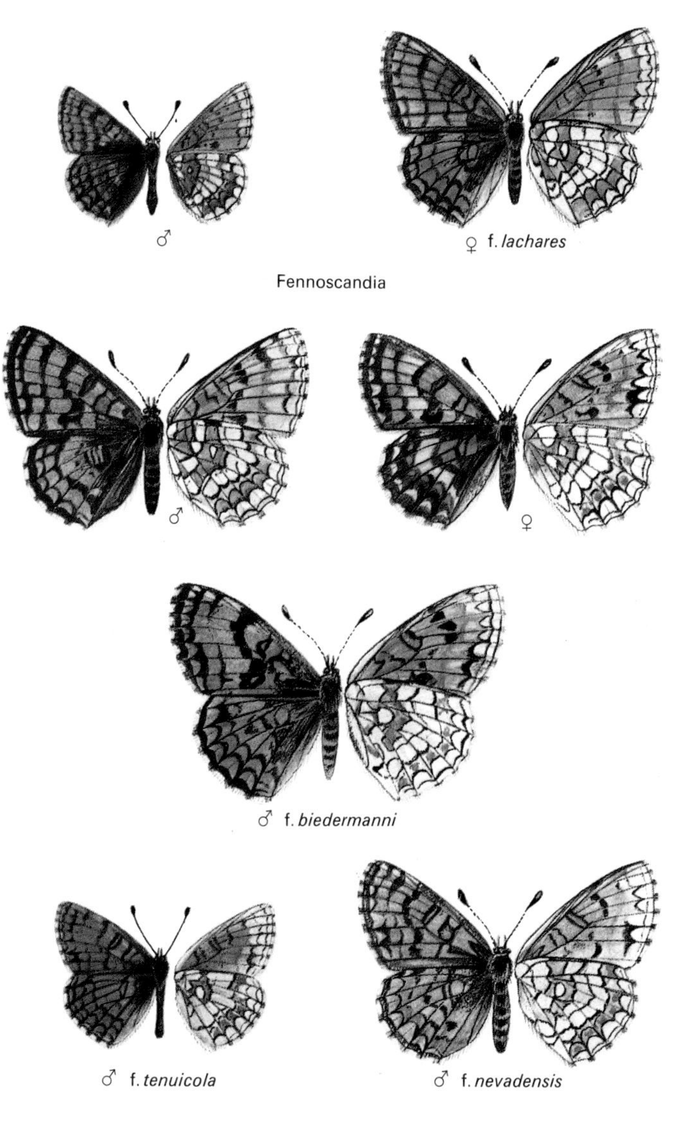


**Heath Fritillary**

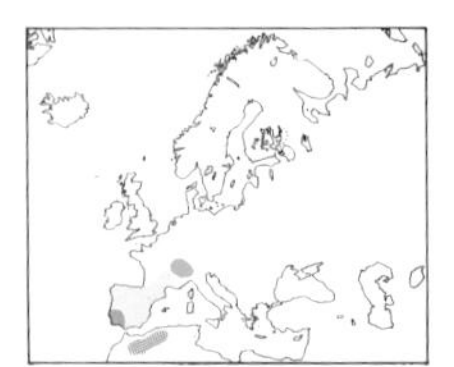

*M.d. deione*
*M.d. berisalii*
*M.d. rosinae*
*M.d. nitida*

**PROVENÇAL FRITILLARY** *Mellicta deione.* Like the Heath Fritillary; upf discal spot in s1b dumb-bell shaped; unf dark inner borders of submarginal lunules in spaces 2+3 vestigial or absent. Occurs in Morocco, Spain, Portugal, Pyrenees, SE France and locally in SW Switzerland and Italian Tirol, flying May–June and later. Larval food plants *Linaria.* Distinction from the Heath Fritillary may be difficult. Locally variable with four subspecies. E.

*M. d. deione* flies in SW Europe; ♂ ups clear orange-yellow; ♀ discal and pd bands often pale yellow with colour contrast. Occurs with two broods, flying over flowery banks from low levels to 1500m.

*M. d. berisalii,* ♂ ups darker fulvous, black markings heavier. Flies in local colonies in SW Switzerland (Rhône Valley, Martigny, Saillon etc.), Piedmont near Ulzio, S Tirol (Eizaktal) etc.

*M. d. rosinae,* ups dark fulvous, black markings heavy. Flies at low altitudes in S Portugal, Cintra, Monchique. This is the largest form known, unlike the rather pale, yellowish forms that fly in S Spain and in the Serra da Estrela in N Portugal.

*M. d. nitida* ♂ ups fulvous-yellow, black markings thin, forewing apex rounded. Flies at 1500m or more in Morocco, Middle Atlas and Er Rif.

**GRISONS FRITILLARY** *Mellicta varia.* Small, ♂ unf pd area unmarked, upf edge of black discal mark in s1b is vertical. ♀ ups often suffused grey. Occurs from Maritime Alps to the Hohe Tauern, flying July–August in a single brood over short grass slopes at 2000m or more, and locally in the C Apennines (Gran Sasso). At lower altitudes sometimes larger, f. *piana.* Markings are very variable. Larval food plants Gentians. E.

In western mountains distinction from the Meadow Fritillary may be difficult.

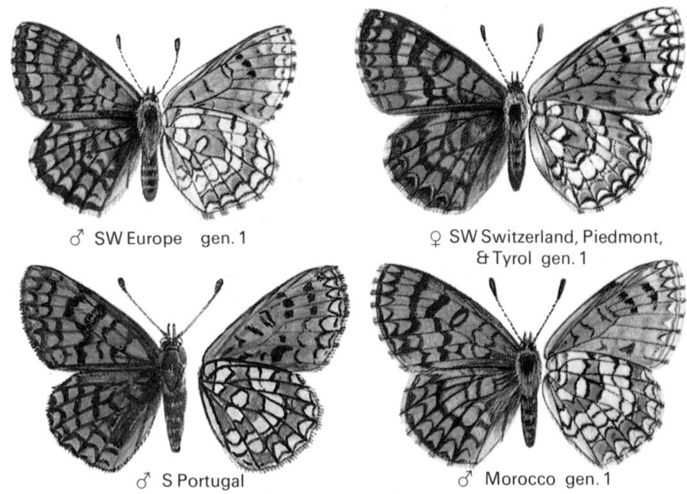

♂ SW Europe gen. 1

♀ SW Switzerland, Piedmont, & Tyrol gen. 1

♂ S Portugal

♂ Morocco gen. 1

**Provençal Fritillary**

**MEADOW FRITILLARY** *Mellicta parthenoides.* Like the Grisons Fritillary. Distinguished by black discal spot unf in s1b *lies obliquely*; ups markings thin, regular; upf discal band often strongly marked. ♀ ups paler yellow, postdiscal and submarginal bands wide. Widespread in Spain, Portugal, France to the Jura Mts, SW Bavaria and SW Switzerland. In Italy only in the Maritime Alps. Flies *at low altitudes* in two broods; May–June and August–September; exceptionally in the Pyrenees *M. p. plena* at higher altitudes to 2000m; ups darker, markings more complete. Larval food plant *Plantago, Scabiosa*. E.

**NICKERL'S FRITILLARY** *Mellicta aurelia.* Like the Grison's Fritillary. ♂ ups black markings in postdiscal areas complete and regular; unh submarginal lunules pale. Locally common in C Europe from Hautes Alpes and Ligurian Apennines to Jura, Swiss and Bavarian moorlands and eastwards to Austria and the Balkans. Absent from Spain, Portugal, the Pyrenees, C and SW France; in Italy, rare south of the river Po. Flies June–July in a single brood over flowery meadows from low altitudes to 1000m or more. Larval food plant *Plantago, Veronica, Melampyrum.* Range extends to the Urals and Caucasus? Easily confused with Assmann's Fritillary.

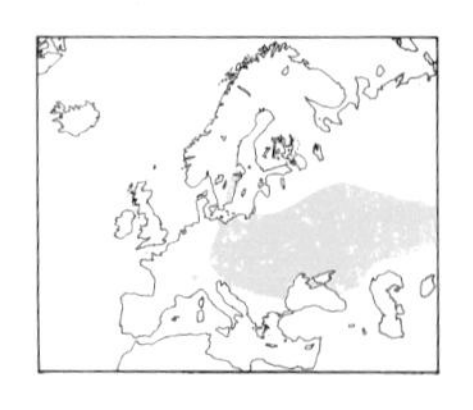

**ASSMANN'S FRITILLARY** *Mellicta britomartis*. Like the Meadow Fritillary. Ups markings complete, hind-wing sometimes dark; unf postdiscal markings often present; unh *narrow marginal line yellow*, darker than submarginal lunules. May fly with the Meadow Fritillary; external distinctive characters too variable for confident identification without exam. of genitalia for confirmation. Occurs near the river Ticino at Galliate, Turbigo etc., very local; more widespread in E Europe from Bulgaria northwards to Hungary, Poland and SW Sweden (Ophem Og, Bollnäs; Regnsjo etc.). Flies in two broods, May–June and August–September. Range extensive, including Dniepopetrovsk, Transbaical and Altai Mts.

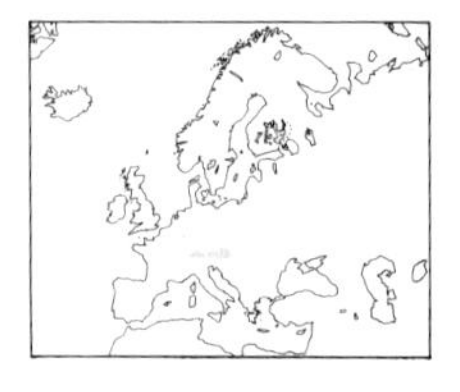

**LITTLE FRITILLARY** *Mellicta asteria*. Very small. ♂ ups dark, unh a single black marginal line. ♀ ups less dark but markings poorly defined. Occurs in E Switzerland (Chur), and Unter Engadin, and in scattered colonies in Ober Engadin, Brenner and Hohe Tauern. A high alpine species; flies July in a single brood over *Vaccinium* fields at 2000m or more. Larval food plant not known. E.

♂

Assman's Fritillary

♀

Little Fritillary

♂

Scarce Fritillary

♀

Asian Fritillary

The four following species are all closely related, and each one presents a different distribution pattern; one on the arctic tundra; one at low levels in woodlands; one as a high alpine member of the Vaccinium group, and one as a species of the middle levels spruce forest zone. The alpine species is a European endemic; the other three are all associated with the deciduous forest zone and with extensive distributions extending east to Siberia, with related species in N America. In all the palpi are short with bushy red hair. Each flies in a single annual brood.

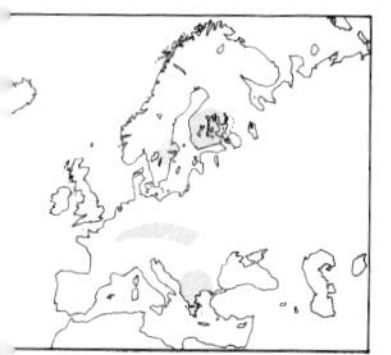

**SCARCE FRITILLARY** *Hypodryas maturna*. ♂ ups black markings heavy; unf pale marginal lunules irregular. Sexes similar. In Europe occurs near Paris and eastwards *north of the Alps* across Germany, Austria, S Fennoscandia; local but widely distributed in Romania and the Balkans to Bosnia, Bulgaria, Macedonia and NW Greece. Flies late May–June at low or moderate altitudes in woodlands. Very local and often scarce in W Europe. Larval food plants beech, ash, poplar, living in nests before hibernation; after hibernation singly on *Plantago, Scabious, Veronica*. Range extends across Russia to the Altai Mts and W and S Siberia. Larva p. 234.

**ASIAN FRITILLARY** *Hypodryas intermedia wolfensbergeri*. Like the Scarce Fritillary; unh the pale postdiscal band includes a fine black line running from costa to anal angle; ♀ similar, often larger. Occurs along the S Alps in light spruce forest, flying at 1600–1800m, from the Savoie Alpes eastwards to the Triglav. Not recorded from the Balkans. Flies July. Distinguished from the Scarce Fritillary by locality and ups by *absence* of small, pale costal and submarginal markings; and unh small black spots in orange submarginal band are rare. Larval food plants not known. Range extends to the Altai Mts, Amur, Sutchan and Korea.

♂

♀

**Cynthia's Fritillary**

**CYNTHIA'S FRITILLARY** *Hypodryas cynthia*. ♂ ups white markings distinctive. ♀ differs, ups buff, lacking colour contrast, like the Asian Fritillary, but unh pale postdiscal band is without the enclosed black line. Occurs along the main chain of the Alps, from Maritime Alps to the Oetztal, including Bavarian and Austrian Alps; also in Bulgaria, in the Pirin and Rilo Dagh. Flies July, usually at high altitudes in the alpine zone, at 2000m or more, over *Vaccinium* slopes and Junipers, but sometimes at lower levels in the E Alps. In its western range at high altitudes, f. *alpicola (spuleri)*, ♂ ups red markings reduced by dark suffusion; ♀ ups paler buff, sometimes with yellowish markings. Larval food plants *Plantago, Alchemilla*. E.

**LAPLAND FRITILLARY** *Hypodryas iduna*. Ups off-white with orange-red spots and bands. Sexes similar. Only in boreal Fennoscandia, not south of 64°N. Flies June–early July over scrub and scattered Pines, often in a wet area, in scattered local colonies often abundant. Larval food plant not known. Range extends across boreal Europe and Asia to NE Siberia, perhaps to Alaska; also in a restricted area in the Caucasus, involving a disjunction of about 4000 miles.

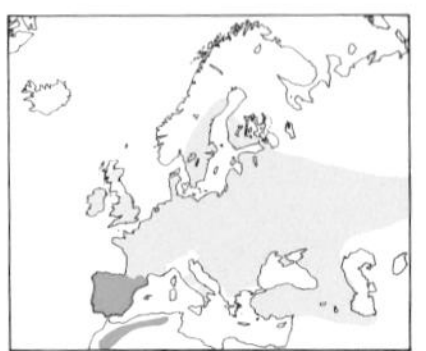

*E.a. aurinia*
*E.a. beckeri*

**MARSH FRITILLARY** *Eurodryas aurinia*. Uph submarginal orange band wide, a well-defined black spot in each space; *unf without prominent black discal markings*; unh margins pale. ♀ often larger. Widespread from Morocco and Algeria across Europe including Britain, Balkans and Fennoscandia to 62°N. Rare and local in Peninsular Italy and Greece; absent from Mediterranean islands. Flies May–June often at low altitudes, on damp moorlands etc., rising sometimes to 1600m or more. Larval food plants *Plantago*, *Scabiosa*, *Centaurea* etc. Range extends across Russia and temperate Asia to Korea. Very variable, with two principal European subspecies. Larva p. 232.

**Map 38**

*E. a. aurinia*, in C and N Europe. Of moderate size, ups usually with some colour-contrast with orange-red and yellow markings.

*E. a. beckeri*, in Spain, Portugal and Morocco and Algeria. Large, ♂ ups sandy-red, often uniform, colour contrast almost or quite absent. ♀ similar, larger or very large. In SE France (Provence), f. *provincialis*, transitional specimens of slightly smaller size. Similar also in Dalmatia, f. *rotunda*, fore-wing wide, apex rounded, ups orange-yellow, black markings thin.

**ALPINE FRITILLARY** *Eurodryas debilis*. Like the Marsh Fritillary but smaller this small alpine form occurring on the E Pyrenees and Alps eastwards to the Grosser Glockner. Flies July–August at 2000m or over, on alpine slopes, rarely at slightly lower levels (Bavarian Alps, Carnic Alps). Principal larval food plant *Primula viscosa*. In some areas, f. *glaciegenita*, ups broadly suffused dark grey.

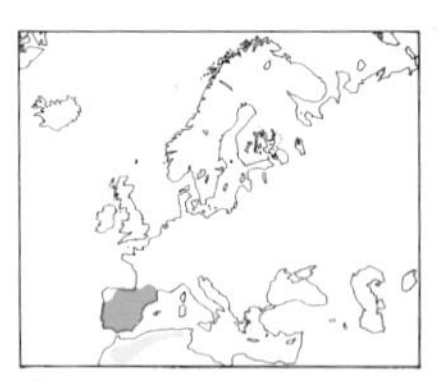

*E.d. desfontainii*
*M.d. baetica*

**SPANISH FRITILLARY** *Eurodryas desfontainii*. Like the Marsh Fritillary. Ups more brightly marked with greater colour contrast; *unf black discal spots prominent*. Sexes similar but ♀ larger. Occurs in N Africa and SW Europe, flying May–June in hilly and mountainous country; local but often common in established colonies. Larval food plant *Centaurea*. Two principal subspecies. E. Larva p. 230.

*E. d. desfontainii*, in Algeria and Morocco, not known from Tunisia. Large, ups orange-red, markings brilliant; Moroccan specimens, f. *gibrati*, especially striking. Flies in the Middle Atlas at 1500m or more over *Cistus* slopes. Larval food plant *Knautia* in Algeria.

*E. d. baetica*, widespread in scattered colonies across Spain and Portugal. Smaller, ups orange-yellow; unh rather variable, f. *zapateri*, black striae well developed. Occurs especially in mountainous areas, Sierra Nevada, Cuenca, Catalonia etc.; very local in SE France (E Pyrenees). Usually flies at 1000–1200m.

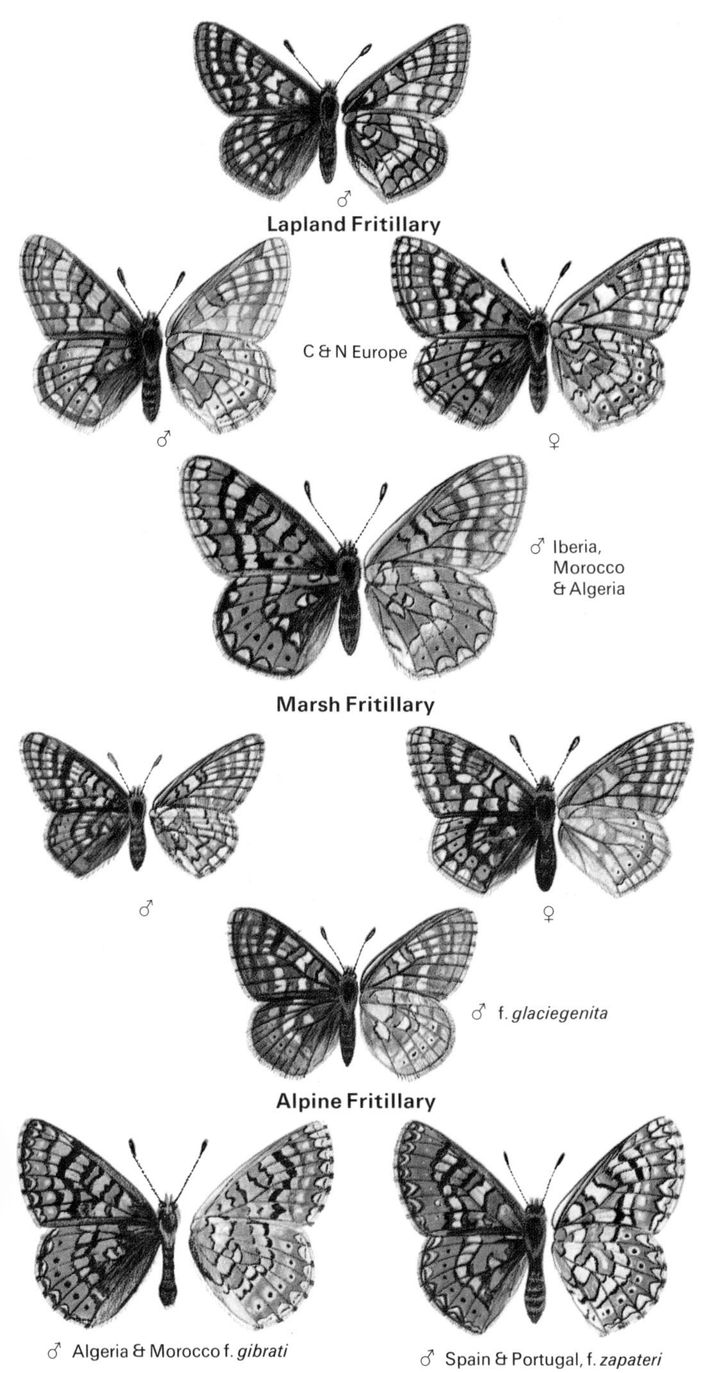
♂
Lapland Fritillary
C & N Europe
♂
♀
♂ Iberia,
Morocco
& Algeria
Marsh Fritillary
♂
♀
♂ f. glaciegenita
Alpine Fritillary
♂ Algeria & Morocco f. gibrati
♂ Spain & Portugal, f. zapateri
Spanish Fritillary

# SATYRIDAE

This large and important family includes more than 30% of our European butterflies. Almost all can be recognized at a glance as members of the family, their characters are so outstanding. The wings are usually brown or buff, marked with eye-spots on one or both sides, and with one or more of the main veins in the fore-wing basally dilated. The front legs are small in both sexes, lacking claws and useless for walking, showing close relationship to the Nymphalidae. The structure of the antennae varies, often with the terminal club well developed, but in some species the apices are scarcely thickened. The ova are oval or truncate, taller than wide, ribbed and reticulate, like those of the Nymphalidae. The larvae are slender, without long hair or spines, with characteristic small flaps covering the anal orifice. All feed upon grasses or similar plants (Monocotyledons), and all hibernate in winter among the grass stems. The pupae are suspended by the tail, or lie free upon the ground, or among the grass stems, which may be lightly spun together to give extra shelter.

**The Marbled Whites.** The milk-white colour of their wings makes these butterflies look out of place among the Satyrids. They are restricted to the Palaearctic Region, with an interesting group of species in the western Mediterranean. All are of medium size, with rather scanty but bold black markings, which vary very little between species. The sexes are similar, but unh often yellowish or pale buff in the ♀; males without a sex-brand.

**MARBLED WHITE** *Melanargia galathea*. Upf cell clear white, not crossed by a black bar. Generally distributed and often common in N Africa and Europe to the Baltic coast at 54°N, recently spreading into the Baltic countries. Flies June–July on grassy slopes at all altitudes to 1800m. Locally variable with three major subspecies. **Map 39**

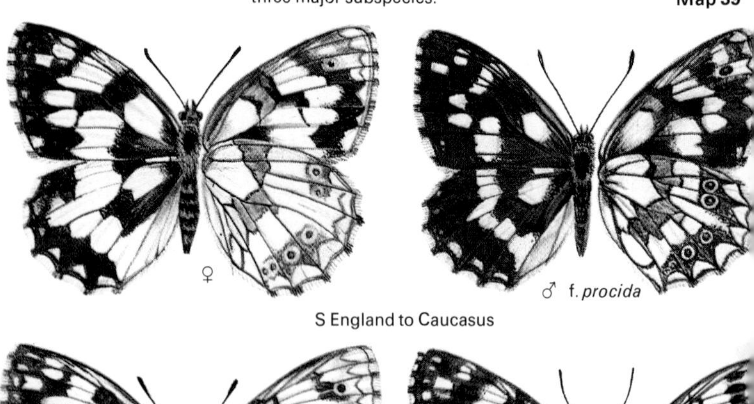


S England to Caucasus

♂ Iberia & SE France

♂ N Africa

**Marbled White**

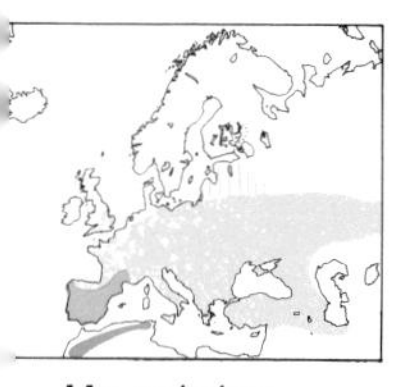

M.g. galathea
M.g. lachesis
M.g. lucasi

*M. g. galathea*, in the Cantabrian Mts, W and C Pyrenees and W and C France to S England and Germany, and eastwards across Europe to Bulgaria and Greece, including Sicily and peninsular Italy. Replaced in SE France and south of the Pyrenees by *M. g. lachesis*. In SE Europe, Bulgaria, Greece and Jugoslavia f. *procida*, ups black markings extensive, white areas greatly reduced, replaces the type form. Recurrent abnormal forms include ♀-f. *leucomelas*, unh plain white, unmarked, and f. *galene*, much less common, uph lacking ocelli. Larval food plant *Phleum pratense*. Range extends across Russia to the Caucasus, N Iran, S Urals and Asia Minor.

*M. g. lachesis*, in Spain and Portugal, south of the Cantabrian Mts and Pyrenees, and in the E Pyrenees and SE France west of the Rhône. Ups like *M. g. galathea*, usually larger, black markings reduced; upf cell elongate; unh grey discal band narrow on costa. A recurrent ♀-f. *cataleuca*, unh plain white, unmarked, is common. At frontier areas between *lachesis* and *galathea*, f. *duponti*, with characters somewhat intermediate, is not rare. Larval food plant *Lamarckia aurea*.

*M. g. lucasi*, in Morocco, Algeria and Tunisia. Like *M. g. galathea* but unf with a grey area beyond the white cell; distinct also by genitalia characters. Flies June–July at 1500m in the Middle Atlas to 2500m in the High Atlas, at lower levels in the Rif. The single brood appears at various dates, later in the High Atlas. E.

M.r. russiae
M.r. japygia
M.r. cleanthe

**ESPER'S MARBLED WHITE** *Melanargia russiae*. Upf cell-bar complete; uph with conspicuous white basal spot. Occurs in S Europe from Spain to the Balkans. Flies June–July at 1000–1500m in grassy places in mountainous country. Locally variable with two major subspecies. Larval food plants *Brachypodium, Poa* etc. Range extends across Russia to Iran, C Asia and W Siberia, in occasional, widely separated colonies.

*M. r. japygia*, in Italy, very local in the Apennines, Lazio (Monte Autore), Bolognola, Pizzo Tre Viscovi and southwards to Puglia and Lucania; in Sicily, often large (Fonte Larocca, Nebrodi Mts, Pian di Battaglia), and Balkans, Mt Perister etc. in Macedonia. Specimens usually heavily marked.

*M. r. cleanthe*, in Spain, not uncommon locally in C and N mountains, Cuenca, Albarracin, Muscadon, Riano etc.; Portugal, on Serra da Estrela; E Pyrenees and SE France, very local in Gironde, Aveyron, Lozère etc. Specimens usually large, ups markings thin, reduced; ♀ ups markings slightly heavier.

♂ Iberia & SE France

♂ Italy & Balkans

**Esper's Marbled White**

Balkan Marbled White

**BALKAN MARBLED WHITE** *Melanargia larissa*. Like Esper's Marbled White. Ups wing bases broadly suffused with grey or black; upf cell crossed by a fine black line. Occurs in Yugoslavia, Bulgaria, Albania and Greece. Flies June–July, usually at low altitudes, on rough, rocky ground. Very variable, black ups suffusion at wing bases and in postdiscal areas, may be most extensive, but in hot, dry localities f. *herta*, black markings can be greatly reduced, but ups wing bases are always dark. Larval food plant not known. Range extends to Asia Minor, and perhaps more widely.

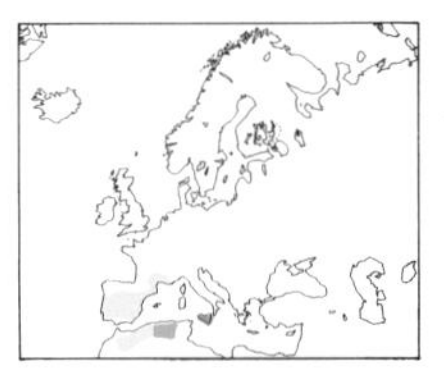

*M.o. occitanica*
*M.o. pelagia*
*M.o. pherusa*

**WESTERN MARBLED WHITE** *Melanargia occitanica*. Upf a black mark at cell-end encloses a pale blue central spot; unh veins firmly lined brown, ocelli blue-pupilled. Widely distributed in SW Europe, locally variable with three subspecies. Flies May–June from valley levels to 1600m or more; usually occurs in mountainous country. Larval food plants *Brachypodium, Dactylis, Lygeum spartum*. E.

*M. o. occitanica*, rather local in Portugal, Spain, widely distributed; SE France, in E Pyrenees, Var, Bouches du Rhône, Maritime Alps, Capo Mele and Capo Berta. Blue spot at cell-end very small; unh a longitudinal dark line present in space 1b.

*M. o. pelagia*, in Algeria. Like *occitanica* but upf blue spot at cell-end larger, unh linear brown markings more delicate. Specimens from Middle Atlas, Morocco, are usually very close to the European *occitanica*.

*M. o. pherusa*, in Sicily. Upf like *pelagia*, upf blue spot at cell-end larger, black markings slightly reduced; unh linear markings further reduced, pale, ocelli often vestigial, sometimes f. *plesaura*, absent on both surfaces. Flies near Palermo at 800m (Monreale).

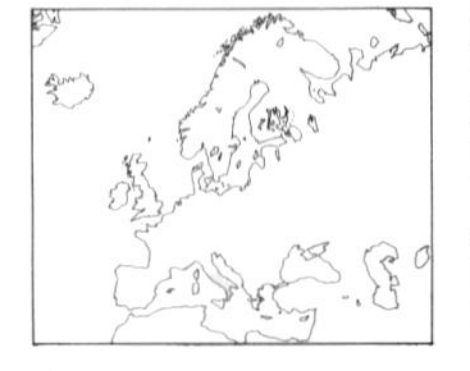

**ITALIAN MARBLED WHITE** *Melanargia arge*. Like the Western Marbled White (*M. o. pherusa*). Ups black markings reduced; upf black cell-bar incomplete, blue spot at cell-end large; unh veins lined black, lacks a longitudinal line in space 1b. Occurs in the Apennines of Italy, from the Gran Sasso southwards to Reggio and the Gargano Peninsular, flying May–June in small, localized colonies at all altitudes to 1500m. E.

**SPANISH MARBLED WHITE** *Melanargia ines*. Ups like *M. occitanica*, cell-bar wide, complete; unh veins delicately lined black; ocelli blue-pupilled and red-ringed, prominent.

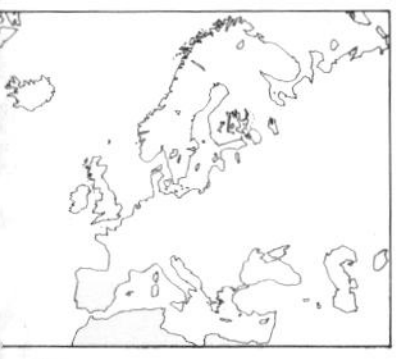

Occurs in Spain and Portugal, widely distributed south of the Pyrenees; also in Morocco, Middle Atlas and High Atlas, Algeria and Tunisia. Flies late April–June, on rocky slopes with grass, from low altitudes to 2000m or more in the High Atlas. At high altitudes, f. *jehandezi*, with upperside markings extended, is not rare. Generally a common species in Spain and in N Africa. Larval food plants *Brachypodium* etc. Range extends to Cyrenaica and Tripolitania.

♂ Iberia & SE France

♂ Sicily f. *plesaura*

♂ Algeria

**Western Marbled White**

♂

**Spanish Marbled White**

♂ f. *jehandezi*

♂

**Italian Marbled White**

**The Graylings.** These butterflies and their close relatives form a large group, very characteristic of the mountainous areas of S and C Europe and N Africa. In almost all species ups are brown, fore-wing with postdiscal ocelli in space 2 and space 5, often best developed on the underside in ♀; ♂ ups with an oblique sex-brand below the fore-wing cell. In the fore-wing, vein 12 and the median vein are basally dilated; the antennal club is well formed. Wing markings of ♂♂ and ♀♀ differ.

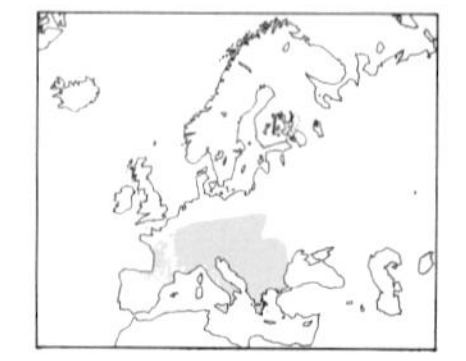

**WOODLAND GRAYLING** *Hipparchia fagi*. ♂ fw 33mm or over, but often slightly smaller in SE Europe; uph postdiscal pale band obscure. ♀ larger, postdiscal bands white, much better defined. Occurs in S and C Europe to 52°N, including Bulgaria and Greece. Absent from S and C Spain, Portugal, NW France, N Germany and NW Europe including Britain, and Mediterranean Islands except Sicily. Often flies at low altitudes, rarely to 1200m, in a single brood, July–August, usually in light woodland. Larval food plants esp. *Holcus*. Range uncertain.

In SE Europe distinction from the Eastern Rock Grayling is most difficult without genitalia examination.

**ROCK GRAYLING** *Hipparchia alcyone*. Like the Woodland Grayling but usually smaller, ♂ fw less than 33mm; uph pale band often yellowish, paler and wider in ♀. Locally variable with two subspecies distinguished by small anatomical char-

**Woodland Grayling**

**Rock Grayling**

*H.a. alcyone*
*H.a. caroli*

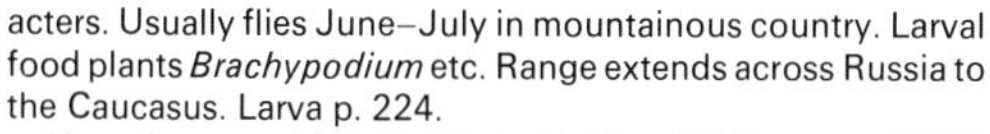

acters. Usually flies June–July in mountainous country. Larval food plants *Brachypodium* etc. Range extends across Russia to the Caucasus. Larva p. 224.

*H. a. alcyone*, widely distributed in S and C Europe to 62°N, including Lithuania and S Fennoscandia. Absent from NW Europe. In Spain, Portugal, France, Switzerland and C Apennines it occurs as a mountain butterfly, flying at 1200m or more around precipices, in torrent beds etc. In N Europe it occurs at lower levels, often on flat, open moorlands.

*H. a. caroli*, in Morocco, Middle Atlas, flying on barren, stony slopes at 1600–1800m. Closely resembles *H. a. alcyone* of Europe, distinguished by a small anatomical character.

**EASTERN ROCK GRAYLING** *Hipparchia syriaca*. Like the Rock Grayling and the Woodland Grayling, probably indistinguishable by external markings but identified by a small character in the male genitalia. Larval food plants not known. Range extends to S Russia (Sarepta) and S Caucasus (Borjom).

*H. s. serrula*, occurs in late June–July at low or moderate altitudes, often in light woodland or in dry river beds. Flies in the Balkans, in Dalmatia, Montenegro, S Bosnia, and Greece, esp. in western areas near the coast of Adriatic Sea.

**Eastern Rock Grayling**

**Algerian Grayling**

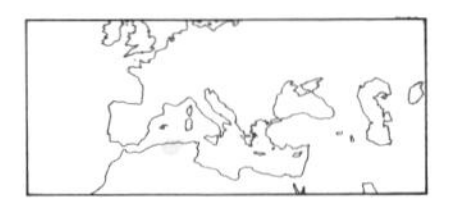

**ALGERIAN GRAYLING** *Hipparchia ellena*. ♂-fw apex pointed, pd band white, slightly oblique. ♀ larger, similar. Occurs locally in woodlands of E Algeria and Tunisia, flying in late July–August at 1200m or more.

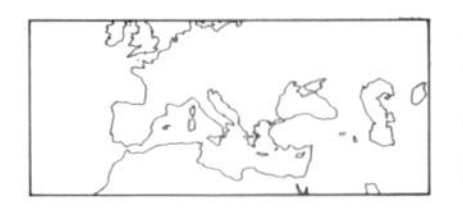

**CORSICAN GRAYLING** *Hipparchia neomiris*. ♂ ups dark brown with fulvous pd bands, upf a single ocellus is present in s5. ♀ upf fulvous band more complete. Flies June–July in a single brood at 1200m or more, on Corsica, Sardinia, and at lower levels on Elba. Larval food plants not known. E.

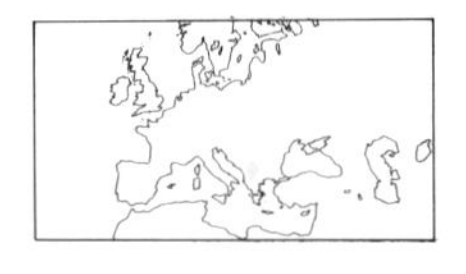

**DELATTIN'S GRAYLING** *Hipparchia delattini*. In both sexes like the Grecian Southern Grayling (*H. a. senthes*), without distinctive external characters. Specific characters are present in the male genitalia. Flies at low or moderate altitudes over barren, stony ground. Occurs in SE Jugoslavia (Pristina), NW Greece and on Mt Chelmos (Peloponnesos). At present the distribution is imperfectly understood. Not illustrated.

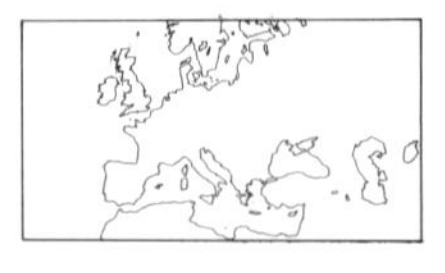

**CRETAN GRAYLING** *Hipparchia cretica*. Like the usual form of the Common Grayling in S Europe (*H. s. cadmus*), lacking distinctive external features. Markings ups rather light in both sexes, in ♀ pale areas distinctly yellowish. Distinctive characters well marked in genitalia of both sexes. Flies June–July on rough ground, road-sides etc. from sea level to about 500m altitude. Known only from Crete. Perhaps better treated as a subspecies of *H. semele*). L. Not illustrated.

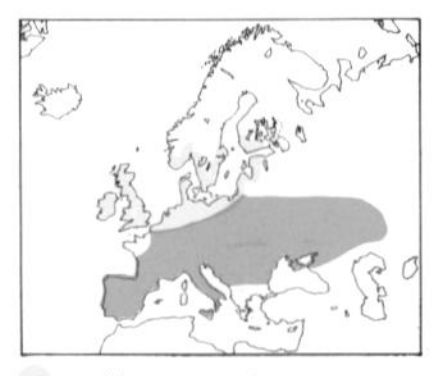

*H.s. semele*
*H.s. cadmus*

**COMMON GRAYLING** *Hipparchia semele*. ♂ upf ocelli present in s2 and s5, yellowish pd area usually small. ♀ upf yellow pd area larger. Widely distributed in C and S Europe to 60°N, including S Scandinavia and S Finland. Flies June–July at low altitudes, often over dry stony slopes. Absent from Corsica, Sardinia, Elba and the Balearic Islands, but range in Balkans and further east not well understood. Larval food plants *Deschampsia, Agropyron* etc. Two European subspecies.
**Map 40**

♂

**Corsican Grayling**

♂ Fennoscandia, Britain, Denmark & Netherlands

♂ ♀

C & S Europe

**Common Grayling**

*H. s. semele* in Fennoscandia, Britain, Denmark and Netherlands. Small, ♂ ups grey suffusion not dense. Flies at low levels, often in coastal areas.

*H. s. cadmus*, in C and S Europe, esp. in mountainous areas of Spain, Portugal, Pyrenees, Alps and Balkans north of Greece and Macedonia. Large, ♂ ups suffused fuscous, fulvous markings greatly reduced. Flies at all altitudes to 1500m or more.

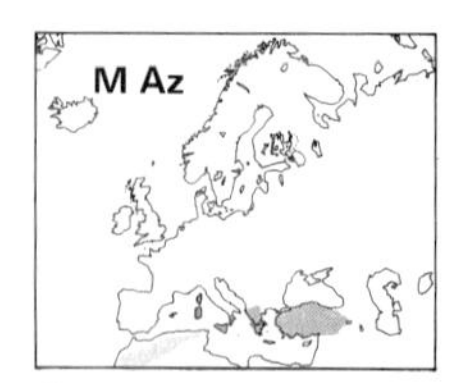


*H.a. algirica*
*H.a. blachieri*
*H.a. aristaeus*
*H.a. senthes*

**SOUTHERN GRAYLING** *Hipparchia aristaeus*. Like the Common Grayling, a genitalia character is distinctive; ♂ ups usually more brightly marked, grey suffusion less dense. Flies in June–July on stony slopes, roadsides etc. at altitudes up to 1500m or more in N Africa. Widely distributed in Europe, N Africa, Madeira and the Azores. The range extends to N Turkey. Larval food plants not known. Five subspecies within our region.

*H. a. algirica*, in Morocco, Algeria, Tunisia. ♂ ups fulvous markings clearly defined. Flies in the Middle Atlas to 1500m or more. Local in the High Atlas. In S Italy (Mt Faito) and Sicily (*H. a. blachieri*) ups orange-yellow areas often brighter, in ♀ usually more extensive in large specimens.

*H. a. aristaeus*, on Corsica, Sardinia and Elba; ups ♂ suffused bright orange fulvous, unf ocellus in space 2 often absent; ♀ ups fulvous areas more extensive. Specimens from Giglio are larger, esp. ♀♀ with fw to 33mm and ups a deeper tone of orange-fulvous.

*H. a. senthes*, in Greece and Asia Minor. ♂ like *H. semele cadmus*, ups darker than *H. a. aristaeus*, pale markings obscured by dusky suffusion; ♀ upf markings yellow-buff, greatly reduced.

*H. a. maderensis*, only on Madeira, ♂ ups both wings heavily suffused dark grey. ♀ also very dark, specimens rather small.

*H. a. azorina*, only on the Azores islands, Fayal and Isola de Pico etc., both sexes small, markings pale; ♂ ups ocelli very small; uph pd pale band sharply angled.

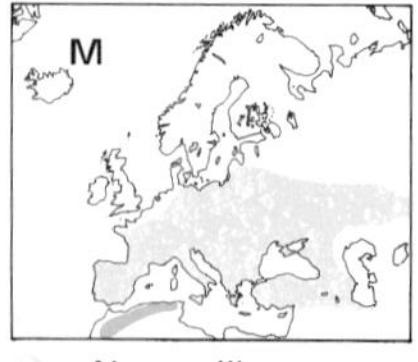


*N.s. statilinus*
*N.s. sylvicola*

**TREE GRAYLING** *Neohipparchia statilinus*. ♂ upf white pd spots in s3 and s4 vestigial, ocelli usually blind. ♀ ups markings better defined, upf white pd spots conspicuous. A very variable species, widely distributed in N Africa, S and C Europe to 50°N.

*N. s. statilinus* unh brown, irregular dark lines outline the discal band but few other markings. A common form in many localities in C Europe. In S and C Spain and in other warm districts, *N. s. allionia*, unh more or less variegated with pale grey, often with a dark band along margin of hw: Granada, Sicily, SE France etc. In N Africa *N. s. sylvicola*, local characters not well defined, unh rather pale grey-brown, usual markings partly obsolete. The butterfly is absent from quite extensive areas in Bavaria, N Switzerland, N Tirol and scarce and local in Romania. It flies late July–September, usually at low altitudes, often on hot, stony slopes, and it is fond of hiding in trees. Larval food plant esp. *Bromus sterilis*. Range extends to Asia Minor and Madeira.

**Tree Grayling**

♂ Morocco, Algeria & Tunisia

♂ ♀

Corsica, Sardinia & Elba

♀ Madeira

♂ ♀

Azores

**Southern Grayling**

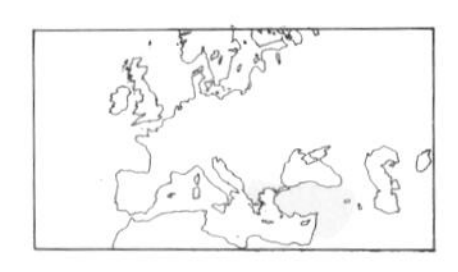

**FREYER'S GRAYLING** *Neohipparchia fatua.* Like the Tree Grayling but slightly larger, ups brown with few markings; hw outer margin strongly scalloped; unh darker brown or grey, irregular sub-basal and median transverse lines distinct, other markings variable, often irrorated dark. Flies July–August at low or moderate levels. An asiatic species which spreads to Turkey, Greece and S Yugoslavia (Macedonia). Often shelters among trees, local, most common in coastal areas.

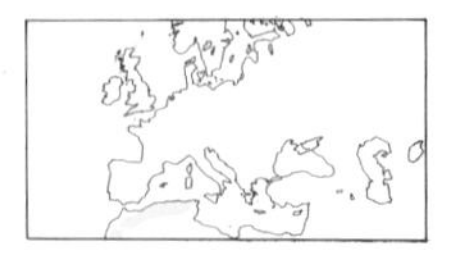

**AUSTAUT'S GRAYLING** *Neohipparchia hansii.* ♂ upf medium-brown with prominent oblique sex-brand; unh postdiscal band pale grey. ♀ upf yellow postdiscal area well defined. Occurs in Morocco, Algeria and Tunisia, flying September–October at 1500m or more in the Middle Atlas Mts, on stony slopes, sometimes in semi-desert. A most variable species. Larval food plant not known. E.

**POWELL'S GRAYLING** *Neohipparchia powelli.* ♂ fw apex pointed; upf sex-brand not prominent, markings obscure, ocelli yellow-ringed; unh veins lined white. ♀ slightly larger, markings similar. Occurs in E Algeria (Oran) and Tunisia, flying September–October over semi-desert. E.

**Freyer's Grayling**

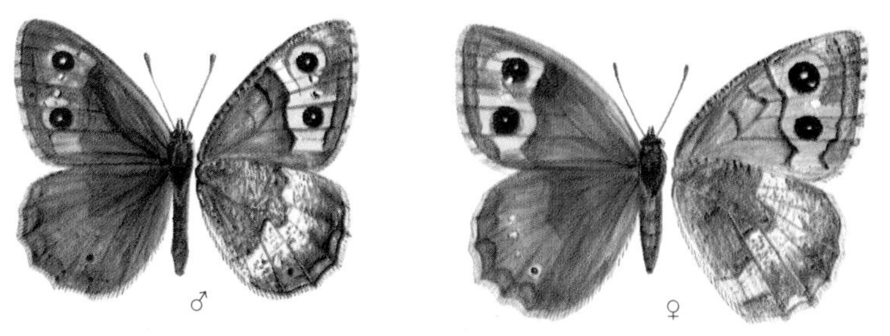
♂ ♀

Austaut's Grayling

♂

Powell's Grayling

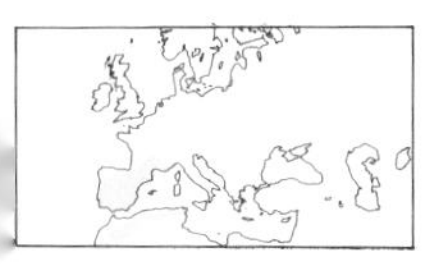

**STRIPED GRAYLING** *Pseudotergumia fidia*. ♂ unh with striking, dark, zig-zag lines. ♀ similar, upf scanty yellowish postdiscal markings often present. Occurs in Morocco, Algeria, Tunisia, Portugal, Spain, Balearic Islands, E Pyrenees and SE France (Provence). In N Africa f. *albovenosa*: unh veins conspicuously pale lined, not rare. Usually flies July–August among trees, at 1000m or more, sheltering from the hot sun, in mountainous country. Larval food plant *Oryzopsis*. E.

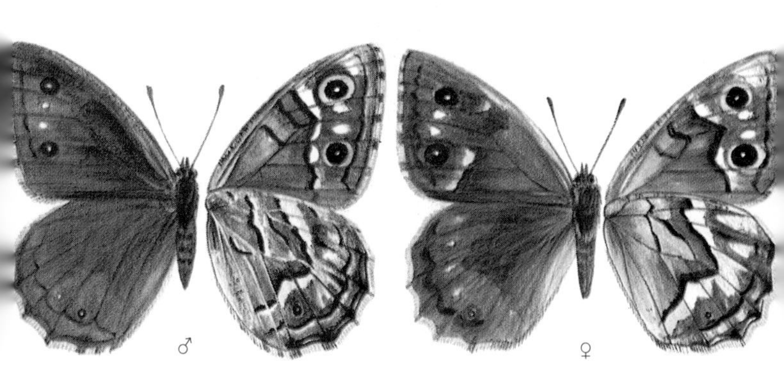
♂ ♀

Striped Grayling

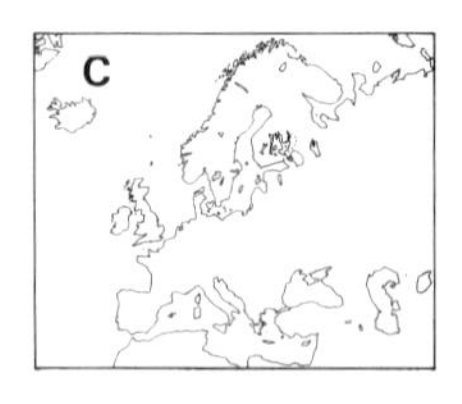


**CANARY GRAYLING** *Pseudotergumia wyssii.* Like the Striped Grayling. Unh pale grey-brown with darker lines and white markings. ♀ ups with scanty pale postdiscal markings. Occurs in the Canaries on Tenerife and Gran Canaria, flying May–September among pine trees at 1500–2200m. Local and uncommon. On El Gomera and El Hierro, *P. w. bacchus*, larger, wings broader and darker brown, especially unh in ♀, brightly marked with prominent white areas. Larval food plant not known. E.

**Canary Grayling**

**HERMIT** *Chazara briseis.* Size variable; ♂ upf costa yellow-grey; uph white, discal band white, regular. ♀ uph white band wider. Generally common and widely distributed in N Africa and S Europe to 50°N. Absent from NW France, Britain, Balearic Islands, Corsica, Sardinia, Elba and Crete. Flies June–July over rough stony slopes and dry mountainsides at all altitudes to 2000m. In the ♀–f. *pirata*, the white markings replaced by buff, rare in S Europe. Larval food plant *Sesleria coerulea*. Range extends across S Russia and Asia Minor to the Caucasus and W Asia from the Altai Mts to the Pamirs. Larva p. 224.

**SOUTHERN HERMIT** *Chazara prieuri*. Like the Hermit, ♂ upf a buff mark in the cell; both sexes unh pale pd band followed by sagittate dark markings. Local in Morocco and Algeria in the Middle Atlas, flying June on dry uplands at 2000m or over; also in C Spain, local at altitudes of 1000m, in Teruel, Zaragoza and in Murcia and Alicante. A ♀–f. *uhagonis*, with white markings replaced by buff, is not rare in C Spain. Larval food plant not known. E.

**Hermit**

**Southern Hermit**

**MOROCCAN GRAYLING** *Pseudochazara atlantis.* ♂ ups orange pd areas wide. ♀ similar, ocelli larger. Occurs in Morocco in the Middle and High Atlas Mts. Flies June–July on barren, stony slopes at 2200–2700m. Recorded also from the South Atlas.

In Er Rif, *P. a. benderi*, ♂ small, expanse 42mm, ups gc and all dark markings paler, reduced; unh grey, almost unmarked. Recorded from Chaouen and Laakra near Bab-Taza, in late July, flying at 2100m. E.

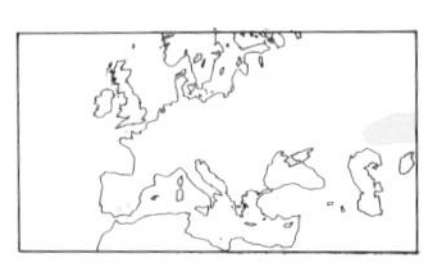

**NEVADA GRAYLING** *Pseudochazara hippolyte williamsi.* ♂ ups pd band very pale buff, well-defined, crossed by dark veins. ♀ upf dark basal area slightly extended along v4. Occurs in S Spain in Granada, on the Sierra Nevada, Sierra de los Filabres, Sierra de Espuña and Sierra Maria in Murcia and Almeria. Flies July–August on barren slopes at altitudes of 1400–2700m. Larval food plants not known. Range (*P. h. hippolyte*) extends to the S Ural Mts, Asia Minor and Tian Shan in C Asia.

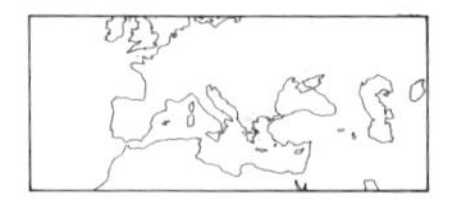

**BROWN'S GRAYLING** *Pseudochazara amymone.* ♂ upf pd band pale buff, white pupilled ocelli present in s2 and s5, white pd spots present in spaces 3–4; uph pale pd band wide. Occurs in NW Greece, flying July on rough ground at 650m. Larval food plant not known. E.

**GRECIAN GRAYLING** *Pseudochazara graeca.* ♂ upf pd band pale buff, crossed by dark veins and broken at v4 by ground-colour, ocelli usually blind; white pd spots in spaces 3+4 *absent*; uph pd band orange-buff. ♀ larger, pd bands paler off-white but variable. Occurs in Greece on the Taygetus, Mt Veluchi, Mt Chelmos and Mt Parnassos. Flies July–August at 1400–2100m over rough, grassy slopes. Larval food plants not known. Range uncertain, possibly extends to Asia Minor and Iran. In N Greece (Pindus Mts) f. *coutsisi*, ups very dark, usual pale markings partly obscured: ♀ dark with buff markings. E.

**MACEDONIAN GRAYLING** *Pseudochazara cingovskii.* ♂ upf black, white-pupilled ocelli in spaces 2+5, prominent white spots in spaces 3+4; unh heavily irrorated and powdered with smokey grey on pale buff. Occurs in S Yugoslavia and in NW Greece. Flies late July over steep rocks at 1250m in mountainous country. Larval food plant not known. The butterfly appears to be extremely local, not identified elsewhere. E.

**Macedonian Grayling**

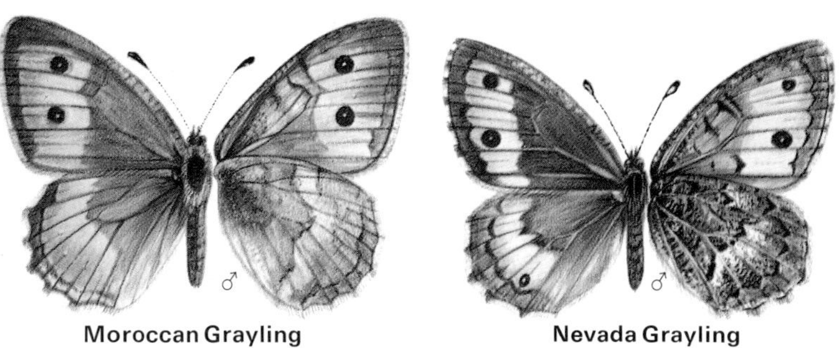


**Moroccan Grayling** **Nevada Grayling**

**Brown's Grayling**

**Grecian Grayling**

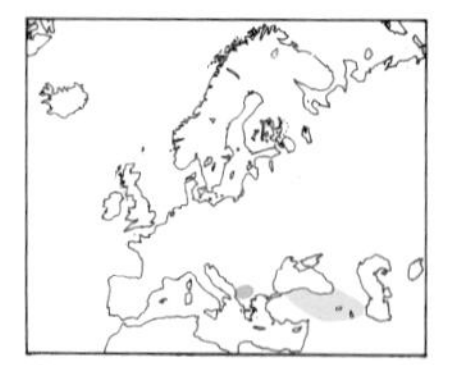

P.g. geyeri
P.g. occidentalis

**GREY ASIAN GRAYLING** *Pseudochazara geyeri.* ♂ unh with a series of V-marks in submarginal area. ♀ slightly larger, ups pale markings better defined. Within the region, known only from Macedonia and Albania. Flies July–August on dry stony slopes at altitudes of 1200–1800m. Larval food plant not known. Range extends to Asia Minor (Mt Ararat), and Turkestan.

**Grey Asian Grayling**

*Note.* An Asiatic specimen is illustrated, as a Macedonian specimen (*P. geyeri occidentalis*) is not available.

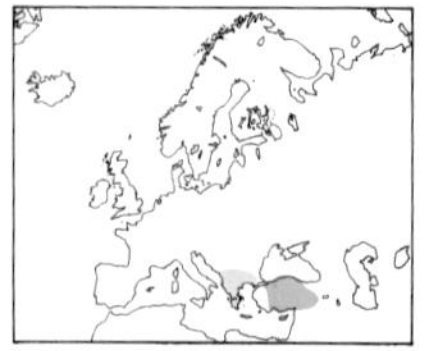

P.a. anthelea
P.a. amalthea

**WHITE-BANDED GRAYLING** *Pseudochazara anthelea amalthea.* ♂ upf with white postdiscal band prominent, a dark sex-band in cell, black ocelli large but white pupils small if present. ♀ larger, uph white postdiscal mark often reduced. Flies June–early July in Greece, Albania, S Yugoslavia, Bulgaria and on Crete. Not rare on rough ground, from low levels to 1500m or more. Larval food plant not known. In the nominate subspecies *P. a. anthelea* (Asia Minor) the female ups is yellow. E.

**White-banded Grayling**

**The Arctic Graylings.** The following four butterflies are the only European representatives of a large group especially associated with the far north, including several truly circumpolar species which occur in Europe, Asia and America. Among the peculiarities are their short antennae; not one of their basal wing-veins is truly dilated, as it would be in all other members of the Family; the discoidal cell of the fore-wing is very long. In some cases it is thought that the larva will hibernate through two winters before the pupa is formed.

**NORSE GRAYLING** *Oeneis norna.* ♂ ups yellow-grey, postdiscal bands buff; unh irrorated grey, dark discal area well defined. ♀ ups basal areas paler, ocelli usually larger. Occurs in Fennoscandia from 62°N to the North Cape. Flies July over rough moorland, from sea level to 300m altitude. Larval food plant not known. Range extends to boreal N Asia, including the Altai and Tarbagatai Mts.

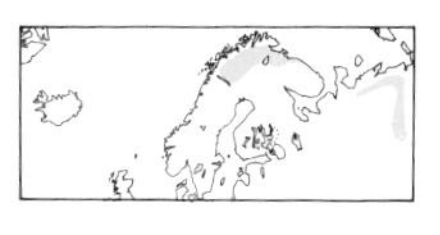

**ARCTIC GRAYLING** *Oeneis bore.* Ups both sexes wings thinly scaled, ocelli absent; uph poorly defined buff postdiscal band present in some specimens. Occurs in Lapland from 67°N to North Cape. Local, flies June–July from sea level to 700m, often seen on hill-tops. Larval food plant *Festuca ovina*. Range extends across boreal Asia and N America.

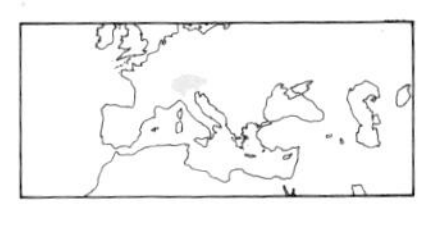

**ALPINE GRAYLING** *Oeneis glacialis.* Like the Norse Grayling, but unh irrorated dark brown, veins lined grey-white. ♀ ups dark basal suffusion reduced or absent. Occurs on the main chain of the Alps in C Europe, from the Maritime Alps to the Hohe Tauern. Flies late June–July, usually on mountain paths at 1600m or over. Larval food plant *Festuca ovina.* E.

Baltic Grayling

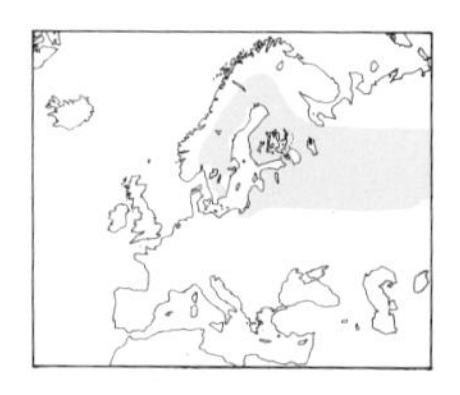

**BALTIC GRAYLING** *Oeneis jutta.* ♂ ups grey brown, ocelli blind, yellow-ringed on both wings, rarely joined to form a band; unh very dark, markings obscure. ♀ similar, ups yellow markings extended. Occurs in Fennoscandia, Estonia, Lithuania and in S Poland (rare). Flies May–June usually at low altitudes on barren moorland or among sparse pine woods on peat mosses. Larval food plant not known. Range extends across N Europe and Asia to the Amur and Sakhalin.

**The True Satyrids.** This is a small group of middle-sized to rather large butterflies. All have a large ocellus on the fore-wing in space 5, with or without a second ocellus in space 2. Well-defined sex-brands are present in ♂♂. The fore-wing vein 12 is basally dilated in all species, the median vein dilated only in the False Grayling. Wing markings are variable.

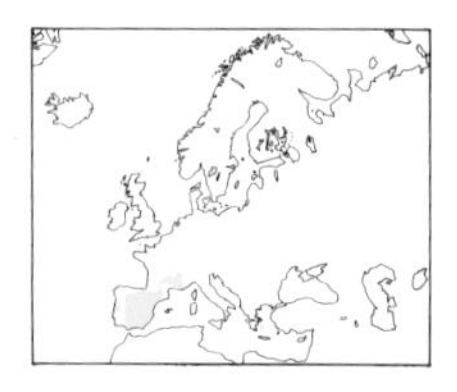

**BLACK SATYR** *Satyrus actaea.* ♂ upf a single postdiscal ocellus in space 5; sex-brand present below cell; unh basal area bordered pale grey. ♀ ups paler brown; ocellus in space 5 often ringed yellow. Occurs in Portugal, Spain, widely distributed; S and C France including Maritime and Basses Alpes; N Italy, only in Maritime Alps and northwards to Susa. Flies July–August in a single brood, over stony slopes, at 1000–2000m. Larval food plants *Brachypodium, Bromus* etc. Range extends to Lebanon and Asia Minor(?).

**GREAT SOOTY SATYR** *Satyrus ferula.* ♂ upf with ocelli in space 2 and space 5; *sex-brand absent.* ♀ ups paler brown, ocelli usually set in orange postdiscal band. Flies July–August on rocky hillsides at 500–1500m or more. Larval food plants grasses. Range extends across Asia Minor, Iran, C Asia to the Himalayas and Amur. Two subspecies in the region.

*S. f. ferula*, in S Europe, not north of 47°N, local but not rare in mountains, extending to the Balkans and Greece.

*S. f. atlanteus*, in Morocco. ♂ upf usually with single ocellus in space 5; sex-brand absent. ♀ ups without orange discal band, often with small ocellus in space 2.

**DRYAD** *Minois dryas.* ♂ upf dark brown, small, blue-pupilled ocelli in space 2 and space 5; hw outer margin scalloped. ♀ larger, upf ocelli larger, ringed orange. Local in widely scattered

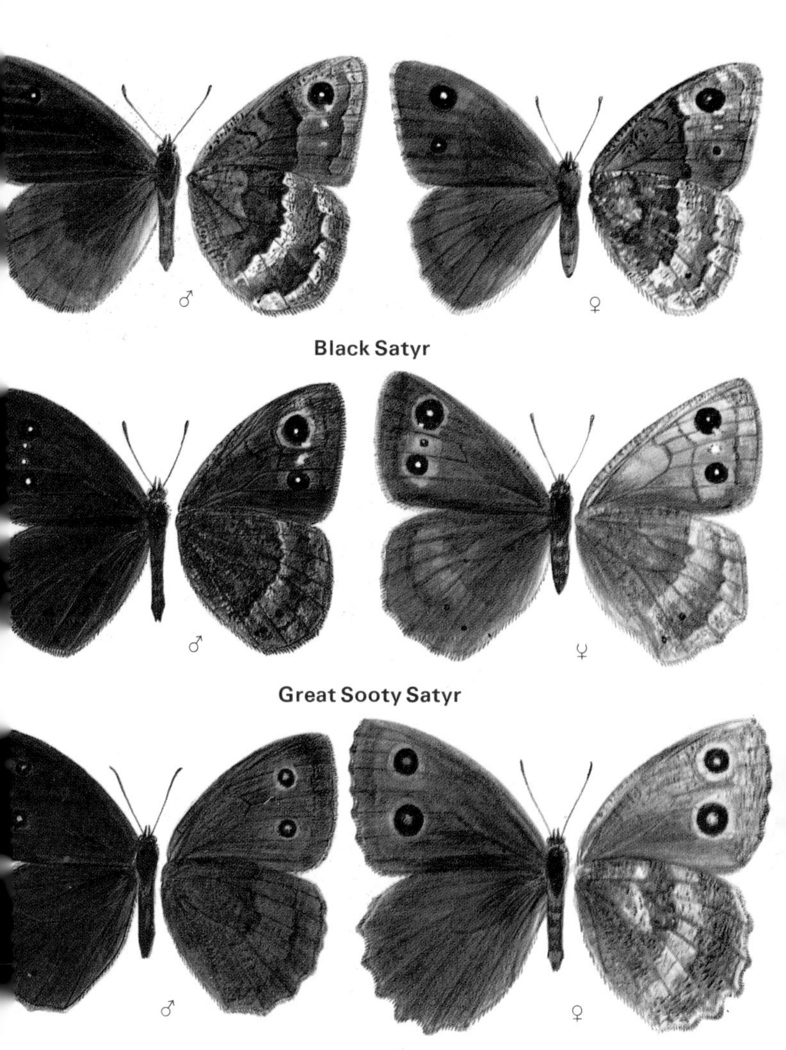

**Dryad**

colonies from N Spain, Pyrenees and France to the Baltic coast (54°N) and east to Romania, Yugoslavia and Bulgaria. Flies in a single brood July–August, at low altitudes in open country or light woodland. Absent from S Spain, Peninsular Italy, Greece and Mediterranean islands. Larval food plant *Avena elatior*. Range extends across Europe to the Caucasus, temperate Asia the Amur and Japan. Larva p. 226.

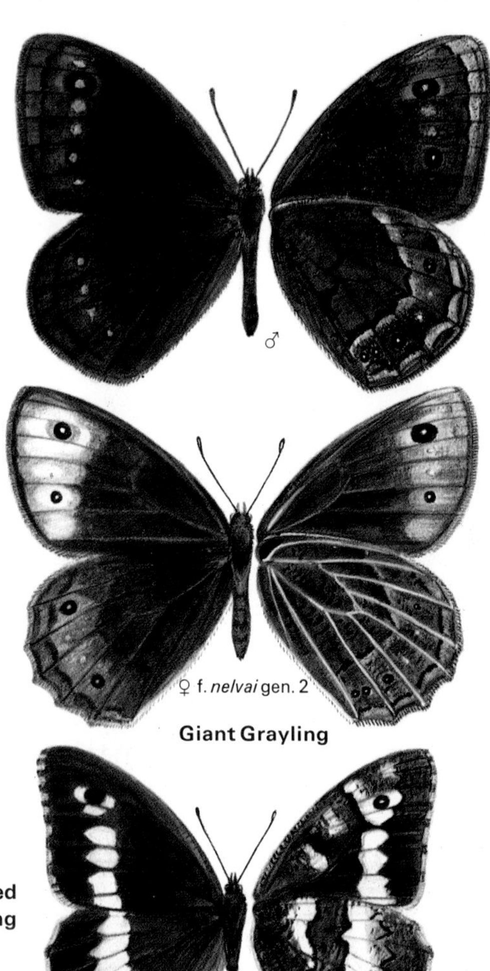


**Great Banded Grayling**

**GIANT GRAYLING** *Berberia abdelkader.* Large; ♂ upf ocelli in space 2 and space 5 blue-pupilled, with small blue spots between; unh postdiscal line prominent, angled. ♀ unh veins lined pale yellow. Occurs in Algeria, Morocco, Tunisia and Tripolitania. Flies in two annual broods, May–June and August–September. Gen.1 upf dark brown; gen.2, f. *nelvai*, upf with broad cream-yellow postdiscal band enclosing ocelli. Larval food plant *Stipa tenacissima* (l'Alfa). E. Two subspecies in the region.

*B. a. abdelkader*, in Morocco and Algeria. Flies in the Middle Atlas and High Atlas at altitudes of 1800–2200m.

*B. a. marteni*, in Tunisia and Tripolitania. Smaller, ♂ upf postdiscal ocellus in space 2 vestigial, ocellus in space 5 well developed, ringed with pale buff (gen.1); probably locally variable. Flies in hilly country near the Mediterranean coast and probably here and there in the Libyan desert.

**GREAT BANDED GRAYLING** *Brintesia circe.* ♂ upf a prominent, interrupted white postdiscal band with a single blind ocellus in space 5. ♀ similar, larger. From Portugal, Spain and France to S Germany (50°N) and east across Europe to the Balkans and Greece, including Corsica, Sardinia and Sicily. Absent from Britain, Holland, Belgium, Crete and the Balearic Islands and N Africa. Flies June–July in a single brood, often in mountains, at all altitudes to 1500m or more. Larval food plants *Bromus, Lolium* etc. Range extends across Russia and W Asia to the Caucasus and Iran.

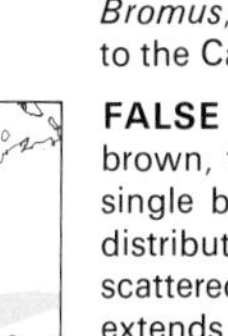

*A.a. arethusa*
*A.a. dentata*
*A.a. boabdil*

**FALSE GRAYLING** *Arethusana arethusa.* ♂ ups medium brown, fulvous postdiscal bands broken into macules; upf a single blind ocellus. ♀ unh veins often lined white. Widely distributed in S and C Europe to 50°N, flying July–August in scattered, local colonies. Larval food plant *Festuca.* Range extends across Russia and Asia Minor to the Caucasus and W Siberia.

*A. a. arethusa* in Austria. Czechoslovakia etc. Ups fulvous postdiscal band not well defined; unh markings obscure.

*A. a. dentata* in Portugal, N and E Spain, Pyrenees, France and N Italy, upf fulvous postdiscal bands well developed and very bright; unh markings variable often with prominent white postdiscal band.

*A. a. boabdil*, in S Spain, ♂ ups dark brown, fulvous markings vestigial if present; unh brightly marked, veins lined white, postdiscal white band often conspicuous. ♂ genitalia differ slightly.

*A. a. alphea*, in S Yugoslavia and Greece, small, ups very dark, fulvous markings well defined; unh base and discal area rather dark grey with vague markings, white postdiscal band fully developed and prominent.

♂

♀

Austria, Czechoslovakia etc.

♀ Portugal, N & E Spain, France & N Italy

♂ S Spain

**False Grayling**

**The Ringlets.** With forty-six species, most of them endemic in the Pyrenees, Alps and Balkans, these form an important group in our fauna. In appearance their wings are usually almost black with postdiscal fulvous bands or yellow-ringed ocelli. On the fore-wing postdiscal ocelli in spaces 4 + 5 form an important generic character. These butterflies are widely distributed in Europe, Asia and North America, especially in mountains, and in arctic and sub-arctic regions. The different species can be so much alike that identification may be difficult. Fortunately the ♂ genitalia and chromosome numbers provide characters which are of the greatest assistance in precise identification.

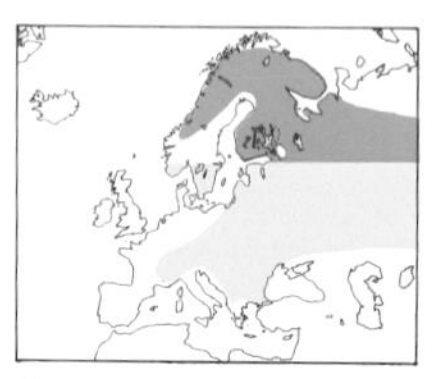

E.l. ligea
E.l. dovrensis

**ARRAN BROWN** *Erebia ligea.* Fringes chequered black and white; on fore-wing upperside the *male sex-brand is prominent*; on the hind-wing underside the dark basal area is defined by white marks. Female similar, often more brightly marked. Flies July from valley levels to 1500m, usually in light woodland, especially Spruce. Two subspecies.

*E. l. ligea*, markings are well developed. Widely distributed from S France eastwards in mountainous areas in S, C and E Europe to N Greece, to about 60°N. Absent from Spain, the Pyrenees, C and N Germany (excepting the Harz Mts), S Italy and all Mediterranean islands. Larval food plants *Digitaria*, *Milium* etc. Range extends, with minor variation, across Russia and Siberia to Japan.

*E. l. dovrensis*, smaller, markings reduced, unh white pd markings vestigial but rarely absent. Widespread in boreal regions from Dovrefjeld northwards to North Cape.

S France eastwards

♂ Dovrefjeld to North Cape

**Arran Brown**

Cantabrian Mts, Pyrenees, C France etc

W Alps, S Switzerland, N Italy etc

♂ SE Alps, Dolomites etc.

## Large Ringlet

*E.e. euryale*
*E.e. adyte*
*E.e. ocellaris*

**LARGE RINGLET** *Erebia euryale.* Like the Arran Brown. ♂ ups fringes chequered, *sex-brand absent.* ♀ unh dark basal area followed by a white or (f. *ochracea*) yellowish band. A variable species. Occurs in the Cantabrian Mts, Pyrenees and across mountainous areas of Europe to 50°N. Flies July–August at sub-alpine levels from 1000–2000m, often among Spruce trees. Larval food plants various grasses. Range extends to the Ural Mts. Three European subspecies. Larva p. 232.

*E. e. euryale*, in Cantabrian Mts, Pyrenees, C France, Jura, N Switzerland, Germany, Czechoslovakia, Bohemia, Austria, Carpathians, Balkans and Bulgaria. Ups postdiscal band red, often wide, ocelli small, usually blind. ♀ similar, ups ocelli often have small white pupils. In some areas, f. *isarica*, ups bands more yellow than red, fringes indistinctly chequered.

*E. e. adyte*, in W Alps, S Switzerland and N Italy to the Ortler Alps and Abruzzi (Gran Sasso). Ups postdiscal band often constricted at vein 4, ocelli larger, white pupils prominent; unh often brown, markings very simple.

*E. e. ocellaris*, in SE Alps, Dolomites, Alto Adige, Hohe Tauern etc. Ups red postdiscal bands greatly reduced or absent. Intermediate races with ups markings reduced, leading to *E. e. euryale* are common, e.g. Glarus, Gemmi, Lenzerheide etc.

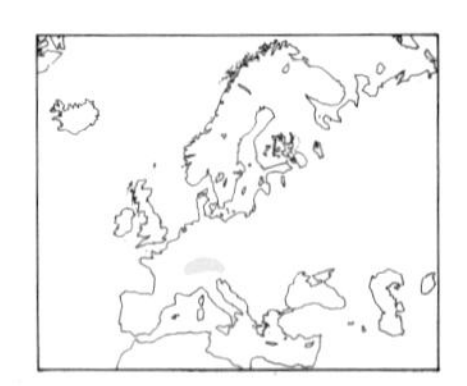

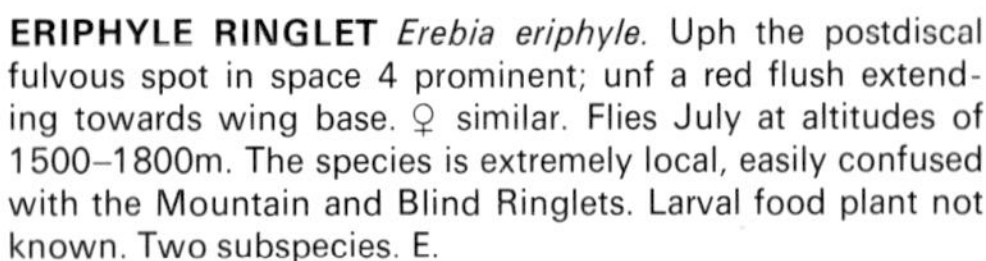

**ERIPHYLE RINGLET** *Erebia eriphyle.* Uph the postdiscal fulvous spot in space 4 prominent; unf a red flush extending towards wing base. ♀ similar. Flies July at altitudes of 1500–1800m. The species is extremely local, easily confused with the Mountain and Blind Ringlets. Larval food plant not known. Two subspecies. E.

*E. e. eriphyle*, in Switzerland; Grimsel, Furka and Flüela Passes, Davos, Val Tschitta etc. Upf markings obscure, often only a small red postdiscal mark in space 5.

*E. e. tristis*, in Bavaria, Austria, including Styria, Carinthia (Gr Sau Alp, Gr Glockner, Innsbruck etc.). Markings better developed, upf usually with a postdiscal band broken by dark veins, enclosing black dots in spaces 2,4,5. ♀ similar, ups often brightly marked.

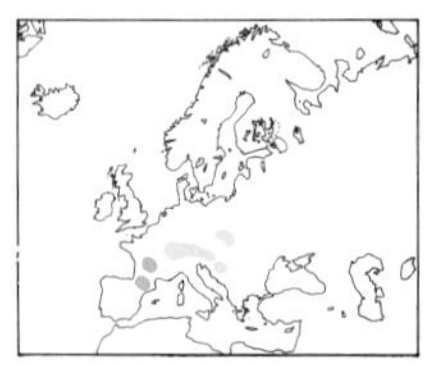

*E.m.manto*
*E.m.constans*

**YELLOW-SPOTTED RINGLET** *Erebia manto.* ♂ ups with fulvous postdiscal bands, often incomplete; upf with black dots in spaces 2,4,5. ♀ ups postdiscal bands yellow, unh with basal and postdiscal markings. Flies July–August on high sub-alpine meadows at 1800m or more. A most variable species. Larval food plants not known. Four subspecies. E.

*E. m. manto*, in the E Alps, Styria, Carinthia, Bavaria; Switzerland and N Italy, markings reduced, Haute Savoie etc. Fulvous markings most developed in the eastern range.

*E. m. pyrrhula*, at high altitudes, Engadin (Albula Pass, Guarda). Very small, ups dark, markings often reduced or obsolete. Less typical in Dolomites, Triglav etc.

*E. m. vogesaica*, in Vosges Mts. Upf black dots absent from fulvous markings. ♀ dimorphic, unh markings often white; ♀-f. *bubastis.*

*E. m. constans*, ♂ ups both wings black, unmarked; ♀ similar or rarely with traces of fulvous mark upf in pd area. Occurs in Pyrenees, Gavarnie to Aulus, flying on damp slopes at 1700–1900m. Also in France, in small specimens, Le Lioran, Plomb de Cantal, Auvergne etc.

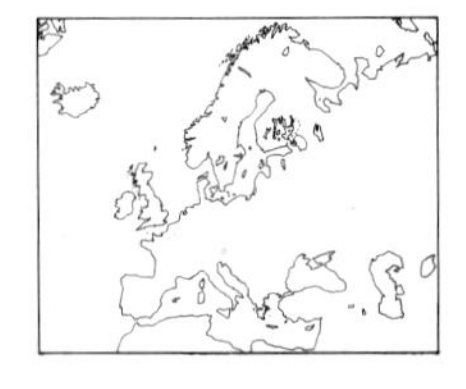

**WHITE SPECK RINGLET** *Erebia claudina.* ♂ unh brown with six white postdiscal dots between veins. ♀ similar, unh yellowish. Occurs in the Carinthian Alps, Gr Sau Alp, Zirbitzkogel, Mallnitz etc. Very local and uncommon. Flies July at altitudes of 2000m or over, on alpine grass slopes. Larval food plant esp. *Deschampsia caespitosa.* E.

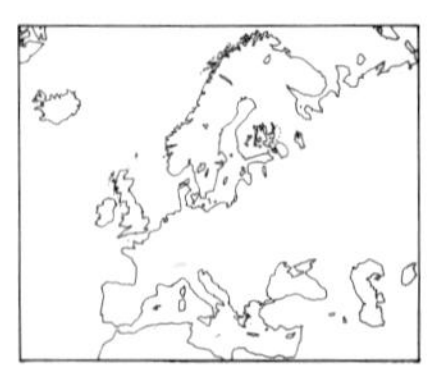

**YELLOW-BANDED RINGLET** *Erebia flavofasciata.* ♂ unh with yellow postdiscal band enclosing small ocellar spots. ♀ similar, ups markings more complete. Restricted to a few localities in Switzerland, in Tessin (Campolungo Pass). In the Engadin (Pontresina etc.), f. *thiemei*, unh yellow band narrower. Flies July. Larval food plant *Festuca ovina.* E.

♂ Switzerland ♂ Bavaria & Austria ♀

**Eriphyle Ringlet**

♂ ♀

E Alps, Styria, Carinthia, Bavaria, Switzerland & N Italy

♂ Engadin

♀ Vosges Mts f. *bubastis*

♂ Pyrenees etc

♂

**Yellow-spotted Ringlet**

♂

**White Speck Ringlet**

♀

♂

**Yellow-banded ringlet**

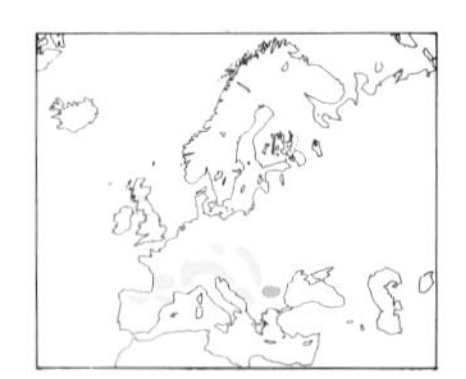

E.e. epiphron
E.e. orientalis

**MOUNTAIN RINGLET** *Erebia epiphron.* In both sexes upf with fulvous postdiscal markings like *E. manto* and other small species; unh *plain brown* with or without small postdiscal spots or ocelli. ♀ ups slightly paler, markings often larger and better defined. Very variable in both sexes. Widely distributed as a mountain butterfly in S and C Europe. Absent from Portugal, S and C Spain, S Italy and Greece. The nominate subspecies (Harz Mts) extinct. Flies July–August. Larval food plants esp. *Deschampsia caespitosa.* E. Five subspecies. **Map 41**

*E. e. silesiana*, on the Altvater Mt. Upf postdiscal band bright enclosing four ocelli. ♀ ups ocelli often white-pupilled. Flies at 1000m or more among Spruce trees. In the Tatra Mts f. *transsylvanica* ups markings slightly reduced. In S Carpathians (Bucegi Mts) almost similar.

*E. e. mnemon*, in Scotland. Smaller, ups markings not prominent, but upf usually with four ocellar spots. Closely related forms occur in N England, the Vosges Mts and in C France.

*E. e. faveaui*, in the E Pyrenees. Large, upf fulvous band reduced, dark and often broken, but usually with four ocellar spots. In the Maritime Alps f. *cydamus*, also large.

*E. e. aetheria*, in Carinthia etc., E Alps, flies at high altitudes. Often small, ups fulvous band narrow and ocellar spot absent in space 4. Similar forms occur in the S Alps of Switzerland, Italy, France, Abruzzi, W Pyrenees and Cantabrian Mts, all usually have three ocellar spots upf; f. *nelamus* ups markings vestigial or absent.

*E. e. orientalis*, on the Rila Mts, Bulgaria. ♂ upf ocelli in spaces 4,5; uph three ocelli, all with prominent white pupils. An outstanding subspecies.

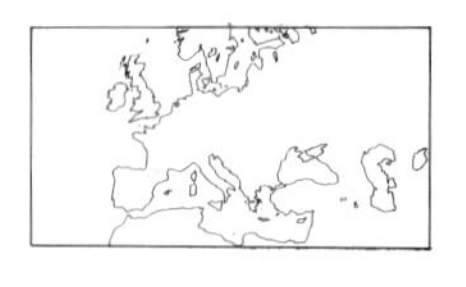

**DESCIMON'S RINGLET** *Erebia serotina.* Like the Mountain Ringlet but larger. About 40 specimens have occurred near Cauterets in the C Pyrenees, flying there at 1000m in September. Only ♂♂ have been seen, and these have disappeared during the last ten years. By genitalia characters it is closely related to the Mountain Ringlet. Taxonomic position uncertain, probably a hybrid form. E.

**RÄTZER'S RINGLET** *Erebia christi.* Like the Mountain Ringlet, but ♂ upf fulvous band regular, with small black spots in a straight row; unh the postdiscal area slightly paler than base. ♀ similar, upf fulvous marking more extensive. Occurs in S Switzerland (Valais) in a few restricted localities, Laquintal, Simplon Pass (Berisal), etc. Flies at altitudes of 1500–1800m. Larval food plant not known. E.

**Rätzer's Ringlet**

**Mountain Ringlet**



**Descimon's Ringlet**

**BLIND RINGLET** *Erebia pharte.* Ups like the Mountain Ringlet but lacks spots or ocelli in the fulvous postdiscal bands. Occurs on the mountains of the main Alpine chain and Tatra. Locally variable with three subspecies. Flies July at altitudes of 1600m and upwards. Larval food plant not known. E.

*E. p. pharte*, in Savoie Alps, Valais, Vosges and N Switzerland. ♂ of moderate size, markings well defined, occupies a central position on the cline of variation. ♀ similar, ups paler brown, markings yellow.

*E. p. eupompa*, Bavarian Alps, E Alps and Tatra Mts. ♂ larger, ups postdiscal bands wider, brighter fulvous. ♀ ups bands yellow.

*E. p. phartina*, at high altitudes from the Dauphiné to Gr Glockner, esp. Engadin, and Dolomites, flying at 2000m and over. ♂ smaller, ups fulvous markings reduced or absent.

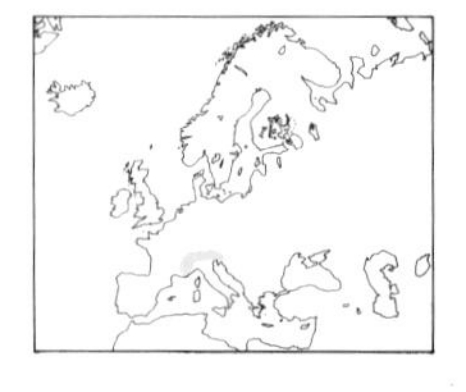

**LESSER MOUNTAIN RINGLET** *Erebia melampus.* ♂ ups postdiscal fulvous bands narrow or broken, unh orange postdiscal spot in space 4 displaced slightly basally, series irregular. ♀ similar, unh yellowish, paler. Local but widely distributed in the Alps from Larche to the Dolomites. Absent from the Pyrenees, Jura, Vosges, Apennines, Carpathians and Balkans. Flies at altitudes of 1000–2000m late June–July, on short alpine pastures. Larval food plants *Poa* species. E.

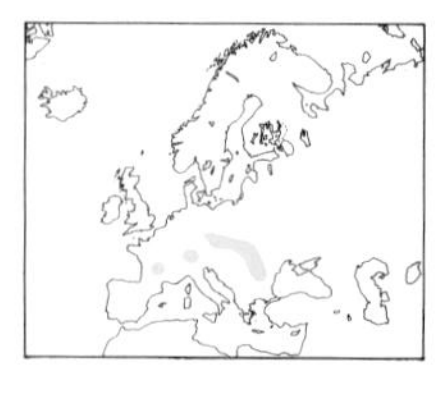

**SUDETEN RINGLET** *Erebia sudetica.* Like the Lesser Mountain Ringlet but all markings more regular. ♂ unh up to six postdiscal spots in well-graded row. ♀ unh spots form a wide band with yellowish suffusion. Local in the Carpathians, Retezat and Bohemian Mts (Altvater etc.). In C France (Le Lioran), f. *liorana*, ups markings less bright; unh usually only 4–5 spots; in Lozère, Puy de Dôme etc. In Switzerland, in a restricted colony (Bernese Oberland), f. *inalpina*, ups markings further reduced. Flies early July, at 1000m or more, often among light woodland in grassy places. Larval food plants not known. E.

**SCOTCH ARGUS** *Erebia aethiops.* ♂ unh discal band dark, postdiscal band grey, with minute white ocelli in spaces 2,3,4. ♀ larger, ups paler brown, postdiscal bands yellow; unh paler, postdiscal band often violet-grey (f. *violacea*). Widely distributed in C Europe, from France, north to N England and C Scotland, eastwards esp. in hilly and mountainous districts to the Baltic coast, Lithuania, Carpathians and Balkans, including N Italy. Absent from SE France, Pyrenees, Denmark and Fennoscandia. Flies late July–September at low levels, 200m and upwards, rare above 1500m, often among woodlands, pines or fir-trees but also in damp meadows and shady places. In Scotland, f. *caledonia*, often small in both sexes. Larval food plants esp. *Molinia caerulea*. Range extends to Asia Minor, S Russia, the Caucasus, Urals and W Siberia. **Map 42**

♂ Savoie Alps, Valais, Vosges & N Switzerland

♂ Dauphiné to Gr Glockner

♂

Bavarian Alps, E Alps & Tatra Mts

♀

**Blind Ringlet**

♂

**Lesser Mountain Ringlet**

♂

♀

**Sudeten Ringlet**

♀

♂

f. *caledonia*

♀

**Scotch Argus**

**DE PRUNNER'S RINGLET** *Erebia triaria.* ♂ upf with three apical ocelli in series within the fulvous postdiscal band; unh very dark, rough, with obscure transverse markings. ♀ upf postdiscal band yellow; unh paler brown. Local but widely distributed in the mountains of N Portugal, Spain (Cantabrian Mts, Cuenca, Albarracin, Sierra de Guadarrama, Sierra de Gredos etc.); Pyrenees; France (Isère, Vaucluse, Basses Alpes etc.), also in S Switzerland, and along the main alpine chain to the Julian Alps, Herzegowina, Montenegro and Albania. Flies June–July at high sub-alpine levels, 1500–1700m, usually associated with Spruce forests, very local and often scarce in its Alpine range, most common in Spain and W Switzerland. In the Spanish provinces of Teruel and Cuenca, f. *hispanica*, small, upf the postdiscal band rather narrow, ocelli small. Larval food plants *Lolium*, *Poa*. E.

**LAPLAND RINGLET** *Erebia embla.* Both sexes uph with 3–4 yellow-ringed blind ocelli, larger in ♀. Occurs in Fennoscandia, not south of 60°N. Flies late May–June from valley levels to 500m on barren moorland with conifers; local but not rare. Doubtfully recorded from Latvia. Larval food plant not known. Range extends across boreal Europe and Asia to the Amur, Sakhalin and Tian Shan at high altitudes.

**ARCTIC RINGLET** *Erebia disa.* Like the Lapland Ringlet. In both sexes uph unmarked. Sexes similar. Occurs in Fennoscandia, not south of 64°N. Flies June–July over wet moorland, bogs etc. at valley levels. Larval food plant not known. Local but not rare. Range most extensive, circumpolar, across boreal Europe and Asia to N America in Alaska, Yukon, British Colombia and Alberta; occurs also in the Sajan Mts, and in S Siberia at high altitudes.

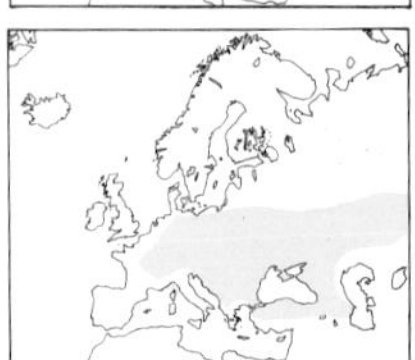

**WOODLAND RINGLET** *Erebia medusa.* In both sexes ups markings usually orange-yellow; unh smooth brown with yellow-ringed postdiscal ocelli; antennal apex brown. ♀ unh paler, often yellowish. Widely distributed in C Europe, often common in lowlands and mountains to 58°N. Absent from S France, SW Alps, Spain, Portugal, Peninsular Italy. Flies late May–June at low altitudes in its northern range, at higher levels in mountains in the southern range. There is marked clinal variation, the forms treated as three subspecies. Larval food plants *Milium effusum, Digitaria sanguinale.* Range extends across Asia Minor, and S Russia to the Caucasus and Ural Mts, and across Siberia to the Amur. The butterfly is easily confused with the Bright-eyed Ringlet (antennal apex black), and the Almond-eyed Ringlet.

*E. m. medusa*, from Belgium (Ardennes), Jura, Vosges and Alps of Savoie to Austria (Vienna area). Ups orange markings well developed.

*E. m. psodea*, in Austria, Hungary, S Carpathians, Bulgaria, Yugoslavia. Ups wing-markings extended, esp. in ♀. Not uncommon in E Europe but inconstant, fully developed only in some colonies.

*E. m. hippomedusa*, in SE Alps, Styria, Carinthia, Dolomites, Monte Baldo, Yugoslavia. Small, ups wing-markings greatly reduced, often darker fulvous. Flies at 1500–1800m. A constant form in some areas, e.g. Dolomites, Venezia Giulia. Flies in July.

♂

**De Prunner's Ringlet**

♂

**Lapland Ringlet**

♂

**Arctic Ringlet**

♂ Ardennes, Jura, Vosges, Alps of Savoie to Austria

♀ Austria, Hungary, S Carpathians, Bulgaria & Yugoslavia

♂ SE Alps, Styria, Carinthia, Dolomites, Monte Baldo, Yugoslavia

**Woodland Ringlet**

**Arctic Woodland Ringlet**

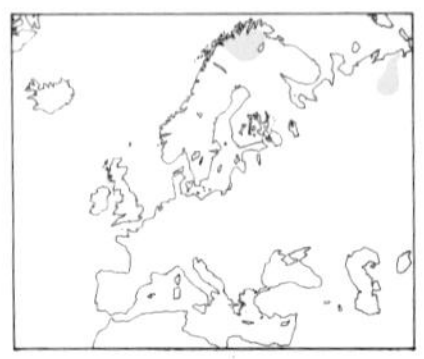

**ARCTIC WOODLAND RINGLET** *Erebia polaris.* Like the Woodland Ringlet, ♂ unh postdiscal area *faintly paler.* ♀ unf red-brown; unh pale postdiscal band better defined. Occurs in Fennoscandia, not south of 68°N, Porsanger Fjord, Kautokeino, Utsjoki etc. Flies July in lightly wooded valleys and hills from sea level to 300m. Larval food plants not known. Range extends to the Polar Urals and N Siberia.

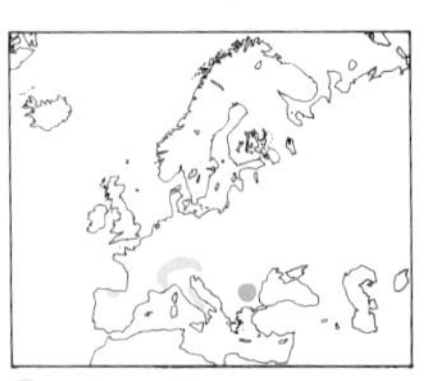

*E.a. alberganus*
*E.a. phorcys*

**ALMOND-EYED RINGLET** *Erebia alberganus.* Ups ocelli small, white-pupilled, in oval or elongate fulvous marks. ♀ uns paler brown, often yellowish. Occurs in the southern Alps, from the Maritime Alps and Switzerland to the Hohe Tauern; also on the C Apennines. Flies late June–July at 1200m or more, over sub-alpine meadows. Locally variable. At low altitudes, 1200m or little more f. *tyrsus*, larger, ups orange markings extended and brighter (Val d'Aosta, Abruzzi). At altitudes of 1800m or more, f. *caradjae*, small, orange markings greatly reduced (Albula, Gr Glockner etc.). In Bulgaria, *E. a. phorcys*, in an isolated area in the Balkan Mts near Karlovo, large, unh lanceolate spots pale yellow to white. Larval food plants *Poa, Festuca.* E.

**SOOTY RINGLET** *Erebia pluto.* Upperside dark brown or black, with or without fulvous markings. Four distinct types of wing-markings occur, the characters often not constant; in some colonies two or even three forms may fly together. The species occurs throughout the main alpine chain, from the Maritime Alps to the Hohe Tauern. Flies July–August always over rocks or moraines at altitudes of 2000m or over. Larval food plant *Poa* species. E.

The distribution of the different forms is confused, lacking defineable geographic frontiers, but generally described as subspecies.

*E. p. pluto*, in the Maritime Alps, Bernese Oberland, Urschweiz (Gadmen), Brienz, Todi Group, Bavaria, Triglav, Abruzzi. ♂ ups black, unmarked. ♀ ups paler, dark grey-brown, unf often with red postdiscal band, unh postdiscal area paler.

*E. p. oreas*, in Bernese Oberland (common), Valais, Ober Engadin etc. Characters often constant, ups in both sexes black; upf often with red postdiscal bands.

*E. p. nicholli*, in Brenta Group and Monte Baldo. ♂ ups black, pupils of the postdiscal ocelli brilliant white, upf in spaces 2,3,4,5, and uph in spaces 2,3,4. ♀ uns paler; unf reddish. A constant form within its restricted distribution.

*E. p. alecto*, in the Bavarian Alps, eastern Alps, and often in mixed races east of Switzerland. Ups black, with white-pupilled fulvous ocelli upf in spaces 4,5; and uph in spaces 2,3,4. Upf often with red postdiscal band. May fly with other forms, esp. *E. p. oreas.* Eastern Switzerland, f. *velocissima*, ups markings more extensive.

**Almond-eyed Ringlet**



**Sooty Ringlet**

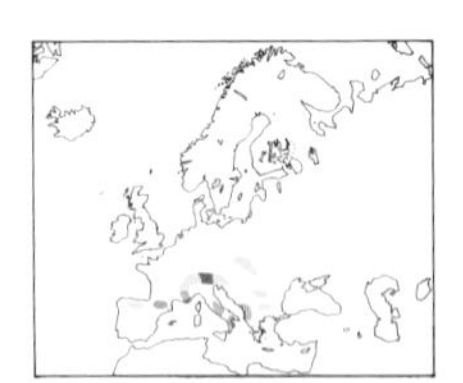

*E.g.gorge*
*E.g.erynis*
*E.g.ramondi*
*E.g.triopes*
*E.g.albanica*

**SILKY RINGLET** *Erebia gorge.* Ups dark brown (black), with gleaming fulvous-red postdiscal bands, with or without white-pupilled ocelli. Locally variable with five distinctly different forms, more or less confined to geographically defined areas, described below as subspecies. Flies July–August over rocks and moraines, at altitudes of 2000m or over. Larval food plants *Festuca, Poa.* E.

*E. g. gorge*, in E Pyrenees, western Alps of France, Switzerland, also in the Balkans (local). ♂ upf ocelli present in spaces 4,5; uph with or without one or two small ocelli. ♀ similar. In N Spain (Asturias Mts) and in Bavaria (Karwendal Mts) f. *gigantea*, very large but ups markings similar.

*E. g. erynis*, upf lacks ocelli in both sexes. In Basses Alpes and Maritime Alps constant; frequent in the Alps of Savoie; constant also f. *carboncina*, in the Abruzzi (Gran Sasso); almost constant in Triglav (Slovenia), elsewhere occasional.

*E. g. ramondi*, in the Basses and Hautes Pyrénées, eastwards to Mont Louis. Like *E. g. gorge*, but uph with three or four prominent postdiscal ocelli; also present unh in both sexes.

*E. g. triopes*, in Ober Engadin, Ortler and Brenta Alps, sometimes large (Monte Baldo). Upf with three ocelli placed in an oblique row within the postdiscal red band; uph postdiscal ocelli present as in *E. g. ramondi.*

*E. g. albanica*, in Albania only. Upf red postdiscal band reduced, ocelli present in spaces 4,5, in a small red mark; uph plain black.

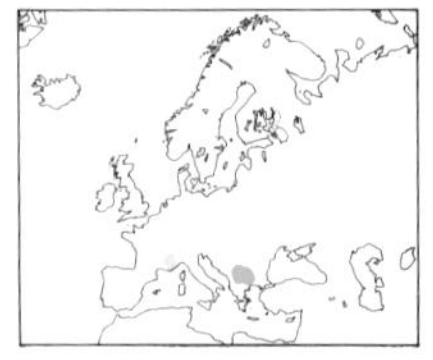

*E.a.aethiopella*
*E.a.rhodopensis*

**FALSE MNESTRA RINGLET** *Erebia aethiopella.* Like the Silky Ringlet. ♂ upf sex-brand prominent, ocelli white-pupilled and *very small*; unh brown with paler postdiscal band, all heavily powdered with white scales. ♀ ups paler brown, postdiscal band yellow; uns paler. Flies late June–July, at altitudes of 1800m or over. Two subspecies.

*E. a. aethiopella*, in France (Maritime Alps) and N Italy (Cottian Alps). Upf postdiscal ocelli often absent; uph lacking postdiscal ocelli. Local, flying over high alpine grass slopes, near Limone Piemonte and Col di Tenda; Sestrières, local but abundant in established colonies.

*E. a. rhodopensis*, in Bulgaria, in Rhodope Mts, slightly larger, ♂ ups ocelli larger, upf ocelli present in spaces 2,4,5 and uph in spaces 2,3,4. ♀ similar but paler. In Macedonia (Shar Planina), f. *sharsta*, slightly smaller, with or without small uph ocelli. Flies at 2200m over grass and heather slopes. Larval food plant not known. E.

♂ ♀

France, & N Italy

**False Mnestra Ringlet**

♂

♂ f. *gigantea*

E Pyrenees, W Alps, Switzerland & Balkans

♂ Basses Alpes,
Maritime Alps, Alps of Savoie

♂ Abruzzi
f. *carboncina*

♂

♀

Basses & Hautes Pyrénées E to Mont Louis

♂ Ober Engadin, Ortler & Brenta Alps

**Silky Ringlet**

♂ Bulgaria in Rhodope Mts

♂ f. *sharsta*

**False Mnestra Ringlet**

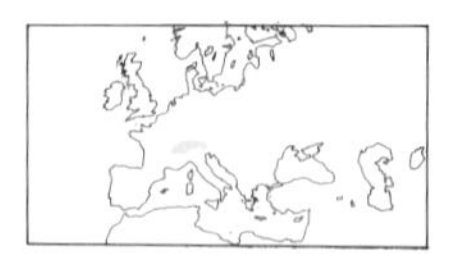

**MNESTRA'S RINGLET** *Erebia mnestra.* ♂ ups like the Silky Ringlet, but slightly larger; upf red postdiscal band wide, extending basally into the cell, ocelli absent (rarely very small), no sex-brand. ♀ upf apical ocelli present; unh with pale postdiscal band. Local and uncommon in W Alps of France and Switzerland. Flies July–August over alpine grass slopes at 2000m or over, on the Simplon Pass; O. Engadin; Ortler etc. Larval food plant not known. E.

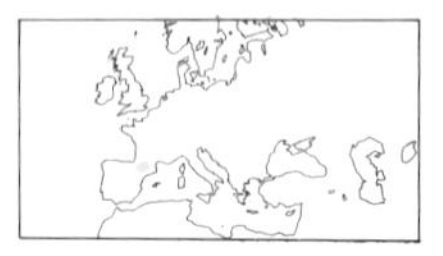

**GAVARNIE RINGLET** *Erebia gorgone.* ♂ ups like the Silky Ringlet (*E. gorge ramondi*). Upf red postdiscal band dark, sex-brand prominent; unh brown. ♀ ups paler brown; unh basal area brown, postdiscal band yellow-grey, veins lined white. Occurs in the Basses Pyrénées and Hautes Pyrénées, from the Lac Lanoux westwards across Ariège to Luchon and Gavarnie. Flies July–August over alpine grass slopes at 2000m or over. Larval food plant not known. E.

**SPRING RINGLET** *Erebia epistygne.* ♂ upf postdiscal band pale yellow; unf ground-colour red-brown. ♀ similar. Occurs in S France, in the Basses Alpes, Maritime Alps, Mont Ventoux, Bouches du Rhône, Gard and Hérault. In N and C Spain smaller, f. *viriathus*, near Barcelona, Cuenca, Albarracin. Flies in France at low levels, but in Spain at higher altitudes up to 2300m (Moncayo), April–June, depending upon the altitude. Larval food plant *Festuca.* E.

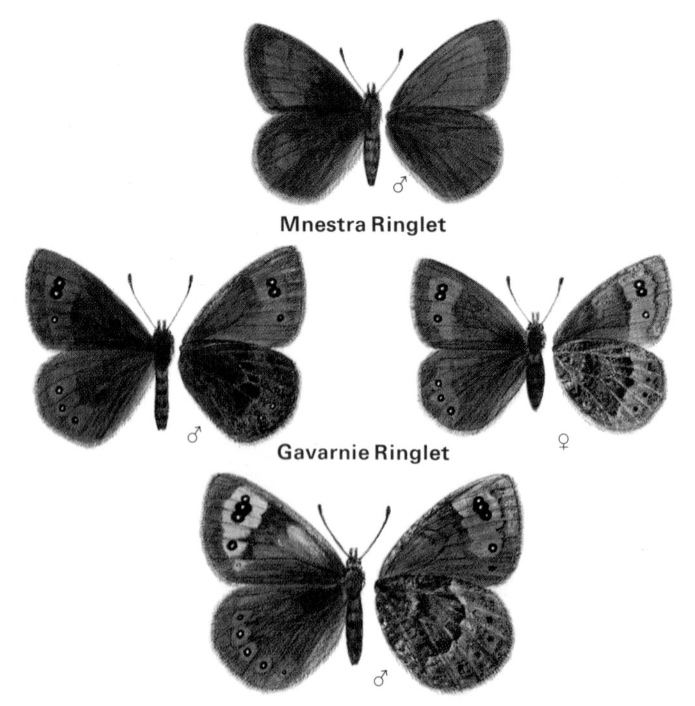

♂ Mnestra Ringlet

♂ Gavarnie Ringlet ♀

♂ Spring Ringlet

**The Brassy Ringlets.** These rather small butterflies occur on all the higher European mountains, from the Cantabrians to mainland Greece. The six species are all very similar, often difficult to recognize by their wing-markings. Much effort and great refinements of techniques have been employed to define the different species. All are European endemics (excepting *E. ottomana*), and for confident identification it is important to remember the distinct areas of distribution.

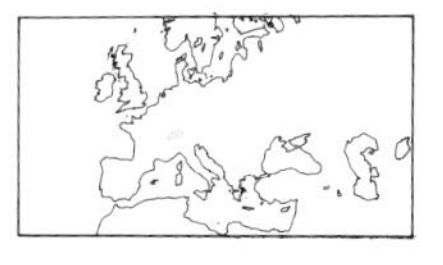

**SWISS BRASSY RINGLET** *Erebia tyndarus.* ♂ fw short, apex blunt, postdiscal ocelli very small; uph plain brown, traces of ocelli very rare. ♀ uns paler, variable. Occurs from the Haute Savoie across Switzerland to the Ortler Group, Bavarian Alps, Allgäuer Alps and Bergamasker Alps. Flies July–August, over grassy alpine slopes at 2000m and over. Larval food plant *Nardus stricta.* E.

**COMMON BRASSY RINGLET** *Erebia cassiodes.* Like the Swiss Brassy Ringlet, slightly larger, fore-wing apex more pointed; upf postdiscal ocelli larger; uph with three well-formed ocelli. ♀ ups paler brown, upf coloured area orange-red. Slightly variable with many named races. Flies July–August over grass slopes at 1800m or more in the Cantabrian Mts, Basses Pyrénées, Hautes Pyrénées (f. *pseudomurina*), Pyrénées Orientales, C France (Mont Dore, f. *arvernensis*), and rather erratically from the Basses Alpes to the Hohe and Niederer Tauern; also in the Apennines (Gran Sasso) and south to Lucania. In the Balkans local and rather uncommon in Romania (Retezat Mts) and S Yugoslavia; absent from the Carpathians. Larval food plant *Nardus stricta.*

**Swiss Brassy Ringlet**

**Common Brassy Ringlet**

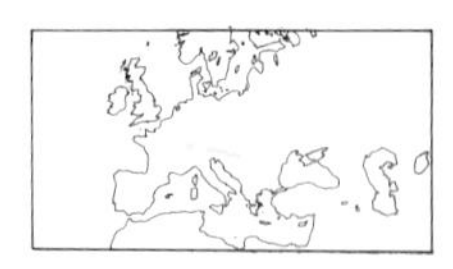

**DE LESSE'S BRASSY RINGLET** *Erebia nivalis.* ♂ fw apex not pointed; upf dark, red postdiscal band inconspicuous, extends basally into cell; uph dark, ocelli absent. ♀ ups paler, unh small ocelli often present. In fresh specimens ♂ unh grey with striking steel-blue lustre. Occurs July–August in Austria, east of the Ötztal, common on the Hohe and Niederer Tauern, where it appears to replace the Swiss Brassy Ringlet. Larval food plant *Nardus stricta.* E.

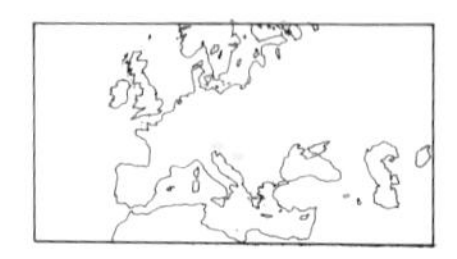

**LORKOVIĆ'S BRASSY RINGLET** *Erebia calcaria.* ♂ ups very dark, ocelli small or vestigial; uph lacks red postdiscal markings. ♀ ups paler, unh yellow-grey. Occurs in the Karawanken and Julian Alps (Triglav etc.); also in NE Italy, with restricted distributions on Mt Cavallo and Monte Santo near Piave di Cadore. Flies late July–August over grass slopes at 1500–1600m. Larval food plant not known. The chromosome number 8 is the lowest so far recorded among butterflies. E.

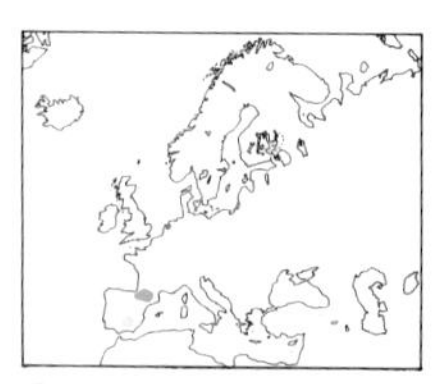

*E.h. hispania*
*E.h. rondoui*

**SPANISH BRASSY RINGLET** *Erebia hispania.* ♂ upf postdiscal band orange-yellow, well defined, twin postdiscal ocelli large. ♀ ups usually paler brown, markings similar, unh yellowish. Occurs in SW Europe in two subspecies. E.

*E. h. hispania*, in S Spain on the Sierra Nevada, distribution range very restricted. Large, fw elongate, esp. the ♀; uph postdiscal ocelli absent or vestigial. Flies late June–July over barren stony slopes at 2200m and upwards (Mulhacen etc.). Larval food plant *Poa, Festuca*, perhaps other grasses.

*E. h. rondoui*, in the Pyrenees on French and Spanish slopes (Huesca, Lerida). Smaller, ups orange markings not quite so brilliant; uph postdiscal ocelli usually well developed. In the E Pyrenees, in France and Catalonia, f. *goya*, small, ups markings more brilliant. Flies July–August at 1800–2000m.

**OTTOMAN BRASSY RINGLET** *Erebia ottomana.* Large; ♂ upf fulvous pd band short, enclosing twin ocelli. ♀ ups paler; upf fulvous area enlarged. Occurs in S Europe as a mountain butterfly, in widely separated colonies from Greece to C France, flying July. Larval food plant not known.

*E. o. bulgarica*, in Bulgaria, S Yugoslavia (Mt Perister) and mainland Greece. Large, upf pd ocelli prominent; unh grey suffusion often extensive. Flies on grass slopes from 1600m upwards; appears to be local and rather uncommon.

*E. o. balcanica*, in Yugoslavia, in Serbia, Croatia, Bosnia and Montenegro; like *E. o. bulgarica* but smaller uph pd ocelli often present but variable. Flies from 1500m upwards, widely distributed, not uncommon.

*E. o. tardenota*, on Massif Central in France, Ardèche, Mont Mézenc etc., slightly smaller than *E. o. balcanica*; ♀ uns yellowish. Flies at 1400m or over. In NE Italy on Monte Baldo, *E. o. benecensis* very similar, ♂ ups tawny patch reduced; unh markings well defined.

♂

**De Lesse's Brassy Ringlet**

♂

**Lorković's Brassy Ringlet**

♂ S Spain

♂ Pyrenees

**Spanish Brassy Ringlet**

♂ Bulgaria, S Yugoslavia & Greece

♀ Yugoslavia

♂ Massif Central, France

**Ottoman Brassy Ringlet**

E.p. pronoe
E.p. vergy

**WATER RINGLET** *Erebia pronoe.* ♂ ups with or without fulvous markings; unh violet-grey, discal band dark and wide. ♀ unh pale brown powdered dark scales, discal band dark brown. Flies July–August at 1000–1800m on damp mountain slopes from the Pyrenees to Romania and Bulgaria. Larval food plant *Poa.* E.

*E. p. pronoe*, in Austria, Styria, Bavarian Alps, Julian Alps, Tatra, Romania and on the Pyrenees. ♂ ups ocelli present on both wings enclosed in fulvous markings, most constant in Bavarian and Styrian Alps, well developed in ♀.

*E. p. vergy*, in France, Haute Savoie, Doubs, Grande Chatreuse; Switzerland, Jura, St Gall, Appenzell, Berne, Vaud, Valais and Grisons. ♂ ups dark, fulvous markings absent or vestigial, ocelli small or obsolete. ♀ ups paler, pd ocelli small but constantly present. In Pyrenees, Bavaria etc., colonies with intermediate characters are common.

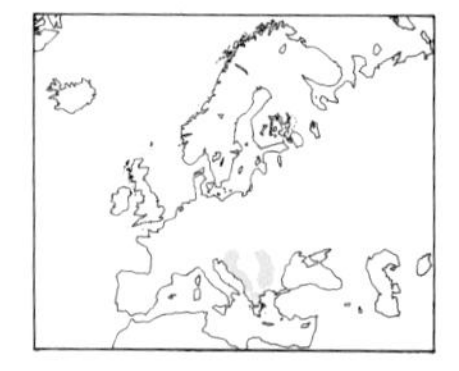

**BLACK RINGLET** *Erebia melas.* ♂ ups black, with or without fulvous markings; uph ocelli, if present, close to the outer margin. ♀ ups brown, ups ocelli larger, enclosed in fulvous rings. Extremely local in the Carpathians, Balkan, Grecian and Albanian mountains, most often on calcareous rocks, reaching furthest west on Mt Nanos in Slovenia. Flies late July–August over moraines and rock-falls. Larval food plant not known. Most variable with two subspecies.

*E. m. melas*, in Romania, Retezat Mts, Greece, Albania and Yugoslavia. ♂ ups black, lacking fulvous markings, ocelli often reduced (variable); ♀ uph ocelli small or vestigial. Flies in Romania at 200–1400m, in Retezat Mts up to 2200m. In Yugoslav Velebit, f. *leonhardi*, small, ♂ markings obscure; flies at 1600–1800m, and at rather higher altitudes in Greece.

*E. m. carpathicola*, in E Carpathians and Transylvania. ♂ larger, ups fulvous-red postdiscal markings present, ocelli well developed. ♀ ups brightly marked with large ocelli. Flies in different colonies at various altitudes of 500–1900m, slightly smaller at the higher levels.

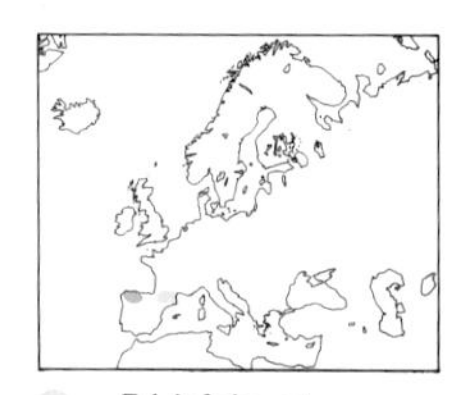

E.l. lefebvrei
E.l. astur

**LEFÈBVRE'S RINGLET** *Erebia lefebvrei.* ♂ ups black; upf ocelli prominent, with or without a fulvous-red postdiscal band. ♀ dark brown, markings variable. Widely distributed in the Cantabrian Mts and Pyrenees. Flies late June–July at 2000m or more on moraines and rocky slopes. Locally variable with two subspecies. Larval food plant not known. E.

*E. l. lefebvrei*, on most of the higher mountains of the Hautes and Basses Pyrénées from Ariège westwards. ♂ upf usually with traces of a red postdiscal band, ocelli often present in spaces 2,3. ♀ more brightly marked, ocelli larger. In the Eastern Pyrenees, from Mt Canigou to Fourmiguères and on Pic Carlitte, f. *pyrenaea*, markings ups usually reduced, ♂ upf often lacks the postdiscal red band, ocelli smaller. ♀ ups markings often less prominent.

*E. l. astur*, on the Picos de Europa in the Cantabrian Mts, ♂ upf red postdiscal markings absent, ocelli small, sometimes absent. ♀ ups black, ocelli reduced, sometimes represented by white pupils only.

*Note.* Distinguish between the Black and Lefèbvre's Ringlets by their different distributions. Anatomical characters do not suggest a close relationship.

♂ Austria, Styria, Bavarian Alps, Julian Alps, Tatra

♀ Romania & Pyrenees

♂

♀

France & Switzerland

**Water Ringlet**

♂

♀

f. *leonhardi*

**Black Ringlet**

♂ Cantabrian Mts

♀ Hautes & Basses Pyrenees

**Lefèbvre's Ringlet**

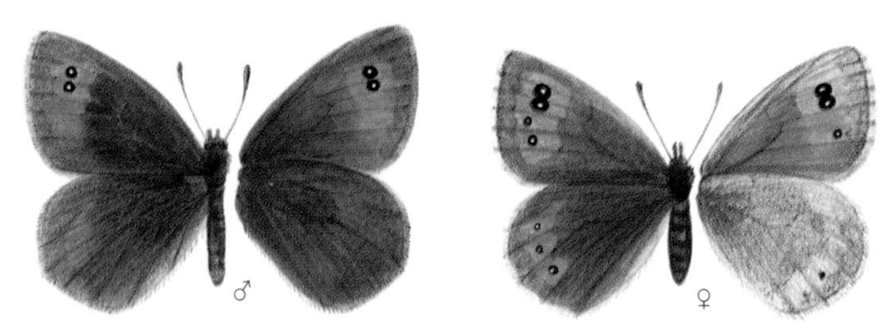


**Larche Ringlet**

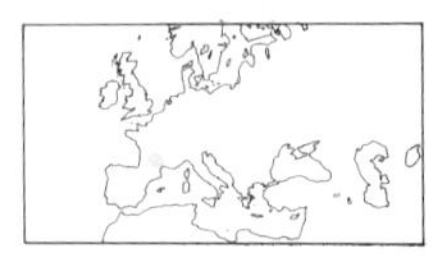

**LARCHE RINGLET** *Erebia scipio.* ♂ upf with twin postdiscal ocelli in a fulvous band; unf discal area chestnut red-brown. ♀ unh palest grey. Occurs in SE France, in a restricted area in the Maritime Alps, Basses Alpes and Vaucluse; very local, associated with calcarious rocks. Flies late July–August at 2000m or more on moraines and rocks. Larval food plant not known. The species is becoming increasingly rare. E.

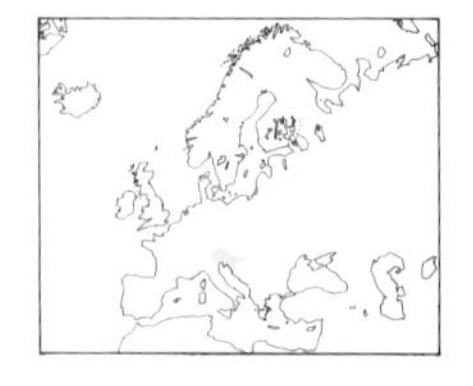

**STYRIAN RINGLET** *Erebia styria.* ♂ ups velvet-black; upf red postdiscal band narrow; unf discal area chestnut brown; unh *smooth dark brown* with three white-pupilled postdiscal ocelli. ♀ paler; unh grey, postdiscal band pale with three–five ocelli. Occurs in the E Alps, from the Seiser Alp and Brenta Group, including Monte Baldo, eastwards to the Slovenian Alps and Karawanken range; widely distributed. Flies late July–August at 800–1500m, usually over rocks. On the Seiser Alp and elsewhere at higher altitudes, f. *morula*, smaller, ups markings reduced. Larval food plant *Poa, Sesleria coerulea.* E.

**STYGIAN RINGLET** *Erebia styx.* ♂ ups like the Styrian Ringlet; unh not smooth, dark brown, basal area usually bordered by vestigial white band, postdiscal area paler, *ocelli rarely present* (distinction from Styrian Ringlet). ♀ paler; unh brown irrorated with darker, postdiscal area paler, small ocelli sometimes present. Widely distributed in the eastern Alps, from N Switzerland to Slovenia. Flies late July–August, at 900–2000m on precipices or among rocks. Locally variable with three subspecies. Larval food plant probably *Sesleria.* E.

*E. s. styx*, Switzerland (U-Engadin, Stelvio), N Tirol (Brennero), Austria (Karwendel Mts). ♂ medium size, unh postdiscal ocelli rarely present in either sex. Flies from 1500m upwards.

*E. s. triglites*, in S Switzerland on Bergamasker Alps and Monte Generoso. Often larger, ♂ ups more brightly marked, fulvous postdiscal band more extensive, unh often with postdiscal ocelli. ♀ ups ocelli often larger. Flies at valley level.

*E. s. trentae*, in Slovenia (Trenta Valley etc.). Large, ups white-pupilled ocelli more prominent, unh very dark grey marbled pale grey and white, dark discal band defined, ocelli usually present in postdiscal area; ♀ large, ups brightly marked with additional ocelli upf; unh pale grey brightly marbled with darker. Flies in the Trenta Valley at about 900m.

**Styrian Ringlet**

Switzerland, N Tirol & Austria

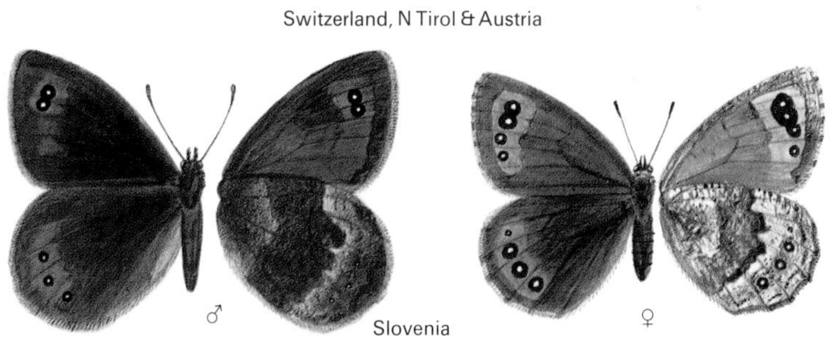


**Stygian Ringlet**

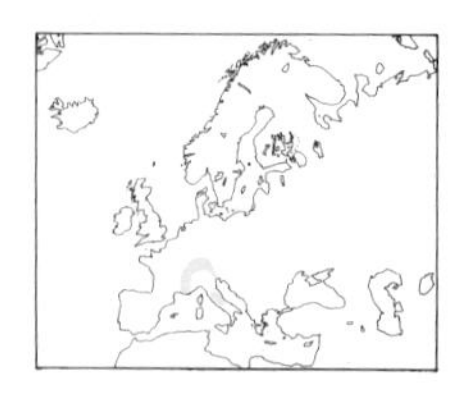

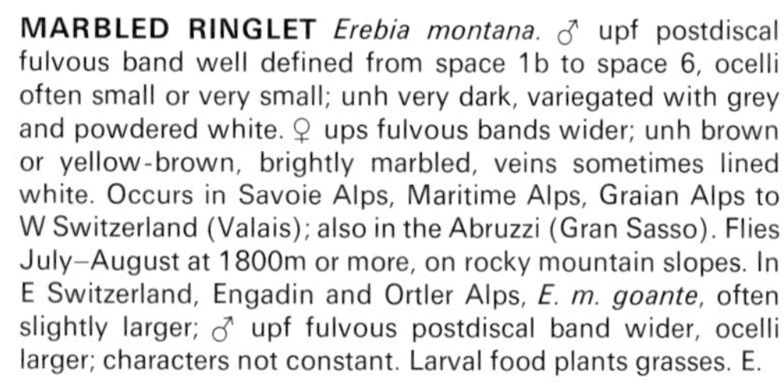

**MARBLED RINGLET** *Erebia montana.* ♂ upf postdiscal fulvous band well defined from space 1b to space 6, ocelli often small or very small; unh very dark, variegated with grey and powdered white. ♀ ups fulvous bands wider; unh brown or yellow-brown, brightly marbled, veins sometimes lined white. Occurs in Savoie Alps, Maritime Alps, Graian Alps to W Switzerland (Valais); also in the Abruzzi (Gran Sasso). Flies July–August at 1800m or more, on rocky mountain slopes. In E Switzerland, Engadin and Ortler Alps, *E. m. goante*, often slightly larger; ♂ upf fulvous postdiscal band wider, ocelli larger; characters not constant. Larval food plants grasses. E.

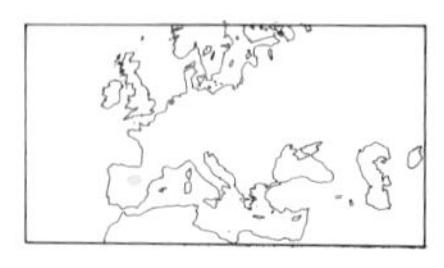

**ZAPATER'S RINGLET** *Erebia zapateri.* ♂ small, upf fulvous postdiscal band yellow; uph ocelli absent. ♀ paler, uph vestigial ocelli sometimes present. Occurs in C Spain, in the mountains near Cuenca and Albarracin. Flies August at 1000–2000m in Pine woods. Larval food plants *Poa, Festuca.*

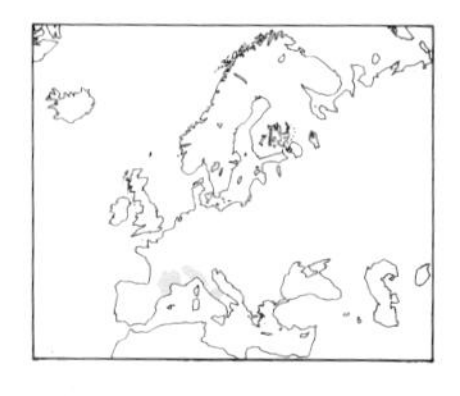

**AUTUMN RINGLET** *Erebia neoridas.* ♂ like Zapater's Ringlet but larger, upf postdiscal band fulvous, tapering from costa to anal angle, with a small ocellus in space 2; uph with or without postdiscal ocelli. ♀ similar. Flies August–September at 1000–1500m in foothills of mountains, locally variable with two subspecies. Larval food plants *Panicum sanguinalis, Poa* species. E.

*E. n. neoridas*, in N Spain (Catalonia etc.); E Pyrenees; S France in Cantal, Lozère, Hautes Alpes, Maritime Alps and Cottian Alps. ♂ ups markings well developed, uph with postdiscal ocelli.

*E. n. sibyllina*, in Italy, in the Sibyllini and Apuane Alps and Abruzzi (Gran Sasso). Small, in both sexes uph ocelli absent.

**BRIGHT-EYED RINGLET** *Erebia oeme.* ♂ ups fulvous markings small, ocellar pupils gleaming white; *antennal apex black.* ♀ unh ocelli variable, sometimes very large. Very widely distributed but local in the Pyrenees, Alps and Balkan Mts. Absent from Peninsular Italy and Carpathians. Flies June–July at altitudes of 1500–2000m or more, usually on damp meadows or in light woodland. Locally variable with three subspecies connected by intermediate races. Larval food plant *Luzula* (Woodrush). E.

*E. o. oeme*, in the Pyrenees, C France (Mont Dore, Isère, Aveyron), Savoie, S Jura, Bavaria, Slovenian Alps and Balkans. ♂ ups fulvous markings small but well defined; unh 3 or 4 ocelli.

*E. o. lugens*, in Switzerland, Allgäuer Alps, the common form north of the Rhône. ♂ ups ocelli often vestigial, very dark, fulvous markings almost obsolete; unh ocelli few or absent.

*E. o. spodia*, in Styria, Austria; some Balkan races (Velebit, Bulgaria). ♂ ups markings well developed; unh 5 or 6 ocelli. ♀ ups fulvous markings enlarged, ocelli large; unh postdiscal ocelli large, joined in a striking submarginal band. In E Pyrenees very similar.

♂ E Switzerland, Engadin & Otler Alps

♀ Savoie Alps, Maritime Alps, Graian Alps to W Switzerland & Abruzzi

**Marbled Ringlet**

♂

♀

**Zapater's Ringlet**

♂

♀

**Autumn Ringlet**

♂ Pyrenees, C France, Savoie, S Jura, Bavaria, Slovenian Alps & Balkans

♂ Switzerland, N of Rhône

♀ Styria, Austria, Balkans

**Bright-eyed Ringlet**

♂ S. Switzerland

♂ C Spain

## Piedmont Ringlet

**PIEDMONT RINGLET** *Erebia meolans.* ♂ ups black, fulvous-red postdiscal markings and ocelli variable; unf *discal area black, red postdiscal band including ocelli well defined*; unh very dark, ocelli lacking yellow rings. ♀ ups paler, postdiscal band yellow; unh brown. A mountain species, widely distributed and often common in C and N Spain, Pyrenees, France and in Switzerland, including the Jura and Vosges, to Bavaria, and W Austria. Flies late June–July, at 1500–2000m, over grassy alpine slopes. Locally variable with four subspecies. Larval food plants species of *Poa* and *Festuca*. E.

*E. m. meolans*, in Maritime Alps, Basses Alpes, Massif Central of France, Graian Alps and Savoie to Jura and Vosges. ♂ of moderate size, ups markings often variable, sometimes slightly reduced. In C France (Le Lioran, Mont Dore etc.) often small.

*E. m. bejarensis*, in C Spain. Larger, ups markings brighter; unf red postdiscal band wide. The largest races fly in the Sierra de Guadarrama and at La Granja. In the Cantabrian Mts and Pyrenees smaller, transitional to *E. m. meolans.*

*E. m. stygne*, in N Switzerland, Bavaria and east to the Brenner and Hochschwab, local and rather scarce. ♂ medium size, ups dark, red postdiscal band and markings reduced.

*E. m. valesiaca*, S Switzerland (Grisons). Small, ups all markings greatly reduced; unf red postdiscal band short, usually from space 2 – space 5. This race differs from all other forms, and is easily confused with *Erebia oeme*, but ♂ *E. meolans* lacks the red postdiscal band unh.

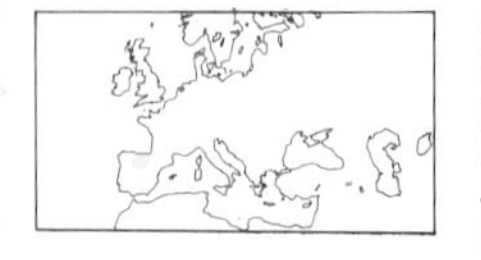

**CHAPMAN'S RINGLET** *Erebia palarica.* ♂ large, unh dark brown with grey marbling and 'rough' looking surface. ♀ ups paler, postdiscal band orange-yellow, ocelli large. Occurs in NW Spain, Galicia, Asturias and Leon. Flies in mountains late June–July, at 1100–1800m, often associated with a tall broom. Larval food plants *Festuca* species. E.

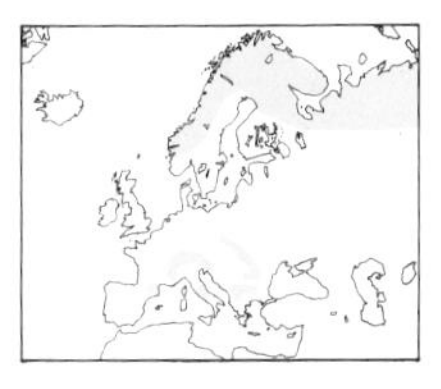

**DEWY RINGLET** *Erebia pandrose.* ♂ upf fulvous postdiscal area dull, enclosing four small black spots in a row. ♀ similar. Widely distributed in Europe from the E Pyrenees and high alps to the Carpathians, Balkans, Rila Mts Bulgaria, Apennines (Monti della Larga), the race recently named *sevoensis*, and in Fennoscandia to 70°N. An alpine species in C Europe, flies late June–July at 1800m and over, above the trees, on grass slopes, but in Fennoscandia at low altitudes over the tundra. In the S Carpathians, ♀–f. *roberti*, unh the discal band is dark grey-brown. Larval food plant *Festuca, Poa*. Range extends across N Russia to the Altai Mts and Siberia.

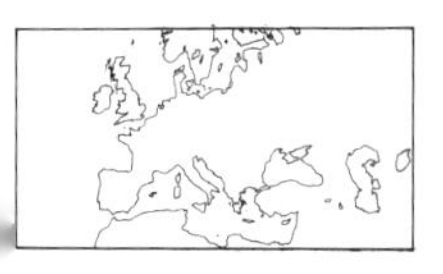

**FALSE DEWY RINGLET** *Erebia sthennyo.* ♂ ups like the Dewy Ringlet, slightly smaller, upf fulvous postdiscal area reduced, the black spots placed closer to the outer margin. ♀ similar. Occurs on the Basses and Hautes Pyrénées, on Spanish and French slopes, eastwards to Salau in Andorra. Flies late June–July at 1900m and over, on alpine grass slopes. Larval food plants probably *Festuca* etc. E.

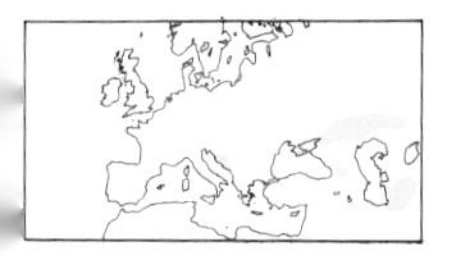

**DALMATIAN RINGLET** *Erebia phegea.* ♂ ups twin post-discal ocelli large, oblique, with small, yellow-ringed ocelli in all other spaces of both wings; ♀ similar, ocelli larger. Occurs in a restricted area in Dalmatia, near the coast (Zara, Sibenik). Flies May on rough ground near the coast. Appears to be very local and rare. Larval food plant not known. Range extends to S Russia, C Asia (Turkmenia), and Iran.

**Chapman's Ringlet**

♀ f. *roberti*

**Dewy Ringlet**

**Dalmatian Ringlet**

**False Dewy Ringlet**

**The Meadow Browns.** This is an extensive group in the warmer regions of C Asia.

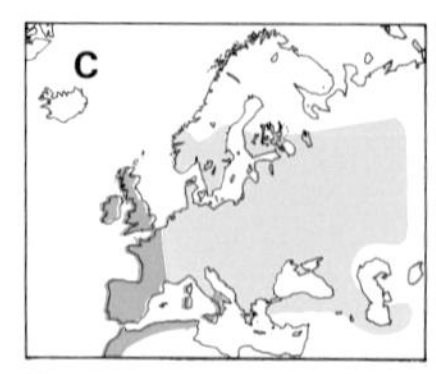


**MEADOW BROWN** *Maniola jurtina.* ♂ upf with a single pd ocellus, with or usually without, fulvous pd markings, sex-brand prominent. ♀ ups with extensive orange-yellow markings. Widely distributed and usually common throughout the region, from the Canary Islands and N Africa to 62°N, and east to the Baltic countries, Carpathians, Greece and Mediterranean islands. Locally variable with two major subspecies defined by genitalia characters. Flies June–July from sea level to 1800m, over rough, grassy places, in a single protracted brood. Larval food plants *Poa* etc. **Map 43**

*M. j. jurtina.* ♂ upf fulvous discal mark vestigial or more often absent, specimens small or rather small. ♀ upf ocellus small. Both sexes locally variable. Occurs in NE France, S Scandinavia, Italy and across C and S Europe to Balkan countries and Greece. Usually small in northern range but larger and more brightly marked in Greece and Crete.

*M. j. hispulla,* Large in SW Europe and N Africa; ♂ upf fulvous discal patch rarely absent, otherwise marked as in *M. j. jurtina.* Occurs in Britain, including Ireland, Isle of Man, Scotland including Orkney Isles, W France, Pyrenees and Spain, and all larger Mediterranean Islands excepting Crete. ♀ ups usually more brightly marked, ocellus large. Specimens from W Scotland, f. *splendida,* are often surprisingly brightly marked; similar specimens are found on the Isle of Man.

*M. j. fortunata* occurs on the Canary Islands (Tenerife). Both sexes very large, ♂ upf with vestigial pd flush; ♀ usually very handsome, ups with extensive brilliant fulvous markings. These large brightly marked forms appear in S France, and become more striking in Spain and N Africa in an obvious cline. All are referable to *M. j. hispulla* by genitalia characters. The two subspecies *M. j. jurtina* and *M. j. hispulla* integrate over a wide belt in Holland, Belgium and NE France to the Rhine in W Germany.

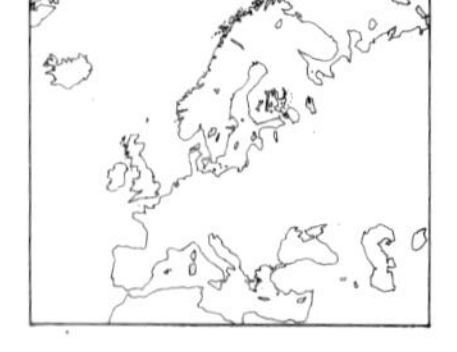

**SARDINIAN MEADOW BROWN** *Maniola nurag.* Ups in both sexes like the Meadow Brown, smaller, ups postdiscal fulvous areas extensive. Occurs in Sardinia. Flies mid-June–July, from 350–1500m, locally common on heaths and roadsides, but very local. Larval food plant not known. E.

**MOROCCAN MEADOW BROWN** *Hyponephele maroccana.* ♂ upf with fulvous postdiscal area, sex-brand narrow. ♀ upf fulvous area extensive, ocelli large. Occurs in Morocco, local in the High Atlas. Flies May–August over dry, rocky slopes at altitudes of 1800–2700m, in a single brood; often common. In the Middle Atlas at 2000m or more, on the Taghzeft Pass, *H. m. nivellei*, smaller and paler. Occurs also in Er Rif. E.

NE France, S Scandinavia, Italy, C & S Europe to Balkans & Greece

♀ SW Europe
& N Africa

**Meadow Brown**

**Sardinian Meadow Brown**

High Atlas
Middle Atlas

♂ Taghzeft Pass

**Moroccan Meadow Brown**

Dusky Meadow Brown

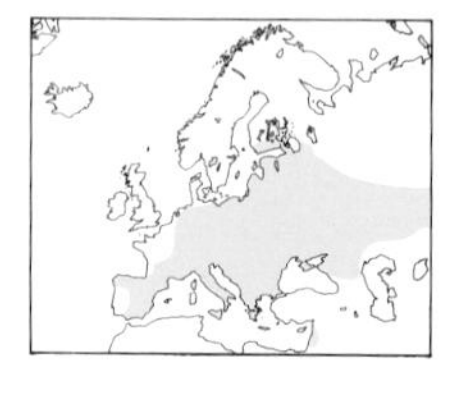

**DUSKY MEADOW BROWN** *Hyponephele lycaon.* ♂ ups grey-brown; upf sex-brand narrow, ocellus in space 2 uncommon, *sex-brand narrow*, hw outer margin scalloped. ♀ upf yellow-fulvous, ocellus in space 2 constant. From C Spain, S and C France to Lithuania and Finland at 62°N, and across Europe to S Romania, Bulgaria and Greece. Absent from Portugal, NW Europe and Mediterranean islands except Sicily. Flies late June–August, from lowlands to 1800m, on dry stony slopes and heaths. The range extends east to the Lebanon and across Russia to the Altai Mts. Larva p. 224.

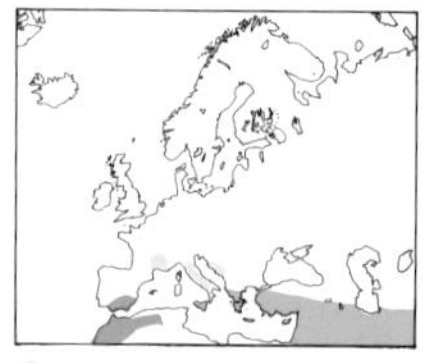

*H.l. lupina*
*H.l. rhamnusia*
*H.l. mauretanica*

**ORIENTAL MEADOW BROWN** *Hyponephele lupina.* Like the Dusky Meadow Brown. ♂ ups grey-brown, often with yellowish gloss, *sex-brand* wide; hw outer margin scalloped. ♀ upf ocelli prominent, broadly ringed pale fulvous. Occurs in N Africa, Spain and across S Europe, north to 48°N in Czechoslovakia, and east to the Balkans and Greece. Flies July–August in a single brood. Larval food plant not recorded. Range extends across S Russia and Asia Minor to C Asia and S Siberia. Locally variable, three subspecies.

*H. l. lupina*, in C Italy (local), S Italy. Orvieto, Lecce etc. ♂ small, ups with golden reflections; in Dalmatia and Macedonia very similar.

*H. l. rhamnusia*, ♂ large, fw 26–28mm, ups golden gloss very marked, hw outer margin deeply scalloped. ♀ often larger, unh pale grey, obscurely marbled white. Flies in bushy country at 700–800m; Sicily at Isnello, Ficuzza etc., local but not rare; Crete, Greece (Peloponnesos) slightly smaller.

*H. l. mauretanica*, ♂ rather small, ups grey-brown, lacks golden suffusion. Common and widely distributed in Morocco, Algeria, Portugal, Spain, flying at 800m or more on hot, dry slopes; sits for shade in bushes. Very local in SE France.

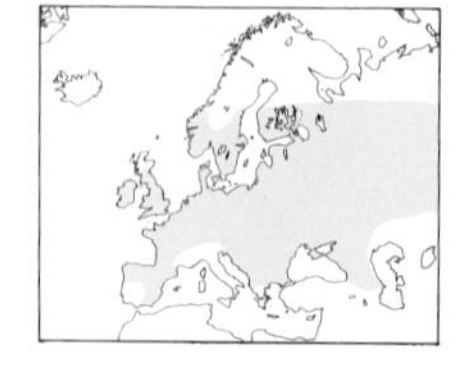

**RINGLET** *Aphantopus hyperantus.* ♂ ups almost black, often unmarked; uns paler, ocelli yellow-ringed, prominent. ♀ ups paler brown, ocelli present on both surfaces. Widely distributed and usually common from N Spain across C Europe to S Fennoscandia (64°N), and eastwards to N Greece. Absent from S and C Spain, Portugal, peninsular Italy and Mediterranean islands. Flies June–July in damp, grassy places, often in open woodland, from sea level to 1500m. In N Europe specimens often small. Larval food plants *Poa, Milium, Carex.* Range extends across Russia and Siberia to the Amur. Larva p. 226.

**Map 44**

♂ C & S Italy ♀ Morocco, Algeria & Iberia

**Oriental Meadow Brown**

♂

**Ringlet**

**The Pyronias.** An interesting feature of this small group is its distribution, so characteristic of the Mediterranean Subregion. A single species, the Gatekeeper, has been able to extend its distribution to southern England. Specific characters are most prominent on the undersides of the hind-wings. ♂ sex-brands extensive in all species.

**GATEKEEPER** *Pyronia tithonus.* ♂ upf apical ocellus with twin white pupils, sex-brand prominent. ♀ larger. Rather local but widely distributed in S and C Europe to 52°N, including S Ireland, S England, Spain and Greece; also N Morocco (Er Rif), Sardinia, Corsica and Elba. Absent from S Italy, Sicily and other Mediterranean islands, and broadly absent from the high Alps. Larval food plants *Poa* and other grasses. Flies July–August. Range extends to Asia Minor, S Russia and the Caucasus. **Map 45**

♂ ♀

**Gatekeeper**

♂ **Southern Gatekeeper** ♀

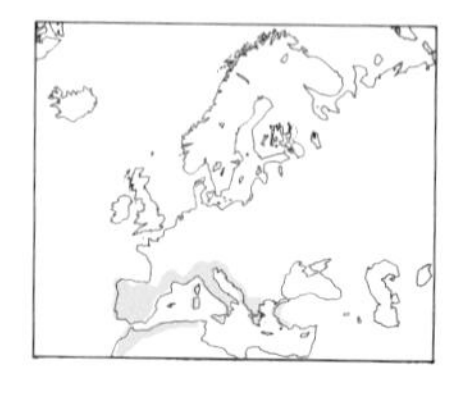

**SOUTHERN GATEKEEPER** *Pyronia cecilia.* ♂ ups like the Gatekeeper, upf sex-brand conspicuous, divided by veins; unh brown, marbled pale grey. ♀ larger. Widely distributed and often common in Morocco, Algeria, Tunisia, Portugal, Spain, north to S Switzerland and across S Europe to Dalmatia, Albania and Greece, including the Balearics and other Mediterranean islands except Crete. Flies May–August over rough ground, from lowlands to 2000m or more in Morocco. Larval food plant *Deschampsia*. Range extends to Asia Minor. Larva p. 226.

*P.b. bathseba*
*P.b. pardilloi*

**SPANISH GATEKEEPER** *Pyronia bathseba.* ♂ unh brown, a yellow discal stripe is prominent; upf base usually dark brown. ♀ larger. Occurs locally in N Africa and SW Europe. Flies April–July, perhaps in more than a single brood, on rough ground or light woodland, usually at low altitudes rising to 1500m in Morocco. Larval food plant *Brachypodium*. Locally variable with two subspecies. E.

*P. b. bathseba*, in Morocco, Algeria and S Spain. ♂ small, unh yellow discal band narrow, ocelli small or vestigial.

*P. b. pardilloi*, in Portugal, C and N Spain, E Pyrenees and SE France. ♂ larger, unh yellow discal band wider, ocelli well developed. ♀ larger.

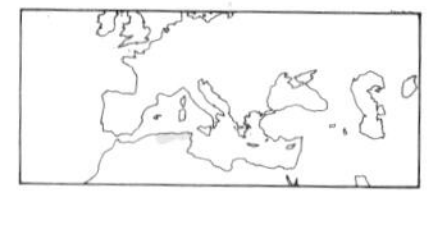

**FALSE MEADOW BROWN** *Pyronia janiroides.* ♂ upf base brown, fulvous postdiscal area reduced. ♀ upf fulvous area extensive. Occurs in E Algeria and Tunisia. Flies July–September on rough ground, usually at low altitudes. Larval food plant not known. E.

♂ Morocco, Algeria & S Spain ♀ Portugal, C & S Spain, E Pyrenees & SE France

**Spanish Gatekeeper**

♂ ♀

**False Meadow Brown**

**The Small Heaths.** Small butterflies, the sexes similar or nearly so. On the upperside buff or brown, the fore-wing often has a single apical (postdiscal) ocellus; the hind-wing underside has five or six submarginal ocelli, but few other markings. The group is well defined, with the bases of vein 12, median and sub-median veins all greatly swollen; the precostal vein of the hind-wing absent. In other anatomical characters the members are exceedingly uniform. With a single exception (Large Heath, widespread in N America), the species are confined to the Palaearctic Region, especially numerous in W Europe and N Africa.

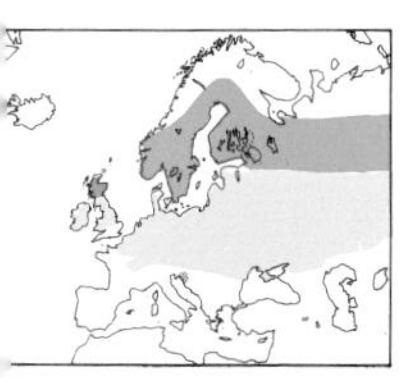

*C.t.tullia*
*C.t.demophile*
*C.t.scotica*
*C.t.lorkovici*

**LARGE HEATH** *Coenonympha tullia.* ♂ ups pale buff to medium brown, without dark marginal borders (distinction from the Small Heath); unh with or without submarginal ocelli. ♀ ups usually paler, markings better defined. Flies late June–July over bogs and moorlands where Cotton Grass grows. Larval food plants *Eriophorum* and *Rhynchospora alba*. Very variable with numerous named forms. Range extends across Russia to the Amur and in N America through the Rocky Mts to Colorado and California. Three major subspecies defined in Europe. **Map 46**

*C. t. tullia*, from Britain and Denmark across north-central Europe. ♂ ups pale buff to light brown, unf a pale pd stripe well developed, unh grey, shading to brown, white markings and ocelli usually prominent. In N England and parts of Bavaria f. *rothliebii*, ♂ darker brown, in both sexes uns heavily marked, unh ocelli in complete series.

*C. t. demophile*, in mountainous and boreal regions of Fennoscandia to 70°N. Small, ♂ ups paler, ♀ yellow-buff, uns white markings often prominent, unh grey, ocelli vestigial or absent. In Ireland, Scotland north of 56°N, including Orkney Islands and Hebrides, *C. t. scotica*, similar but larger.

*C. t. lorkovici*, a remarkable race recently described from Bosnia, where it flies July, and perhaps August near Jaice at low altitudes in rather sparse, scattered colonies. ♂ ups gc dark, like f. *rothliebii*, the usual markings well developed. ♀ ups paler and larger. A special feature is the large size of both sexes, ♀-fw 19–25mm, as large as a Meadow Brown. It is interesting to compare this with the much smaller *Coenonympha rhodopensis* which flies in the neighbouring Dinaric Alps at altitudes of 1000m or more.

♂

Britain & Denmark across N central Europe

♂ f. *rothliebii*

♂ Ireland & N Scotland

♂ Fennoscandia

**Large Heath**

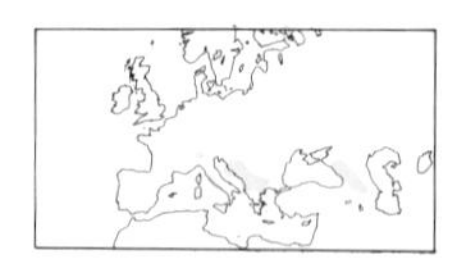

**BALKAN HEATH** *Coenonympha rhodopensis.* Small, ups yellow-brown, ♀ yellow-buff; unf pale pd stripe absent in both sexes, rarely vestigial; unh grey, often shading to yellow-brown, pale markings reduced to a single small white spot beyond cell, ocelli variable, often reduced or absent. A mountain species flying June–July at 1500m or more, rarely down to 1000m, in Bulgaria, Yugoslavia, Albania and N Greece; Romania (Retezat Mts), Italy on Monte Baldo and C Apennines (Monte Terminillo etc.) f. *italica*.

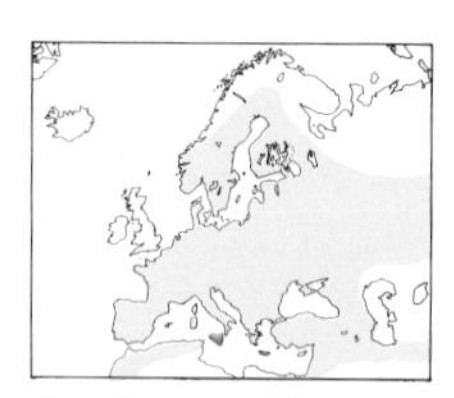

C.p.pamphilus
C.p.thyris
C.p.t.f.sicula

**SMALL HEATH** *Coenonympha pamphilus.* Like the Large Heath; ups yellow-buff, wings with *grey marginal borders* (distinction from the Large Heath). Sexes similar. Common and generally distributed in N Africa and Europe to 68°N. Flies April–September in grassy places, at all altitudes to 1800m. Seasonal and local variation is marked, with two subspecies. Larval food plants *Poa, Nardus stricta, Cynosurus.* Range extends across S Russia and Asia Minor to the Caucasus, C Asia and S Siberia. **Map 47**

*C. p. pamphilus*, occurs in N Africa and all Europe except Sicily and Crete. First brood unh grey, basal area often darker, bordered externally by a white mark from costa, ocelli obscure. In late broods, July and later, characters scarcely differ in N and C Europe. In S Europe, f. *marginata*, ups marginal borders wider and darker, unh often not grey but brown (f. *latecana*). In N Africa, Portugal, Spain, S France, S Italy and Greece, f–aest. *lyllus*, unf with a reddish, postdiscal stripe and silvery premarginal line; unh pale buff, the basal area and ocellar region often brown.

*C. p. thyrsis*, on Crete. Ups always f. *marginata*, unh pale buff, ocelli well defined with silver pupils, base and ocellar area shaded grey-brown. On Sicily, f. *sicula*, in second brood very similar, but unh dark markings less emphasized (normal in first brood). In Crete the subspecific characters are present also in the first brood.

♂

**Corsican Heath**

♂

**Elban Heath**

**CORSICAN HEATH** *Coenonympha corinna.* ♂ small, ups bright fulvous; unh basal area bounded by very irregular yellowish band, ocelli inconspicuous, absent in space 5, most prominent in space 6. ♀ ups paler. Common on Corsica and Sardinia. Flies May and throughout the summer with a succession of broods, from sea level to 1500m in grassy places. Larval food plants not known. E.

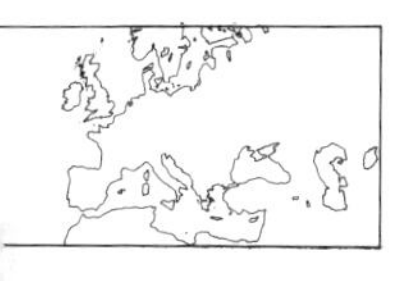

**ELBAN HEATH** *Coenonympha elbana.* Ups like the Corsican Heath but unh yellow postdiscal band more regular, narrower, ocelli well developed, usually present uph. Occurs on Elba, Giglio and in Italy on Monte Argentario and surrounding mainland. Flies June–September at low altitudes. Larval food plant not known. E.

*C.d.dorus*
*C.d.fettigii*

**DUSKY HEATH** *Coenonympha dorus.* ♂ ups variable; uph fulvous below vein 5, often enclosing 4–5 black ocellar spots in curved row. ♀ ups fulvous. Widely distributed in SW Europe, Morocco and Algeria, with marked local variation and two major subspecies. Flies June–July in a single brood, often on barren slopes, from lowlands to 2000m or more. Larval food plants *Agrostis alba, Festuca* etc. E.

*C. d. dorus*, in Spain, Portugal and SE France. ♀ ups grey-brown; unh ocelli well developed. Widely distributed, often common. In NE Spain and N Portugal (Galicia, Alijo) f. *bieli*, ups dark brown, uph fulvous area vestigial if present. In C Italy (Abruzzi) f. *aquilonia*, upf has a fulvous discal band.

*C. d. fettigii*, in Morocco, Algeria. ♂ ups like *C. d. aquilonia*, upf grey-brown with fulvous postdiscal band; uph postdiscal spots usually absent; unh pale yellow-grey, ocelli minute if present. ♀ ups fulvous.

♂

♀

♂ f. *bieli*

Spain, Portugal & SE France

♂ Morocco & Algeria

**Dusky Heath**

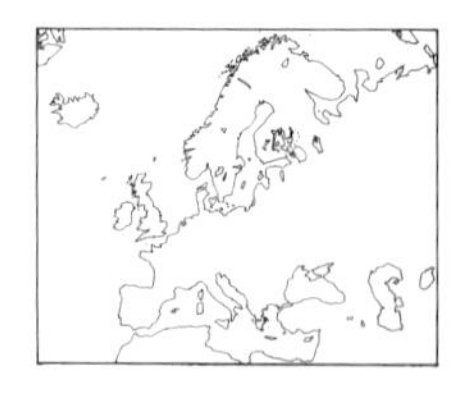

**AUSTAUT'S ALGERIAN HEATH** *Coenonympha austauti.* ♂ Like the Dusky Heath (*C. d. fettigii*) but upf apical ocellus larger and postdiscal area suffused buff; unh dark basal area bordered by a narrow, silvery white stripe. ♀ ups like the Dusky Heath. Occurs in Algeria in Oran, near Nemours at Masser Mines, Lalla Marnia, Zough-el-Beghal etc., probably at low altitudes near the coast. The Dusky Heath (*C. fettigii*) is known to occur on the neighbouring mountains. Flies June–July and later, over a long period. Larval food plant not known. E.

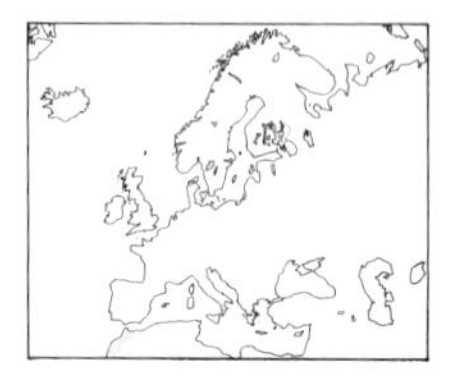

**VAUCHER'S HEATH** *Coenonympha vaucheri.* Upf apical ocellus large, white pupil absent. Occurs in Morocco, in the High Atlas, flying over barren slopes with grass at 2700m. In the Middle Atlas, *C. v. annoceuri*, small, markings similar but less brilliant. Flies June–July at 1800–2000m at Annoceur, Taghzeft Pass etc. A rather similar small race, *C. v. rifensis*, occurs in Er Rif. On upf the size of the ocellus is reduced, the dark marginal border narrow. Recorded from Targuist and Ketama in late July flying at 2000m. Larval food plant not known. E.

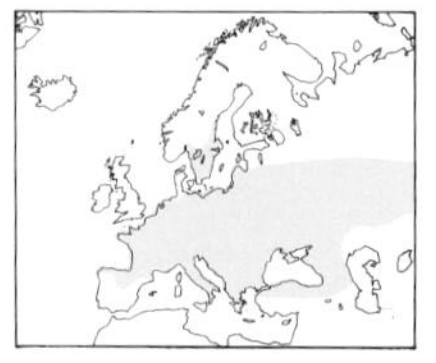

**PEARLY HEATH** *Coenonympha arcania.* Unh irregular white postdiscal band conspicuous, ocellus in space 6 is internal to band, within the dark basal area. Locally common in C and N Spain and almost all W Europe to 60°N, including peninsular Italy, Balkans and Greece. Absent from Britain, S Spain and Mediterranean islands. Usually has a single brood, June–July, sometimes a partial late brood in S Europe; most common at valley levels but occasionally to 2000m (Pyrenees), on grassy slopes, light woodland etc. Larval food plant *Melica, Bromus, Festuca.* Range extends across S Russia, Asia Minor and Caucasus to the Ural Mts.

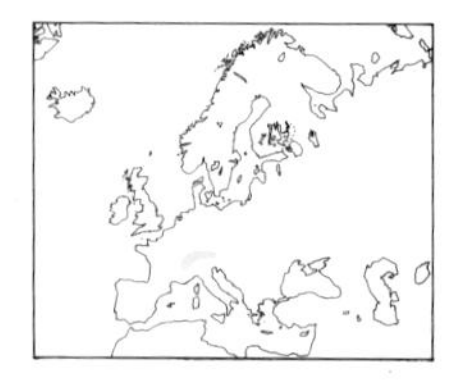

**DARWIN'S HEATH** *Coenonympha darwiniana.* Like the Pearly Heath but smaller. Uph very dark; unh the white postdiscal band is narrower, the ocellus in space 6 is within the band. ♀ ups slightly paler. Local in Maritime Alps, Basses Alpes, and in S Switzerland in the Valais, Tessin, Graubünden and eastwards to Mendel, Schlern and ?Dolomites. Flies July–August in localized colonies over subalpine meadows, rarely below 1500m. The species is easily confused with the Alpine Heath which occurs in the same districts, usually flying at higher altitudes. E.

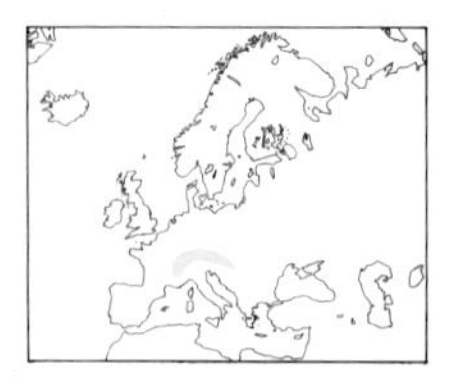

**ALPINE HEATH** *Coenonympha gardetta.* Ups both wings grey-brown, slightly variable; upf with or without fulvous discal suffusion; unf apex grey; unh grey, white postdiscal band regular, often rather wide, enclosing small ocelli. Occurs in the Alps of Savoie and eastwards across Switzerland, including the Bavarian Alps and Tirol to the Dolomites, Hohe Tauern and Karawanken Alps; absent from Carpathians and Balkans. Flies July–August over flowery alpine slopes at 2000m or more. In the Carnic Alps, Venezia Giulia etc. sometimes at 1500m, f. *macrophthalmica*, unf grey apical shade sometimes absent; unh ocelli larger, in a regular row. Larval food plant not known. E.

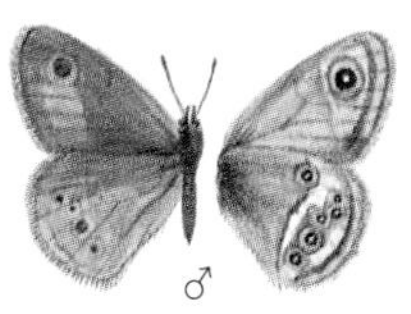

♂

Austaut's Algerian Heath

♂

Vaucher's Heath

♂

Pearly Heath

♂

Darwin's Heath

♂ f. *macrophthalmica*

♂

Alpine Heath

♂

Moroccan Pearly Heath

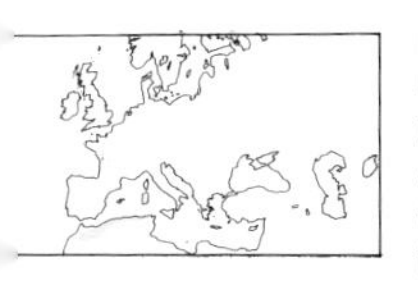

**MOROCCAN PEARLY HEATH** *Coenonympha arcanioides*. Unh dark brown with a narrow white postdiscal stripe. Occurs in Morocco, Algeria and Tunisia. Flies April–September with continuous broods, common near the coasts and in mountains to 1500m on the northern slopes of the Middle Atlas. Larval food plants not known. E.

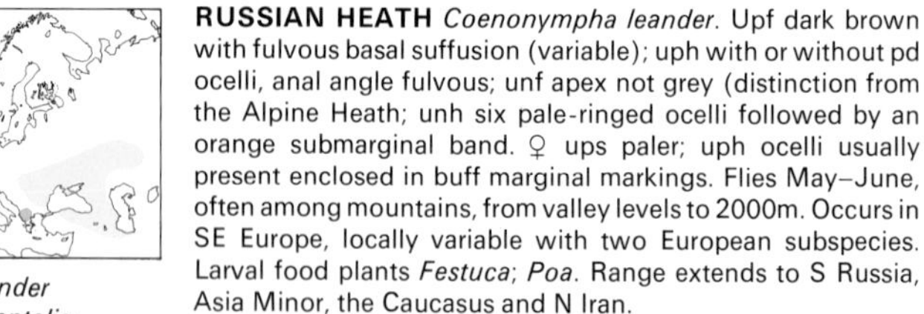

*C.l. leander*
*C.l. orientalis*

**RUSSIAN HEATH** *Coenonympha leander*. Upf dark brown with fulvous basal suffusion (variable); uph with or without pd ocelli, anal angle fulvous; unf apex not grey (distinction from the Alpine Heath; unh six pale-ringed ocelli followed by an orange submarginal band. ♀ ups paler; uph ocelli usually present enclosed in buff marginal markings. Flies May–June, often among mountains, from valley levels to 2000m. Occurs in SE Europe, locally variable with two European subspecies. Larval food plants *Festuca*; *Poa*. Range extends to S Russia, Asia Minor, the Caucasus and N Iran.

*C. l. leander*, unh ocelli ringed pale buff to whitish, which may extend slightly into pd area. Very local in the Carpathians, Bulgaria and NW Greece.

*C. l. orientalis*, unh the pale ocellar rings extend widely into the pd area, forming a prominent white pd band, best developed in females. Occurs in S Bosnia (Stolac) and NW Greece (Pindus Mts).

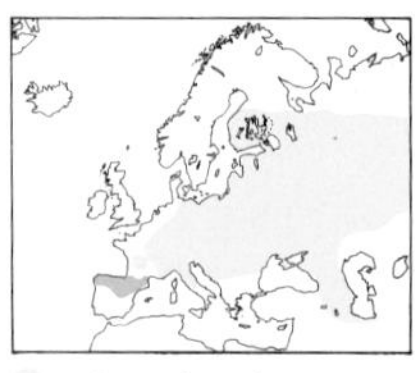

*C.g. glycerion*
*C.g. iphioides*

**CHESTNUT HEATH** *Coenonympha glycerion*. ♂ ups chestnut-brown; unh with small, white postdiscal mark in space 4, internal to the ocelli; a narrow, orange marginal line is sometimes incomplete. ♀ ups paler. Widely distributed in W Europe to 56°N, absent from the W Pyrenees, NW Europe and Mediterranean islands. Locally variable with two major subspecies. Flies June–July in a single brood, often in damp grass, usually in mountains at 700–1500m or more. Larval food plants *Brachypodium, Melica* etc. E.

*C. g. glycerion*, from E Pyrenees and C France to Switzerland and S Germany, Lithuania, Hungary and the Balkans (Sarajevo); isolated colonies also in N Spain (Huesca, Albarracin) and in Italy (Abruzzi). Small, unh ocelli small or vestigial, white post-discal markings often extended near anal angle. Range extends across S Russia to the Altai Mts and W Siberia.

*C. g. iphioides*, in N and C Spain. Larger, size variable; like *C. g. glycerion* but unh ocelli larger, white postdiscal mark in space 4 often very small but never absent. At high levels f. *pearsoni*, smaller, with characters transitional to *C. g. glycerion*. *C. g. iphioides* is graded with specific rank by many authors.

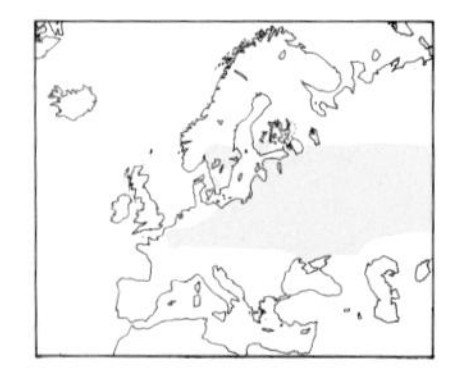

**SCARCE HEATH** *Coenonympha hero*. ♂ ups dark grey-brown; unh ocelli ringed orange, preceded by white post-discal band. A very local species; colonies widely scattered in NE France, S Germany, Czechoslovakia, S Fennoscandia and Baltic countries. Flies May–early June at low altitudes in damp meadows and bogs. Larval food plant *Elymus arenarius*. Range extends across Asia to Siberia and Japan.

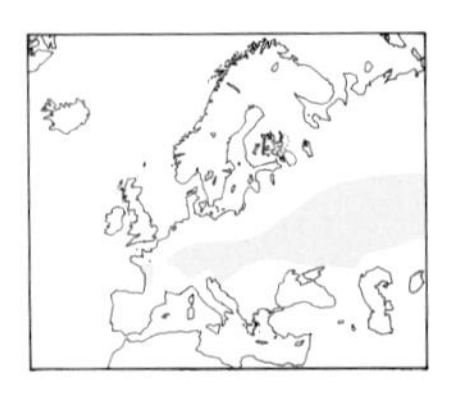

**FALSE RINGLET** *Coenonympha oedippus*. ♂ ups dark brown; unh ocelli usually large, black and yellow-ringed, sometimes present also unf near outer margin, most common in ♀. Very local in widely scattered colonies, in SW France, N Italy (Po valley), Vorarlberg, Slovakia, Austria, Hungary, Venezia Giulia. In some colonies in Hungary, f. *hungarica*, unh ocelli greatly reduced in size. Flies June–July at low altitudes in damp meadows, open woodland etc. Larval food plants *Lolium, Carex, Iris pseudacorus*. Range extends across Russia and Siberia to Japan.

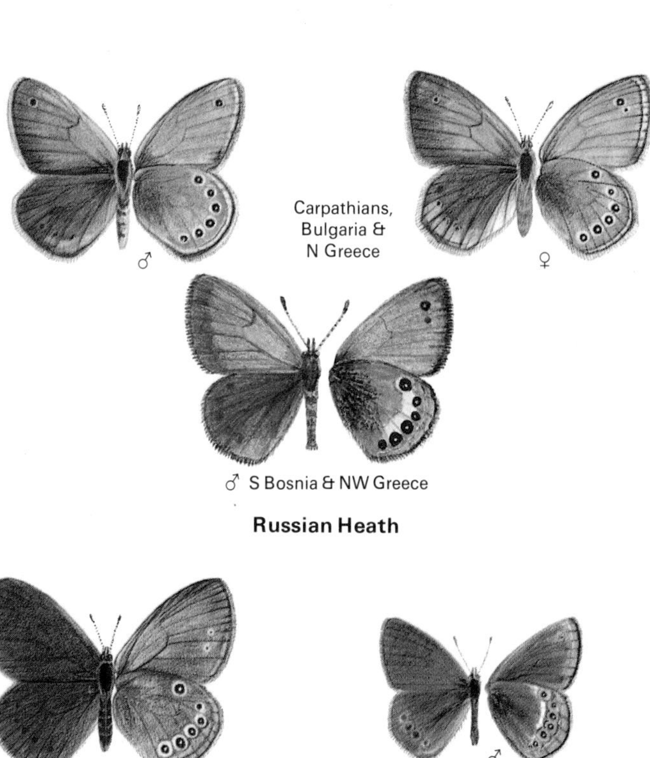

Carpathians, Bulgaria & N Greece

♂ S Bosnia & NW Greece

**Russian Heath**

**False Ringlet**

**Scarce Heath**

E Pyrenees, C France to Switzerland, S Germany, Lithuania, Balkans etc

N & C Spain

**Chestnut Heath**

**The Wall Browns and Speckled Woods.** These butterflies belong to a group which differs in several respects from other European Satyrids. On the upperside the wing-markings are more reticulate or bizarre, all far removed from the common plan with a dark wing-base and a coloured postdiscal band. All have hairy eyes and their wing-veins are arranged differently. Some are distributed across Asia to Japan; others all reach C Asia, none is a European endemic. The males have a prominent sex-brand upf, the absence of which in females makes them more brightly marked.

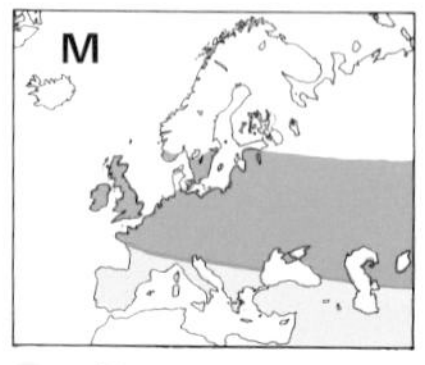


*P.a. aegeria*
*P.a. tircis*

**SPECKLED WOOD** *Pararge aegeria.* ♂ ups fulvous to pale buff, upf with dark brown lattice pattern. Widely distributed in W Europe, including N Africa and Madeira. There is marked local variation with two major subspecies. Flies in successive broods throughout the summer, March–September, in light woodland, often in partial shade, from sea level to 1200m or more. Larval food plants *Agropyron, Triticum repens.*

**Map 48**

*P. a. aegeria*, in S France, Switzerland (Sudschweiz, Valais), Italy south of the Alps, all S Europe including the Mediterranean Islands, N Africa and recently discovered in Madeira, ♂ ups bright foxy-fulvous. Range extends across Asia Minor to Syria and Lebanon.

*P. a. tircis*, in N, C and E Europe to 62°N, in its southern range blending in a cline with *P. a. aegeria*, which it resembles closely, but ups ground-colour pale buff, slightly variable. Flies in N France, Britain, Fennoscandia and across C Europe to Yugoslavia, shading towards *P. a. aegeria* in Greece. Range extends across S Russia to the Caucasus and C Asia.

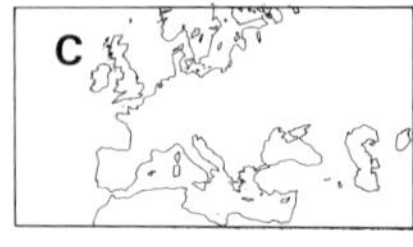


**CANARY SPECKLED WOOD** *Pararge xiphioides.* Like *P. a. aegeria* but slightly larger, unh the basal area is defined by a short white band from the costa. Flies throughout the year on all the larger islands from sea level to 2000m or more. Common and wide-spread.

**MADEIRAN SPECKLED WOOD** *Pararge xiphia.* Like the Canary Island butterfly but larger, the fore-wing more pointed, the hind-wing elongate. Ups the dark brown markings extended. Occurs on Madeira, and there common and widely distributed to 1500m or more, April–October, perhaps flies throughout the year.

*L.m. megera*
*L.m. paramegaera*

**WALL BROWN** *Lasiommata megera.* ♂ ups bright fulvous; upf with two dark bars in cell, and oblique sex brand. Flies March and later from sea level to 1500m in open country, usually in two broods. A common species in W Europe, including the Mediterranean Islands and NW Africa, with two subspecies. Larval food plants *Poa, Dactylis.* Range extends to Russia, the Caucasus, Iran and C Asia. **Map 49**

*L. m. megera*, ups pd brown markings well defined on both wings. Occurs in NW Africa and most of Europe to 60°N, including Britain, Fennoscandia and Mediterranean islands except Corsica, and Sardinia.

*L. m. paramegaera*, like *L. m. megera* but smaller; ups pd brown markings vestigial or absent. Confined to Corsica and Sardinia, the distinctive character best defined in specimens from Corsica.

♂ S France, Switzerland, S Europe
N Africa & Madeira

♀ N, C & E Europe

**Speckled Wood**

♂

**Canary Speckled Wood**

♂

**Madeiran Speckled Wood**

♂

♀

NW Africa & most Europe

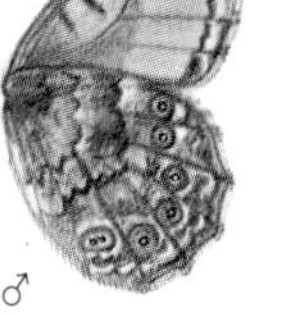

♂

♀

Corsica & Sardinia

**Wall Brown**

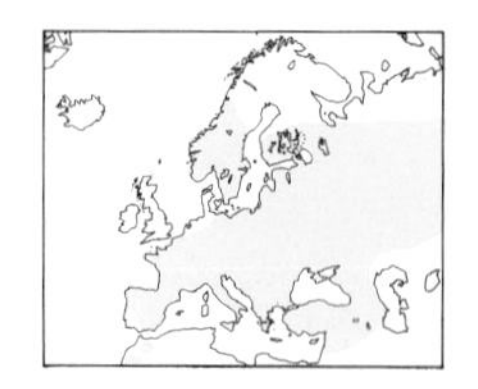

**LARGE WALL BROWN** *Lasiommata maera*. ♂ ups wing-bases brown; upf with a single dark bar in cell. ♀ upf postdiscal fulvous markings prominent. Widely distributed in Europe to 68°N, often common in mountains; less common in S Spain, local and rare in N Africa (Middle and High Atlas). Absent from Britain, Corsica, Sardinia, Elba and Crete. Flies from sea level to 1800m in Europe, and to 2400m in the High Atlas, on rough, open ground and on rocky paths, usually in two broods June–July and August–September, a single brood in the north. Locally variable on a cline, dark forms in the north, fulvous markings increased in southern districts, usually described as subspecies. Larval food plants *Poa*, *Glyceria fluitans* etc. Range extends across S Russia, Asia Minor and Syria to Iran, C Asia and Pakistan. Larva p. 226.

*L. m. maera*, in Europe north of the Alps. ♂ ups postdiscal fulvous markings reduced or vestigial. ♀ upf basal area dark. In Fennoscandia, f. *borealis*, males often small, females postdiscal fulvous bands yellowish.

*L. m. adrasta*, in S Alps, peninsular Italy, Spain etc. ♂ ups fulvous post-discal markings present in a band broken by dark veins. ♀ upf basal area not dark, brightly marked.

*L. m. meadwaldoi*, in S Spain and N Africa. Upf postdiscal markings more extensive but rather obscure; upf apical ocellus large, often bipupilled. In late broods (Aug–Sept) specimens usually smaller, ups fulvous markings more extensive.

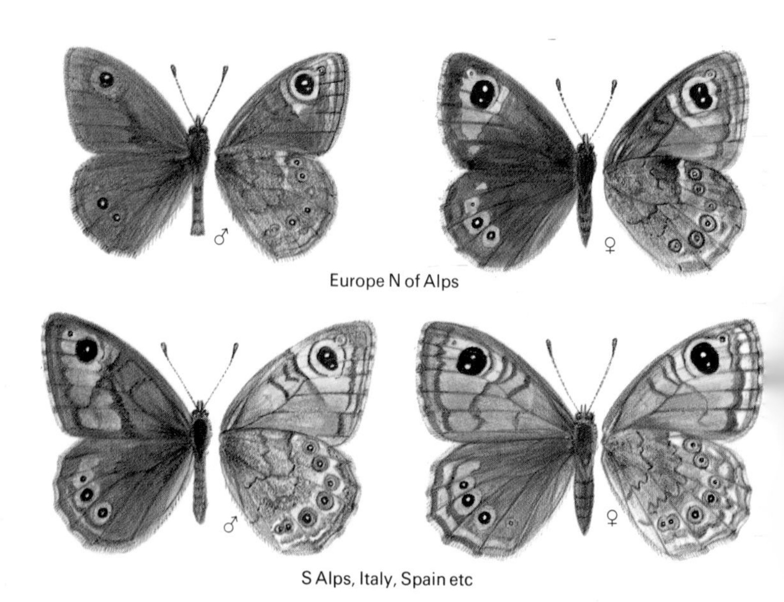


**Large Wall Brown**

Northern Wall Brown

Woodland Brown

**NORTHERN WALL BROWN** *Lasiommata petropolitana.* Like the Large Wall Brown but smaller; uph has an angled, dark discal line, often poorly defined, present in both sexes. Occurs on all the higher mountains in the Pyrenees, Alps, Carpathians and Balkans to N Greece, also in Fennoscandia to 68°N. Absent from Spain, Portugal, Jura, Vosges and Apennines. Flies May–July, at high altitudes to 2000m in C Europe, but at low levels in the far North, usually among Spruce trees or pines; often common. Larval food plant *Festuca.* Range extends across Russia, Caucasus and N Siberia to the Amur.

**WOODLAND BROWN** *Lopinga achine.* Ups with large, yellow-ringed, blind ocelli on both wings. Local in widely scattered colonies from N Spain and France to S Fennoscandia and Baltic countries, and eastwards to the Balkans. Absent from Britain and NW Europe, S and C Spain, Portugal, peninsular Italy, Greece and Mediterranean islands. Flies June at valley levels to 1000m in woodlands. Larval food plants *Lolium, Agropyron.* Range extends across Russia and Asia to the Amur, Ussuri and Japan. Larva p. 244.

**LATTICE BROWN** *Kirinia roxelana.* ♂ fw narrow, distorted by sex-brand, apical ocellus very small. ♀ ups brightly marked. Occurs in Romania, S Balkans, Bulgaria and Greece. Flies late May–July in lowlands, not above 1000m; often shelters in low bushes, rarely flies unless disturbed. Larval food plants esp. *Poa*. Distribution extends across Asia Minor to Syria and Iraq.

**Lattice Brown**

**LESSER LATTICE BROWN** *Kirinia climene*. Like the Lattice Brown, but smaller, ♂ upf sex-brand absent, venation not distorted; unh yellow-grey, ocelli small and with vague paler markings. ♀ slightly larger, ups marking better defined. Single specimens have been reported from Romania, Bulgaria and Yugoslav Macedonia, flying June–July in rough grassy places. Its status as a breeding species within the region is uncertain. Distribution extends to Armenia, Iraq and N Iran.

**Lesser Lattice Brown**

# DANAIDAE

These are large butterflies with tough, flexible wings and an unpleasant smell, unacceptable as food by insect-eating birds and other creatures, i.e. 'protected.' On this account they are often a basis for mimicry by other (edible) butterflies of different groups. In both sexes the front legs are small, without claws and useless for walking, a character that shows relationship to the great Nymphalid butterfly group. Males of many species have sex-brands on their wings, and within their bodies are large hair-pencils, peculiar to this family, which are everted during mating. On the larvae, the usual Nymphalid spines are replaced by soft, finger-like appendages. The pupae, pendant by the tail, often show brilliant metallic reflections.

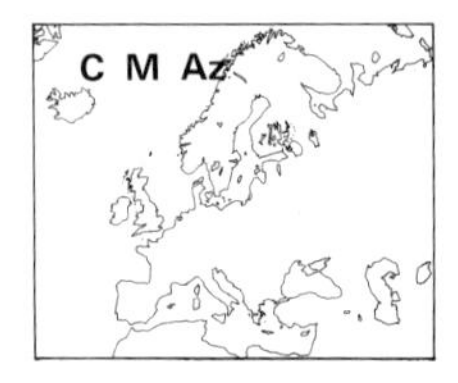


**MONARCH** *Danaus plexippus*. Sexes similar; head, thorax and legs black with small white spots; all veins lined black; uph a small male sex-brand on vein 2. Within the region resident in the Canary Islands on Tenerife, Gran Canary, La Palma, Hierro and perhaps on other islands. It flies throughout the year, especially at low altitudes and in the public gardens, near its food-plant *Asclepias curassavica*, grown as an ornamental plant. It occurs also on Madeira and in the Azores, possibly resident. The species is among the most remarkable migrants known among butterflies. Originally from N America, it is known as an occasional immigrant over coastal areas of Portugal, France, Britain, Holland etc. It is represented by local forms and subspecies over a vast area in C and S America and much of the Indo-Australian Region.

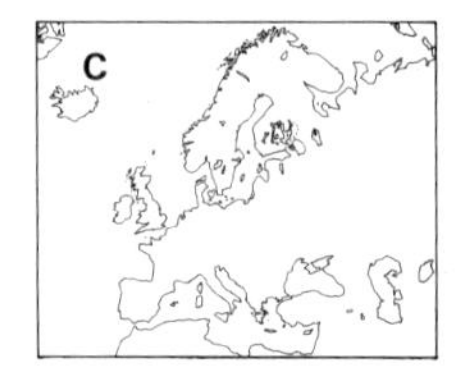


**PLAIN TIGER** *Danaus chrysippus*. Like the Monarch, but ups veins not lined black; ♂ uph sex-brand present on vein 2. In all specimens seen from the Canary Islands, the white apical markings have been present on the fore-wing, and the hind-wing has been buff. Originally from C Africa, the butterfly occurs March–September on Gomera, Gran Canaria, La Palma and Tenerife, usually in the public gardens flying with the Monarch. Occasionally recorded from S Italy, Crete etc. Larval food plants *Asclepias*. Very widely distributed across Africa and S Asia to Japan and N Australia.

Monarch

Plain Tiger

# HESPERIIDAE
## The Skippers

In their physical characters and in their habits these small butterflies differ from all the others. All have a wide head, the antennae set wide apart, and at their bases are short bristles, the 'eyelash,' present only in this family. The thorax is rather massive, like that of certain moths. In venation, all veins arise from the wing-bases or from the discoidal cells, and they run un-branched to the costa and outer margins of the wings. All legs are fully formed, the fore-tibia with a small flap (*epiphysis*) present also in the Papilionidae. The larvae are cylindrical, with a large head, living within shelters of leaves or grass, where they remain as a pupa, so that they never move about freely. This is a very large family with hundreds of different species distributed around the world. In Europe we have members of the two principal groups, the Pyrginae, which feed upon flowering plants, making their shelters from leaves, and the Hesperiinae, which feed only upon grass (and other Monocotyledons). These make grass shelters within which they pass their lives as larvae and pupae.

**The Pyrgine Skippers.** Small butterflies with upperside markings of white spots on a dark ground in a uniform pattern. On the fore-wing the postdiscal white spots in spaces 4,5, are out of line with the others, displaced towards the wing-margin. Sexes usually similar, but ♂ has a costal fold on the fw, enclosing scent-scales; the hind-tibia with two pairs of spurs and a hair pencil.

The classification of this group and the critical specific characters, are based upon features present in the male genitalia. Identification by external characters is difficult and uncertain. For further information and figures of male genitalia *see* L. G. Higgins, *The Classification of European Butterflies* (Collins, 1975), pp. 33–58.

*P.m.malvae*
*P.m.malvoides*

**GRIZZLED SKIPPER** *Pyrgus malvae.* Small, ♂ uph pale discal spot prominent, submarginal spots often irregular, small or partly absent; unh yellow-brown, main veins yellowish. ♀ similar. Widespread in Europe, flying from sea level to 2000m in open country with flowers; usually has two broods at low altitudes April–June and August. Larval food plants *Fragaria, Potentilla* etc. Several subspecies are based upon anatomical characters, of which two occur in Europe. Larva p. 230.

**Map 50**

*P. m. malvae*, in C, N and E Europe to 65°N. External markings not distinctive. Ranges across Russia to C Asia and the Amur.

*P. m. malvoides*, occurs from Portugal and Spain across France and S Switzerland to Italy and Sicily. Absent from Corsica, Sardinia, Elba, the Balearic Islands and Crete.

*Note.* In several districts these two butterflies are known to breed freely together.

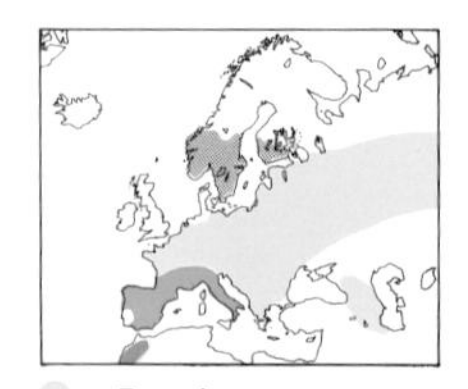

*P.a.alveus*
*P.a.centralhispaniae*
*P.a.numidus*
*P.a.scandinavicus*

**LARGE GRIZZLED SKIPPER** *Pyrgus alveus.* Larger than the Grizzled Skipper, a variable species. ♂ unh pale discal band usually complete, well-defined, pale marks in spaces 4,5 and 6,7, broad. ♀ ups markings somewhat reduced. Widely distributed throughout Europe to 60°N, except in NW, especially common in mountainous districts. Flies June–August at all altitudes to 2000m. Larval food plants *Rubus, Potentilla, Helianthemum.* Range extends to Altai Mts, W Siberia and Tibet.

*P. a. alveus*, in Maritime and Savoie Alps and across C and E Europe to the Tatra, Balkans and N Greece. Absent from Britain and from all Mediterranean islands, except Sicily (?).

Maritime & Savoie Alps, C & E Europe, Tatra Mts, Balkans & N Greece

♂ C Spain, Castile & Aragon

♂ Morocco & Algeria

♂ N Fennoscandia

**Large Grizzled Skipper**

**Grizzled Skipper**

**Foulquier's Grizzled Skipper**

♂ ups white markings usually small, uph dark, markings vestigial. ♀ ups markings small, obscure. Flies July–August.

*P. a. centralhispaniae*, in C Spain, Castile, Aragon (Albarracin) etc. ♂ ups pale markings prominent, uph discal and submarginal markings well defined, easily confused with the Safflower Skipper, in which cell-spot and discal mark are close together (see illustrations). In C Italy, *P. a. centralitaliae*, similar but smaller, very local in the Abruzzi. In the Cantabrian Mts, Pyrenees and through C France, *P. a. accretus*, pale markings well developed, like *P. a. centralhispaniae*, a small distinctive character present in ♂ genitalia. Flies July–August.

*P. a. numidus*, in Morocco and Algeria, large, ups pale markings well developed. Flies June–July in the Middle Atlas at 1500m or more. A well-defined character is present in ♂ genitalia.

*P. a. scandinavicus*, in N Fennoscandia, small, ups white markings rather prominent. A distinctive character is present in ♂ genitalia. Flies July–August.

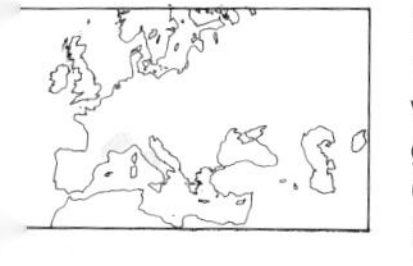

**FOULQUIER'S GRIZZLED SKIPPER** *Pyrgus foulquieri (bellieri)*. Like *P. alveus centralhispaniae*; ups pale markings well developed. Well defined specific characters present in ♂ genitalia. Occurs in S and SE France; also in N Italy in the Cottian Alps, and in C Italy, Abruzzi (*P. f. picenus*), often small. Flies July–August in mountainous country, from valley levels to 2000m. E.

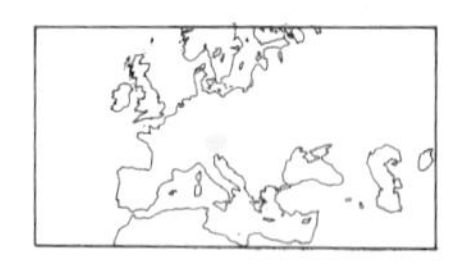

**WARREN'S GRIZZLED SKIPPER** *Pyrgus warrenensis.* Very small, upf white markings minute, uph dark, markings vestigial. Local but not rare at high altitudes 2000m and over, in the E Alps, Engadin, Brenner, Grosser Glockner. May fly July–August with the Large Grizzled Skipper (*P. alveus*). Recorded (not seen) from the Pennine Alps and Grisons. Specific characters present in the ♂ genitalia. E.

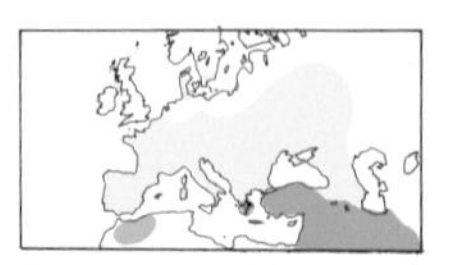

*P.a. armoricanus*
*P.a. maroccanus*
*P.a. persicus*

**OBERTHUR'S GRIZZLED SKIPPER** *Pyrgus armoricanus.* Small, like the Large Grizzled Skipper, but uph pale markings usually better defined. Widely distributed in Europe to 55°N or a little more; also in Morocco and Algeria. Flies May–June and August–September at low altitudes in Europe. Somewhat variable, but geographical races difficult to define. In Morocco, *P. a. maroccanus,* rather large, ups pale markings well defined. Flies in two broods at 1500m. Grecian specimens, *P. a. persicus,* differ in a small character of the genitalia. Range extends to S Russia, Asia Minor, Lebanon, N Iran and C Asia.

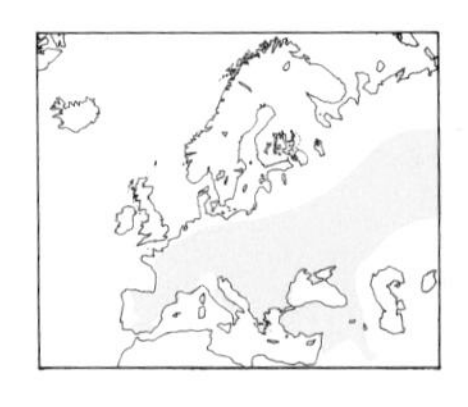

**OLIVE SKIPPER** *Pyrgus serratulae.* Like Oberthur's Grizzled Skipper, ♂ uph markings vestigial; unh olive-grey, without mottling, soon fading to yellow-grey. ♀ upf white markings reduced, often suffused yellowish. Widely distributed from S Spain to 52°N, common in mountainous districts, flies July–August from lowlands to 1800m or more. Size variable, often small, but f. *planorum* in SW France larger; in S Balkans and Greece *P. s. major,* a constant geographical race, also much larger. Larval food plants *Potentilla, Alchemilla.* Range extends across Russia to the Caucasus, C Asia and Suchan.

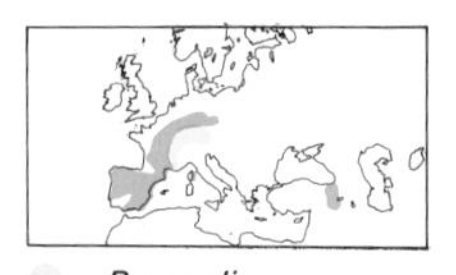

*P.c. carlinae*
*P.c. cirsii*

**CARLINE SKIPPER** *Pyrgus carlinae carlinae.* Like the Olive Skipper, ♂ unh red or yellowish-grey, a pale marginal mark on v4 prominent (distinction from Olive Skipper). ♀ upf white markings greatly reduced. Flies July–August at altitudes of 1600–2300m in the W Alps in France, S Switzerland, Piedmont and the Ticino. Larval food plant *Potentilla verna.* E.

*Pyrgus carlinae cirsii.* Like the Carline Skipper, ♂ ups white markings *prominent,* esp. upf the spot at base of s2; unh discal band narrow. Flies at low altitudes, rarely above 1500m. Occurs widely in Spain, Portugal, France, Corsica, Swiss Jura, S Bavaria and recorded from C Turkey and Armenia. Larval food plant *Potentilla verna.*

Although distinct in external characters and in genitalia structure, these two butterflies are closely related and are known to breed together in areas where their distributions are in contact. Recorded as semi-species by many authors.

**ROSY GRIZZLED SKIPPER** *Pyrgus onopordi.* Ups markings well developed; uph a pale postdiscal mark near costa is usually present and characteristic; unh the 'anvil-shaped' discal pale mark and an elongate mark in space 1c are useful characters. Occurs in Morocco, Algeria, Portugal and Spain (absent in NW), Pyrenees, S and C France to 46°N, S Switzerland and Italy south to Puglia. Absent from Mediterranean islands. Not E of the Adriatic. Flies April–September in two or three broods, in lowlands rising to 1000m in the Apennines, but in Morocco at 1500–2500m, often on flowery meadows. E.

♂

♂ Morocco only

**Oberthur's Grizzled Skipper**

♂

**Warren's Grizzled Skipper**

♂

♀

♂ S Balkans & Greece

**Olive Skipper**

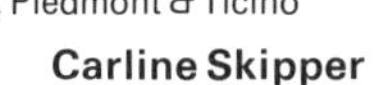

♂

♀

♂

W Alps, S Switzerland, Piedmont & Ticino

Iberia, France, Corsica, etc

**Carline Skipper**

♂

♂

♀

**Rosy Grizzled Skipper**

**Sandy Grizzled Skipper**

*P.c. cinarae*
*P.c. clorinda*

**SANDY GRIZZLED SKIPPER** *Pyrgus cinarae.* Large; ♂ ups all white markings prominent; upf cell-spot large. ♀ ups grey-brown, pale markings small, yellowish, indistinct. In Europe occurs in Macedonia, Bulgaria and N Greece. Local in hilly and mountainous country, usually at a low altitude but rising to the tree-line, flying June on rough, stony ground. Also in C Spain. (*P. c. clorinda*). Larval food plant not known. Range extends to Asia Minor, S Russia, the Crimea, Caucasus and C Asia.

The five species following are of special interest. Their anatomical characters are all very similar, unlike those of the species already described. It is thought that these butterflies represent a primitive group, dating back perhaps for many million years to Tertiary geological times.

♂ Istria, Dalmatia, Yugoslavia to Bulgaria, Macedonia & N Greece

♂ Italy, Provence

**Yellow-banded Skipper**

♂

**Safflower Skipper**

♂

**Alpine Grizzled Skipper**

♂

**Dusky Grizzled Skipper**

♂

**Northern Grizzled Skipper**

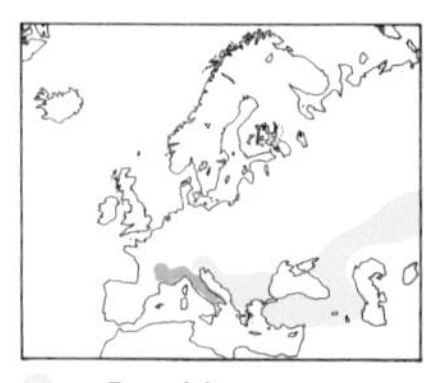

*P.s. sidae*
*P.s. occiduus*

**YELLOW-BANDED SKIPPER** *Pyrgus sidae.* ♂ uph a regular row of submarginal white spots; unh both sexes pale grey, markings bright yellow bordered dark. ♀ similar, often larger. Occurs in SE France, peninsular Italy and SE Europe. Flies June–July at low or moderate altitudes, rarely to 1800m, in flowery meadows. Two subspecies in Europe.

*P. s. sidae*, in Istria, Dalmatia and across Yugoslavia to Bulgaria, Macedonia and N Greece. Very large, not found north of Sarajevo. Larval food plant *Arbutilon avicennae.* Range extends across S Russia, Asia Minor and Iran to the Pamirs, Turkestan and Tian Shan.

*P. s. occiduus*, Italy, from Florence south through the Apennines to Gargano and Lucania; France, only at low levels in Provence (Alpes Maritimes, Var, Hérault etc.). Much smaller, uns colours less brilliant, pale yellow. Variable, in some localities specimens with intermediate characters not rare.

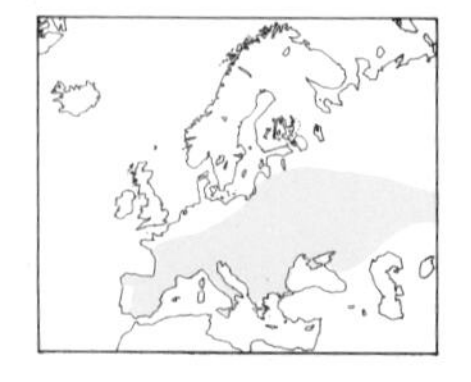

**SAFFLOWER SKIPPER** *Pyrgus carthami (fritillarius).* Ups white markings well developed; uph a regular row of submarginal pale spots; unh yellow-grey between markings. Widely distributed in S and C Europe to Baltic coast, from Spain and Portugal across SE France, Switzerland and eastwards to the Balkans. Absent from NW Europe and the Mediterranean islands. Flies May–July in a single brood, at all levels to 2000m in the Sierra Nevada. Variable in size and development of markings, but subspecific groups not well defined. Larval food plants *Althaea, Malva, Carthamus.* Range extends across S Russia, and Asia Minor.

**ALPINE GRIZZLED SKIPPER** *Pyrgus andromedae.* Ups rather variable; upf a specific character is present in *a small spot at base of space 2, with two small pale spots below* it in space 1b; unh a pale streak and a round spot below it in space 1c. ♀ similar. Occurs in the Pyrenees and high Alps eastwards to the Grosser Glockner. Also in Macedonia on the Schar Planina. In Norway from the Dovrefjeld northwards. Flies June–August in the Alps at high altitudes, 1800m and above. In Norway at lower levels, on Dovrefjeld at 1000m. Larval food plant not known. E?

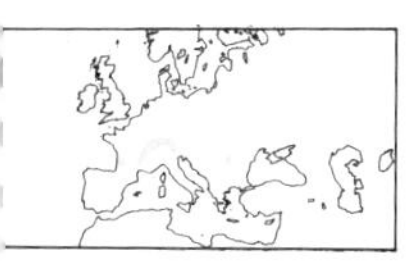

**DUSKY GRIZZLED SKIPPER** *Pyrgus cacaliae.* Upf white markings *very small, lacks a spot at base of space 2* and lacks also markings in space 1b at this position; unh markings like the Alpine Grizzled, but in space 1c the stripe is short. Occurs in the Pyrenees, Alps, S Carpathians and Balkans (Rilo Mts). Local but widespread, always at high altitudes, 1800m or over, flying over short grass slopes July–August. Larval food plants *Potentilla, Sibbaldia.* E.

**NORTHERN GRIZZLED SKIPPER** *Pyrgus centaureae.* Ups grey-black, upf no spot at base of space 2; unh dark, veins lined white, basal, discal and submarginal markings all well developed. Widely distributed in Fennoscandia between 60–70°N. Flies June–July in a single brood, around low scrub on bogs and mosses. Larval food plant *Rubus chamaemorus.* Range very extensive, circumpolar in Asia and America, and to Colorado, New York and N Carolina.

In the following species the white pd spots upf in spaces 4+5 are in line with the spots in spaces 3+6. In both wings ups the rows of submarginal spots are usually complete. Sexes similar; ♂ fw without costal fold.

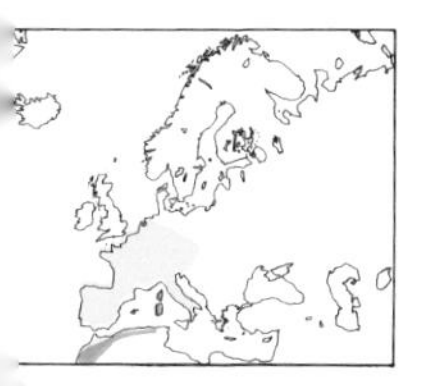

*S.s. sertorius*
*S.s. therapne*
*S.s. ali*

**RED-UNDERWING SKIPPER** *Spialia sertorius.* Small, unh red-brown; a large, round, white spot is present at mid-costa in spaces 7+8. Widespread and usually common in N Africa and W Europe to about 51°N, and eastwards to Slovakia, W Hungary, and N Yugoslavia (Croatia), including Corsica and Sardinia. Flies April–June and July–September in two broods at low altitudes, a single brood at high altitudes, at all levels from lowlands to 2200m or more. Most common in flowery meadows and slopes. Larval food plants *Sanguisorba, Potentilla* and *Rubus.* Three subspecies. E.

*S. s. sertorius*, all continental European area. Uph discal spot very small.

*S. s. therapne*, only in Corsica and Sardinia. Very small, uph discal spot relatively larger.

*S. s. ali*, in N Africa. Unh discal spot irregular, shining white.

♂ Continental Europe

♂ Corsica & Sardinia

♂ N Africa

**Red-underwing Skipper**

**HUNGARIAN SKIPPER** *Spialia orbifer.* Larger than *S. sertorius*; unh olive green or greenish-grey, costal spot round. Occurs in Sicily, Hungary, Czechoslovakia, Romania, Yugoslavia and Greece. Widespread in E Europe in mountainous districts, usually at 1000–1500m, rising to 2000m in the Balkans. Flies April–September in two or three broods, on flowery open ground. Larval food plant *Sanguisorba.* Range extends eastwards across Russia and W Asia, Iran, Fergana, the Amur and Mongolia.

**PERSIAN SKIPPER** *Spialia phlomidis.* Ups all white markings large, fore-wing costa shaded grey. In Europe occurs in Macedonia, Greece, Albania. Flies June–July in a single brood, at low or moderate altitudes, attracted by flowers. A very local species, usually rare or uncommon. Larval food plant *Phlomis.* Range extends across Asia Minor and Lebanon to N Iran.

**ADEN SKIPPER** *Spialia doris daphne.* Small; ♂ ups white markings relatively large; uph white discal band prominent. ♀ not seen. Occurs in S Morocco (Ifni etc.) and in southern valleys of the Atlas Mts. Flies March–April at sea level or rising to 1500m in mountains. Larval food plant not known. Range with other subspecies extends widely to Egypt, Ethiopia, Iran and Pakistan. An Ethiopian intrusion into our fauna.

In the following species the male hind-tibia does not have a hair-pencil; on upf postdiscal spots in spaces 4,5, are absent.

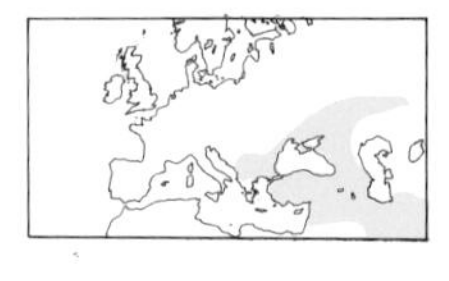

**TESSELATED SKIPPER** *Syrichtus tessellum.* Large; uph an oval discal spot below costa. In W Europe only in Macedonia and N Greece. Flies late May–June in a single brood, usually at low altitudes over flowery meadows not above 1000m. Larval food plant not known. Range extends across W Asia to N Iran, Caucasus and S Siberia.

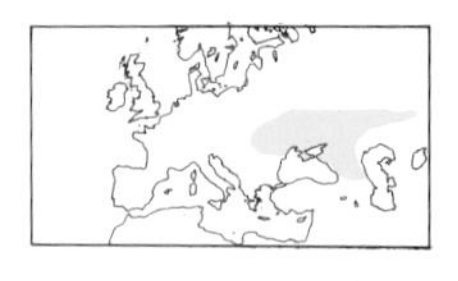

**SPINOSE SKIPPER** *Syrichtus cribrellum.* Like the Tesselated Skipper but smaller, ♂ ups white markings larger; upf two pairs of discal spots in space 1b; uns all white markings very large. ♀ similar. In Europe only found in N Romania (Cluj district). Flies late May–June on flowery meadows of the Pannonian plain. Larval food plant not known. Range extends across S Russia to the Caucasus, S Urals and eastwards to the Amur.

**SAGE SKIPPER** *Syrichtus proto.* ♂ ups grey-brown, often yellowish with grey suprascaling, markings slightly obscure, uph discal band small; unh yellowish or faintly sandy. ♀ similar, ups suprascaling absent. Occurs in S Europe, Portugal, Spain, SE France, C and S Italy, Sicily and Greece. In N Africa, Morocco and Algeria, f. *fulvosatura*, larger, with similar markings. Flies April–June in a single brood, usually among mountains, at 1000m or more to 1700m, on waste ground and open heaths. Larval food plant *Phlomis.* In N Africa, distinguish from the Barbary Skipper. Range includes S Russia, Crimea, Caucasus, Asia Minor.

Hungarian Skipper

Persian Skipper

Aden Skipper

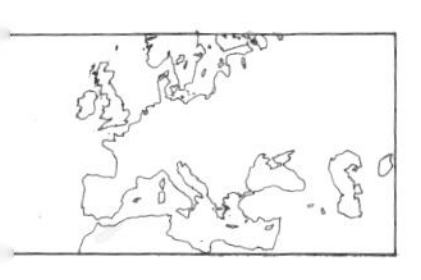

**BARBARY SKIPPER** *Syrichtus mohammed.* Like the Sage Skipper. Ups darker brown, markings yellowish, better defined; unh yellow-brown, veins lined pale brown, markings white bordered dark grey. Occurs in Morocco and Algeria. Flies in two broods, March–June and August–September on rough open ground at 1600m or over, in the Middle Atlas. Gen.1 f. *caid*, small, unh darker. Larval food plant *Phlomis*. E.

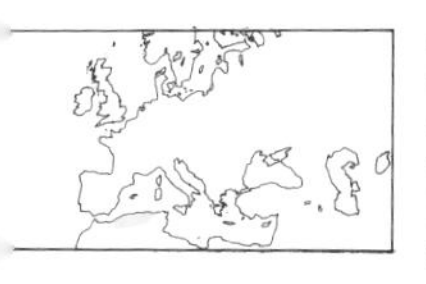

**ALGERIAN GRIZZLED SKIPPER.** *Syrichtus leuzeae.* Like the Sage Skipper. Upf the pale cell-spot very large; unh basal, discal and postdiscal pale markings fused to form three bands curving across the wing. ♀ not seen. Only known from Algeria. Flies in two broods, May–July on flowery open meadows at sub-alpine levels. E.

Tesselated Skipper

Spinose Skipper

♀ f. *fulvosatura*

Sage Skipper

Barbary Skipper

Algerian Grizzled Skipper

**The Marbled Skippers.** These little butterflies are easily recognized as a group for the wing-markings differ entirely from the usual pattern of white spots on a dark ground. In the five European species the most striking characters are three small pre-apical spots on the fore-wings, with two discal spots and the cell-spots all hyaline (transparent). The fringes are long, the margins scalloped, especially prominent on the hind-wings. Specific characters are not well defined and identification is difficult. The male upf has a costal fold enclosing scent scales and in three species a dark hair tuft uns at base of fore-wing.

**MALLOW SKIPPER** *Carcharodus alceae*. ♂ unf hair-tuft absent; ups brown, marbled darker; uph *pale markings vestigial.* Widespread in N Africa, S and C Europe to 52°N. Absent from Britain, Fennoscandia and Baltic countries. Flies April–August through the summer, on open ground with flowers, commonly at low altitudes rising to 1600m. Larval food plants *Malva, Althaea, Hibiscus*. Range extends across S Russia and Asia Minor to the Caucasus, Altai Mts, N Iran and E Siberia. Specimens from NW Africa, S Portugal and SW Spain, *C. a. tripolinus*, differ slightly from other European races, with a small distinctive character in the male genitalia. Wing markings are not distinctive.

**MARBLED SKIPPER** *Carcharodus lavatherae*. ♂ unf hair-tuft absent; ups grey brown, sometimes with greenish tones, brightly marbled; uph dark, pale basal spot and discal markings prominent. Widespread in Morocco, Algeria, Tunisia; more local in S Europe in Spain, Pyrenees, southern Alps, Abruzzi, Balkans, Bulgaria, and N Greece. Flies May–August in a single brood, often at low altitudes, but rising to 1600m. Larval food plant *Stachys*. Range extends to Asia Minor, Crimea and the Caucasus.

*C.b. boeticus*
*C.b. standeri*

**SOUTHERN MARBLED SKIPPER** *Carcharodus boeticus*. ♂ unf dark hair-tuft present; like the Oriental Marbled Skipper, but ups often dove-grey (variable), pale markings more complete, with basal spot, discal and sub-marginal macular bands; unh pale grey, white transverse bands easily seen. Flies May–August in two or three broods, usually on flowery slopes among mountains, to 1600m. Larval food plants *Marrubium, Ballota* etc. Two named subspecies.

*C. b. boeticus*, local in Spain, Portugal, France (E Pyrenees and Provence), Piedmont (Susa), C Apennines (very local), Lucania, Sicily(?). E.

*C. b. stauderi*, external features similar, distinguished by a small character in the ♂ genitalia. Occurs from Morocco to Cyrenaica, often at low altitudes, rising to 1500m in the Middle Atlas. Range extends to Asia Minor, Lebanon.

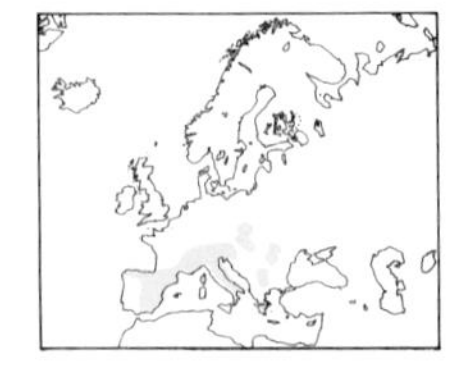

**TUFTED MARBLED SKIPPER** *Carcharodus flocciferus*. ♂ unf dark hair-tuft present; ups brown marbled grey; uph dark, but basal and discal pale spots usually present; unh elongate, pale marginal marks prominent. Local in S Europe from Spain and Pyrenees to 48°N, and in southern Alps and Apennines to Julian Alps, Macedonia and Greece. Flies May–June and August, in two broods, at valley levels, but more often at high altitudes to 1800m. Absent from N and W France, Corsica, Sardinia. Larval food plants *Marrubium, Stachys*. Ranges to S Russia, Crimea, Caucasus and C Asia (needs confirmation).

**ORIENTAL MARBLED SKIPPER** *Carcharodus orientalis*. ♂ unf dark hair-tuft present; ups like the Tufted Marbled, but general colour tone is grey instead of brown; uph dark, basal and discal spots well defined; uns pale grey; unh elongate marginal marks not present. Only in SE Europe. Albania, S Yugoslavia, Bulgaria and Greece. Flies, April–August probably in two broods, on flowery banks, at valley levels, rarely above 1000m. The distribution overlaps the range of the Tufted Marbled, which flies in Macedonia at altitudes of 1500–2000m. On ups the colour varies, paler or darker, sometimes very near the Tufted Marbled; distinction is not then reliable without anatomical examination. Larval food plant uncertain. Range extends across Asia Minor, Lebanon and Iraq to Iran and Turkmenistan.

**DINGY SKIPPER** *Erynnis tages*. Ups dark brown; uns paler brown almost unmarked. Widely distributed in S and C Europe to about 60°N; scarce and local in S Germany and in the Baltic countries. Absent from the Mediterranean islands. In Ireland, *E. t. baynesi*, ups variegated with grey. Other colour forms have been named; f. *brunnea*, medium brown, very common in S Europe in second brood. Flies May–August in two broods, on open ground with flowers and brushwood at all altitudes to 2000m. Larval food plants include *Lotus*, *Eryngium*, *Coronilla*. Range extends across E Europe and Asia to Siberia and China. Larva p. 228. **Map 51**

**Oriental Marbled Skipper** **Marbled Skipper** **Tufted Marbled Skipper**

**Southern Marbled Skipper**

**Mallow Skipper** **Dingy Skipper**

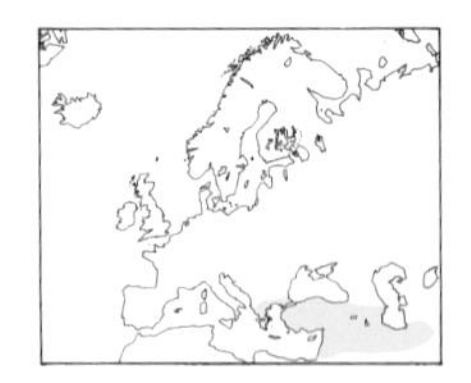

**INKY SKIPPER** *Erynnis marloyi.* Ups very dark; upf two oblique cross lines and small but conspicuous costal spot before the apex. In Europe known only from Greece, Albania and Bulgaria (?). Flies May–August in rocky places, often at low altitudes. Larval food plant not known. Range extends to Asia Minor, Lebanon, Iraq, Iran, Pakistan.

**Inky Skipper**

**The Chequered Skippers.** These interesting little butterflies are somewhat isolated by their unusual characters. Compared with the great majority, the head is relatively less wide, the thorax less bulky, the abdomen slender, longer than the hindwing, males without a sex-brand.

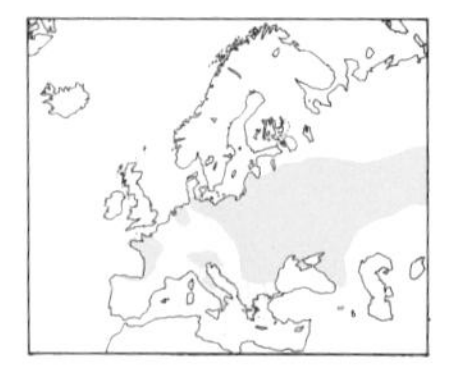

**LARGE CHEQUERED SKIPPER** *Heteropterus morpheus.* ♂ upf very dark with small pre-apical markings; unh yellow, with large white, dark bordered spots. ♀ fringes chequered; upf yellow markings slightly more prominent. Always local in widely scattered colonies, from N Spain and C France north to Lithuania, and across Germany and Italy, including the C Apennines, to Romania and the Balkans. Flies in a single brood June–July, often in shaded areas or in light woodland, rare above 300m. Larval food plants *Brachypodium*, *Molinia* and other grasses. Range extends across temperate Asia to the Amur and Korea. Throughout this extensive range variation is negligible.

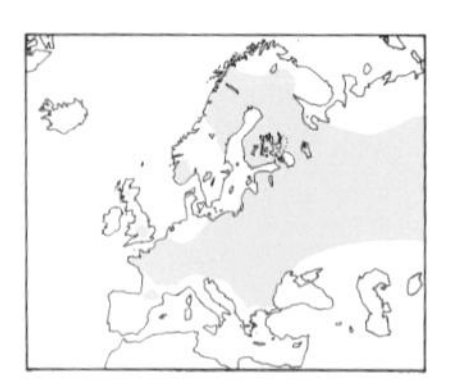

**CHEQUERED SKIPPER** *Carterocephalus palaemon.* ♂ ups black with orange-yellow markings. ♀ similar. Local in the Pyrenees, France, England and Scotland to Fennoscandia to 66°N, and east across the Alps and Carpathians to the Balkans and Bulgaria. Absent from SE France and Peninsular Italy, Mediterranean islands and Greece. Flies June–July in a single brood. usually in light woodland, forest roads etc., from low altitudes to 1200m in the S Alps. Occurs in Spain in the Val d'Aran. Larval food plants grasses, esp. *Bromus*. Range extensive, circumpolar, across temperate Asia to N America in Canada and the northern States of USA, in Connecticut, Pennsylvania, Michigan etc. **Map 52**

**Large Chequered Skipper**

**Chequered Skipper**

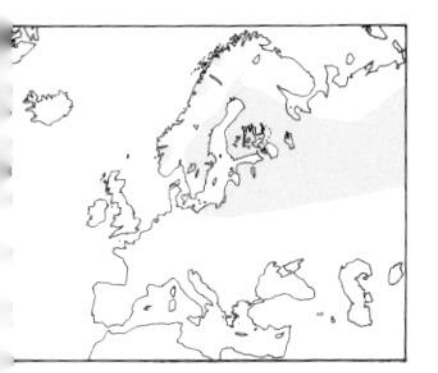

**NORTHERN CHEQUERED SKIPPER** *Carterocephalus silvicolus.* ♂ upf yellow with scanty dark markings. ♀ upf dark markings extended. Occurs in N Poland, the Baltic countries and in Fennoscandia to 66°N or more, but generally absent in northern Lapland. Flies June–July in a single brood, at low altitudes in light woodland. Larval food plant grass, esp. *Cynosurus.* Range extends in subarctic latitudes across N Russia and Siberia to Amurland and Kamschatka. Larva p. 226.

**Northern Chequered Skipper**

**The Hesperine Skippers.** The remaining Skipper butterflies all belong to the Hesperiinae, the second and largest section of the Family. The larvae live on grasses (Monocotyledons), which are spun together to make a hollow case in which the creature spends its entire larval and pupal life. The external specific characters of these butterflies are not always distinctive, but in the fore-wing vein 5 at its base is almost always nearer to vein 4 than to vein 6. The entire group is enormous, including a very large number of tropical species, although in Europe it is poorly represented. Many species have a sex-brand on the upf, an oblique black stripe below the cell.

The four species following are all small, yellow butterflies which occur in local colonies, often very common where they are found. On the male fore-wing upperside there is an oblique, black stripe (sex-brand) with moniliform androconial scent scales; in the hind-wing vein 5 is vestigial or absent. The antennal club is well developed, without an apiculus.

*T.a. acteon*
*T.a.a.* f. *oranus*

**LULWORTH SKIPPER** *Thymelicus acteon.* Upperside yellowish to rather pale olive-brown (variable), a paler stripe in the cell and four or five postdiscal, pale yellowish spots near the costa, not always well defined. Flies May–July in a single brood, at all altitudes to 1600m. Larval food plants *Brachypodium, Agropyron* etc. Range extends to Asia Minor, Cyprus and Lebanon. Two subspecies. Larva p. 230. **Map 53**

*T. a. acteon*, local in N Africa, S and C Europe to the Baltic coast and east to Romania, Balkans and Greece, including Crete, Sicily and S England. Absent from Corsica, Sardinia and the Balearic islands. Ups in southern areas often darker, e.g. in N Spain (f. *virescens*), and in S Spain and N Africa (f. *oranus*), and in Crete, Elba etc.

*T. a. christi*, in the Canary Islands, on the western group, Tenerife, Gran Canaria, La Palma and La Gomera. Ups brighter, yellow markings more prominent, well defined. Flies in May and later through the summer, at all altitudes to 2000m or more.

N Africa, S & C Europe including S England

♂ Canary Is

**Lulworth Skipper**

Moroccan Small Skipper

Essex Skipper

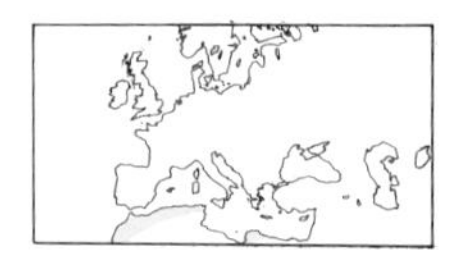

**MOROCCAN SMALL SKIPPER** *Thymelicus hamza*. ♂ like the Lulworth Skipper. Ups brighter fulvous, lacking pd spots; uph *veins not lined black*. Antennal apex *grey* beneath. ♀ ups costal margin and cell often paler yellow. Local in Morocco, Algeria and Tunisia. Flies May–June up to 1600m on flowery slopes. Larval food plants not recorded. Not reported from Europe. E.

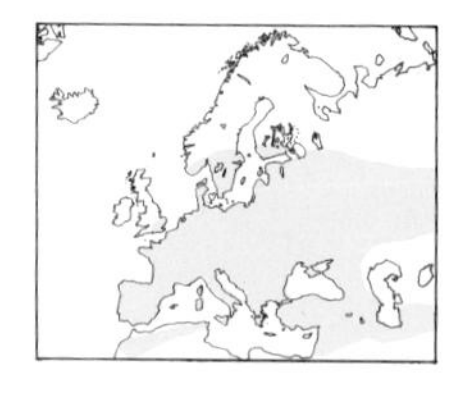

**ESSEX SKIPPER** *Thymelicus lineolus*. Upf fulvous, marginal borders dark, 0.5–2mm wide, *veins partly lined black*, sex-brand inconspicuous, broken at vein 2. Antennal *tip black* beneath. Flies May–July at all altitudes to 2000m, in open spaces with grass. Range extends across C Asia to the Amur, also in N America. **Map 52**

*T. l. lineolus.* size variable, often small, widespread across Europe at all altitudes to 2000m, to 62°N, including S and E England.

*T. l. semicolon*, in N Africa, widely distributed but not recorded from Tunisia. ♂ ups veins conspicuously lined black.

**SMALL SKIPPER** *Thymelicus flavus* ('sylvestris'). Ups clear yellow, sex-brand prominent, slightly broken at vein 2. Widespread and common in N Africa, S and C Europe to 56°N. Absent from Ireland and Scotland. Flies June–July in open spaces with grass, at all altitudes to 2000m. Large specimens, f. *syriacus*, ups bright orange-yellow, are often common in S Europe. Larval food plants *Deschampsia*, *Oryzopsis*, *Holcus* etc. Range extends to W Asia, the Caucasus, C Asia and Iran. **Map 53**

♂

♂ f. *syriacus*

**Small Skipper**

**LARGE SKIPPER** *Ochlodes venatus faunus.* Unh markings pale yellow, obscure. Sexes similar, apart from prominent sex-brand upf in ♂. A common and widespread species throughout S and C Europe to 64°N. Absent from Ireland, N Africa and Mediterranean islands except Sicily. In northern areas flies June–July in a single brood, but often two or three broods in S Europe, at all altitudes to 2000m. At high altitudes often f. *alpinus*, ups darker. Larval food plants *Festuca, Agropyron, Poa* etc. Range extends across Russia to Siberia and the Kurile Islands. **Map 54**

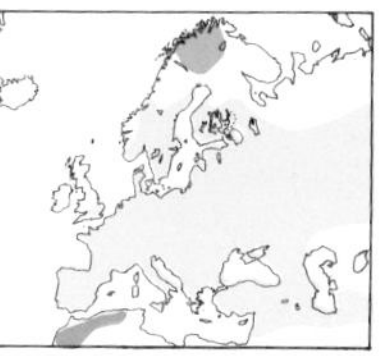

*H.c. comma*
*H.c.* f. *catena*
*H.c.* f. *benuncas*

**SILVER-SPOTTED SKIPPER** *Hesperia comma.* Unh greenish, markings silver white, well defined. Sexes similar apart from prominent sex-brand upf in ♂. Widely distributed but local, confined to calcareous soils, from Portugal and Spain across Europe to 70°N in Fennoscandia, and east to Romania, the Balkans and Greece. Absent from Ireland, Sardinia and Crete. In the far north f. *catena*, smaller and ups dark; in N Africa f. *benuncas*, ups markings often brighter. Larval food plants *Lotus, Festuca, Poa* etc. Flies July–August. Range extends across Europe and Asia to W North America **Map 55**

♂

♀ f. *alpinus*

**Large Skipper**

♂

♀

**Silver Spotted Skipper**

In the three species following the antennal apex is expanded rather gradually but at the tip (apiculus) is diminished abruptly, elongate and curved backwards in the shape of a hook. Males without sex-brands.

**PIGMY SKIPPER** *Gegenes pumilio*. Small; ♂ ups very dark, unmarked. ♀ paler brown; upf two or three small, pale pd marks. Antennal club short, apiculus small. Widely distributed along the Mediterranean coasts, especially on E coast of Spain, W coast of Italy, Sicily, Sardinia, Corsica and Elba, flying April and later at low altitudes, is fond of resting on hot paths, rocks etc. Larval food plants grasses. Range extends to Iran and Himalayas; it is widely distributed in Africa.

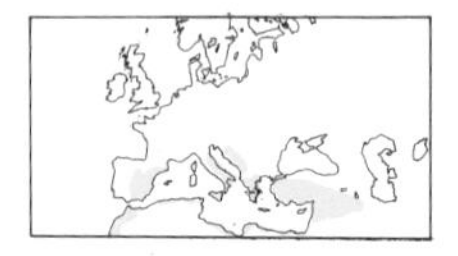

**MEDITERRANEAN SKIPPER** *Gegenes nostrodamus*. ♂ like the Pigmy Skipper but larger, ups dark brown, unmarked. ♀ larger, ups grey-brown; upf with several pale spots; unh grey. Widely distributed but uncommon along the coasts of Morocco and N Mediterranean to Greece, also in Spain near Saragossa and Aranhuez, Flies May and later, most common in late summer, often sits on hot paths, rocks etc. Range extends through Egypt and Turkestan to India.

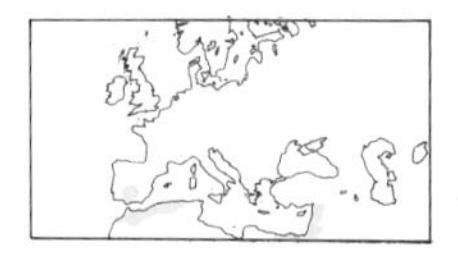

**ZELLER'S SKIPPER** *Borbo borbonica zelleri*. ♂ ups very dark, with small vitreous discal markings. ♀ similar, upf with five well-defined discal spots. Flies late summer. Recorded from Morocco (Rabat), Algeria and Gibraltar, most often in September. Probably an occasional immigrant. Widely distributed in Ethiopian Africa.

**Pigmy Skipper**

**Mediterranean Skipper**

**Zeller's Skipper**

## The Early Stages: Larvae and Pupae

This handbook on our European butterflies would be incomplete without some account of their early stages. These are now illustrated for 79 species on the six pages following in paintings based on those published by the German entomologist Dr Ernst Hofmann in 1893. It is obvious that there is great diversity in appearance of both larvae and pupae, and important groups are quite as well defined as they are in wing-shape and markings of the perfect insects. It is noteworthy that in almost all our butterflies the stages of development take place entirely exposed in the open air. Only in the Apollo is the pupa on the ground protected by a fragile cocoon of silk threads, and in a different family, the Grayling makes a more complete shelter for its pupa (not illustrated). This is in contrast with our moths in which the pupa almost always is enclosed in a cocoon, buried in the earth or otherwise protected.

Our butterflies can be divided into two large groups. In the first the pupa is fixed by hooks on its tail ('the cremaster') to a silken pad, often supported further by a silken girdle, on a twig or the stem of a plant. This group includes the Swallowtails, Whites and Blues. In the second group are the Purple Emperor, Fritillaries, Tortoiseshells and most of the Browns. In these the pupa is also fixed by its cremaster, but it hangs pendulous without further support.

### GROUP 1:

**Swallowtails.** In this small group the butterflies vary greatly as do their larvae. Some of these are smooth, others slightly hairy or with soft, finger-like processes. All larvae have one character in common, a curious little organ called an *osmaterium*, a small, forked, red filament which appears behind the head when the insect is agitated.

**The Whites.** The members of this very large group are remarkable for their eggs which are about twice as tall as they are wide. The larvae are usually smooth, often green with pale stripes down the back and sides. These (cryptic) markings are clearly intended to hide the larvae, making them difficult to see as they feed on the green leaves of rough herbage. In many larvae the skin looks velvety, covered with a down of short, very fine hairs. Most pupae are angular, with a sharp process anteriorly and often with a crest over the thorax, especially evident in the important sections of the Dappled Whites, Orange Tips and Wood Whites, in all of which the pupae are somewhat bent and pointed at each end. The pupae of the Clouded Yellows and Brimstones are more robust but still have the sharp, anterior prominences and the thoracic regions are dilated.

**The Blues** form another large family with individual characters exceptionally well defined. The eggs are domed or compressed, the sculpture of the shells most striking in the eggs of the Coppers. In our European species the larvae are unmistakable, short, the body flattened like that of a woodlouse, the head minute. Markings on the larval bodies is variable, usually basically green on those species which feed on such low plants as *Lotus*, *Hippocrepis* etc. The pupae also are short, fixed to a twig or plant stem by the cremaster and with a silken girdle. The flattened shape is rather less striking in larvae of the Coppers.

## GROUP 2:

**Tortoiseshells and Fritillaries.** In these species which are often larger the larvae may be dark, brown or even black, or sometimes quite brightly coloured and with spines or bristled tubercles in rows on the back and sides. In some species it appears that concealment is unimportant, perhaps because the spines and bristles make these larvae look unpalatable. This is especially true, for example, of the Peacock, whose black, spiny larvae may be seen feeding exposed and unmolested on a bed of stinging nettles. Most of the pupae can be recognised by their peculiar shape, crested on the head, with a double row of shorter spines or tubercles down the back. The eggs are barrel-shaped or pyramidal, more or less deeply grooved, beautiful objects under the microscope. This description does not apply to a few species, including the Purple Emperor and the Two-tailed Pasha, in which the larvae are green with smooth skins. These belong to a section of the family with few representatives in Europe.

The ova (eggs) of a butterfly from each main group (enlarged about twenty times): 1 Swallowtail, *Papilio machaon*; 2 Chalk-hill Blue, *Lysandra coridon*; 3 Small White, *Artogeia rapae*; 4 Small Tortoiseshell, *Aglais urticae*; 5 Dingy Skipper, *Erynnis tages*; 6 Meadow Brown, *Maniola jurtina*; 7 Monarch, *Danaus plexippus*.

**The Browns,** including the Meadow Brown, Grayling and Speckled Wood are very different. In this important family of grass-feeders, all larvae have characteristic features, smooth-skinned, slender and with a pair of small flaps covering the anal orifice. Most are coloured greenish or buff, with paler or darker longitudinal stripes, making them inconspicuous as they rest on the stems of grass. The pupae are smooth, usually pendulous, but sometimes they lie loosely among the stems of a tuft of grass, unattached. The eggs are barrel-shaped, usually weakly ribbed.

**The Danaids**. Two species belonging to this large tropical family are seen occasionally in southwestern Europe. Their larvae are unlike any truly European species being smooth-skinned and rather brightly coloured with one or more pairs of remarkable long filaments that spring from the body segments. An American species, the Milkweed, is established in the Canary Islands. Its larvae is striped cream and brown.

**The Skippers** differ from the true Butterflies in several ways, especially in the life-styles of their early stages. All European species are small, the larvae smooth, rather slender anteriorly, the head separated from the body by a short neck. The larvae of the yellow species may live entirely within a grass shelter, making the change into a pupa without ever emerging from their shelter. In other species the larvae are normally mobile, but it appears that they all make the change to pupae within a shelter of leaves. The pupae are slender, without special features.

1 Cleopatra *Gonepteryx cleopatra, p. 50*

2 Woodland Brown *Lopinga achine, p. 201*

3 Rock Grayling *Hipparchia alcyone, p. 142*

4 Hermit *Chazara briseis, p. 150*

5 Dusky Meadow Brown *Hyponephele lycaon, p. 188*
**a** larva
**b** pupa

6 Clouded Apollo *Parnassius mnemosyne* (on *Corydalis solida*), *p. 30*

7 Adonis Blue *Lysandra bellargus* (on *Melilotus officinalis*), *p. 92*

8 Black-eyed Blue *Glaucopsyche melanops, p. 71*

9 Black-veined White *Aporia crataegi* (on *Crataegus oxyacantha*), *p. 32*
**a** larva
**b** pupa

10 Wood White *Leptidea sinapis* (on *Lotus corniculatus*), *p. 53*
**a** larva
**b** pupa

11 Pale Clouded Yellow *Colias hyale* (on *Vicia sativa*), *p. 48*

12 Mountain Clouded Yellow *Colias phicomone* (on *Vicia sativa*), *p. 44*

13 Clouded Yellow *Colias crocea, p. 46*

1
3
7
2
6
4
5b
8
5a
9b
9a
13
10a
11
12
10b

1 White-letter Hairstreak *Strymonidia w-album, p. 58*

2 Moorland Clouded Yellow *Colias palaeno* (on *Vaccinium*), *p. 44*

3 Orange Tip *Anthocharis cardamines* (on *Cardamine pratensis*), *p. 40*

4 Green-veined White *Artogeia napi* (on *Raphanus sativus*), *p. 34*

5 Lesser Purple Emperor *Apatura ilia, p. 98*

6 Northern Chequered Skipper *Carterocephalus silvicolus, p. 217*
**a** larva
**b** pupa

7 Swallowtail *Papilio machaon* (on *Daucus carota*), *p. 24*
**a** larva (juvenile)
**b** larva (adult)

8 Violet Copper *Lycaena helle* (on *Rumex acetosa*), *p. 61*
**a** larva
**b** pupa

9 Small Copper *Lycaena phlaeas* (on *Rumex acetosa*), *p. 61*

10 Duke of Burgundy Fritillary *Hamearis lucina, p. 95*
**a & b** variable larvae

11 Dryad *Minois dryas, p. 156*

12 Ringlet *Aphantopus hyperantus, p. 188*
**a & b** variable larvae

13 Large Wall Brown *Lasiommata maera, p. 200*

14 Southern Gatekeeper *Pyronia cecilia, p. 190*

1
2
3b
3a
4
5a
5b
6a
6b
7a
7b
8a
8b
9
10a
10b
11
12a
12b
13
14

1 Bath White *Pontia daplidice* (on *Alyssum calycinum*), *p. 36*

2 Purple Emperor *Apatura iris, p. 98*

3 Southern Festoon *Zerynthia polyxena* (on *Aristolochia clematitis*), *p. 27*
**a** larva with osmaterium erect
**b** larva with osmaterium retracted

4 Black Hairstreak *Strymonidia pruni, p. 58*

5 Damon Blue *Agrodiaetus damon, p. 86*
**a** larva
**b** pupa

6 Small White *Artogeia rapae* (on *Brassica rapa*), *p. 32*

7 Large White *Pieris brassicae* (on *Brassica rapa*), *p. 31*

8 Purple Hairstreak *Quercusia quercus, p. 56*

9 Purple-edged Copper *Palaeochrysophanus hippothoe, p. 66*
**a** larva
**b** pupa

10 Sooty Copper *Heodes tityrus, p. 64*
**a** juvenile larva
**b** adult larva

11 Chalk-hill Blue *Lysandra coridon, p. 91*

12 Purple-shot Copper *Heodes alciphron, p. 64*

13 Brown Argus *Aricia agestis, p. 80*

14 Nettle-tree Butterfly *Libythea celtis, p. 96*
**a** juvenile larva
**b** adult larva
**c** pupa

15 Dingy Skipper *Erynnis tages, p. 215*
**a** larva
**b** pupa

1
2
3a
3b
4a
4b
5a
5b
6
7
8
9a
9b
10a
10b
11
2
13
14a
14b
14c
15a
15b

1 Scarce Swallowtail *Iphiclides podalirius* (on *Prunus spinosa*), *p. 26*
**a** larva
**b** pupa

2 Lang's Short-tailed Blue *Syntarucus pirithous, p. 67*

3 Iolas Blue *Iolana iolas, p. 74*

4 Provence Hairstreak *Tomares ballus, p. 60*

5 Long-tailed Blue *Lampides boeticus* (on *Colutea arborescens*), *p. 67*
**a** larva
**b** pupa

6 Silver-studded Blue *Plebejus argus* (on *Colutea arborescens*), *p. 78*
**a & b** larva, variable forms

7 Lulworth Skipper *Thymelicus acteon* (on *Briza media*), *p. 217*

8 Holly Blue *Celastrina argiolus, p. 71*
**a & b** larva, variable forms

9 Little Blue *Cupido minimus* (on *Melilotus officinalis*), *p. 70*
**a** larva
**b** pupa

10 Idas Blue *Lycaeides idas* (on *Melilotus officinalis*), *p. 78*

11 Lesser Fiery Copper *Thersamonia thersamon, p. 64*

12 Grizzled Skipper *Pyrgus malvae* (on *Rubus idaeus*), *p. 206*
**a & b** variable larvae
**c** pupa

13 Apollo *Parnassius apollo* (on *Sedum album*), *p. 29*

14 Blue-spot Hairstreak *Strymonidia spini, p. 58*
**a** larva
**b** pupa

15 Cranberry Blue *Vacciniina optilete, p. 79*

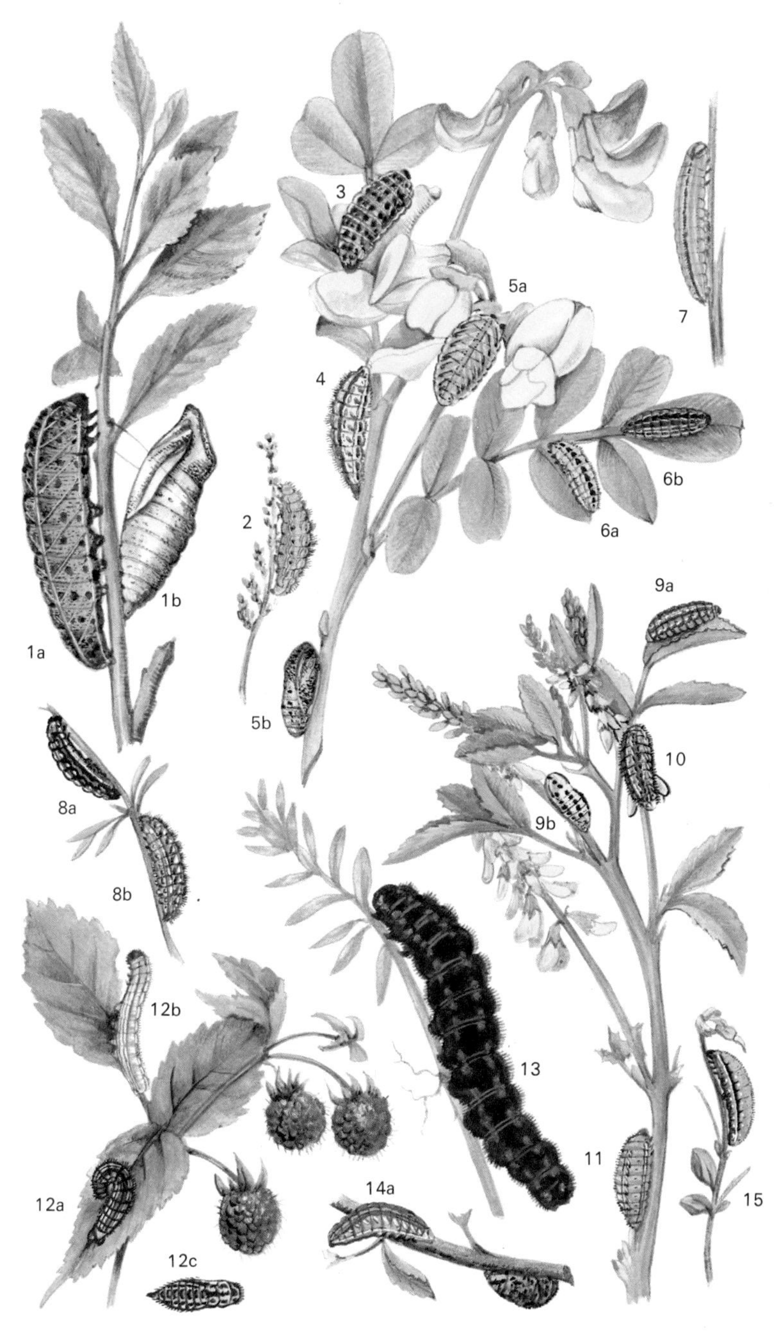

1a
1b
2
3
4
5a
5b
6a
6b
7
8a
8b
9a
9b
10
11
12a
12b
12c
13
14a
15

1 Titania's Fritillary *Clossiana titania* (on *Polygonum bistorta*), *p. 120*
**a** larva
**b** pupa

2 Map Butterfly *Araschnia levana* (on *Urtica dioica*), *p. 108*
**a & b** variable larvae
**c** pupa

3 Small Tortoiseshell *Aglais urticae* (on *Urtica dioica*), *p. 106*
**a & b** variable larvae
**c** pupa

4 Peacock Butterfly *Inachis io* (on *Urtica dioica*), *p. 104*

5 Red Admiral *Vanessa atalanta* (on *Urtica dioica*), *p. 104*
**a, b, c & d** variable larvae

6 Comma Butterfly *Polygonia c-album* (on *Urtica dioica*), *p. 108*

7 Marsh Fritillary *Eurodryas aurinia, p. 136*

8 High Brown Fritillary *Fabriciana adippe, p. 112*
**a & b** variable larvae

9 Large Ringlet *Erebia euryale* pupa, *p. 161*

10 Shepherd's Fritillary *Boloria pales* (on *Viola mirabilis*), *p. 116*

1a
2a
2b
3a
5b
7
8a
1b
3b
2c
5c
6
3c
4
8b
5d
5a
10
9

1 Scarce Fritillary *Hypodryas maturna* (on *Populus tremula*), *p. 135*

2 Poplar Admiral *Limenitis populi* (on *Populus tremula*), *p. 101*

3 False Comma *Nymphalis vau-album* (on *Populus tremula*), *p. 104*

4 Southern White Admiral *Limenitis reducta* (on *Lonicera tartarica*), p. 101
**a** larva
**b** pupa

5 White Admiral *Limenitis camilla* (on *Lonicera tartarica*), *p. 101*

6 Hungarian Glider *Neptis rivularis* (on *Lonicera tartarica*), *p. 102*

7 Niobe Fritillary *Fabriciana niobe* (on *Viola tricolor*), *p. 114*
**a & b** variable larvae

8 Queen of Spain Fritillary *Issoria lathonia* (on *Viola tricolor*), *p. 115*

9 Dark Green Fritillary *Mesoacidalia aglaja* (on *Viola tricolor*), *p. 112*

10 Pearl-bordered Fritillary *Clossiana euphrosyne* (on *Viola mirabilis*), *p. 120*

11 Small Pearl-bordered Fritillary *Clossiana selene* (on *Viola mirabilis*), *p. 120*

12 Silver-washed Fritillary *Argynnis paphia* (on *Viola canina*), *p. 110*

1
4a
4b
2
5
7a
6
3
7b
10
8
9
11
12

## English Index

This Index includes the English (vernacular) names of the butterflies described in this book. Page references to the main text are given in ordinary type, but references to the larval and pupal figures are in *italics*. Also included are references to technical English words, most of which are explained in the Glossary on p.21.

# Scientific Index

This index includes the scientific name of every butterfly mentioned in this book. Page references to larval and pupal figures are printed in *italics*; all others are printed in ordinary type. Names of Families and Genera are in Capitals; names of species and subspecies are followed by the names (in brackets) of the Genera to which they belong. The two names are necessary because a common specific name, such as *algirica*, may be given to different butterflies, placed in different genera.

## British Distribution

The special distribution maps of British Butterflies are based upon the maps prepared by Mr John Heath of the Nature Conservancy Centre, Monks Wood Experimental Station, Abbots Ripton, Huntingdon. These maps provide the first fully documented records of distribution of our native butterflies, and so are of the greatest importance in this respect, showing the collective records of a large number of workers up to 1970, the date of publication of the last official edition. A few small alterations were made in 1973 by T. G. Howarth in his book *South's British Butterflies*. Unfortunately our British Butterflies are under constant pressure from various quarters, as they are also elsewhere in Europe, for example in Denmark (see P. Svendson, *Entomologist's Record* p.47, 1976). Our native forests and woodlands are disappearing to give place to conifer plantations; hedgerows are cut down and destroyed on a grand scale, bogs and wetlands are drained and open heaths and wild places are ravaged by man's destructive activities and by fires. The entire countryside is especially poisoned by insecticides. All this had led to changes in environments and to gaps in our fauna. In fact we have been losing butterflies for about 150 years, with loss of the Large Copper about 1848 and of the Mazarine Blue somewhat later (1871?). The Black Veined White finally disappeared about 1925. The Large Tortoiseshell is now a rarity with doubtful status as a breeding species, although thought to survive in its south-eastern habitats, but everywhere rare, and occasional captures in widely separated localities suggest records of rare immigrant specimens. The Large Heath, and especially its finely marked form *rothliebii* (*philoxenus*) has disappeared from most of its well-known localities in Westmorland, Cheshire, Shropshire, Yorkshire and Staffordshire, and from many other localities. The Large Blue, in 1979 officially reported extinct from its strongholds in Devon and Cornwall, may yet survive in a few remote colonies in the Cotswolds, but again, its status as a breeding species in England is uncertain. During the last ten years most of the Elm trees in Britain have died. We have yet to learn what effect this loss will have upon our populations of the White-letter Hairstreak. It is against this background of recession that these maps are to be interpreted. On the other hand, I believe the distribution of the Chequered Skipper in southern Scotland, and of the Brown Hairstreak in England, to be more extensive than the maps suggest.

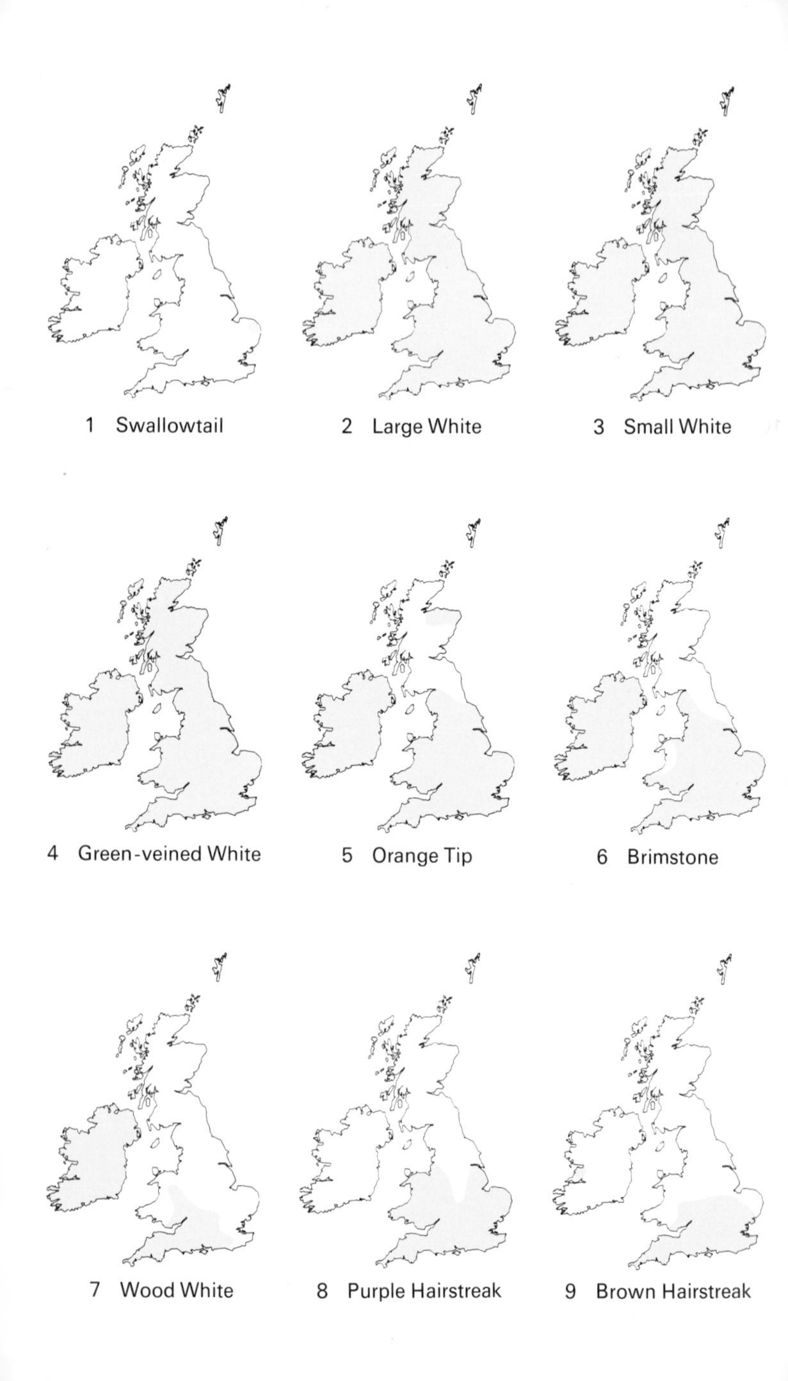
1 Swallowtail
2 Large White
3 Small White
4 Green-veined White
5 Orange Tip
6 Brimstone
7 Wood White
8 Purple Hairstreak
9 Brown Hairstreak

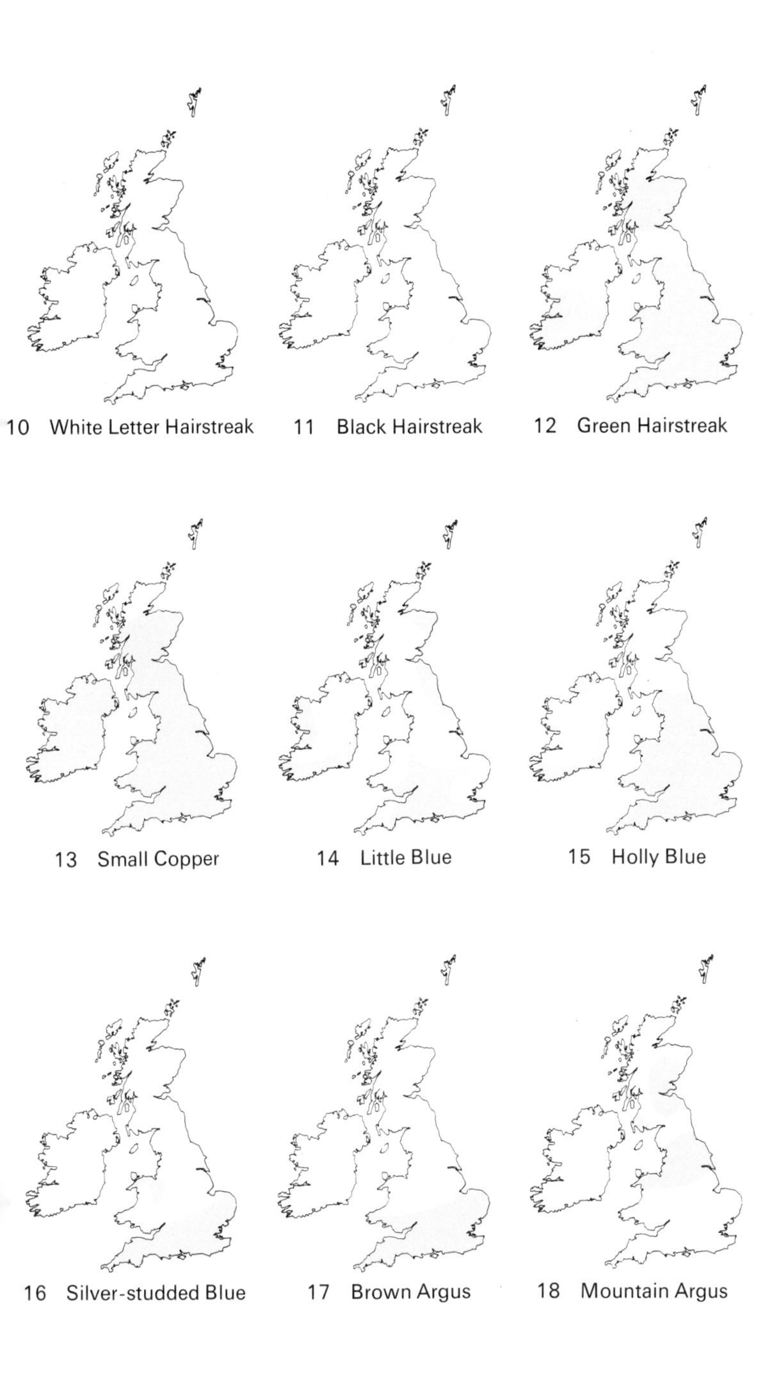

10 White Letter Hairstreak

11 Black Hairstreak

12 Green Hairstreak

13 Small Copper

14 Little Blue

15 Holly Blue

16 Silver-studded Blue

17 Brown Argus

18 Mountain Argus

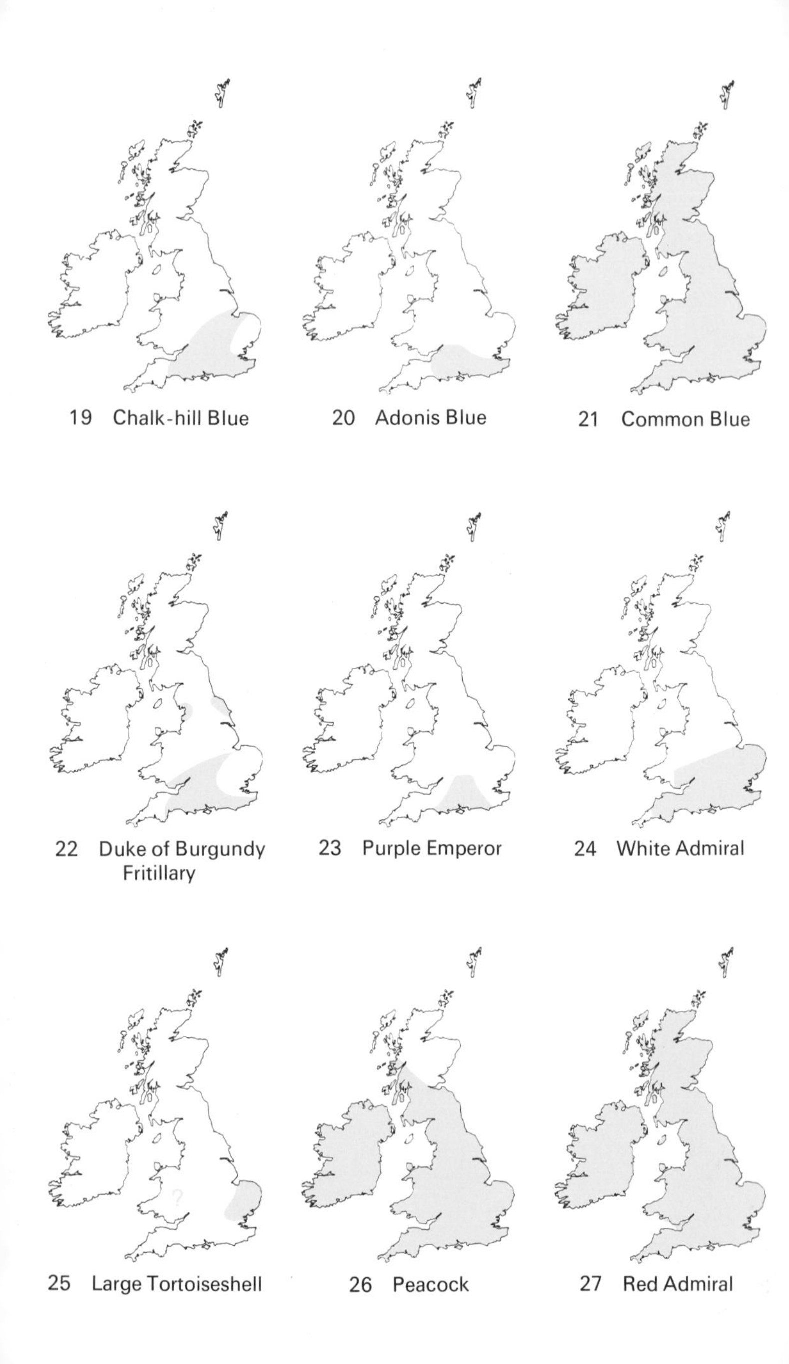
19 Chalk-hill Blue

20 Adonis Blue

21 Common Blue

22 Duke of Burgundy Fritillary

23 Purple Emperor

24 White Admiral

25 Large Tortoiseshell

26 Peacock

27 Red Admiral

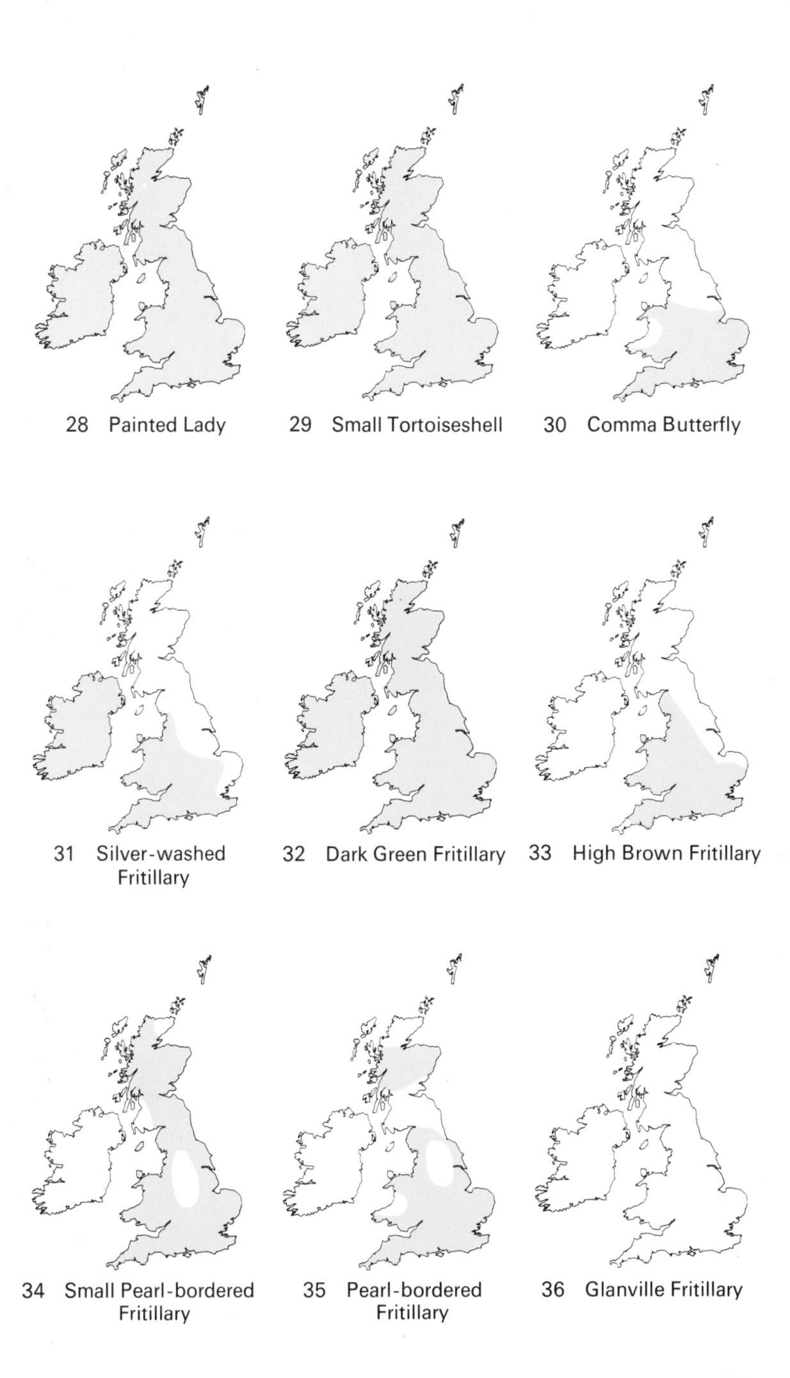

28 Painted Lady

29 Small Tortoiseshell

30 Comma Butterfly

31 Silver-washed Fritillary

32 Dark Green Fritillary

33 High Brown Fritillary

34 Small Pearl-bordered Fritillary

35 Pearl-bordered Fritillary

36 Glanville Fritillary

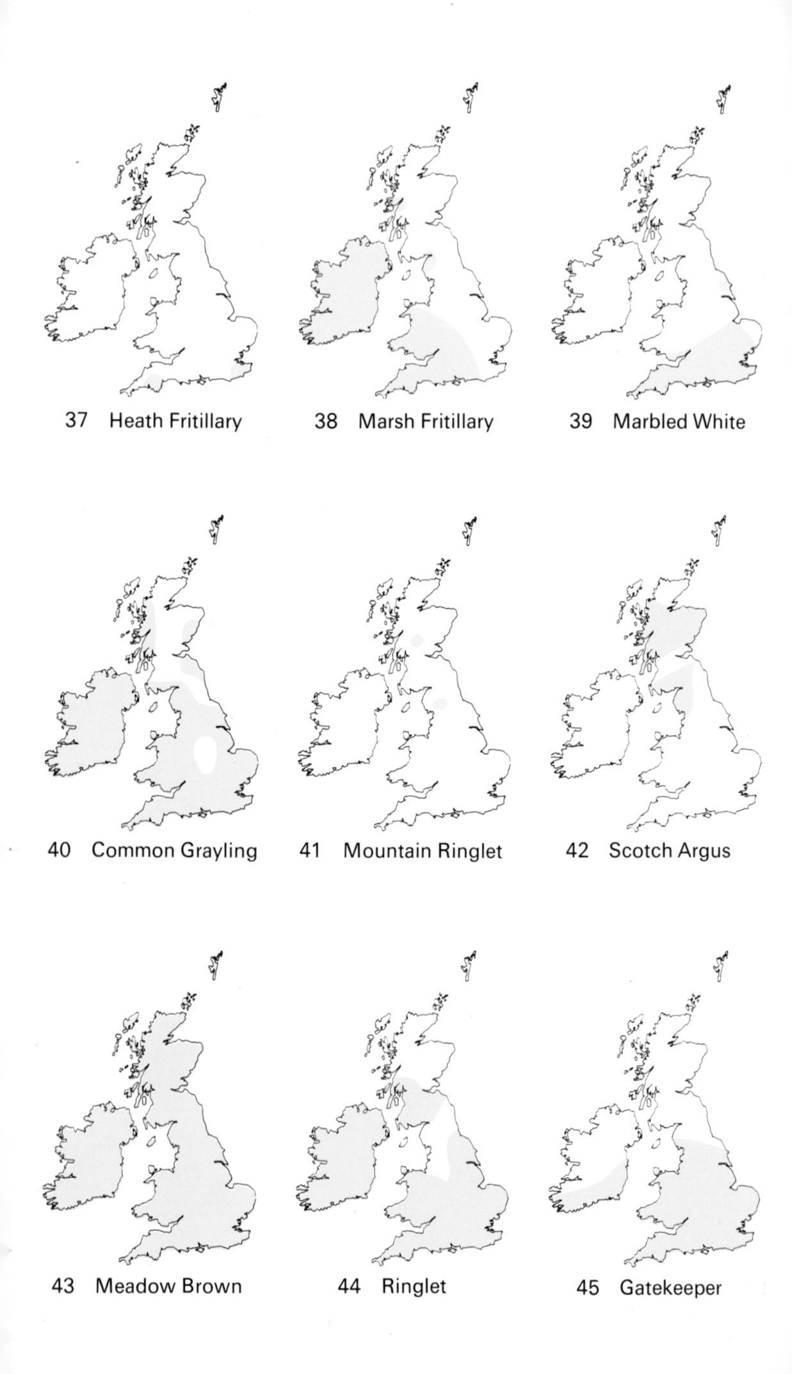
37 Heath Fritillary
38 Marsh Fritillary
39 Marbled White
40 Common Grayling
41 Mountain Ringlet
42 Scotch Argus
43 Meadow Brown
44 Ringlet
45 Gatekeeper

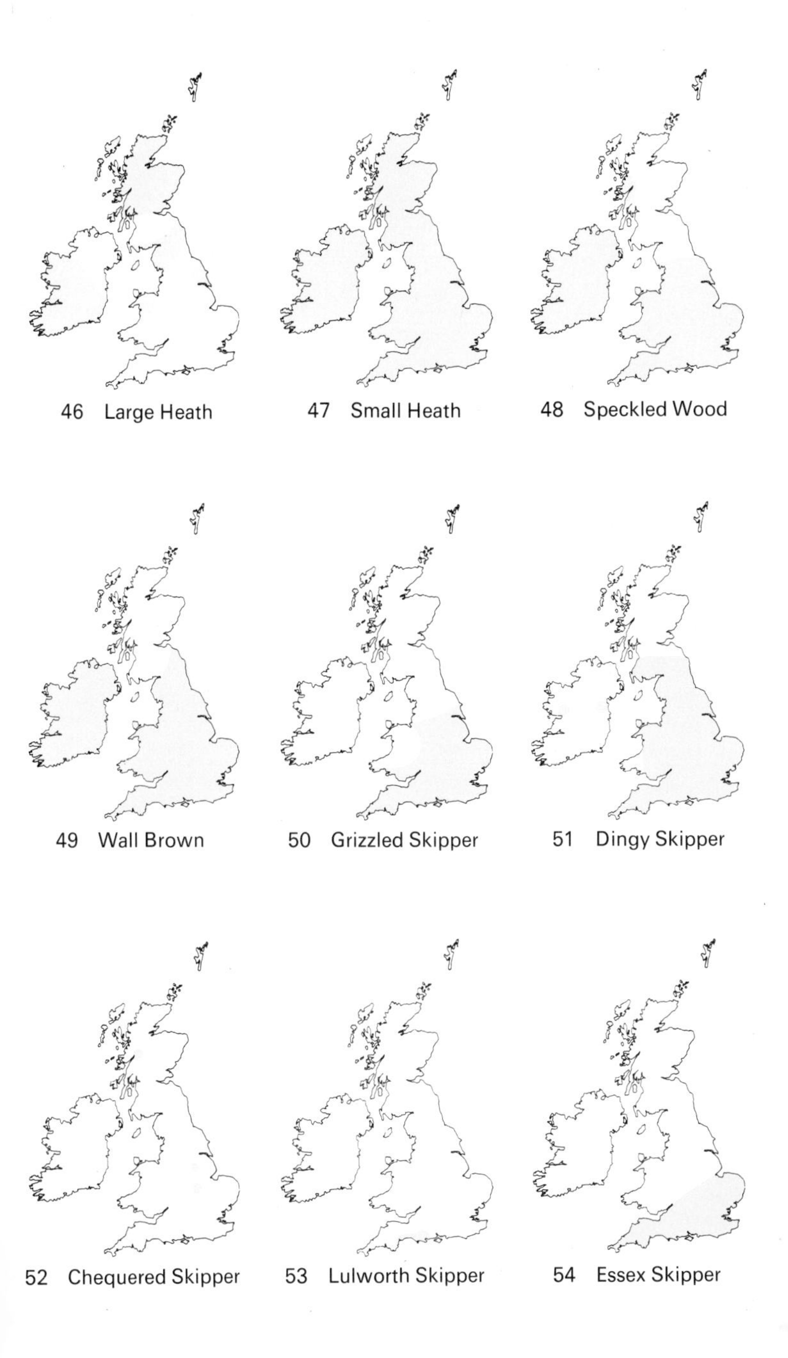
46 Large Heath
47 Small Heath
48 Speckled Wood
49 Wall Brown
50 Grizzled Skipper
51 Dingy Skipper
52 Chequered Skipper
53 Lulworth Skipper
54 Essex Skipper

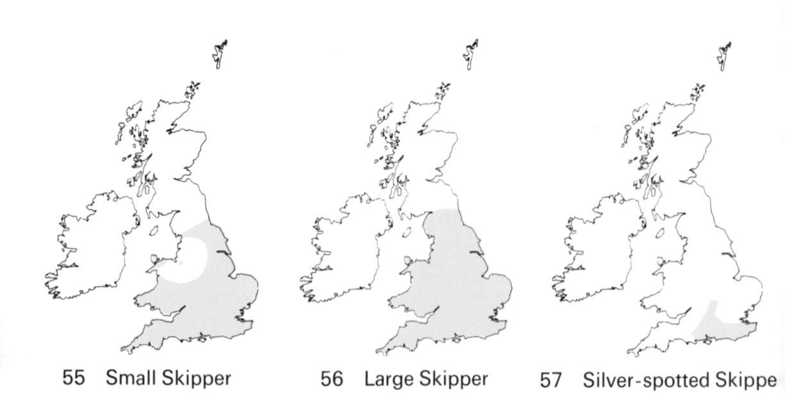

55 Small Skipper    56 Large Skipper    57 Silver-spotted Skippe